top50 ski & snowboard resorts in europe 2007

top50 ski & snowboard resorts in europe 2007

pat sharples   vanessa webb

foulsham

LONDON • NEW YORK • TORONTO • SYDNEY

foulsham

The Publishing House, Bennetts Close,
Cippenham, Slough, Berkshire, SL1 5AP
England

Foulsham books can be found in all good bookshops or
direct from www.foulsham.com

ISBN 13: 978-0-572-03270-8
ISBN 10: 0-572-03270-6

Cover photograph © Getty Images

Photographer: Ross Woodhall

A CIP record for this book is available from the British
Library.

Train information provided by Daniel Elkan

Design and layout by Ben Cracknell Studios
Printed in China through Colorcraft Ltd.,HK

Contents

Acknowledgements   7
Introduction   9
About the authors   9
How to use this book   11
Our top 50 resorts   11
Our top 5s   13
Equipment guide   16
For the gadget mad   24
Safety   26

Ski and snowboard
    banter   410
Index   413

Andorra

Arinsal	34
Pas de la Casa	40
Soldeu	46

Austria

Bad Gastein	58
Hintertux	64
Ischgl	70
Kitzbühel	76
Lech	84
Mayrhofen	90
Saalbach-Hinterglemm	98
St Anton	104
Sölden	112
Zell am See	118

France

Alpe d'Huez	126
Les Arcs	132
Avoriaz	140
Chamonix	148
Courchevel 1650	156
Courchevel 1850	164
Les Deux Alpes	174
La Grave	184
Meribel	192
Morzine	200
La Plagne	206
St Foy	214
Serre Chevalier	220
Tignes	228
Val d'Isère	238
Val Thorens	246

Italy

Alagna	256
Cervinia	260
Cortina d'Ampezzo	266
Courmayeur	272
Gressoney	278
Selva in Val Gardena	286

Norway

Hemsedal	296
Oppdal	302

Sweden

Åre	310
Riksgransen	316

Switzerland

Arosa	322
Champéry	330
Crans Montana	336
Davos	344
Flims	352
Klosters	358
Laax Murschetg	366
Saas-Fee	374
St Moritz	384
Verbier	392
Zermatt	400

Acknowledgements

We would like to thank all the people who helped us throughout the winter, allowing us to travel to each of the Top 50 Resorts. We could not have done this without them. Thank you to tourist offices and their press and marketing departments, and to friends and family who have helped us out along our way, providing information and accommodation. In particular we would like to thank the following:

Andorra: Arinsal: Pete and Adrian. Pas de la Casa and Soldeu: Silvia Encinas and Sira Puig, Tyler Charlton.

Austria: Bad Gastein: Markus Papai. Kitzbühel: Sascha Reitsma and Tamara Prömer. Lech: Claudia Lengenfelder. Mayrhofen: Kathren Egger and Jon Weaver. Saalbach-Hinterglemm: Jason Hough. St Anton: Wilma Himmelfreundpointner.

France: Les Arcs: Helen. Chamonix: Glen and Caroline. Courchevel: Laurence Bourgeois and all the regulars at the Signal. Les Deux Alpes: Elodie Lavesvre, Héléna Hospital, Pete and Lynn and Matt Sharples. La Grave: Robin and Marlene, Niels and Didier, and Jean-Charles. Meribel: Adam Johnson, The Taverne hotel/bar. Morzine: Sturan Erskine, Johnny Mclaren, Bruno Robinet. La Plagne: Giles and Claire, Marcus, Paul and Monica Sharples. St Foy: Anne Royer, Adrian Myers. Serre Chevalier: Ben Hawker aka Bungle. Tignes: Simi Johnson, Euan at Les Mélèzes, James Vernon. Val d'Isère: Chris Howarth, Jane Jacquemod. Val Thorens: Stefanie.

Italy: Alagna and Gressoney: Lara, Hotel Villa Tedaldi. Cervinia: Elsa and Andy North. Selva in Val Gardena: Jolanda Senoner.

Sweden: Jon Olsson, Jens H. Bond. Åre: Bengt Ullström.

Switzerland: Heidi Reisz at Swiss Tourism. Arosa: Beatrice Gerber and our film crew Rachel and Simon. Champéry: Yannick Ducrot, Kina Ojdahl, John Mitchell, Paul and Rhonda. Crans Montana: Stefanie Ambuehl. Davos: Clair Southwell, Daniel Waechter, Chris Southwell, Carin Gisep-Caligari, Othmar Thomann. Klosters: Clair Southwell, Daniel Waechter, Hotel Alpina, Lukas Durr, Al Thony and Chris Southwell. Saas-Fee: Robbie and Therese, Adrian Schnyder. St Moritz: Alexandra Blaha. Verbier: Warren Smith, Melody Sky, Nick Southwell, Pierre-Yves. Jamie and Kerry. Zermatt: Karin Schmid.

Photographers: Adrian Myers, Ross Woodhall, Melody Sky. Magazines: Zack Ragg and Daniel Crawford at Dark Summer.

A big shout out to all of Pat's sponsors who have supported him in his career as a professional skier and now are considered close friends. *Thank you.* Oakley Marketing Manager, Stewart Morgan. Oakley team manager, Jeremy Festa. Salomon Marketing, Sonia Prior, Richard Seymour, Andy Topping and Eric Davis. Natives.co.uk, Iain Martin, Snow and Rock, Kevin Young and Gregor Brealey, Ignite, Neil Thompson, Ortovox, Richard Want, Giro, Gregor Urquhart.

A special thanks to all at Foulsham Publishing who believed in us and gave us the chance to write our book.

Also, we would like to thank our families and friends for their support. A special thanks to David and Carol Webb, Vanessa's parents, who have let us take over their home, and provide unconditional help and support and to Paul and Monica Sharples, Pat's parents, for our European base, and for re-fuelling us when we needed a break.

We are so sorry if we have missed people out, but you know who you are and we won't forget all the support you have given us.

Many thanks, Vanessa and Pat.

Photograph acknowledgements

Photographs for the following resorts are tourist board copyright: Alagna Tourist Board. Alpe d'Huez. Åre Tourist Board. Arosa Tourismus. Avoriaz Tourist Board. Bad Gastein Tourist Board. Cervina. Champéry. Cortina Turismo. Courchevel. Crans-Montana Tourisme. Davos. Hemsedal Tourist Board. Hintertux. Rick Hutchings. Ischgl Tourist Board. Kitzbühel Tourist Board. Klosters Tourismus. Laax. La Plagne. Lech Arlberg. Les Arcs Tourist Board. Les Deux Alpes. Mayrhofen Tourist Board. Meribel Tourist Board. Monterosa. Morzine Tourist Board. Riksansen. Saalbach. Saas Fee. St Moritz Tourist Board. Ski Andorra. Ste Foy Tarentaise FR/A Royer. Serre Chevalier Tourist Board. Swiss Tourist Board. Tignes. Val D'Isere. Val Gardena Tourist Board. Val Thorens. Verbier. Zell am See (fotorush). Many thanks to all the tourist boards for their help and support.

Introduction

We are very proud to introduce the second edition of the *Top 50 Ski and Snowboard Resorts in Europe*.

In April 2004 we had the idea of writing a travel guide on the best locations to ski and snowboard whilst we were sitting on a ski bus, giving birth to the first edition, published in 2005. Since then, we have worked hard to improve on the first year, and we have updated every morsel of information that the book provides.

We have changed some of the resorts, as we felt that a few we didn't mention in our Top 50 last year deserved recognition. Again, we travelled and researched these resorts ourselves, with plenty of help from locals, tourist offices and friends. We skied with some of the world's best skiers and snowboarders and checked out some of the biggest events in the world. We have also been lucky to get hold of amazing photos from some of the best mountain photographers from around Europe.

Don't forget to check out our new equipment and gadget chapters so you can find out about what's hot to be wearing and using on the mountain, and don't even think about venturing out into the backcountry or off-piste without reading our avalanche safety chapter and equipping yourself with the essential gear. In fact, 2006 had one of the highest avalanche records in the last ten years, and the fatality rate was high, so you should make sure you know your stuff.

So sit back and find out which resort will suit you best for your next ski holiday or season. We hope you enjoy this year's edition of the *Top 50 Ski and Snowboard Resorts in Europe*.

About the authors

Pat Sharples: Pat is a big name on the British freestyle scene. He is head coach of the British Freeski camps and a former England Freestyle team captain. Pat has earned many titles, such as England Champion and European Mogul Challenge champion. His sponsors include Oakley, Salomon, Snow and Rock, Ortovox, Giro, Ignite hats and Natives.

Pat is currently the team manager for Salomon and Oakley's skiers and spends his time looking for and coaching new talent. He has also started his own training camps in the UK and France (www.patsharples freestylecamps.co.uk), providing high-performance coaching for all abilities and ages.

The information in this book about the mountains – including parks, and off-piste and backcountry – was compiled by Pat, with the help of many of his contacts and friends in the industry.

Vanessa Webb: Vanessa has always had a passion for skiing, travelling and writing. She has skied all her life and has spent winters in Canada, France and New Zealand and is also a qualified ski instructor and coach. Vanessa has a first class degree in Psychology and Philosophy, and has recently been the manager for a number of events in the mountains, including the ever popular Snowbombing in Mayrhofen, Austria.

Vanessa is responsible for writing about the resorts themselves, including the hotels, restaurants, activities and nightlife, and for the editing of Pat's dubious spelling.

How to use this book

Use this book exactly how you like, but if you want to find the best resort for you, we recommend that you start by checking out the list of 'Top 5s' (page 13). Decide which features of a resort you value the most (nightlife, lift pass price, off-piste/backcountry, parks...) and see which resorts we recommend in these categories; you might find that some overlap. Make a shortlist of three or four that you think would suit you, then refer to them in the main text of the book and decide which one you think is more your cup of tea. If you think you might like similar resorts to us, you could also check out how we rank all 50 resorts.

Our top 50 resorts

Please be clear that these ratings are based purely on our opinion and have been included for interest and as a talking point. Some people may hate our favourite resorts, while others may fall in love with some we are not so keen on. A favourite resort is a very personal thing and should be chosen on the qualities *you* think are the most important. It is also important to note that we would not have included a resort that we do not rate highly, so even those at the bottom of our personal list have some great plus points and might shoot to the top of your list.

Travelling by train

We are grateful to Daniel Elkan for providing the information on train travel.

- All journeys have been quoted in standard class, based on one person sharing a 6-berth standard-class couchette accommodation.
- Most fares shown are specially reduced and once confirmed do not permit change or refund.
- Train and bus times and fares are based on the most up-to-date information available at the time of going to press so readers must check all details of their journey when booking as times and fares may vary, although this is not likely to be by very much.
- All trains and times are daily, except journeys that use the Bergland Express, which leaves on a Friday night.
- On all routes, children under 4 travel free of charge unless they require their own accommodation. The exception is the Bergland Express where a reduction only applies in a sharing couchette cabin.
- On the fares to Swiss resorts, children under 16 do not pay the rail fare in Switzerland if travelling with their parents.
- Special fares apply for groups of 6 or more (10 or more for Eurostar and in France).

#	Resort	#	Resort
1	St Anton, Austria (page 104)	27	Crans Montana, Switzerland (page 336)
2	Chamonix, France (page 148)	28	La Plagne, France (page 206)
3	Saas-Fee, Switzerland (page 374)	29	Meribel, France (page 192)
4	La Grave, France (page 184)	30	Saalbach-Hinterglemm, Austria (page 98)
5	Zermatt, Switzerland (page 400)	31	Arosa, Switzerland (page 322)
6	Verbier, Szitzerland (page 392)	32	Laax Murschetg, Switzerland (page 366)
7	Mayrhofen, Austria (page 90)	33	Kitzbühel, Austria (page 76)
8	Courchevel 1650, France (page 156)	34	Zell am See, Austria (page 118)
9	Courchevel 1850, France (page 164)	35	Selva in Val Gardena, Italy (page 286)
10	Champéry, Switzerland (page 330)	36	Courmayeur, Italy (page 272)
11	Morzine, France (page 200)	37	Val Thorens, France (page 246)
12	St Moritz, Switzerland (page 384)	38	Alpe d'Huez, France (page 126)
13	Tignes, France (page 228)	39	Arinsal, Andorra (page 34)
14	Lech, Austria (page 84)	40	Hintertux, Austria (page 64)
15	Val d'Isère, France (page 238)	41	Alagna, Italy (page 256)
16	St Foy, France (page 214)	42	Cervinia, Italy (page 260)
17	Klosters, Switzerland (page 358)	43	Sölden, Austria (page 112)
18	Bad Gastein, Austria (page 58)	44	Hemsedal, Norway (page 296)
19	Ischgl, Austria (page 70)	45	Davos, Switzerland (page 344)
20	Les Deux Alpes, France (page 174)	46	Riksgransen, Sweden (page 316)
21	Serre Chevalier, France (page 220)	47	Pas de la Casa, Andorra (page 40)
22	Avoriaz, France (page 140)	48	Oppdal, Norway (page 302)
23	Åre, Sweden (page 310)	49	Flims, Switzerland (page 352)
24	Soldeu, Andorra (page 46)	50	Cortina d'Ampezzo, Italy (page 266)
25	Les Arcs, France (page 132)		
26	Gressoney, Italy (page 278		

Our top 5s

Top 5 resorts for off-piste/backcountry

1. La Grave, France (page 184)
2. Chamonix, France (page 148)
3. Verbier, Switzerland (page 392)
4. St. Foy, France (page 214)
5. Gressoney/Alagna, Italy (pages 278/256)

Top 5 resorts for parks

1. Laax Murschetg, Switzerland (page 366)
2. Les Crosets park in Champéry, Switzerland (page 330)
3. Les Deux Alpes, France (page 174)
4. Soldeu, Andorra (page 46)
5. Mayrhofen, Austria (page 90)

Top 5 resorts favoured by the rich and famous

1. St Moritz, Switzerland (page 384)
2. Courchevel, France (page 156)
3. Klosters, Switzerland (page 358)
4. Lech, Austria (page 84)
5. Kitzbühel, Austria (page 76)

Top 5 resorts for après ski

1. St Anton, Austria (page 104)
2. Ischgl, Austria (page 70)
3. Saalbach-Hinterglemm, Austria (page 98)
4. Mayrhofen, Austria (page 90)
5. Zell am See, Austria (page 118)

Top 5 resorts for guaranteed snow

1. Hintertux, Austria (page 64)
2. Tignes, France (page 228)
3. Sölden, Austria (page 112)
4. Zermatt/Saas-Fee, Switzerland (pages 400/374)
5. Les Deux Alpes, France (page 174)

Top 5 most expensive lift passes

1. Les Deux Alpes, France (page 174)
2. Laax Murschetg, Switzerland (page 366)
3. Zermatt, Switzerland (page 400)
4. Saas-Fee, Switzerland (page 374)
5. St Moritz, Switzerland (page 384)

Top 5 cheapest lift passes

1. St Foy, France (page 214)
2. Arinsal, Andorra (page 34)
3. Serre Chevalier, France (page 220)
4. Riksgransen, Sweden (page 316)
5. Oppdal, Norway (page 302)

Top 5 resorts to go to with a group of mates

1. St Anton, Austria (page 104)
2. Soldeu, Andorra (page 46)
3. Mayrhofen, Austria (page 90)
4. Morzine/Avoriaz, France (pages 200/140)
5. Val d'Isère, France (page 238)

Top 5 resorts for resort charm

1. Saas-Fee, Switzerland (page 374)
2. Lech, Austria (page 84)
3. Klosters, Switzerland (page 358)
4. Zermatt, Switzerland (page 400)
5. Kitzbühel, Austria (page 76)

Top 5 resorts for a romantic weekend

1. Saas-Fee, Switzerland (page 374)
2. Bad Gastein, Austria (page 58)
3. Klosters, Switzerland (page 358)
4. Lech, Austria (page 84)
5. St Moritz, Switzerland (page 384)

Top 5 resorts for nightlife

1. St Anton, Austria (page 104)
2. Verbier, Switzerland (page 392)
3. Åre, Sweden (page 310)
4. Les Deux Alpes, France (page 174)
5. Ischgl, Austria (page 70)

Top 5 resorts for value for money

1. Soldeu, Andorra (page 46)
2. Pas de la Casa, Andorra (page 40)
3. Les Deux Alpes, France (page 174)
4. Arosa, Switzerland (page 322)
5. Mayrhofen, Austria (page 90)

Top 5 resorts for heliskiing

1. Riksgransen, Sweden (page 316)
2. Alagna/Gressoney, Italy (pages 256/278)
3. Hemsedal, Norway (page 296)
4. Courmayeur, Italy (page 272)
5. Selva in Val Gardena, Italy (page 286)

the community project

Equipment guide

BOARDS

Prospect: *Freestyle*

Land on rails with ease thanks to the sidewall rubber; the P-Tex 2000 base will give you the speed needed to take on any kicker, no matter what size. The board is a machine for progress. Its limits are yours ... infinite.

Benedek: *Freestyle*

This year's DB pro model has changed technically as well as visually. It is lighter than last year and looks better too. The flex has been adjusted to make it a little softer and more aggressive to ride. Mr Benedek says that it's the best board he's ever had.

Loft: *Freestyle*

Now even lighter, with more intuition and still just as fast, this new LOFT still has the exclusive Zeolit base known to be the fastest on the market and combining selected light wood and Nomex for dynamic support and surgical precision. The ultimate weapon.

Patrol: *Versatile*

The ERA concept is finally available as a wide size! This board has incredible torsion for more manouevrability and mad pop thanks to the Carbon Booster. It is, without doubt, the high end reference in Wide.

Special: *Versatile*

This board works well on all types of terrain. Lively and dynamic, it gives you the feeling you can adapt to anything. Its versatility is exceptional, allowing you to be at ease on the slopes, as well as in parks or backcountry. Light and aggressive, it is the board that makes its own path.

Society: *Versatile*

Wow, what a board! All who have tested it have said if they could have only one board for the rest of their days, this would be the one. All mountain, freestyle, jib, park – it does the lot.

DH: *Freestyle*

The DH has an easy, clean, classic twin shape, and all the carbon array pop you could ever need: the meaty centre of the freestyle world.

Fever: *Freestyle*

The Fever is the perfect female board for jibs and the park ... good flexibility, light and solid.

Verona: *Versatile*

Tuned for today's accomplished women who like every aspect the mountain has to offer, focused on refinement and finesse. Drawing on Ride's ten years of women-specific history.

The Warren Smith Ski Academy brings together some of the sports top professionals to create the ultimate performance coaching team. The Academy trains Professional Freeskiers, up and coming British Athletes, Ski Instructors from Ski Schools across Europe, recreational skiers who have surpased ski school instruction and skiers who are either stuck on a plateau or wish to gain confidence.

The performance coaching develops your skill and builds your **confidence** to a level that gives you the power and technique to blast through powder, ski steep terrain, have the range of movement to master moguls, carve dynamically and become an all mountain freeskier.

www.warrensmith-skiacademy.com

UNLOCK YOUR
ALL MOUNTAIN POTENTIAL

PERFORMANCE COACHING
INSTRUCTOR TRAINING
SKI BIOMECHANICS CLINICS
FREERIDE
RACE TRAINING
NEW SCHOOL / FREESTYLE
HELI - SKIING
DVD SERIES
PODCAST AND 3GP SKI TIPS

ALSO FOR THIS SEASON

GAP VERBIER
PROGRAM 2007

CONTACT:
sales@snowsportsynergy.com
+44 (0)1525 374757

2006/07 COURSES

Winter 2006/07 - Verbier, Switzerland
25 Nov, 2 Dec, 9 Dec, 16 Dec, 6 Jan, 20 Jan,
10 Mar, 24 Mar, 14 Apr, 21 Apr (5 day courses)

Winter 2007 - Courcheval, France
6 Jan, 13 Jan, 10 Feb (5 day camps)

Spring 2007 - Snozone @ Xscape
3, 10, 17, 24 May - Milton Keynes
7, 14, 21, 28 May - Braehead
8, 15, 22, 29 May - Castleford

Summer 2007 - Saas-Fee, Switzerland
4 Aug, 11 Aug, 18 Aug (5 day courses)

ARMADA

T-Hall: *Freestyle*

The T-Hall is lighter and stronger than ever. At the heart of it all, the model remains jib-specific; the skis' profile is considerably more progressive, allowing for flex points before and after the binding. These flex points provide the ideal flex for nose presses and butters, while remaining stiff under boot for stability. No longer including a factory de-tuned edge under boot, the T-Hall is also more conducive to all-mountain riding than ever before, dispelling any preconceptions that Tanner's brainchild could not serve much of a purpose outside a park setting.

JP vs Julien: *Backcountry Freestyle*

The original backcountry jumping/jib specific ski from the Armada quiver enters its junior year. The JP vs Julien Signature Model is the ultimate tool for those who want to elevate their backcountry jumping/jibbing game to the next level. No doubt this model opened a lot of eyes this past fall as Tanner Hall attacked Chad's Gap with these under his feet. JP and Julien designed this model with little sidecut and camber and a wide waist, which allows the skier to stomp landings and makes it easier to control while skiing switch into backcountry booters. The tip radius remains progressive, proving extra float in powder, while the tail sits 10mm higher than the tip for those wanting to land, or ski, switch in deep snow.

ARW: *Versatile*

Designed by X Games gold medalist, Grete Eliassen, the ARW is a performance twin tip built specifically for women. The ARW is completely revamped with wider overall dimensions and more sizing options, and also has the additional weight savings, due to a new wood core and sidewalls, and a softer flex profile fit for girls. Please don't be fooled, this is no ordinary women's ski as Grete designed it to perform at a high level everywhere from the park to all-mountain riding, and as an added bonus, the ARW comes with its own beefcake to stare at on the lift.

Pipe Cleaner: *Freestyle*

The newest model to the Armada line, the Pipe Cleaner has been behind closed doors for over a year. Once exclusively used by the pro-team in major pipe competitions, the ski is now offered to everyone. The PC is the fastest ski in the Armada fleet; edges reduced in thickness and a high-grade downhill race base makes it ideal for those looking to boost out of the pipe. Not to be limited in its scope, the construction characteristics of this model make it an equally impressive all-mountain ski. This formula has provided a number of super pipe wins at X Games, US Open and the World Superpipe Championship. Only 500 pairs will be available globally.

LINE

Prophet 90: *Freestyle*

Line introduced the ground-breaking Prophet range in 2005/6, featuring matrix technology throughout and the humvee of big-mountain skis; the Prophet 130 measuring 130mm under each foot! For 2006/7, LINE has given the Prophet range distinctive graphics and introduced the new Prophet 90 ski – the most versatile, go anywhere, do anything, all-terrain ski you could hope to own!

Elizabeth: *Backcountry/Freestyle*

The Elizabeth, designed by Eric Pollard, is the undisputed leader of today's backcountry freestyle revolution. Eric designed the entire ski – graphics, dimensions and construction – his goal was for the Elizabeth to handle less like traditional skis and more like a snowboard. Eric has found the winning combination, incorporating a unique symmetric flex pattern with extra deep eliptical snowboard-like sidecut, a slant sidewall construction – and a bunch of other secret ingredients they can't share. The result is a fun, freestyle snowboard-like feel with incredible freestyle agility, especially in the deep stuff.

Chronic Blend: *All-terrain freestyle*

LINE have complemented the bombproof Chronic with the slightly wider Chronic Blend, a special new blend of powerful Chronic freestyle construction with precision freeride geometry to create the most versatile, high-performance all-terrain freestyle ski ever made. The Chronic Blend dominates every aspect of freestyle skiing with power and strength; its Freeride geometry delivers versatility, its Maple Macroblock fuels the power, the Carbon Ollieband provides the pop and the solid flex maintains stability above and beyond the call of duty.

Celebrity: *Versatile*

LINE's women's range created great interest when it launched last year, the vision of some of today's most progressive girl skiers who are taking freestyle and freeride skiing to the next level. The all-mountain Celebrity and its sister ski, the Shadow, have been very popular and for 2006–7 LINE have 'beefed up' the Celebrity even more, offering Carbon Matrix technology, new lengths and new graphics. (A shorter, youth version of the Celebrity is also available.)

SALOMON

1080 Guns: *Backcountry Freestyle*

The ultimate weapon for backcountry junkies, the Gun is super fat and shreds the whole mountain. Perfect for ripping off massive cliffs and killing backcountry kickers. If you live the extreme life, you'd better make sure you have the Gun in your holster.

1080 Foil: *Backcountry Freestyle*

Cast your eyes on this bad boy. The new and improved 1080 Foil with rock solid monocoque lite double wall construction. This complete freestyle tool gives you the ultimate performance on any obstacle that gets in your way.

1080 SPK: *Freestyle*

New to the 1080 range is the SPK superpark. If you want to be the next gold medalist at the X Games this is the ski that will get you there. Throw down your best tricks and you will find that this ski rocks the whole park.

Temptress: *Freestyle*

Stun the guys in the park by busting out your sick tricks on these little puppies. With the Temptress, the park is your oyster. Designed by Salomon's pro riders with all you rock chicks in mind.

XW Sandstorm: *Freeride*

Fat and fast, this weapon of choice provides riders with no limits, especially for speed. With massive sidecuts, you can fly over any mountain that is before you. No obstacles can keep you from conquering them all!

BODY ARMOUR

There is no doubt that skiing and snowboarding are dangerous sports. Whether you are sticking to the pisted runs, hitting the parks or venturing into the backcountry, we strongly advise the use of safety equipment. There are numerous examples of people who have seriously injured themselves, sometimes fatally, who could have protected themselves simply by wearing the basic safety equipment of a helmet and a back and short protector. I hope that the loved and hugely respected professional skier and in-line skater Rich Taylor, who died from a severe head injury in August 2004, would not mind us mentioning that a helmet could have saved his life.

Helmets

In America, there are a number of resorts in which it is illegal not to wear a helmet and this attitude is spreading to Europe. You should consider a helmet as important as your skis/board, if not more so, as it could be a lifesaver. There is no excuse for not wearing one. And they make you look hardcore. We don't go anywhere without our Giro helmets. In particular we recommend...

G10, The Freestyle Boss:
This super light freestyle/freeride helmet has a skate-styled shape with progressive lines and wide-angle cut for great peripheral vision and gapless goggle fit. Its features make it a versatile helmet for a variety of weather conditions, and include EPS liner and 14 vents with Thermostat ventilation control system. In addition, the removable earpads detach for springtime sessions and are compatible with TuneUps™ (so you can hear your favourite beats in full stereo with your helmet on).

Bad Lieutenant: This is standard issue for hardcore riders. Its styling is one of a kind and it has a high-impact ABS shell with an impact-absorbing EPS (expanded polystyrene) liner. The earpads are removable and compatible with TuneUps™.

For further information on Giro ski and snowboard helmets, and to find your nearest stockist contact Big Bear Sports on 020 8991 9244 or giro@bigbear.co.uk.

Back protectors

If you fill your days in the park hitting huge kickers and sketchy rail slides or going off cliff drops in the backcountry then you need a back protector. Your spine is pretty vulnerable when you crash and needs protecting; if you value the use of your limbs invest in one. Contrary to popular opinion they are perfectly comfortable and don't restrict body movement at all. We like the **Dainese Shield 8-7-6**, which has polypropylene hard plates and perforated polyethylene soft padding. The protector is tested at −20° C.

Short protectors

Not everyone feels the need to wear a short protector but it can be very handy in a crash over rocks or on a rail in the park. The **Dainese Short Protector Plus** features soft composite protection for the hipbone, sides and gluteus with rigid composite femur protectors.

Venturing into the backcountry is a risky (albeit fun) business no matter how good your knowledge of the terrain. Each year there are more reports of avalanches taking people's lives because an increasing number of skiers and boarders are exploring off-piste without the required experience or equipment. There are a few *essential* pointers. For starters, *never go alone*. No one will be there to witness your amazing Rodeo 720 off the 24m cliff and if you get caught in an avalanche – you're stuffed. Ensure that at least one person in the group has extensive experience and substantial knowledge of the local terrain. If your group does not have these qualities, hire a guide.

Additionally, it is vital to invest in the right equipment – it could save your life or someone else's…

Avalanche transceivers

This is arguably the most important piece of equipment to have when exploring off-piste. It is used to locate someone who has been enveloped in an avalanche and also allows a fellow transceiver carrier to find you. It should be worn under your jacket at all times. Remember, it is completely useless unless you know how to use it. Details on vitally important courses can be found at www.natives.co.uk.

We recommend the **Ortovox X1 avalanche transceiver**, which we carry with us religiously on the mountain. The new fully automatic X1 brings extra accuracy with greater simplicity.

Digital/analogue functions are microprocessor controlled to limit user faults. They are also safe, fast and compatible with all transceivers.

The **S1** is the first sensor-controlled avalanche transceiver. This spectacular piece of technology can simultaneously locate up to five people within a radius of 60m. It has a large, illuminated display showing the position and distance to all buried persons. Additional features include an electronic compass, and displays of temperature, inclination and depth of burial.

Probe pole

The probe is used to stick into the snow to find someone who has been buried. Ortovox do a wide range of probes from mega lightweight to carbon-based probes. We use the **Ortovox Carbon 280 Probe**, which is high-flex, lightweight and impact resistant with a compact length of 40cm, extending to 280cm.

Avalanche shovels

Shovels are now ultra light so you can't use weight as an excuse for not carrying one. They are designed for digging people out of an avalanche, but also come in handy for building big backcountry kickers.

The **Ortovox Professional shovel** has a light, telescopic shaft with an ergonomic left-/right-hand grip and an unbreakable, torsion-free polycarbonate blade. This is our choice, but Ortovox's range will have something to suit your personal preferences.

Backpacks

The **Ortovox Tour Rider 30+ backpack** is the perfect backcountry companion. Avalanche shovel and probe can be attached outside, to be quickly accessible. The spacious main compartment can accommodate the hydration system and other accessories, and smaller items have a place in the front compartment or in the hip-belt pocket. All pockets have waterproof zippers. If you'd rather tote your board or skis, you can attach them with the Clip Fix buckles. An emergency signal whistle is integrated in the chest strap; the drinking tube line is on the shoulder strap. Ortovox also have a wide range of other packs.

ABS backpacks

This is one of the most recent and invaluable avalanche safety devices. It is designed to keep you above the surface during an avalanche by making the body less dense than moving snow.

Why you need it
Burial is a huge factor in avalanche fatalities (see pages 26–7) and an ABS backpack can massively increase your chances of survival, witness 30 documented cases in Europe.

How it works
The airbags are stowed in the backpack until the trigger on the shoulder strap is pulled, when the nitrogen-air cartridge is activated, releasing two 75-litre air bags within two seconds. The ABS has to be released by the user and practising this is vital.

Find out more information on http://www.abssystem.com.

Simon Dumont

Charles Garnier

SalomonSki.com

For the gadget mad

Mio A701 integrated GPS handheld mobile phone PC

Save yourself from disappearing in the backcountry by using the GPS to pinpoint exactly where you are on your map. The handset is stylish, and equipped with a 68mm, 240x320 display and a 1.3 megapixel camera. Its radio supports tri-band GSM with GPRS and you will also find Bluetooth 1.2 connectivity. There's a SD/MMC slot on the side for memory expansion. The GPS receiver is integrated within the body of the device, so there's no cumbersome flip up antenna or receiver stub.

Helmet cameras

Helmet cameras are the ultimate toy for use on the piste, in the park and in the backcountry, and a great way to make your mates go green with envy at your tricks on the slopes. You can view an extensive range at www.actioncameras.co.uk (E-mail: info@actioncameras.co.uk), where you can also purchase any of the cameras mentioned below.

1. For the beginner...

Wireless helmet cameras are perfect for those new to on-piste filming as they are self-contained units that record on to SD cards, eliminating the need for a camcorder. The tiny cameras clip or Velcro to your helmet and off you go.

ATC-1000 action camera (around £130) This camera is both shock- and splash-resistant, the perfect gadget to capture your challenging feats. There are three resolutions,

the highest 640x480 and the lowest 160x120. Using the built-in 32Mb SD card you can record in low resolution for 16 minutes or in high res for 1 minute, but this can easily be increased by splashing out a few pounds on a bigger SD card. Also included is a TV cable for instant replay on the big screen and USB cable for easy uploads onto your PC.

Tony Hawk's helmetcam (around £110) This camera, endorsed by skateboarding legend Tony Hawk, isn't a serious camera, but is nevertheless huge fun. It even comes with a laser pointer for targeting so you can see where you are filming. This product is for people who want ease of use and no cables, rather than for those who want DVD-quality images. The Tony Hawk camera comes with 32Mb removable SD memory card and has a normal resolution of 320x240. It contains a microphone with 3m range and there are some decent software features. Also included are a docking station with attached mini USB cable and removable bezel for fish eye lens attachment.

2. For the all-round entertainment package...

AV 500 digital mini camera (around £160) This is the option if you want a fantastic media machine

at your fingertips for music and movies (that you can rip straight from DVD) on those long journeys or even on the lifts. The DigiMini Cam PAL is a helmet camera that has been developed by Archos to go with its Archos AV500 range. The camera has a 420 TV line resolution and comes with a 6mm Sony CCD lens. The helmetcam, which is powered off the Archos unit, can record several hours of footage directly onto the hard drive of the Archos AV500. The camera has some fantastic features: it can capture in any environment without an extra light source, even in near darkness; the MPEG-4 SP files are compatible with both PCs and Macs; data can be transferred via USB 2.0 directly to a computer and, it has slow motion capability ($\frac{1}{2}$, $\frac{1}{4}$, $\frac{1}{8}$ speeds) in order to record detailed actions.

The disadvantage is obviously the cost, as you have to buy the Archos (£250–350), in addition to the DigiMiniCam above.

3. For the pro...

If you have ever fancied yourself as a budding film maker, there are a variety of top quality helmet cameras on the market providing DVD-quality footage. All that you will need is a compatible camcorder with AV-In.

520 TV line helmet camera with low light chip (around £175) This is one of the highest spec helmet cameras on the market, coming with the top of the range Sony Ex-View CCD Lens capturing DVD-quality images. It is used by professionals worldwide to film all kinds of extreme sports. It has a tough, sleek compact design (21x72.5mm), is waterproof and produces high-quality images. With a minimum illumination of 0.05 Lux, it performs extremely well under darker conditions, such as at dusk or in forests. Go for this camera if you want the best lens on the market and you want the highest resolution helmet camera available.

Oakley Thump 2

The world's first digital music eyewear is now available in a new design with the option of even greater memory. Built around the hard-edged style of Oakley's GASCAN™ eyewear, THUMP 2 offers memory storage up to 1 gigabyte (240 songs). Listen to music virtually anywhere with speaker booms that adjust easily for a customised fit, and just swing them out of the way when you need to hear your environment. The Thumps will play up to 6 hours of playback time on a single charge.

O ROKR™

The O ROKR™ from Oakley and Motorola provides stereo music and wireless connectivity, using the next generation of BLUETOOTH® eyewear, letting you stay connected to calls and music while you're riding. O ROKR™ can wirelessly stream music from a compatible Bluetooth-enabled phone or a portable music

player with an add-on Bluetooth adapter (you can use O ROKR™ with your iPod by adding the optional NAVIPLAY© adapter). When you want to pause the music, adjust the volume or change songs, just use the buttons on O ROKR™. You can switch instantly between stereo music and wireless communication – when you need to take a call, answer it from O ROKR™ while your compatible mobile phone rests up to 10 metres away. You get up to 5 hours of talk time and more than 100 hours of standby time in a hands-free link that is part of something you're already wearing. Impressive…

Suunto wristop computers

Depending on the model that you choose (with costs of £100–500), you will be able to take advantage of a range of features such as an altimeter, barometer, compass, chronographic functions, logbook and on certain models, GPS (SUUNTO X9i). The Suunto S6 has been designed specifically with skiers and snowboarders in mind, providing you with information enabling safe and responsible decisions on- and off-piste, as well as tools for analysing your downhill skiing or snowboarding performance.

The altimeter gives you an insight into your vertical speed, online cumulative descent and number of runs and altitude profile. The barometer will show you the sea level pressure, absolute pressure, weather trend graph, temperature and has a 48-hour memory and weather alarm. The compass provides information on bearing and bearing tracking and the ski chronograph shows the degree of the slope, maximum speed, average speed and vertical drop for

individual runs. The logbook keeps record of the total and cumulative vertical ascents and descents, as well as the number of runs. Most models also store data for later analysis – you can view, compare, and analyse your riding performance through a specially designed PC interface and compare it with others over the internet.

Portable boot dryer

Around £40. The Thermic-Air dryer dries all kinds of boots or gloves overnight and warms them up again for cosy feet and hands in the morning. It also gets rid of unpleasant odors. It dries ski boots in 60–90 minutes and the compact collapsible design makes it easy to pack away.

Nixon watches

£50–500. The snowboarders' choice, and an instant eyecatcher, these watches are superb presents. The range is massive, check out www.nixonnow. com and make your choice. Some of our favourites include The Banks, The Rotolog and The Boss for men, and The Siren, The Cougar and The Chalet for girls.

Surfster Ice

Around £60. The Surfster Ice is an inflatable toboggan, with neolite knuckle guards, webbing handles and left and right leash tags. Its Dual Density core makes for a comfortable and exhilarating ride. Traditional toboggans can be very cumbersome; the joy of the Surfster Ice is that it packs down to little more than a roll mat, and yet inflates in a couple of minutes (it comes with a pump).

Radica SSX Snowboarder

Around £40. Play SSX for real, in the comfort of your own lounge. Grab a few mates, a few beers, and hit the pipe.

Safety

Avalanche safety

For anyone who is venturing off-piste, it is vitally important to be equipped, not only with all the gear mentioned in the previous chapters, but also with the required knowledge.

Skiing and snowboarding are not without risk. Around 100 people die every year in the Alps as a result of avalanches; they do happen, so you need to be physically and mentally prepared.

Ultimately there are three key areas of knowledge in which skiers and boarders should be proficient before they step off pisted areas. These are:

1 **Avalanche avoidance:** This is by far the best method of avalanche safety!
2 **Avalanche survival:** What to do if the worst occurs.
3 **Search and rescue:** How to rescue an avalanche victim effectively.

Avalanche avoidance

While it is vitally important to carry avalanche survival equipment such as transceivers, probes and shovels, it still remains that 55–65 per cent of buried victims die even when they are equipped with all the gear. Therefore, the most successful way to deal with avalanches is to avoid them, and the key to this is skiers'/boarders' knowledge and experience, and their ability to engage in effective risk analysis. Here are a few pointers to get you started.

Plan your route
Your route should be well considered and carefully planned, taking into account:
• **Slope aspect and gradient.** Carry an inclinometer and compass for gauging slope aspect and steepness. Remember that the majority of avalanches occur on north-west to east aspects on slopes greater than 30 degrees. Slopes between 30 and 60 degrees have a potential to slide, and the gradient most likely to slide is 38 degrees.
• **Recent weather conditions.** Include new snowfall. Rain on fresh snow leads to a high risk of avalanches.
• **Evolution of the snowpack.**

• **Predominant wind direction and speed.**
• **Humidity.**

Gain experience
The better your knowledge and experience, the better able you will be to cope with problem situations. Find ways to expand your knowledge:
• **Attend courses.**
• **Read up on the subject.**
• **Go out with experienced people and listen to their advice.**
• **Study the avalanche bulletin.** Do this in great detail, especially if there is a mention of local risk factors.

Don't fall into common traps
A run is not safe just because:
• you've done it before; familiarity is dangerous and can mean that you do not assign the risk-analysis procedure that you would to an unknown slope;
• you can see other people doing it;
• you've already started so you'll finish; always be prepared to admit the danger and head back, even if it does mean a long hike;
• you've got an avalanche transceiver and all the other equipment: a transceiver is a search-and-rescue device, it should not affect the risk-analysis procedure.

Avalanche survival

In the case of an avalanche there are three main factors that will affect whether a victim survives and there are a few things you can do to enhance your chances of survival.

Depth of burial
Approximately 90 per cent of victims caught in avalanches are alive when the avalanche has stopped moving but most are buried beneath the surface and cannot free themselves. Their chances of survival decrease rapidly with time, and statistics show that 55–65 per cent of buried avalanche victims are recovered dead.

Help yourself
If you can, try to swim in the slide, this may avoid you being entirely buried.

The ABS Airbag (a fantastic but expensive piece of equipment) has been designed to protect the victim from complete burial; airbags are triggered by the victim, making their bodies less dense than moving snow (see page 21).

Air supply

Suffocation accounts for 50 per cent of all avalanche fatalities and is not easily avoided if your rescuers cannot reach you quickly.

Help yourself

Try to clear your airways to breathe. It is sometimes possible to clear an air pocket around your mouth as you feel the slide slowing down.

The Avalung is a unique piece of equipment that can be used to buy the victim valuable time. Working on the principle that avalanche debris is mostly air, it extracts air from the surrounding area and deposits exhaled air into the snow behind the victim.

Rescue time

It has been found that victims recovered during the first 15 minutes of burial have a 93 per cent chance of survival. The only fatalities tend to be those who sustained injuries as a result of the fall during the avalanche itself. Between 15 minutes and 45 minutes recovery time is a crucial half hour known as the asphyxiation phase. After 45 minutes, the chances of survival decrease to less than 30 per cent. After 45 minutes, even if you have managed to find an air pocket, the risk of death from hypothermia is high.

Help yourself

Visual clues can give rescuers an indication of your location, and speed up the rescue process. If you can push a ski pole or arm out to the surface, statistics show you have a much greater chance of being rescued.

The Avalanche Ball is another useful piece of equipment that will give a visual clue to the victim's location. Pull a cord on the waist belt and the ball inflates and floats to the surface of the slide, whilst remaining attached to the victim via a cord. This will greatly increase the victim's chances of a swift rescue.

An effective rescue team is by far the best way to decrease rescue time. If all parties have avalanche transceivers it is vital that the rescuers start the search immediately and have prior training. The rescuer can alert the rescue services quickly if they have a phone (be aware that using a phone may interfere with the transceiver signals) but they *should not go for help*; they should start their rescue immediately as the avalanche ceases.

Search and rescue

Using transceivers

We have talked about the importance of carrying transceivers and equipping yourself with the knowledge of how to use them. However, there are a few details that are very important and not immediately obvious. For example, think about the impossibility of trying to find more than one buried body using transceivers; the signals given out by a number of transceivers will cause confusion and may render them useless. The best way to avoid this is to ensure that only one person is skiing/boarding at a time. Others should wait in safe areas, not in the way of a potential avalanche. This also provides a greater number of rescuers should the worst occur.

Help yourself
- Ensure that one person at a time is skiing or boarding.
- Ensure that transceivers are functioning and turned on.
- Practise using them in the local park, back garden or on snow; in a time of need you want use of the transceiver to be a reflex action.
- Do not carry your transceiver in your rucksack as this can be easily lost in an avalanche. Wear it as close to the body as possible to avoid it being torn from you.
- Assign a leader to ensure that every member of the group has a functioning transceiver.
- Turn your transceiver off at the end of the day and remove the batteries if it is to be stored for a long period of time. Use new batteries at the start of each season.

FREESKI BRITAIN

BRITISH FREESKI CAMPS

PERFORMANCE COACHING FOR
SLOPE STYLE / HALF PIPE / BIG AIR
RAILS / SKIER CROSS / BIG MOUNTAIN
AND PERSONAL PERFORMANCE

SUMMER 2007, SAAS-FEE, SWITZERLAND 7-14, 14-21, 21-28 JULY £499
MORE INFO AT WWW.BRITISHFREESKICAMPS.COM OR CALL 01525 374757

Switzerland. get natural.

Saas-Fee
BERGBAHNEN

DARK SUMMER

SKI CLUB of Great Britain

ifyouski.com

natives.co.uk
knowledge is powder

WARREN SMITH
SKI ACADEMY

POPCORN
SHOP & BAR · SAAS-FEE

Unique people & Popcorn

FREESKI BRITAIN

Saas-Fee
SAASTAL

ride
Freesport

Park rules and etiquette

1 No snaking. Make sure you know when it is your turn to take your run up to the jump or rail; never cut people off by jumping in front of them and stealing their turn.

2 Never stand on top of the jumps unless you are marking the fact that there has been an accident, in which case you should make this obvious to those waiting at the top of the jump – make a cross sign with your arms or poles.

3 Never stand or sit on the landing of a jump for obvious reasons – the jumper can't see you, could land on you and this could lead to death.

4 If you crash on a landing, try to get out of the way of the landing area as quickly as possible, and alert those around you to indicate your crash to those at the top.

5 Never start your run in until you know the person before you has landed safely and made their way out.

6 Always stick to jumps within your ability. Don't try something that you don't feel comfortable with.

7 Wear a helmet, and back and hip protector. Landings can be hard-packed and it's easy to mess up on rails. Many people have died when a helmet could have saved them, although resorts obviously try not to advertise this fact. Helmets are not unfashionable, you can get some wicked-looking ones (see page 20), and they could save you from a crushed skull.

8 Don't walk out across run-ins or landings unless you can see exactly where everyone else is and what they're doing, and they can see you.

9 Never ride down the park in a group, always go one at a time.

10 Store the resort's mountain rescue/emergency number in your phone so that you're prepared if you witness an accident. The international emergency number from a mobile phone is 112.

11 Don't intimidate people who have just started using the park – you were there once.

In your backpack should be:

- shovel
- probe
- map
- compass
- inclinometer
- first aid kit
- torch
- emergency food and water
- pocket-knife.

EMINENT
EXCLUSIVE
INSPIRED
SKI COACHING

Coaches:
Chris Haworth
Pat Sharples
Stephan Mongellaz

Dates
Summer:
Tignes, France

Autumn:
Tignes, France

Winter:
Val d'Isere
Tignes
Courcheval
Megeve
Chamonix

Fast
High speed and
race training

Bespoke
Private coaching
tailored for you.

Free
Powder, Park & Pipe,
Freeride & Big Air

www.dissent-ski.com
France: 0033 603 281 16*
UK: 07973 577 671

Andorra

The Brits' choice: perfect for beginners,
an amazing party scene and it won't break
the bank

Arinsal

If you've been once, you'll want to come back to this fun and friendly resort

Pic de Comapedrosa 2942m

Pic Alt de la Capa 2572m

Pic Negre 2569m

Pic dels Lacs

Port de Carbus 2301m

SETURIA AREA

Pic de Cubil 2356m

ARINSAL AREA

Comallempla 1950m

Cota 1550m

Carving Area

PAL 1550m

Xixerella 1450m

ARINSAL 1450m

Pla de la Cot 2052m

PAL AREA

Els Fontanals 1970m

Erts 1350m

LA BORDA

La Caubella 1950m

Escas 1375m

L'Aldosa 1350m

La Massana 1300m

Sispony 1375m

On the slopes	
Snow reliability	❄ ❄ ❄ ❄
Parks	❄ ❄ ❄ ❄
Off-piste	❄ ❄ ❄
Off the slopes	
Après ski	❄ ❄ ❄ ❄
Nightlife	❄ ❄ ❄ ❄
Eating out	❄ ❄
Resort charm	❄ ❄ ❄

The resort

Arinsal might not be known as one of the great resorts in Europe, but we loved it. It's the friendliest place ever, has some wicked bars, cheap accommodation and lift passes, and the fact that 40 per cent of visitors return says it all. It's packed with Brits, which has its good and bad points. It's better for beginners than experts, although the park is pretty good.

The mountains

Height: 1550–2560m

Ability	Rating
Expert	❄ ❄
Intermediate	❄ ❄ ❄
Beginner	❄ ❄ ❄ ❄

Getting about

There are 89km of pistes in Valnord (Arinsal and Pal, its neighbour), most of them geared for beginners and intermediates. Pal's slopes (linked to Arinsal by cable car) are less crowded and there is more to keep the keener riders happy.

The park

The Arinsal park was a big hit with us. The resort recently spent €20,000 on a massive selection of rails, and the shapers are enthusiastic and friendly. The park has something to keep all standards of riders happy: kickers of all sizes, a spine, quarter pipe, ski- and boardercross, and the new rails. There are a few local skiers and snowboarders who hang out here, like pro skier Peter Kaplansky, sponsored by Atomic, and owner of the popular snowboard, skate and freestyle ski shop in town, Loaded. He's always on hand to give tips and point you in the right direction. To add the cream on top of the cookie, there's an alluring super pipe. The walls are approximately 3.5m high and are always well maintained. Good work, boys.

Off-piste and backcountry

Arinsal seems to get its fair share of snow each year, which means you can always find a bit of fresh powder. There are a few good tree lines around and a couple of faces but nothing over-challenging. On the plus side, Arinsal attracts mostly beginners so the off-piste that there is won't get tracked out and you can find fresh powder weeks after it has dumped. The La Cappa area is one of the best and there's a massive cornice that's great for getting huge air. Here is also, allegedly, the steepest marked run in Andorra.

Lift passes	High season	Low season
1 day	€32	€27
6 days + (price per day)	€24	€20
Children receive discounts.		

Instruction

Arinsal Ski School
T: 00376 73 70 29

Pal Ski School
T: 00376 73 70 08
Group lessons cost €19.50 for 2 hours, and €81 or €95 for 15 hours (depending on the time of season). Private lessons are €31. 50–49 per hour depending on the time of season and the number of people. Prices are relevant to both skiing and snowboarding.

Other activities

Shopping: The main activity in Andorra is shopping on all the duty-free delights: alcohol, clothes, electronics – everything is as cheap as chips. Take care, though, as you are only allowed to take back certain quantities and values of products.

Skibikes, paragliding, hot air balloon rides, mushing: Other activities in Arinsal include skibikes (€34.50–50 per hour, depending on number of people), paragliding (€51), hot air balloon rides, and mushing in Pal. For more information, contact the tourist office, located in La Massana, about 4km down the road.

Thermal water centre: Andorra la Vella is the best place for this, and it's only about 10–15 minutes' drive from Arinsal. The Caldea Andorra (80 09 99, www.caldea.ad) is Europe's biggest mountain thermal water centre. It is an impressive place offering 6000m^2 of indoor and outdoor lagoons, Jacuzzis, Turkish baths, pools, waterfalls, with a variety of cultural influences – from Roman to Japanese. On top of this there is a fitness room and a variety of beauty treatments available. Entry to Caldea costs €22.80.

And if you don't manage any of the activities, drinking is a popular and cheap alternative!

"If you don't manage any of the activities, drinking is a popular and cheap alternative!"

of town. The **Micolau** (00376 83 50 52, www.arinsal.com/hmicolau) is a cosy and charming stone house, with simple, snug rooms and a relaxed restaurant, with an inviting log fire. Half-board accommodation is €47 per person per night.

> ## "Simple, snug rooms and a relaxed restaurant, with an inviting log fire"

The 3-star **Hotel Solana** (00376 73 79 99, www.uha.ad/solana) is a large hotel with pool and sauna facilities. Half-board accommodation is €49 a night. Bed and breakfast is €32.

For ritzy accommodation, head to the 4-star **Princesa Parc** (00376 73 65 00, www.hotelprincesa parc.com, hotelprincesaparc@andorra.ad), which has swish spa facilities as well as ten-pin bowling and a games area. Rooms aren't ridiculously priced either, with a choice of a standard room (€51–100 for half board), or a room with a hydromassage bath (€60–110) or a junior suite (€68–120). Price differences depend on the time of season. Finally the **Sant Moritz apartments** (00376 73 78 78, santmoritz@santmoritz.com, www. santmoritz.com) are recently built and fully equipped, perfect for families or groups of friends with 13 apartments for two to four people and 2 for two to six people, ranging from 50 to 85m². Prices are available on the website (€65–135 per night for a 4-person apartment).

Events

There are a couple of events in Arinsal including the **Arinsal Challenge** in February and the **UFO Funtime** in March.

Accommodation

If you're planning a holiday in Arinsal there are a number of cheap options to consider.

Just take care that you're not too far away from the action – there's no need to be as you can get some great deals right in the centre of town and next to the gondola. **Hostel Poblado** (00376 83 51 22, info@ hotel-poblado.com) is really cheap, costing €22–45 a night and it's right next to the gondola in the centre

Eating out

On the mountain
The restaurants on the mountain are mainly self-service, and usually crowded, offering the usual assortment of snack food. **Panoramix**, a British bar-restaurant, has a good reputation for its extensive sun terrace and Pal's main building has a decent

array of options, including a large cafeteria and a proper restaurant, **La Borda**, serving Andorran cuisine. There are also Mexican, Chinese and Italian restaurants on the mountain!

In town

Our favourite restaurant in Arinsal is **Cisco's**, which does fab Tex-Mex food in a converted cattleshed, with a relaxed and wooden feel. The fajitas are especially tasty, as is the mango chicken. The staff are a riot, and the bar downstairs is really popular with the locals and those in the know. All in all, this is a great place for a night out. **El Moli** is a cute pizzeria in the centre of town, with great food and even better cocktails. They also do takeaway. **Surf** is a great place to munch on a plate of steak and chips. **Micolau** is open all day and serves some great snacks such as all-day breakfasts,

bacon and sausage sandwiches, and good tasty salads. At night the warming fire is very inviting and cosy. **Borda d'Erts** is a few minutes' drive down the road, and is great for a posh(er) night out away from the squalor.

Bars and clubs

The bars in Arinsal are plentiful and it's pretty difficult not to have a good night here (although that could be something to do with the size of the measures). All of the bars are open from après ski (unless they serve food at lunchtime) and stay open until 3am on weekdays and 4am on Friday and Saturday. **Cisco's** is a favourite with the locals and is a snowboarder hangout. It has a great atmosphere, wicked staff, table football, free internet and the awesome Tex-Mex restaurant upstairs.

El **Derbi** is an Irish pub (even though its owner is from Bristol), that thankfully allows no tour operator pub crawls. It's especially heaving on karaoke night. **El Cau** is a bar for the real locals. They have giant TV screens for sports too. **Quo Vadis** is famous as the longest running bar in Arinsal, has a small restaurant and is very popular with tourists. The **Solana** hotel is owned by local instructors and has a big open log fire to chill out by. **Red X** is a theme bar that often has fancy dress and live music, and at the end of the day they show video analysis from the day's skiing/boarding. **Surf** is a funky bar that has ample room for dancing and is usually the last stop of the evening before you finally collapse.

Useful facts and phone numbers

Tourist office

T: 00376 73 70 20
F: 00376 83 59 04
E: palarinsal@palarinsal.com
W: www.palarinsal.com

Emergency services

- Police: 110
- Ambulance/Fire: 118
- Emergency health care: 116
- Mountain rescue: 112
- Hospital: 87 10 00

Taxis

- Associacion de Taxistas de Andorra (86 30 00)

Getting there

By car

Arinsal is not an easy drive from the UK, but if you are planning a road trip you should take the A 71 motorway from Paris (860km) as far as Clermond Ferrand, then the A 9 motorway through Narbonne and the A 61 to Toulouse. Next, head towards Foix on the N 20 and to Andorra via the Envalira Tunnel (for which there is a toll), towards La Massana. From the La Massana cable car roundabout, Arinsal is signposted.

By plane

Toulouse (190 km) Transfer to Arinsal by the novotel airport transfer service costs €39 one way and €66 return.
Barcelona (200 km) Transfer to Arinsal by the novotel airport transfer service costs €36 one way and €61 return.

By train

Take the 17.09 Eurostar from London Waterloo to Paris; then an overnight train to L'Hospitalet, then a bus to Andorra la Vella (90 minutes), and then another bus (25 minutes) arriving in resort at 09.55. Return fares from £111 in a 6-berth couchette. Contact Rail Europe (08705 848 848, www.raileurope.co.uk) or European Rail (020 7387 0444, www.europeanrail.com). The combined bus journey costs €11 single, and tickets are purchased on the bus.

Pas de la Casa

Take Blackpool, add some snow and remove the crime and you've got Pas de la Casa

On the slopes	
Snow reliability	❄ ❄ ❄
Parks	❄ ❄
Off-piste	❄ ❄
Off the slopes	
Après ski	❄ ❄ ❄
Nightlife	❄ ❄ ❄ ❄
Eating out	❄ ❄
Resort charm	❄

The resort

If you don't like drinking and shopping to excess, stop reading now. Pas de la Casa is the biggest, and most well known, of the six resorts in Granvalira (the others being Grau Roig, Soldeu, El Tarter, Canillo and Encamp). It is big and pretty ugly, but it's very friendly and it's very cheap, so the shopping is tremendous and loads of people come here to buy electrical gadgets, alcohol and perfume, etc. The nightlife could be a plus or a minus point depending on how you look at it. The comparison with Blackpool is, we feel, fairly accurate (and we're not dissing Blackpool) – it's a 'lads on a stag night' kind of place and when night falls the urge comes over you to wave your hands around, shout 'Wehey' and drink until you drop. The dropping bit might not be completely your fault as Andorran drinks are as cheap as British pub prices and you get around a triple measure into the bargain. So it does tend to get a tad rowdy. We prefer to stay in Soldeu (see page 46) – you get all the benefits of cheap drinks and there's still a great night-time scene but you're in much nicer surroundings and you can always pop over for an afternoon's shopping in Pas de la Casa or Andorra la Vella.

If you are thinking of coming to Pas de la Casa, it is worth checking out the Soldeu chapter too as the resort is only 20 minutes away by car and the mountain areas are directly accessible.

The mountains

Height: 1710–2640m

Ability	Rating
Expert	❄ ❄
Intermediate	❄ ❄ ❄ ❄
Beginner	❄ ❄ ❄ ❄

Getting about

The Grandvalira mountain contains six sectors that correspond to the six towns; Pas de la Casa, Grau Roig, Soldeu, El Tarter, Canillo and Encamp. From Pas de la Casa head up the Solana chairlift. From Grau Roig there are a number of options to take you up the hill, all directly accessible from the car park. There are 193km of runs in Grandvalira, all of which come under the same lift pass and most of which are geared towards the beginner/intermediate skier or boarder, with lots of long 'motorway' runs. There is a bit to keep the expert happy though. Grau Roig is home to the best slopes – the masses tend to stay on the beginners' slopes in Pas de la Casa and Soldeu so you can enjoy the sunny slopes in peace.

The park

If you've just got to grips with your skiing or boarding and want to start practising some tricks, the fun park here is a perfect place to learn. There are a couple of small jumps and the odd rail. If you're pretty good and looking for a sick park, make your way over to the superb ACG Snow Park in El Tarter (covered in detail in the Soldeu chapter, see page 46). There is also another small park in the Grau Roig sector with a few OK rails but not much else. If you fancy a shot on a skier/boardercross course, there's one near the bottom of the resort.

Off-piste and backcountry

Pas de la Casa doesn't have much off-piste of its own but within the Grandvalira region there are some good areas to be found. Some of the best riding can be found at the top of the mountain by Grau Roig, where there are a few long powder fields to be had. There is also some decent freeriding over towards Soldeu (see Soldeu chapter, page 46).

Lift passes	High season	Low season
1 day	€37	€35.50
6 days	€180	€175

For seven or more days, multiply the number of days by €29 in high season or €28.50 in low season. For two days or more the only available pass covers the whole of the Grandvalira. For a half day or one day you have the option of a pass for half of Grandvalira (either Canillo–El Tarter–Soldeu or Pas de la Casa–Grau Roig–Encamp) which will cost a little less. Children (between six and 11) get a discount and a beginner's pass is also available for €21 per day giving you access to the beginners' sectors only.

Instruction

The Andorran ski and snowboard school has seven different centres with instructors that speak loads of languages. Group lessons cost from €97.50 per person for 15 hours. Private lessons cost €31–58 per hour depending on the time of season and number of people.

Pas de la Casa
T: 00376 87 19 20

Grau Roig
T: 00376 87 29 20/00376 87 29 27

Other activities

Adventure activities (based in the Cubil in Grau Roig): The Grau Roig Adventure Activities Centre is the place to go to organise any activity you may want to try your hand at. They organise individual activities as well as catering for large groups of 100 or more. Here are a few of the popular choices (contact the tourist office for more details). Other activities offered by the Adventure Activities Centre include cross-country skiing, snowshoeing, igloo building, orienteering and avalanche rescue courses.

Helicopter flights: 10- or 20-minute helicopter flights can be organised (€50 or €100 respectively), taking off from Grau Roig or Soldeu.

Husky sled trip: A romantic husky sled trip, driven by a guide costs €50 for 1.5km, €90 for 5km.

Mushing: There is a mushing circuit at Grau Roig where you can learn to ride a sled pulled by a team of huskies. Thirty minutes costs €55 (1.5km).

Paintball: This takes place in the battlefield in Grau Roig. All equipment is provided and participants buy the first 100 pellets for €30 and extra pellets at a price of €15 for 100.

Parapent flights: Take off from Tossa d'Espiolets (in El Tarter) and land at the bottom of El Tarter. The flights last for 20 minutes and you are accompanied by an instructor. Check prices at the Reservations Centre.

Shopping: Shopping is the main activity of choice here (unless you're too busy drinking). Shop, shop, shop. Remember to check the permitted quantities of alcohol, perfume, cigarettes, etc but take as much as you are allowed or you'll regret it. A 3-litre bottle of Jack Daniel's costs just over £20! It's worth knowing that department stores do not close at midday or on Sundays. On Sundays, most shops open in the morning and some stay open in the afternoon. Shop around before you buy as prices do differ from shop to shop.

Snowmobiling: This takes place along guided routes. Trips can last 15 minutes (€35), 30 minutes (€60), one hour (€100), or you can take a two-hour excursion (€200) to Port d'Envalira which has fantastic terrain for snowmobiling.

Snow track: The Audi snow track is located at the Pla d'Espiolets in Soldeu and you can rent 4WD cars and learn to drive on the snow. Visit www.audi.es for more info.

Sports and socio-cultural complex: Pas de la Casa sports and socio-cultural complex (85 68 30) contains a multi use court with floating floor and spectator seating, squash courts, table tennis, saunas and an indoor pool. The price of a pass covering all the sports facilities is €4.60.

Events

The **Snowgames** take place in March each year (this year will be its 8th edition) and run over consecutive weekends. The main events are a snowrunning competition (a snowshoe race) and the San Miguel Snowbike, a bike-cross for mountain bikers on snow. There is also a cross-country endurance test, 'Snowtop'. The best comps (freestyle festival and freestyle series) happen in Soldeu and El Tarter (see Soldeu, page 46).

Accommodation

Hotel **Himàlaia Pas** (00376 73 55 15) is close to the slopes and offers pretty good accommodation and facilities, including a pool, spa area, gym, games room, internet and disco. There are 98 rooms, equipped with satellite and mini bar. Prices are €36–127 per person, per night, depending on the time of year and whether you require B&B or half board. Hotel **Màgic** (00376 87 55 00), is owned by the same company and is also 4 star (Andorran rating systems, however, appear to be slightly more lenient than their European equivalents).

It has a similar level of comfort and price, and although there is no pool, there is a sauna, Turkish bath, gym and sunbeds.

Apartments are popular because they are often good value, and you can cook for yourself, which (personally speaking) looks more hygienic and enjoyable than eating at some of the dodgy buffets that are around. Being honest, those who don't fall into the '18–30, on a mission for carnage, the cheaper the better' category shouldn't really stay in Pas de la Casa anyway (the neighbouring Soldeu would be far better) and those who do fall into this category probably won't give a monkeys about the type of accommodation they're in as they won't see much of it. In fact, the grottier the better, then they won't mind as much when you throw up all over the lobby.

Eating out

On the mountain

At **Coll Blanc**, at the top of the Pas de la Casa chairlift, is an 80s-looking restaurant with pretty good views. The food comes in takeaway boxes and is OK for a

quick bite but that's about it. You'll find very few places that you want to linger in Pas de la Casa and Grau Roig – apart, that is, from the restaurant at **Llac dels Pessons** (75 90 15), by far the best on the mountain. Reach it from the Comi del Pessons path running from the Llac del Cubil chair. It's sat on the edge of a frozen lake and is cosy and inviting. It's a table-service restaurant with superb food, specialising in grilled meats on their indoor wood fire.

In town

Most of the restaurants in Pas de la Casa serve sketchy food in a dingy atmosphere with shocking service. Then they have the cheek of adding a mandatory 10 per cent service charge onto your bill. If you find comfort in the familiar you could always head to **Burger King** (Pas de la Casa), McDonalds (Pas de la Casa) or **Pizza Hut** (Grau Roig).

However, all is not lost; there are a couple of places that every Pas de la Casa victim should head to. We love the Perla Negra (85 68 38, tavernpirata@hotmail.com), a fun place to take a group of mates, where you can play some darts and then tuck into some tasty ribs (all you can eat for 212) and meat skewers. A main meal will cost you about 218 a head

with wine. El Raco is a Moroccan-style restaurant and smells of incense. A main costs 210–14. Vertigo has a gorgeous, candlelit restaurant, with smart food and the sweet choice of 'big plates' or 'little plates' depending on your appetite. It's a shame it's so eerily quiet though.

A real find this year was a tucked away restaurant called **L'Husky**. It has a big open fire and old wooden skis and woodwork on the walls, creating the cosy ski lodge feel rarely found in Pas de la Casa. The T-Bone steak is very tasty, although at 10oz, it might not satisfy the most hardened steak-eater. To find it you should turn left when facing the Vertigo/Underground bars and walk down some steps to the corner of the courtyard. Across the road from the Underground club is a doorway with stairs leading up to it and here you will find L'Husky overlooking the bottom of the main slopes.

Bars and clubs

If you didn't feel like you were in Blackpool before, you will when you hit the bars. They are cheesy, rowdy and most of the best clubs are down seedy backstreets (don't worry: Andorra has one of the lowest crime rates in Europe). It's great fun though.

Milwaukee is the place to start the evening with a few pints – between 6 and 8.30pm there is a good atmosphere and an enticing happy hour. After this it gets absolutely rammed. The Underground is a great little bar and the Dutch/English owners really make the atmosphere. It's one of the few bars in Pas de la Casa where you can actually have a conversation over the music. Vertigo should be good, but the attempt to compensate for the solitary person sat at the bar by playing pumping music fails miserably. Bilboard (85 62 36) is the place to drink when everywhere else has closed but keep hold of your beer – put it down on the bar and it may well be danced upon. Music is generally commercial hits and the crowd Dutch and British.

Getting there

By car

From Paris, take the A6 to Nantes, the A10 to Toulouse, the A62 to Carcassone, the A61 to Foix (direction Hospitalet – RN 20).

By plane

There are no airports in Andorra although there are plans for one at Seu d'Urgell. Until then, the closest are Toulouse, Barcelona and Girona.
Toulouse (200km) There is a daily minibus service at 10.30am and 7pm, costing around €24.
Barcelona (200km) There is a daily bus service (11.30, 13.00, 17.00, 18.00 and 21.00) with a fare of around €24.
Girona (219km) There is one minibus service a day at 3pm.

By train

Take the 17.09 Eurostar from London Waterloo to Paris; then an overnight train to L'Hospitalet, and then a connecting bus (40 minutes), arriving in resort at 08.15. Return fares from £111 in a 6-berth couchette. Contact Rail Europe (08705 848 848, www.raileurope.co.uk) or European Rail (020 7387 0444, www.europeanrail.com). Bus tickets (€3.35 single from Andorra Bus) are purchased on the bus.

Useful facts and phone numbers

Ski Andorra

T: 00376 86 43 89

Grandvalira General Info/Reservation Centre

T: 00376 80 10 60/ 80 10 64
E: reservas@grandvalira.com,
     info@grandvalira.com

Websites to check out

- www.andorra.ad (Andorra's official website)
- www.grandvalira.com
- www.skiandorra.ad (official website of the Association of Andorran Ski Resorts)
- www.andorra.com
- www.SkiAndorra.info (unofficial – provides ratings of bars, shops, etc)

Emergency services

- Fire brigade: 118
- Police: 110
- Police station: 82 12 22
- Emergency medical service: 116
- Medical centre: 89 05 70
- Hospital: 87 10 00

Taxis

You won't find any taxi ranks out of Andorra la Vella but you can call any of the numbers below to order one. The price set by the Andorran government is €0.99 per kilometre and there are two zones: A is Andorra la Vella and Escaldes, and B is everywhere else.
- Associació de Taxis d'Andorra: 86 30 00
- 86 10 05
- Més Taxis: 82 80 00

Soldeu

One of Andorra's finest resorts. Great slopes for beginners and intermediates and a perfect park for the freestylers

On the slopes	
Snow reliability	❄ ❄ ❄
Parks	❄ ❄ ❄ ❄
Off-piste	❄ ❄ ❄
Off the slopes	
Après ski	❄ ❄ ❄
Nightlife	❄ ❄ ❄ ❄
Eating out	❄ ❄ ❄
Resort charm	❄ ❄ ❄

The resort

The resort is set along the busy main road from Pas de la Casa through to Andorra la Vella. The buildings are far prettier than that of its neighbour, Pas de la Casa, although there are fewer amenities here. The general vibe of the resort is British, fun, friendly and cheap. There are some pretty cool pub-type bars (which are packed every Saturday with British footie fans), and good restaurants and hotels. Another great thing about the six resorts in Grandvalira (Pas de la Casa, Grau Roig, Soldeu, El Tarter, Canillo and Encamp) is that they are so close together that you can be in any one of them in half an hour. The mountains are also linked, making it one of the largest ski areas in Europe. If you are thinking of coming to Soldeu, it is worth checking out the Pas de la Casa chapter too (see page 40) as the resort is only 20 minutes away by car and the mountain areas are directly accessible.

"The general vibe of the resort is British, fun, friendly and cheap"

Andorra is a mad little place. Since it only got its own constitution a few years ago they are still making the rules up as they go along. Apparently (we aren't convinced that this is gospel truth), divorce is illegal and wives are allowed to take their adulterous husbands outside and shout at them in public… but only for one hour! So there we have it, believe it or not. And if that's not enough, here are a few more Andorra facts: apparently, one in ten British skiers have been to Soldeu; Andorra has the lowest unemployment rate in the world (0 per cent) and If you see a farmer, they are almost certainly a millionaire! We obtained this information from Kate and James, the authors of the informative 'Inside Soldeu' booklet (that you can pick up in most bars).

The mountains

Height: 1710–2560m

Ability	Rating
Expert	❄ ❄ ❄
Intermediate	❄ ❄ ❄ ❄
Beginner	❄ ❄ ❄ ❄ ❄

Getting about

The Grandvalira mountain contains six sectors that correspond to the six towns: Pas de la Casa, Grau Roig, Soldeu, El Tarter, Canillo and Encamp. From Soldeu, the cable car takes you up to Espiolets, where you can start your journey through Grandvalira. Alternatively you can head up the mountain from nearby El Tarter, which has a chairlift and a gondola that take you up to the experts' snow park and general meeting place. Canillo and Encamp are slightly more inconvenient places from which to begin your journey up the mountain, being at the far end of Grandvalira, and you also have to take the gondola back down at the end of the day. From Encamp, the long Funicamp might take a while but it does set you down bang in the heart of Grandvalira.

Grandvalira tends to be geared to the beginner/ intermediate skier or boarder with 'motorway' style runs and long paths. It also caters very well for kids, and has a great Disney run (at the top of the El Tarter gondola) past pictures of Mickey, Donald, Cinderella and Buzz Lightyear. There are a few things to interest the more advanced/expert rider though, not least the superb park, sponsored by Nike AGC, in the El Tarter sector. El Tarter also holds the Guinness Record for

Lift passes	High season	Low season
1 day	€37	€35.50
6 days	€180	€175

For seven or more days, multiply the number of days by €29 in high season or €28.50 in low season. For two days or more the only available pass covers the whole of the Grandvalira. For a half day or one day you have the option of a pass for half of Grandvalira (either Canillo–El Tarter–Soldeu or Pas de la Casa–Grau Roig–Encamp) which will cost a little less. Children (between six and 11) get a discount and a beginner's pass is also available which is €21 per day giving you access to the beginners' sectors only.

having the longest bumps run in the world at 1300m long.

The park

There are three parks in Grandvalira, a beginners' park in Pas de la Casa, a slopestyle in Grau Roig, and the amazing ACG park in El Tarter. The latter (accessed from el Pla de Riba Escorxada) consists of three big kickers with a smaller side kicker by the side of each one. They range from 22m to 5m gaps, and are always perfectly shaped. There's a 120m half pipe, a selection of rails and a massive wall ride. The quarter pipe and gigantic hip are also wicked after they've been shaped. Note to skiers: you can only enter the park in El Tarter on twin tips.

One of the guys behind the park is Jamie Phillips, a British pro snowboarder sponsored by Oakley, who always keeps it in top shape. Soldeu is also the home of Tyler Chorlton (British Snowboard Champion, sponsored by Oakley and Ride), who trains here when he's not off travelling around doing comps and photo shoots. He is truly the master of this park!

> "One of the guys behind the park is Jamie Phillips, a British pro snowboarder, who always keeps it in top shape"

Off-piste and backcountry

The off-piste in Grandvalira is all really accessible and requires a minimum of hiking. It isn't over challenging but there's more than you would think and you can find fresh powder in the trees, even when it hasn't snowed for a few weeks. The big tree run back to the bottom of Soldeu is a must after a snowfall and has been nicknamed 'the land of the giants' because the trees are so huge. The hike off to the right of Riba Escorxada is amazing in the right conditions and is a favourite among the locals.

For some low-risk off-piste and an interesting experience (weather conditions permitting), there is a ratrack pistebasher that will drag you with ropes to the Pic d'Encampadana (El Tarter sector), from where there are four possible routes down. It's free, so why not give it a go?

Instruction

The Andorran ski and snowboard school has seven different centres with instructors that speak loads of languages. Group lessons cost from €96–101 per person for 15 hours. Private lessons cost €33–58 per hour depending on the season and number of people.

Soldeu
T: 00376 89 05 91/00376 89 06 15

El Tarter
T: 00376 89 06 41/00376 89 06 44

Canillo
T: 00376 89 06 91

Other activities

In Andorra the main activities are **shopping** for all the duty free delights (alcohol, clothes, electronics – everything is cheap as chips, take care though as you are only allowed to take back certain quantities and values of products) and **drinking**. However, for the more discerning holiday maker (of which there aren't too many), there are a fair few things to try your hand at.

Adventure Activities: The Adventure Activities Centre in the Cubil, Grau Roig (covered in more detail in the Pas de la Casa chapter, see page 40) has a huge number of activities available. These include igloo building, orienteering and avalanche rescue courses, mushing, husky sled trips, snowshoeing, parapent flights, helicopter flights, snowmobile riding, paintballing and cross-country skiing.

Bowling: A two-lane bowling alley can be found in the Hotel Nòrdic in El Tarter (73 95 00).

Ice skating, go-karting and curling: In Canillo, the Palau de Gel D'Andorra contains an ice rink that is

equipped for ice skating, ice go-karting or curling. There is also a large pool, tennis and squash courts, and lots more things to do. An ice-skating pass costs €8.20 and pool pass €5.50.

Snow track: At the Pla d'Espiolets in Soldeu, Audi have designed a snow track where you can learn to drive 4WD cars on the snow. For bookings visit www.audi.es.

Sports: For €4.60 you can use all the facilities in Encamp's Sports and Socio-Cultural Complex. Facilities include badminton, basketball, volleyball, a climbing wall, tennis courts, martial arts room, squash courts,

boules area, gym, solarium, saunas and indoor pool.

Thermal Leisure Centre: The Calbó Thermal Leisure Centre (87 05 00, www.sporthotelcomplex.com) is a brand spanking new complex; a huge, modern centre with 4500m^2 of water including Jacuzzis, Turkish baths, hammam, pools and other facilities such as beauty treatments and a hairdresser. It's connected to the Sport Hotel and only 100m from the Hotel Sport Village, all three buildings belonging to the Calbó family.

Thermal water centre: Caldea Andorra (80 09 99, www.caldea.ad) is Europe's biggest mountain thermal

water centre, located in Andorra la Vella. It is a massive and impressive place offering 6000m² of indoor and outdoor lagoons, Jacuzzis, Turkish baths, pools, waterfalls, with a variety of cultural influences – from Roman to Japanese. On top of this there is a fitness room and a variety of beauty treatments available. Entry to Caldea costs €28 (3 hours).

Events

The ACG park hosts the **Freestyle series** which is composed of three freestyle events and is entered by a mix of pros and amateurs. At the end of the season a **freestyle festival** takes place with ski and board comps, a live DJ in the park, equipment tests and loads of parties and concerts. The festival lasts one week. It's worth looking out for the events whilst you're there as they always have cool stuff on – we pitched up unannounced to find a wicked rail comp (Atomic Night Fever) taking place in a car park. There are also loads of freestyle comps throughout the winter, a mogul competition mid-February and a five-day touring comp at the beginning of March.

Accommodation

Be aware that accommodation ratings in Andorra may be slightly different to what you might expect. For example, two of the three 4-star hotels we visited would probably have been classed as a 3-star anywhere else in Europe although the other 4-star hotel definitely deserved its rating. For the cheapest deals, tour operators (Thompson, Crystal, etc) and the internet can have some real bargains. Just make sure your accommodation isn't too far from town. Apartments are also worth consideration; you will pay less if you self-cater and there are loads of good apartments around.

The best hotel in town (that is if you're after classy sophistication instead of a week of lairy boozing), is the **Sport Hotel Village** (with four well-deserved stars, 00376 87 05 00). You walk into an immense reception area with a gorgeous bar, acres of lounge areas, all in a wooden, modern-chalet-style décor. There are 148 gorgeous rooms (25 with Jacuzzi) and the hotel has a sauna and gym. As if all this isn't enough, the hotel is in the centre of town and built over the lift system so has direct access to the slopes. Prices for half-board

accommodation are €70–126 per person per night. There are supplements for Jacuzzis, lockers and rooms with slope-facing balconies. **Piolets**, also in the centre of town and classed as 4-star, is a pleasant hotel, very spacious, with a massive balcony that's in the sun all day. The pool and spa area is the best feature of the hotel with sun loungers, a huge gym, sauna, solarium, Turkish bath and massage. Prices (half board) are €66–115 per person per night depending on the season and they do special deals from Sunday to Friday for €454 per person for five nights half board and lift pass. For an extra €224 you can stay for the whole week. The 4-star **Himálaia** hotel is once again spacious and comfy with underground parking, sauna, Jacuzzi, Turkish bath and fitness area. It costs €32–97 per person per night

for bed and breakfast and €42–112 for half board.

If you don't need to be near the heart of the nightlife all the time we can recommend staying in a family-run aparthotel in Canillo called **El's Meners** (00376 75 14 54, elsmeners@andorra.ad). It has 15 apartments that contain a bathroom, kitchenette, dining table, lounge area (with double sofa bed) and bedroom. The rooms are beautifully done out with a terracotta, sunlit, Spanish feel. The service and staff are super-friendly and efficient and the hotel also has a bar and restaurant downstairs. It costs €100–215 per apartment per night depending on the time of season. For details of high/low season etc, contact the aparthotel on the E-mail address above.

Eating out

On the mountain

In Grandvalira you don't have the best selection of mountain restaurants but they're comparatively inexpensive compared to other European countries. For starters, decide whether you want a burger stand, self-service restaurant, cafeteria, table-service restaurant or a 'gastronomic' restaurant (the word 'gastronomy' seems to fly around Andorra a little looser than in the UK). Both Soldeu and El Tarter have a collection of restaurants at the top of the bubble cars from the villages which are good meeting points, especially if you have skiers and boarders of different abilities.

At the Soldeu area, **Espiolets**, you have the self-service restaurant (89 05 81) if you don't have much time, and the **Gall de Bosc** building which contains a cafeteria on the ground floor, **Fun Food** (89 06 04), selling sandwiches, burgers and salads (for about €6) and on the upper level a 'gastronomic' restaurant, **Gall de Bosc** (89 06 07). At El Tarter, at the top of the gondola, is Restaurant **Riba** (89 06 36), a self-service restaurant, and a terrace overlooking the ACG Snowpark where you can grab a burger or sandwich.

The **Pi de Migdia** (89 06 35) opened last season next to the arrival of the El Tarter gondola. The restaurant opens for lunches and on Friday and Saturday evenings. Reservation is essential.

At **Collada d'Enradart**, at the top of the Funicamp gondola from Encamp, is a panoramic restaurant with great views and, again, a number of choices of service with a 'gastronomic' restaurant upstairs, a pretty dodgy-looking self-service restaurant on the lower floor and a burger/sandwich counter outside. The terrace is great but there are often large queues for the burger counter.

We recommend heading over to a restaurant called **Llac des Pessons** (75 90 15) in the Grau Roig area; a table-service restaurant that is by far the best in the area with cosy wooden tables, a great view over the frozen lake of the Circ del Colells mountains (so-named because they look like a circus) and superb food, where you choose anything from sandwiches to their meat specialities, grilled on the indoor wood fire.

In town

In Soldeu, there are a fair few decent eateries. For a full English breakfast head to **Slim Jims**, an English-run café where you can also check your E-mails. If you're not up the mountain at lunchtime, **Hotel Bruxelles**, right in the centre of town, has a big terrace in the sun overlooking the mountain. They serve massive sandwiches, paninis, burgers and salads. Anywhere you can get a bacon and cheeseburger for €4.20 on a terrace in the sun gets our vote.

At night-time, there is a cosy and homely Indian, **L'Esquirol** (85 26 55 – English speaking). It's situated on the edge of the village and the food is cooked in their traditional coal-fired Tandoor. The Chicken Tikka Masala is fab. **Fat Albert's** (85 17 65, www.fatalberts bar.com) has a restaurant in a converted barn, serving a mix of meat, fish and pasta. For some traditional cuisine, try **Borda del Rector** (85 26 06), a lovely wooden and stone, chalet-style restaurant. They have an open fire and a gorgeous bar/lounge area. It's a little out of Soldeu, closer to El Tarter, but they'll pick you up from Soldeu if you're eating. The **Red Dragon** is a Chinese restaurant that has recently changed management and has a really cosy and inviting atmosphere. It serves Chinese, Thai and Vietnamese dishes (as well as steaks and other dishes if you prefer) and has an extensive menu (a main dish costs around €9). **La Cava** restaurant in the Alba Hotel in El Tarter (75 11 16) is friendly and serves good food. They'll even pick you up from your hotel or apartment.

Bars and clubs

Going out in Andorra is an experience. Once you've got used to the dirt-cheap booze (actually similar to British pub prices, but compared to typical European ski resorts it's cheap), poured freely (a triple shot is the norm) until there is little room for mixer, you can join in with the other delighted Brits in causing havoc.

The **Aspen Bar** (85 19 74) has a cool atmosphere, very much like a British pub. There are loads of TV screens for the Saturday footie matches (on Saturdays the bars are far more packed than the slopes), tons of comfy seating, and pool tables and video games to keep you entertained. On a Thursday, don't be surprised to walk in and find two guys/girls boxing in big kangaroo

suits, and Saturday night traditionally entails a School Disco theme. From 2pm they serve good Tex Mex food (starters cost €6–8, mains €12–20). The **Avalanche Bar**, also full of Brits, offers live music and a local DJ, and has big plasma screens for sports. **Fat Albert's** is a really popular place, with great après ski, an excellent restaurant downstairs and a locally renowned live band. The **T-bar** is known by the locals for its après ski snacks

and more interestingly, for the opportunity to hang upside down from the roof for a shots challenge. **Pussycat** opens from 9pm until late and is the place to be later on in Soldeu (although you can go early to make full use of the special drinks deals). They have live music, DJs and theme nights and have just introduced pole-dancing competitions to turn the heat up even more. What's even better is that it's free entry.

Useful facts and phone numbers

Ski Andorra

T: 00376 86 43 89

Grandvalira Reservation Centre

T: 00376 80 10 60/80 10 55

Websites to check out

- www.andorra.ad (Andorra's official website)
- www.grandvalira.com
- www.skiandorra.ad (official website of the Association of Andorran Ski Resorts)
- www.andorra.com
- www.SkiAndorra.info (unofficial – provides ratings of bars, shops, etc)

Emergency services

- Fire brigade: 118
- Police: 110
- Police station: 82 12 22
- Emergency medical service: 116
- Medical centre: 89 05 70
- Hospital: 87 10 00

Taxis

You won't find any taxi ranks out of Andorra la Vella but you can call any of the numbers below to order one. The price set by the Andorran government is €0.99 per kilometre and there are two zones: A is Andorra la Vella and Escaldes, and B is everywhere else.
- 86 30 00
- 86 10 05
- 82 80 00

Getting there

By car

From Paris, take the A6 to Nantes, the A10 to Toulouse, the A62 to Carcassone, the A61 to Foix (direction Hospitalet – RN 20).

By plane

There are no airports in Andorra although there are plans for one at Seu d'Urgell. Until then, the two closest are Toulouse and Barcelona.
Toulouse (200km) There is a daily minibus service at 10.30am and 6.30pm, costing around €24.
Barcelona (200km) There is a daily bus service (11.30, 13.00, 17.00, 18.00 and 21.00) with a fare of around €24.

By train

Take the 17.09 Eurostar from London Waterloo to Paris; then an overnight train to L'Hospitalet, and then a connecting bus (65 minutes), arriving in resort at 08.40. Return fares from £111 in a 6-berth couchette. Contact Rail Europe (08705 848 848, www.raileurope.co.uk) or European Rail (020 7387 0444, www.europeanrail.com). Bus tickets (€5.50 single from Andorra Bus) are purchased on the bus.

Austria

You might not expect to find charming traditional towns with crazy après ski parties, but Austria makes it work perfectly

Bad Gastein

The spa facilities, and spectacular scenery, make the Gastein valley an exceptional place to visit

Ski, Berge & Thermen.

GASTEIN

www.skigastein.c

LEGENDE

On the slopes	
Snow reliability	✳ ✳ ✳ ✳
Parks	✳ ✳
Off-piste	✳ ✳

Off the slopes	
Après ski	✳ ✳
Nightlife	✳ ✳ ✳
Eating out	✳
Resort charm	✳ ✳ ✳ ✳ ✳

The resort

The Gastein valley is famous for its spas and wellness facilities – the 17 thermal springs produce 5 million litres of radon-enriched water each day, which are used for their restorative qualities. Many of the hotels have superb facilities, and there are some huge health centres in the resort too.

There are a number of towns along the valley floor. Bad Gastein is the most well-known, but it's not necessarily the best place to stay – it depends completely on what you are looking for. Dorfgastein is the first stop. It's a lovely quiet village, with the disadvantage that the slopes are not connected to the valley's main network. Bad Hofgastein's slopes are connected to Bad Gastein's and it has the major pull of the new Alpen Therme Gastein (see Other activities) – Europe's most modern alpine health and leisure world. Bad Hofgastein is a genuine village, with a pleasant and relaxed atmosphere whereas Bad Gastein's buildings are regal and majestic. Although some of the interiors of the buildings in Bad Gastein could do with updating, it is impossible not to be impressed by the setting – the whole resort is built on the sides of a steep gorge, with a massive waterfall roaring through the centre of town. The furthest resort is Sportgastein, which you wouldn't want to stay in, but it's a great place to visit if the snow is bad elsewhere. The restaurants and nightlife are somewhat lacking in the valley, so it is a better destination for relaxing spa and skiing weeks than for crazy nights of partying.

A car is a good idea to ferry yourself around or you could always look into renting an electric quad bike (contact the tourist office for details).

The mountains

Height: 1080–2230m

Ability	Rating
Expert	✳ ✳ ✳
Intermediate	✳ ✳ ✳ ✳
Beginner	✳ ✳ ✳

Getting about

There are four mountains to choose from in Gastein, providing 200km of slopes, although they are not all connected by lift. The Schlossalm (2050m), above Bad Hofgastein, has a number of easier slopes for the beginner/low intermediate rider. This mountain is connected to the main area in Bad Gastein, the Stubnerkogel (2246m), from which you can ride back down to town. At the end of the valley is the small area of Graukogel (2492m), a blessing only for its tree runs. You could also take the short (15–20 minute) drive to Sportgastein's mountain, Kreuzkogel (2686m), sacred for its snow reliability when all other areas fail. New snowmaking facilities on Sportgastein this year will add to the reliability of the area and extend the season further. Sportgastein is definitely worth a look, and not only when the snow is bad as it has some great runs on- and off-piste, even though it is only served by a two-stage gondola and one drag lift!

The park

The freestyle scene appears not to have captured the hearts of the locals in Gastein so, although they actually have a half-decent park, they aren't fussed about advertising it. You can find the park in Grossarl, above Dorfgastein. It has a half pipe, two quarter pipes, a small selection of jumps (ranging from 3 to 10m long), and a couple of fun boxes. Unfortunately, like a few other archaic Austrian resorts, the park is exclusively for boarders. Why, we do not know.

Off-piste and backcountry

Sportgastein is the highest area, and therefore has the best snow and some of the best powder runs in the Gastein valley. There are some good spots of off-piste that are accessible and they're unlikely to be tracked out, although you should really employ the services of a local guide to make the best of the ski area (contact the ski schools/tourist office to find an available guide). From the top of Sportgastein, at Kreuzkogel (2686m), there's a great run down the valley that is a marked route (Ski route Nord), but is not prepared or patrolled (you do need avalanche equipment and a good skill level for this run). You will come out at Heilstollen, on the road from Sportgastein back to Bad Gastein and from here you can catch the bus back into town (8am–6pm). There is a new ski route this year, 2.2km long, starting south of the prepared piste and culminating at the bottom of the valley.

Lift Passes

1 day	€59
6 days	€171

There are discounts from mid to late January and at the beginning and end of the season (December and April), as well as for children and teenagers.

Instruction

Ski School Schlossalm, Bad Hofgastein

For information and pricing enquiries:
T: 0043 (0)6432 3298
E: office@schischule-schlossalm.at
W: www.schischule-schlossalm.at

Ski and Snowboard School

Group lessons cost €50 (1 day) or €125 (3 day). Private instruction costs €45 per hour for one person and €10 per hour for each additional person.
T: 0043 (0)6434 2260 (Bad Gastein)/ 0043 (0)6432 6339 (Bad Hofgastein)
E: schneesportschule@onemail.at or info@schneesportgastein.com
W: www.schneesportgastein.com

Other activities

Tobogganing: Go up the Schlossalm lift (Bad Hofgastein) and enjoy 3.3km of floodlit fun.
Ice skating: Bad Hofgastein has an artificial ice skating rink and curling lanes.
Tandem paragliding: In Bad Hofgastein (06432 2526, www.tandem-flying.com) and costs €50–105.

Spas: As well as venturing to the wellness area that you are almost guaranteed to have in your hotel, visiting one of the massive spas in resort is an absolute must. Far more than just something to do on a bad weather day, these places rock.

In Bad Hofgastein is the **Alpen Therme Gastein** (06432 82930, www.alpentherme.com, info@alpentherme.com), Europe's most modern alpine health and leisure world covering an area of more than 32 000m^2. It contains six adventure and vitality worlds: leisure world, adventure world (with lazy flow river, 'black hole' slide with flashy lights, etc and a speed slide which really is pretty speedy), sauna world, ladies wellness and beauty world, fitness world and taste world (a restaurant and bar with a 360-degree panoramic view of the mountains). There's also a 360-degree cinema screen in adventure world that you swim into. So that you don't have to faff around with money, you have a band around your wrist that records everything you buy. Clever. If you want to be extra clever, bring your own towel and dressing gown from the hotel because it's extra to hire them. Don't be shy if you're a bloke either, there are loads of men there.

> "There's also a 360-degree cinema screen in adventure world that you swim into"

In Bad Gastein is a similar construction, the new **Felsentherme Gastein** (06434 22230, www.felsentherme.com). This spa was re-opened in 2004 with some fantastic new features. The Felsentherme indoor area includes a pool surrounded by rocks for relaxation, a 600m^2 adventure area with two layered pools, massage beds, geysers and a wild water channel, a 70m water slide and a rock grotto. There is also a fitness area and a new panorama wellness area with seven different saunas, solariums, a juice

bar, a nudist area and two mountain-top pools. Outdoors is a 34°C relaxation pool, a 24°C sport pool and a children's fairytale pool with interactive fairytale figures.

The **Healing Gallery** (06434 37530, office@ gasteiner-heilstollen.com, www.gsateiner-heilstollen .com) is an intensive, natural and rare spa remedy, 2.5km deep inside the Radhausberg mountain. The healing air inside the mountain was discovered by miners searching for gold, but the unique climate they revealed is far more valuable. The healing effects are due to the radon content of the air, a temperature of 37–41.5°, speleotherapy conditions (pure, dust-free, allergy-free and bacteria-free air) and a high humidity (70–100 per cent). The vast majority (80–90 per cent) of visitors have reported alleviation of medical complaints, as well as relaxed muscles and joints. The healing gallery is thought to be the most effective natural treatment of rheumatic illness and may also relieve joint infection, muscular injury, respiratory disease and allergic illness.

Snow-biking, frozen waterfall climbing, and tobogganing: All these are offered by Schneesport schule Gastein (see Instruction), if you can squeeze them in around your spa treatments.

Events

The **FIS Nokia Snowboard World Cup** in parallel slalom takes place in Gastein in early January but apart from that you're looking at **jazz festivals** and **ski and golf competitions**, that kind of thing.

Accommodation

Bad Gastein

In Bad Gastein you should look at location pretty carefully, especially if you're not a fan of walking with skis or board, as some hotels involve a fairly long, steep ascent. The hotel **Cordial Sanotel** (0043 (0)6434 25010, chbadgastein@cordial.at, www.cordial.at) is close to the lifts to the fairly small area of Graukogel but not to the others. It is a beautiful hotel though, with a fantastic wellness facility (Jacuzzi, indoor pool, sauna, steam bath, solarium and treatments), and it is right on the infamous Gastein cascades waterfall. A double room will cost about €69–235 per room per day (no breakfast), depending on room and time of season. The **Hotel Salzbergerhof** (0043 (0)6434 20370, hotel@salzburgerhof.com, www.salzburgerhof.com), is in a fairly good location for the lifts. As well as containing a couple of the best bars in town (see Bars and clubs), and a good wellness area, all rooms now

have plasma TV (family rooms have a DVD player) and mini bars.

The **Grüner Baum** (0043 (0)6434 25160, urlaub@ hoteldorf.com, www.gruenerbaum.info) is in the middle of nowhere and is a beautiful and romantic retreat from the world. The décor is olde worlde and quaint and it's not really a place for the hardcore riders as it takes about 20 minutes to get to the slopes. It is, however, the place to go for the most comprehensive list of beauty and slimming treatments, with packages such as a Shiseido beauty week or a slim and fit purification week. No matter what ailment you go in there with, you're bound to come out feeling as fit as a fiddle.

Bad Hofgastein

Bad Hofgastein is a great place to be based. It's more of an active town than the touristy Bad Gastein, with shops, bars and atmosphere. The **Klammer's Kärten** (0043 (0)6432 67110, info@hotel-kaernten.com, www.hotel-kaernten.com) is our favourite hotel. It is friendly but luxurious, calm and classic. The wooden bar is cosy and welcoming, with new papers each day and free cakes in the afternoon. The rooms are beautiful and spacious, some even with baths in the centre of the room. Yet it is the new wellness area where the hotel really excels. The indoor and outdoor pools, and range of saunas, therapeutic treatments, solarium and plunge pool are set in an idyllic, serene and perfectly designed sanctuary. If you are staying in Bad Hofgastein, stay here.

Some hotels in Bad Hofgastein have partnered up with the Alpen Therme to give free access to their guests. These include the **Hotel Norica** (0043 (0)6432 8391, info@hotel-norica.at, www.hotel-norica.at), **Österreichischer Hof** (0043 (0)6432 62160, info@ oehof.at, www.oehof.at), **Kurparkhotel** (0043 (0)6432 6301-0, appartment@kurpark hotel.at, www.kurpark hotel.at) and **Panorama Apartmenthotel** (0043 (0)6432 6759-0, info@ panoramagastein.com, www.panoramagastein.com).

Eating out

On the mountain

The best places to eat on the mountain are **Jungerstube** (06433 7370) on the Bad Hofgastein side of Stubnerkogel (at the bottom of the Fleischleiten run and Jungeralm lift), **Treff** on Graukogel, at the mid-station of the chairlift up the mountain and **Knappenstub'n** on Sportgastein, a self-service restaurant at the first station of the gondola, with a great terrace and great views.

In town

This is one resort where we would probably opt for half-board accommodation as there isn't a great variety of restaurants to check out. **Mozart's Hotel** (06434 26860) and **Elisabethpark Hotel** (06434 2551-0) do good food and the **Weinfassl** has an old, traditional atmosphere and a good view. For a change, there's the **Sancho** Mexican – the only restaurant in town with a relaxed atmosphere that serves Mexican and British dishes. You will find it next to the waterfall in the centre of town. There's a kebab shop if you get desperate.

Bars and clubs

The Salzbergerhof has all the best bars, with the spirited **Silver Bullet Bar** (great live music at après ski), the **Ritz Cocktail Bar** and the **Gatz Music Club**. Of the other bars in town, the best are **Häggblom´s Bar** and the bar at **Eden**. The casino is also definitely worth a look. In Bad Hofgastein, the **Piccolo** ice bar has a great atmosphere and we loved the pool bar downstairs with three pool tables where you pay a trifling amount for an hour's play. The best club is the **Amschtadl**.

Useful facts and phone numbers

Tourist office

T:	0043 (0)6432 3393-560
F:	0043 (0)6432 3393-537
E:	bad@gastein.com
W:	www.badgastein.at

Emergency services

- Police: 133
- Ambulance: 144
- Fire:122
- Mountain rescue: 140
- Doctors' emergency call out: 141

Doctors

- Emergency service for drugs and medicine: 06432 85000
- Dr Foisner: 06432 8293
- Pharmacy Bad Gastein: 06434 22180
- Pharmacy Bad Hofgastein: 06432 62040

Taxis

- Taxi Rainer: 06432 3000
- Taxi Rudigier: 06432 6611

Getting there

By car

From Innsbruck take the motorway via Wörgl, followed by road number 312 via St Johann/Tirol to Lofer. Take the road number 311 via Zell am See to Lend and then road number 167 into the Gastein valley.

By plane

Salzburg (90km) Transfer takes around 1 hour and costs €58 per person (book online at www.gastein.com).
Munich (290km) Transfer takes around 2 hours.
Innsbruck (200km) Transfer takes around 2 hours.

By train

Take the Friday 16.39 Eurostar from London Waterloo to Brussels; then the Bergland Express overnight skitrain, changing at Wörgl, to arrive in Bad Gastein station, in resort, at 10.40. Return fares start at £212 in a 6-berth couchette. Contact European Rail (020 7387 0444, www.europeanrail.com).

Hintertux

Reliable snow all year round
attracts large numbers of
people to this lovely little resort

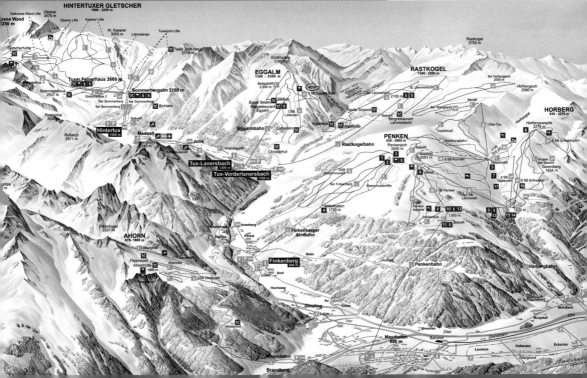

On the slopes	
Snow reliability	✳ ✳ ✳ ✳ ✳
Parks	✳ ✳ ✳ ✳
Off-piste	✳ ✳
Off the slopes	
Après ski	✳ ✳ ✳
Nightlife	✳ ✳
Eating out	✳
Resort charm	✳ ✳ ✳

The resort

The major pulling point of Hintertux is that it is probably the most snowsure resort in Austria, with a peak of 3250m. Snow is guaranteed all year round and the extent of the glacier is far less confining than that of many of the glaciers in Europe. Hintertux is at the end of the Tux valley and is accessible by car or bus from Mayrhofen and from the other towns in the Tux valley: Lanersbach and Vorderlanersbach. Hintertux itself is a compact hamlet with some lovely hotels and guest houses and a few amusing bars and clubs. Though small, it has a definite charm, as all of the buildings maintain a traditional, yet new and glossy feel. The lifts are a few minutes down the road from the village centre, where there are more hotels and one bar with a great après ski vibe. Hintertux is most suited to those who consider guaranteed snow to be the primary requirement of a holiday, with the provision of bars and off-slope activities secondary.

The mountains

Height: 1500–3250m

Ability	Rating
Expert	✳ ✳ ✳
Intermediate	✳ ✳ ✳
Beginner	✳ ✳

Getting about

There are 225km of ski runs, which are collectively named the 'Ski and Glacier World Zillertal 3000'. Of these runs, 86km are on the glacier and to get to the rest you'll need to take a 15-minute bus journey to Lanersbach. In summer, there are 18km of pistes open, and up to ten lifts, with the longest descent being 2km long. Spring also offers good value skiing/boarding, with around 60–70km open until May.

The park

The Hintertux park (www.hintertuxergletscher.at) is on the large glacier, and is one of the highest in the world, so you are almost guaranteed to find good snow. It does mean that it can get windy and cold, but if you keep hiking up instead of catching the lift, you'll keep your muscles warm. They have some of the top pros up on the glacier, shaping the hits, hence their immaculate condition. They also have a perfectly shaped pipe that is used for World Cup Half Pipe events (snowboard), a choice of jumps for different standards and a mixture of rails. One of the best features of this great park, is that it is rideable practically all year round.

> "The off-piste around the marked black runs is a good place to get some powder turns"

Off-piste and backcountry

Hintertux's snowsure glacier mountain makes it one of the best places to go when other resorts are lacking in powder; you can sometimes start exploring the backcountry from as early as October. Make sure you take real care exploring this glacial area. The weather can change totally within minutes and you could easily find yourself lost in winds and mist. It's not a good place to be in bad weather as it's too high up for trees to grow, so you're stuck in vast areas of open terrain. There are also crevasses to watch out for.

When the weather's right, the off-piste around the marked black runs is steep and a good place to get in some powder turns. Don't underestimate the dangers of the glacier – take a guide.

Lift passes	
1 day	€35
6 days	€168
13 days	€309.50
Passes bought for 4 days or more are automatically Zillertal Super Passes.	

Instruction

Luggis Ski and Snowbard School, Tux

Ski course (4 hours per day): 1 day €50, 6 days €122. Snowboard school (2 hours per day): 1 day €36, 3 days €73.

For further information:

T: 0043 (0)5287 86808

E: info@luggis-schiscule.at

W: www.luggis-schischule.at

Ski and Snowboard School Hintertux

Ski course (4 hours per day): 1 day €50, 5 days €122. Snowboard course (2 hours per day): 1 day €45, 3 days €95.

T: 0043 (0)5287 87755

E: info@skischule-hintertux.at

W: www.schischule-hintertux.at

Ski School Tux 3000

Private instruction (4 hours per day): 1 day €165. One-day ski course (4 hours) €50; 1-day snowboard course (2 hours) €36.

For further information:

T: 0043 (0)5287 87747

E: info@tux-3000.at

W: www.tux-3000.at

Other activities

Ice skating and curling: On the natural ice rink in Lanersbach. Open from December until the end of February 3–10pm. Skating costs €3.70 and curling costs €8 per rink per hour. For reservations call 05287 87385.

Shooting range: Air rifle shooting takes place every Monday from 7pm at the shooting range in the Tux primary school in Lanersbach. Contact Tux riflemen's guild: 05287 87337.

Sleigh rides: Cost €90 for four people. Book one day in advance at Café Brentnerstall (05285 87782).

Sports Centre Tux: This offers bowling 3pm–midnight. Squash at €7.50 per 30 minutes and tennis at €20 per court. Call 05287 87297.

Tandem paragliding: Take off from the Hintertux Glacier, the Sommerbergalm or the Eggalm in the double-seater glider (with qualified pilot). Contact Natursport Tirol on 05287 87287 or 0676 307 0000 or Tandem Funflights on 0676 328 1996 or 05287 86109.

Tobogganing: There are three natural toboggan runs on Bichlalm (3km run), Grieralm (5km run) and Höllensteinhütte (4km run). All runs can be accessed by taxi.

"The park is on the large glacier so you are almost guaranteed good snow"

Events

Hintertux host their version of **Oktoberfest** on the first weekend in September. In mid-October there is a **powder weekend** to celebrate the first powder of the winter. The **Snowboard World Cup Half Pipe** event also takes place in Hintertux's superb park.

Accommodation

Hotels and pensions in Austria are a cut above the rest – all you need to worry about is how far it is to the slopes and the bars. **Guesthouse Kössler** (0043 (0)5287 87490, www.koessler.at, info@koessler.at) is a friendly and pretty B&B in the centre of Hintertux. The cost is approximately €42 per night per person. The **Bad Hotel Kirchler** (0043 (0)5287 8570, office@badhotel-kirchler.at, www.badhotel-kirchler.at) is slightly more upmarket, with suites and apartments as well as their standard and superior rooms.

If you are looking for the utmost in quality, choose one of the hotels next to the slopes (and therefore a 20-minute walk to the village). Of these, the smartest is probably the **Neuhintertux** (0043 (0)5287 85 80, hotel@neu-hintertux.com, www.neu-hintertux.com) with stunning pools and large wellness facilities. A standard room costs €77–123 per person per day half board and a deluxe suite (50–70m²) €113–149. **Hotel Vierjahreszeiten** (0043 (0)5287 8525, info@vierjahreszeiten.at, www.vierjahreszeiten.at) and **Der Rinderhof** (0043 (0)5287 8558, hotcl@rinderhof.at, www.rinderhof.at) are also top quality 4-star hotels by the lifts.

Staying in Lanersbach is also an option, as it is now linked to the Mayrhofen and Finkenberg slopes and is only a 15-minute drive from the glacier at Hintertux. We'd prefer to either stay in Mayrhofen or Hintertux though.

Eating out

On the mountain

Gletscherhütte (05285 64470) at 3012m is a lovely hut at the peak of the Gletscher. It is open all year and the views are fantastic. **Spannagelhaus** (05287 87707) is a popular après ski joint, and is a good place

for a bite to eat. It is also open all year. **Tuxer Joch Haus** (05287 87216) at the top of the Tuxerjoch chair lift is good, but is only open December to April. Each of the latter two offer the possibility of staying over – call the restaurant for more details.

In town

There aren't too many independent restaurants, most are hotel-based. **Didi's** is a really nice pizzeria (pizza/pasta €6–9) and **Tuxersübl** has great food in a cosy atmosphere. Tasty burgers can also be picked up from the **Hohenhaus** pub by the lifts.

Bars and clubs

Après ski starts with a couple of beers at the **Spannagelhaus** and continues at the crazy **Hohenhaus Tenne** (05287 8501), just opposite the lifts back in town. Après ski is massive here, in a really atmospheric, big chalet-style bar. This really is how an après ski bar should be, with loads of drinking until around 9pm, when it closes up for the night. Between après and dancing, there aren't too many bars to choose from, mostly hotel bars. Later on, back in Hintertux 'centre' (if you can call it that), there are a couple of amusing places to continue. **Tux 1** (05287 8501) is bizarre, but cool. The atmosphere is mixed up; it has a typical, Austrian-style chalet interior, yet mingled into the décor is an 80s-style DJ box, a dance floor, disco ball, plasma TVs, a dancing pole, pool, darts and table footie. The clientele is equally bizarre, but it's great fun all the same. Look out for karaoke Wednesdays and 70s and 80s nights. At the **Batzen keller** (05287 8570), there are once again the 80s style features – smoke machine and neon – but it's really quite fun after a few pints.

Useful facts and phone numbers

Tourist office

T: 0043 (0)5287 8506
F: 0043 (0)5287 8508
E: info@tux.at
W: www.tux.at, www.hintertux.com

Emergency services

- Police: 133/05285 622060
- Ambulance: 144
- Rescue helicopter: 0800 207 070
- Mountain rescue: 140
- Fire: 122
- Schwaz District Hospital: 05242 6000
- Innsbruck Hospital: 0512 5040

Doctors

- Dr Katharina Weber-Gredler and Dr Simon
   Gredler: 05285 62550
- Dr Armin Zumtobel: 05285 62054
- Dr Wilfried Schneidinger: 05285 63124
- Dr Pavel Kriz (dentist): 05285 63341

Taxis

- Siegfried's Taxi: 05287 1718
- Taxi Siebzehnwölf: 05287 1712
- The Tuxer nightbus carries on until 2am from
   Vorderlanersbach to Hintertux

"Look out for karaoke Wednesdays and 70s and 80s nights!"

Getting there

By car

From the A12 take the exit for the Ziller valley. Take the Federal Highway B169 to Mayrhofen and then the Tux road to Hintertux.

By plane

Innsbruck (90km)
Salzburg (160km)
Munich (230km)

By train

Take the Friday 16.39 Eurostar from London Waterloo to Brussels; then the Bergland Express overnight skitrain, changing at Jenbach, to Mayrhofen, and then a local bus (41 minutes), arriving in resort at 10.11. Return fares start at £180 in a 6-berth couchette. Contact European Rail (020 7387 0444, www.europeanrail.com). Bus tickets (€4.30 single) are purchased on the bus.

Ischgl

Glamorous and chic, with great terrain and après

On the slopes	
Snow reliability	❄ ❄ ❄ ❄
Parks	❄ ❄ ❄ ❄
Off-piste	❄ ❄ ❄
Off the slopes	
Après ski	❄ ❄ ❄ ❄ ❄
Nightlife	❄ ❄ ❄ ❄
Eating out	❄ ❄ ❄ ❄
Resort charm	❄ ❄ ❄ ❄

The resort

If you like comfort and style, and return year after year to big-name resorts such as Val d'Isère, Zermatt, Verbier or St Anton, you should give Ischgl some serious consideration. The hotels are just as glamorous and plush, the après ski is as crazy as it gets, and the terrain is superb. You can also ride over to the duty-free Samnaun, pack your bags with cheap booze for the evening and clink your way back to Ischgl.

The resort is compact and focused around a pedestrianised street. The most convenient place to stay is close to the Silvrettabahn lift in the centre of town. There is a moving walkway from town to the other two lifts, the Pardatschgratbahn and Fimbabahn. There are also some really good après ski bars here.

The mountains

Height: 2000–2872m

Ability	Rating
Expert	❄ ❄ ❄
Intermediate	❄ ❄ ❄ ❄
Beginnner	❄

Getting about

Ischgl has over 200km of snowsure terrain to explore, as well as a superb park and some great backcountry areas.

Ischgl is good for most intermediates and for experts, but beginners should perhaps look elsewhere, partly due to the lack of decent slopes to learn on and also because many instructors speak less English than you would expect.

The park

Ischgl claims to have one of the biggest and best parks in Europe, 'Boarders' Paradise'. It was one of the first resorts in Europe to start pushing the freestyle ski and snowboard scene, and it held the first official World Championships for snowboarders. The park has a long list of features: tons of different sized kickers (from beginner to professional), one quarter pipe, World Championship half pipe named 'the tube', rails for all levels of rider, a big fun box, a boarder/skier-cross course, a giant slalom (boarders only), wave rides (from advanced to pro), and a kindercross (boarder/skier-cross for children with waves and jumps). Though called 'Boarders' Paradise', the park welcomes skiers and boarders.

"Ischgl claims to have one of the biggest and best parks in Europe"

Off-piste and backcountry

Ischgl mainly attracts intermediates who stick to the pisted areas, so there are plenty of fresh untracked areas around. Like a lot of other resorts, Ischgl has marked areas for freeriding. The Palinkopf (2864m) is a favourite and not too challenging and the Greispitz (2872m) also has a freeride trail. For the more advanced is the extreme trail on the Hollenkar face; this is one of the most challenging parts of the mountain and should be undertaken only by those in the know. Even though these runs are marked on the map, there is still the danger of avalanches so check out the avalanche danger rating and ask pisteurs if you're not sure. Also make sure you, and those you're riding with, have all the necessary avalanche equipment. Towards the bottom of the resort are some good tracks through the trees; a great place to head in flat light.

Lift passes	VIP (Ischgl and Samnaun)	Silvretta (Ischgl, Samnaun, Galtür, Kappl and See)
1 day	€50	-
6 days	€177.50	€208
13 days	€309.50	€363

Flexible passes are also available for if you want to ski/board for 5 days out of 7 (€173.50/196) or 10 out of 14 (€277/327.50).

Instruction

Ischgl Ski School

Group rates (ski): 1 day €49, 3 days €114, 5 days €156.
Snowboard course: 3 half days (am or pm) €116.
Private lessons (any discipline): half day €174 (€18 per additional person), full day €214 (€25 per additional person).
T: 0043 (0)5444 5257
E: info@schneesport-akademie.at
W: www.schischule.ischgl.at

Other activities

Beauty treatments: Alpenhotel Ischglerhof (05444 5330), Hotel Trofana Royal (05444 600), Hotel Madlein (05444 5226) and Hotel Seiblishof (05444 5424) offer beauty treatments to the public.
Horse-drawn sleighs: Adults pay €11 to ride to Mathon, where they have a short stop. The ride takes around 2 hours. Call 05444 5365 to book.
Ice skating and curling: The ice rink is open daily from 2pm, late night closing twice a week (05444 526611).
Recreation centre: On the outskirts of Ischgl (in the direction of Mathon), the centre has four indoor and four outdoor tennis courts. The courts cost €16–20 for 55 minutes. Call 05444 5264 for court reservations. Private lessons are also available on request.
Silvertta centre: This centre (05444 606950) has an indoor pool, sauna, steam room, sunbed, massage, reflexology, internet café, bowling alley and restaurant.
Squash: At the Hotel Solaria (05444 5205). The courts are open 9am–9pm, with 50 minutes (no equipment) costing €9.50.
Tobogganing: Every Monday and Thursday, from 7pm, take the Silvrettabahn to take a ride down the huge, 7km-long, floodlit toboggan run from Idalp to Ischgl. Toboggans can be rented for €8 from Silvretta Sports.

Events

Ischgl don't seem too fussed about attracting freestyle snowboard or ski events, but they are keen to encourage famous pop stars to play gigs here. Last year Lionel Richie launched the season and Pink did a concert marking the end of the season. Check with the tourist office for this year's line-up.

"Towards the bottom of the resort are some good tracks through the trees; a great place to head in flat light"

Accommodation

There are loads of plush hotels in Ischgl, most with a traditional luxurious feel, the most extravagant of which is the **Trofana Royal** (0043 (0)5444 600, office@trofana.at, www.trofana.at). There are nearly 20 styles of room, each with their own hefty price tag. The 110m² imperial suite can cost up to €320 per person per night, in the height of the season.

The minimalist **Madlein** (0043 (0)5444 5226, info@madlein.com, www.madlein.com), however, is significantly different, with vast open spaces filled only with marble, spotlights and the occasional

square pouf or artily positioned candle. Stylish and glamorous it is, cosy and inviting it isn't. The pool and fire room are very cool, but the jury's still out on the zen garden. A double room will cost somewhere in the range of €110–245, and a design room €165–280 (per person per day, half board).

Other good hotels are the **Yscla** (0043 (0)5444 5275, info@yscla.at), in a very central position on the main street, and the **Elisabeth** (0043 (0)5444 5585, info@ischglelisabeth.com, www. hotel-elisabeth.ischgl.com), another glamorous choice, right opposite the Pardatschgratbahn lift, with a great après ski bar.

The expensive hotels aren't the only option, there are loads of guesthouses and apartments. Call or E-mail the reservations department of the tourist office (see Useful facts and phone numbers). They will help you find something to suit your budget; just make sure it's not out of town, or on the wrong side of the bypass.

Bars and clubs

The two sides of town have their own après scene going on. At the base area of the Pardatschgratbahn and Fimbabahn lifts, our favourite bars are the **Ice bar** and **Schatzi** bar of the Elisabeth hotel, **Niki's Stadl** and the **Nevada Alm**, which all involve drinking, dancing and singing. If you ski down to the other side of town head straight to the **Fire and Ice bar**, which never stops, or the **Trofana Alm**. When the night sets in you need to head either to the **Tenne club** at the

"Ischgl is keen to encourage famous pop stars to play gigs here"

Trofana or go Ibiza style and hit the crazy **Pacha nightclub** in hotel Madlein. If you tire of dancing and would prefer to watch some lovely ladies strut their stuff, the Hotel Madlein also has a Coyote Ugly table dancing club.

Eating out

On the mountain
Towards Fimbatal, the **Paznauner Thaya** and **Bodenalpe** (05444 5285) are atmospheric chalet-style restaurants with busy bars. The Paznauner often has live music. On the Swiss side, the **Alp Trida Sattel** has great views and good food as does the table-service restaurant **Schmuggler Alm** in Samnaun.

In town
Ischgl's restaurants cater to most demands, from après ski munchies to gourmet cuisine. Trofana Royal's gourmet restaurant, **Paznauner Stube** (05444 600), will suit the more refined palate. For a good steak or

pasta, try the **Allegra** (05444 527564) attached to the Hotel Yscla in the centre of town with a Frankie and Benny's style atmosphere and menu, and a happy pasta hour. For pizzas, the **Salz & Pfeffer** (05444 591956) takes some beating, with fantastic wood-fired pizzas and an open feel, reminiscent of Pizza Express. For something a little cosier, try the **Grill Alm** (05444 5293), which serves up tasty traditional treats, or the gorgeous **Tofana Alm** pizzeria (05444 602), which you will find tucked behind the Trofana Royal. If your taste buds demand a change, try the top notch Eurasian food in the **Indochine** (05444 529357).

Useful facts and phone numbers

Tourist office

T: 0043 (0)5444 5266
F: 0043 (0)5444 5636
E: info@ischgl.com
W: www.ischgl.com

Direct reservations

T: 0043 (0)5444 526618
E: reservation@ischgl.com

Emergency services

- Police: 059 133 71 42
- Fire brigade: 122
- Rescue squad/Red Cross: 144
- Mountain rescue: 5234/140 (emergency number)
- Hospital St Vinzenz: 05442 60 00

Doctors

- Dr Walser: 52 00 (in office hours and emergency)
- Dr Treidl in Galtür: 05443 82 76

Taxis

- Alpentaxi Ischgl: 5757/ 0664 4663 373, info@taxi-ischgl.at
- Ischgler Taxi: 5999, info@taxi-ischgl.com
- Taxi Express: 20120 or 5814, taxi@20120.com

Getting there

By car

Take the Inntal motorway towards Arlberg and exit at Pians towards Paznaun. From here it is signed to Ischgl and should take 20 minutes.
Parking is free during the day, so you can pop in for a day on the mountain, but if you stay overnight you will have to pay.

By plane

Innsbruck (100km) Around an hour by road.
Friedrichshafen (170km) Around 1.5 hours by road.
Munich (300km) Around 2.5 hours by road.
Salzburg (300km) Around 3 hours by road.

By train

Take the Friday 16.39 Eurostar from London Waterloo to Brussels; then the Bergland Express overnight skitrain, changing in Innsbruck, to Landeck, and then a local bus (60 minutes), arriving in resort at 10.55. Return fares start at £198 in a 6-berth couchette. Contact European Rail (020 7387 0444, www.europeanrail.com). Bus tickets (€6 single) are purchased on the bus.

Kitzbühel

One of Austria's most beautiful and traditional resorts

On the slopes	
Snow reliability	❄ ❄
Parks	❄ ❄
Off-piste	❄ ❄ ❄

Off the slopes	
Après ski	❄ ❄ ❄ ❄
Nightlife	❄ ❄ ❄ ❄
Eating out	❄ ❄ ❄
Resort charm	❄ ❄ ❄ ❄ ❄

The resort

Kitzbühel's distinguishing feature is its fairytale pedestrianised centre with colourful buildings, sparkly lights and exclusive cocktail bars and shops. Reflected in this cosmopolitan atmosphere are the clientele, most of whom are elegant and sophisticated. Aside from all this, however, is a great après ski scene, in which the less sophisticated Brits can revel. It's a shame that Kitzbühel's charm and character does not extend far out of the square though – you quickly reach far less attractive suburbs and congested roads.

Kitzbühel's slopes are great for cruising, although altitude is a problem and you may have to go searching for good snow on higher peaks. The resort also has a seriously Old School attitude, hiding the snowboarders away on a separate mountain wherever possible. For the typical Kitzbühel skiers, the focus is definitely more on the pit stops than the powder.

The mountains

Height: 760–2000m

Ability	Rating
Expert	❄ ❄ ❄
Intermediate	❄ ❄ ❄ ❄ ❄
Beginner	❄ ❄ ❄

Getting about

Kitzbühel's slopes are extensive, but largely disjointed. The 3S lift has alleviated this problem to an extent by connecting the Hahnenkamm/Pengelstein area to the terrain of Jochberg and Pass Thurn, but the others are still out on a limb. From Pengelstein, you can begin the Ski Safari right over to Pass Thurn, a great place to head to if conditions are bad, as it offers the highest terrain in Kitzbühel. On this route you will cover around 35km of runs. The Hahnenkamm mountain is also home to the Streif piste: the Hahnenkamm downhill run. The run's not as difficult as it may sound, confident red run riders will be fine.

The Kitzbüheler Horn is home to the park (see below) and Bichalm has been left ungroomed to encourage freeriders to make the effort to get to this inconvenient area.

The park

Kitzbühel, along with a few other Austrian resorts, should really move into the 21st century and let boarders and skiers into the same freestyle park. The snowboard-only park, on the Kitzbüheler Horn, consists of a boardercross and half pipe, and a few jumps and rails that are changed regularly according to the snow conditions. The maintenance of the park is decent, if sporadic.

Off-piste and backcountry

Some of the best off-piste is really accessible, so first-time freeriders can easily find some good spots to practise on and even the more experienced backcountry rider won't need to do massive hikes to locate good areas. There aren't too many people looking for it either, so you should find untracked spots.

Look out for the fairly steep Ehrenbachgraben bowl, or try the 'freeriding mountain' Bichalm. To hire a guide, give Alpinschule Kitzbühel a call on 05356 73323.

Lift passes	Low season	High season
1 day	€32	€36.50
6 days	€147.50	€170
13 days	€257	€296

Instruction

Rote Teufel (Red Devil) Kitzbühel

Group lessons (ski or board): half day €35, 1 day €60, 5 days €145.

Private lessons: half day €120/150 (pm/am), 1 day €200, 5 days €1000 (€20 extra per day for each additional person).

New School snowboarding lessons: 1 day €60, 3 days €150, 5 days €185

T: 0043 (0)5356 62500

E: info@rote-teufel.at

W: www.rote-teufel.at

Other activities

Boutique shopping: Shopping and sipping wine in cafés is the usual activity of those who choose not to hit the slopes.

Bowling: This can be found in the nearby town of Reith, open 11am–12pm (05356 72161).

Curling: Available at a couple of places: the Alpenhotel (05356 642540, alpenhotel-hirschhuber@tirol.com, www.alpenhotel-kitzbuehel.at) has ice stick shooting from 1 hour per person for €2. Curling at the Lebenberg (05356 62444) costs €4.

Fitness centre: This fitness centre (05356 63412, www.fitnessforfun.at) is open 9am–10pm weekdays and from 1pm at weekends.

Horse sleigh rides: These cost around €60 per hour plus €8 per additional person. Call Eberl Hubert (05356 66380) or Henntalhof (05356 64624).

Hot air ballooning: For this popular option, call Ballooning Tyrrol (05352 65666, office@ ballooningtyrol.com, www.ballooningtyrol.com). Rides cost €180–360, depending on the length of ride.

Ice skating: You can also skate at the Alpenhotel (see Curling) for €5.

Paragliding: Three schools offer paragliding in Kitzbuhel: Alpin Experts (05356 72012, resl@alpin-experts.at, www.alpin-experts.at); Hermanns Flugschule (05356 67138, herm.krimbacher@tirol.com) and Tandem Flights Kitzbühel (05356 67194, tandem flights@tirol.com, www.tandemflights.at).

Tobogganing: There is a natural 5km tobogganing run at Gaisberg, above the nearby town of Kirchberg. It is free during the day (with valid lift pass) and €7.50 (single ticket) or €13 (all evening) at night. On Thursdays and Fridays there is also nightskiing at Gaisberg. The lifts are open 6.30–9.30pm but the runs stay lit until 11pm so you can stop for a drink or two on your way down. There is another, 2.5km, toboggan run at Bichalm. You can rent toboggans at the lodge and it is open in the evening but is not lit.

Water sports and spa: The Aquarena (05356 64385, aquarena@bergbahn-kitzbuehel.at, www.berghahn-kitzbuehel.at), situated close to the Hahnenkamm lift, is pretty impressive, with a big pool, adventure slides, sauna, hammam, massage and other treatments. It costs €8.50 for adults (€7.20 with guest card), €5.20 for kids.

Wellness facilities: You can find these in many of the smart hotels. For example, at the smart Sport Hotel Reisch you can visit the Aveda wellness facility (05356 63366 336, spothotel-reisch@kitz.net, www.sporthotelreisch.at).

Events

The **Kitzbühel Hahnenkamm Downhill** is now the most famous downhill event in the world. It's held every year in January and thousands of people flock to the resort to watch the best downhill skiers from around the globe battling it out on one of the toughest alpine courses.

Accommodation

There's a great range of accommodation, with lots of places to find 5-star luxury and equally as abundant guest houses and pensions where you can find cheaper

beds. Of the luxury options, we love the **Zur Tenne** (0043 (0)5356 644440, info@hotelzurtenne.com, www.hotelzurtenne,com), a stunning 4-star hotel, right in the heart of the beautiful town centre. The **Schwarzer Adler** (0043 (0)5356 6911, hotel@adlerkitz.at, www.adlerkitz.at) has superb wellness facilities and a gorgeous, traditional atmosphere. If you like the sound of a secluded alpine castle, try the imposing **Hotel Schloss Lebenberg** (0043 (0)5356 6901, schloss.lebenberg@austria-trend.at, www.austria-trend.at/leb). The location is inconvenient for the slopes and town, but there are shuttle buses to take you around.

If you are looking for B&Bs, you can get very good value places on the outskirts of town, such as pension **Thurner** (0043 (0)5356 62275), or something slightly more expensive to be closer to the main lifts, such as pension **Rosengarten** (0043 (0)5356 625280).

Eating out

On the mountain

The mountain restaurants in Kitzbühel have a fantastic reputation. The bars that are dotted around on the snow

> "The bars that are dotted around on the snow make good pit-stops too"

make good pit-stops too. Our two favourite restaurants in the Hahnenkamm sector are the beautiful and rustic **Melkalm** (05356 62119, Melkalm@aon.at), with fantastic food and the friendliest service, and the **Sonnenbuhel** (05356 62776, schialm@tirol.com, www.schi-alm.at), that has a great terrace with deckchairs. Over towards Kirchberg, the **Ski Alm** (05357 3282) has a great little bar out on the snow.

In town

For good, traditional Tyrolean dishes, as well as the odd tasty Asian dish, the **Schwedenkapelle** (05356 65870)

is the place to go. To get into the swing of things, pop along to the dinner dancing on Saturdays. The **Neuwirt** (05356 6911), at the hotel Schwarzer Adler, provides award-winning food (two red rosettes, one Michelin star), with just as astonishing a price tag. For Austrian cuisine in less formal surroundings, the **Chizzo** (05356 62475) is good value and has a lovely terrace and bar outside. You will find it just outside the gated town centre entrance. Our favourite was the Mexican restaurant **La Fonda** (05356 73673), where you can enjoy some fajitas and a margarita in a cosy and well-designed restaurant/bar. The **Shanghai Chinese** (05356 62178) has great Chinese food and an extensive menu, and looks like your typical Chinese restaurant inside. If you're missing Italian food, head to the bustling **Barrique** (05356 62658) in the centre of town. If you get post-après munchies, **McDonald's** is across the street from the Londoner.

Bars and clubs

The ice bars at the bottom of the slopes (**Hahnenkamm Pavilion Bar**, for example) are good places to start the après. Most tourists head straight to the **Londoner** (71427, www.thelondoner.at), which has a great atmosphere but gets really jam packed and is more expensive than other bars. The American-themed **Highways** (0676 3541465) with a diner area and a Cadillac convertible, and the cute **s'Lichtl** with its ceiling of fairy lights are also well-liked. The popular **Holzl Bar** has been taken over and turned into **Flannigan's Irish Bar** (63237). **Jimmy's** wine bar, in the centre of the square, is great for a more civilised glass of wine and a plate bruscetta. The **Bergsinn** (66818), just at the edge of the pedestrianised area, is modern and futuristic, with a great cocktail list. Late-night dancing can be had at **Take 5** (71300), a smarter and more expensive club.

"The Kitzbühel Hahnenkamm Downhill is now the most famous downhill event in the world"

The **casino** (05356 62300, http://kitzbuehel.casinos.at) has French and American roulette, black jack, poker and slot machines and has recently had a €3.5 million revamp.

Useful facts and phone numbers

Tourist office

T: 0043 (0)5356 777
F: 0043 (0)5356 77777
E: info:kitzbuehel.com
W: www.kitzbuehel.com

Emergency services

- Police: 133 or 05356 62626
- Mountain rescue squad: 140 or 05356 62265
- Mountain patrol: 05356 74544
- Rescue squad – Red Cross: 144 or 05356 691000
- Helios Hospital: 05356 6010, postmaster@kitzbuhel.helios-kliniken.at, www.helios-kliniken.at/kitzbuehel

Taxis

- Andi's Taxi: 05356 66222
- Silver Star: 05356 63500
- Taxi Aufschnaiter: 05356 6969-0, info@kitz-tour.at, www.kitz-tour.at

Airport transfer

- Four Season Airport transfer: 0043 (0)512 584 157, www.airport-transfer.com
- Transferbus.net: 0043 (0)820 600802, www.transferbus.net

Getting there

By car

From Munich take the E53, A9, A99 and A8, all in the direction of Salzburg. Then take the A93 to Kufstain Süd, highway 178 towards St Johann and the 161 to Kitzbühel.
From Salzburg take the highway to Walserberg, the 21 towards Bad Reichenhall, the B178 towards St Johann and the 161 to Kitzbühel.

By plane

Salzburg (80km)
Innsbruck (95km)
Munich (135km)

By train

Take the Friday 16.39 Eurostar from London Waterloo to Brussels; then the Bergland Express overnight skitrain to arrive at Kitzbühel station, in resort, at 08.20. Return fares start at £171 in a 6-berth couchette. Contact European Rail (020 7387 0444, www.europeanrail.com).

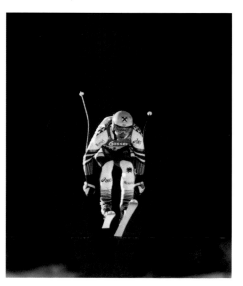

Lech

Chic, yet relaxed, with
something for everyone

On the slopes	
Snow reliability	✼ ✼ ✼ ✼
Parks	✼ ✼ ✼
Off-piste	✼ ✼ ✼ ✼

Off the slopes	
Après ski	✼ ✼ ✼
Nightlife	✼ ✼
Eating out	✼ ✼ ✼ ✼ ✼
Resort charm	✼ ✼ ✼ ✼

The resort

Lech is a stunning resort. Every building has the traditional chalet look and a stream trickles through the town, adding to the relaxed ambience. The resort's planning and construction laws cleverly maintain not only the traditional look of the hotels and chalets, but also space in-between buildings, providing an open feel and the convenience of being able to ski back to many hotels. The Rüfikopf cable-car, can be accessed from the main street and the Schlegelkopf chairlifts are just a short walk from here.

"Lech has off-piste for all levels of backcountry rider"

Oberlech is a small, traffic-free gathering of hotels just above Lech, only accessible by cable car. The cable car does stay open until 1am so you could sample some of the nightlife in Lech and then rush back up to your hotel, but we prefer it for a lunch stop rather than as a base for the holiday. Families might enjoy the seclusion though, and there is the ski-in ski-out option from any of the hotels there.

Lech attracts the rich, famous and royal – residents of Lech are proud that Princess Diana was a regular visitor, whose signed painting hangs proudly from the wall of the Hotel Arlberg. Despite the abundant prosperity, the resort is by no means pretentious or elitist, it's friendly and welcoming.

The mountains

Height: 1450–2450m

Ability	Rating
Expert	✼ ✼ ✼ ✼
Intermediate	✼ ✼ ✼ ✼ ✼
Beginner	✼ ✼ ✼ ✼

Getting about

The main slopes of Lech and Oberlech are accessed by the Schlegelkopf chairlifts. These slopes are great for low intermediates and cruisers as they are primarily wide and flat (boarders may find the flats a tad annoying). As in many resorts now, there are a number of off-piste routes marked on the piste map. In some resorts this is a little infuriating as it can hinder your chances of fresh tracks, but in Lech there are few people to compete with.

From the Rüfikopf cable car on the main street in Lech, you can make your way over to Zurs, although this is a one-way trip; you'll have to catch the bus back. These reds and blues are geared to intermediates, but you'll also find some decent challenges.

The park

Short but sweet! The park is well-shaped and groomed. There are six kickers, ranging from 3m to 12m in length and two rails, including a superb rainbow rail. It would be a great place to learn freestyle, and get your tricks dialled, but could be a little dull for the experts – apart from the rainbow.

Off-piste and backcountry

Lech has off-piste for all levels of backcountry rider. For the less experienced freerider, there are a fair few marked ski and board routes on the map, which are not pisted or patrolled. For backcountry trips, hire a guide. There is quite a bit of hiking and climbing to be done to access some of the big powder bowls, but this all adds to the adventure. On bad weather days, with high winds and flat light, the Krieferhorn area has some good off-piste spots which wind up at the bottom of Lech.

Lift passes	
1 day	€39
6 days	€184
13 days	€321
A €4 deposit is required for your electronic pass.	

Instruction

Alpin Center Lech

A private guide to show you the best backcountry areas will cost €205 for one person for one day, with a surcharge of €16 for each additional person.

T: 0043 (0)5583 39880

E: info@alpincenter-lech.at

W: www.alpin-center-lech.at

Lech Ski School (Ski and Snowboard)

Adult group lessons cost €50 for 1 day, €118 for 3 days and €169 for 6 days. There are discounts in low season. A private instructor will cost €205 for 1 person for 1 day, with a surcharge of €16 for each additional person. They can also arrange guiding.

T: 0043 (0)5583 2355

E: skischule-lech@aon.at

W: www.skilech.info

Other activities

Beauty treatments: The following hotels offer treatments and are open to the public: Burg-Vital-Hotel (05583 2291-930), Romantik Hotel Krone (05583 2551), and Gasthof Rote Wand (05583 34350).

Helicopter rides: For information about helicopter rides call the ski school on 05583 2355.

Horse sleigh rides: Reserve your horse sleigh rides from Haus Angelika (0664 3443 730, 4140), Pension Zugerhorn (0664 5207167, 2749) and Duftner Wilfried (0664 2841645).

Ice skating: Skating is really popular in Lech at the indoor ice skating rink at the Hotel Monzabon (05583 2104). You can also have a go at curling.

Paragliding: Ring the school on 0664 141 5166 for more information.

Tennis, squash and football: The Tenniszentrum Lech (05583 2780) offers tennis, squash and indoor football.

Therapeutic massages and remedies: Call the Physiosport Muxel (0664 1229 923).

Tobogganing: Tobogganing on the 1.2km long slope from Oberlech to Lech is open 9am–10pm. Bobsleds are available for rent from the Bergbahn Oberlech.

Accommodation

For 5-star luxury you could follow in Princess Di's footsteps and choose the central **Hotel Arlberg** (0043 (0)558321340, hotel-arlberg@lech.at, www.arlberghotel.at) with indoor and outdoor pools, sauna, beauty treatments and a gourmet restaurant. Prices are €240–318 per person per night for half-board accommodation in the main season. The **Hotel Post** (0043 (0)5583 22060, info@postlech.com, www.postlech.com), a Relais & Châteaux hotel, is also a favourite of royalty from many countries. The cosy lounge bar is the place for whisky and cigars and the numerous elaborate suites are exceptional. Jackets and ties are essential for meals in the dining room. This hotel was the choice of the Bridget Jones cast when they were filming *The Edge of Reason* in Lech. A night in the Post could set you back €210–880 per person per night for half-board accommodation, so get saving. The more affordable 4-star **Tannbergerhof** (0043 (0)5583 22020, info@tannbergerhof.com, www.tannbergerhof.com) costs from €112 per person per night half board. It is right in the centre of town and has a decent spa area, and one of the best bars in town.

However, you don't need to stay in the gorgeous 4- and 5-star hotels to get quality service and lovely rooms. We stayed in the charming **Hotel-Pension Felsenhof** (0043 (0)5583 2524, reservierung@felsenhof.at, www.felsenhof.at) and would recommend it to anyone. The rooms are lovely and the staff first class. It also costs a very reasonable €47–94 per person per night B&B (half board also available). Alternatively **Pension Angerhof** (0043 (0)5583 2418, www.lech-zuers.at/angerhof) is an attractive and central B&B and the cute **Pension Odo** (0043 (0)5583 2358-0, haus-odo-lech@aon.at, www.lech-zuers.at/haus-odo) is in a great, ski-in ski-out location, has only 17 beds and has reasonable half-board accommodation.

Eating out

On the mountain

The **Rud-Alpe** (05583 418250, rud-alpe@skiarlberg.at, www.rud-alpe.at), on the slopes just above town, is just how you would hope a chalet-style restaurant would look. It's big but still manages to be cosy with a nice fire. Typical Austrian food is on offer and it is very good value. You can also have an evening meal up here. The **Panorama** restaurant at the Rüfikopf top station also serves traditional Austrian food, and the views from the terrace are pretty good.

The sunny terraces in car-free **Oberlech** are one of the best places for lunch. We had a great meal at the Goldener Berg (05583 2205), which has a huge menu, although it was a little pricey. At night the Goldener Berg restaurant is popular for its fondues. The **Kriegeralpe** (0664 442 3697) is a cosy, romantic cabin, and a lovely lunch stop and the **Murmele** is a well-kept secret (until now), where those in the know pop in at lunchtime.

In town

Lech/Zürs has the largest number of gourmet restaurants in Austria. Those wanting to sample such exclusive treats should try the restaurants at the **Arlberg Hotel** (05583 2134), the **Berghof** (05583 2635), the **Burg** (05583 3140) or the **Rote Wand** in Zug (05583 3435). For more information, collect a booklet from the tourist office and look for restaurants with pictures of chefs' hats next to them.

By far the most atmospheric and charming restaurant is **Haus No. 8** (05583 3322), a restored old farmhouse. The restaurant is split into sections of the old house (the owner himself was born in one of the rooms). The food is fantastic, from its traditional Austrian specialities to fondues, raclettes, salads and soups. The best thing about this restaurant is that it's not at all expensive. For a romantic night, the **Älpele** (05583 3388) in Zugertal is beautiful and the evening is completed by the restaurant's seclusion – you cannot reach the restaurant by car, you must walk or take the snowcat. In Zürs, the **Flexenhäusl** (05583 4143) is another special place to dine, largely because it's so small, with only 20 covers. Reservation is a must.

The **Schneggarei** bar (05583 39888), a little hut near the chairlifts, looks like nothing from the outside, but it's beautifully decorated inside and the pizzas and ribs are great and reasonable. The **Italiener** restaurant (05583 3734) is a lovely little pizzeria, serving food from 6pm until midnight. The futuristic **FUX** restaurant and bar (05583 2992) caters for those who tire of local delicacies. Choose between an American steakhouse and the Euro-Asian option with woks, sushi and other oriental dishes. The lounge bar is great for curling up in front of the fire with a whisky and a cigar. If your taste buds ask for nachos and tortillas, head to the relaxed **Charly's Cantina** (05583 2339). The little coffee shop in the centre of town (05583 3734–23) serves great coffee and offers internet access (wireless and otherwise).

Bars and clubs

When après ski kicks off you have two choices. Either join the mainly local crowd at the outdoor S'Pfefferkorndl (05583 2525-424) ice bar in the centre of town, where you can get some good snacks if you're peckish (burgers, oysters, the works), or head to the tourist favourite, the **Tannbergerhof** (05583 2202). This is the most popular après venue, with fab happy hours, a great atmosphere and a heaving crowd until early morning. The **FUX** has a bar/club and is a good place for a whisky in front of the fire, and the **Post** hotel has a cosy, upmarket bar with a comprehensive cigar menu. For seriously late-night partying you'll need to catch a taxi into Zürs, where you will find two great clubs, the **Zürserl** (05583 2662) in the Hotel Edelweiss, and the **Vernissage** (05583 2271) bar/club in the Robinson Club.

Useful facts and phone numbers

Tourist office

T: 0043 (0)5583 21610
F: 0043 (0)5583 3155
E: info@lech-zuers.at
W: www.lech-zuers.at

Emergency services

- Police: 05583 2203 or 0591 338 1051
- In case of emergency call 144

Doctors

- Dr Elmar Beiser: 05583 2032
- Dr Reinhard Muxel: 05583 3300
- Dr Harald Rhomberg: 05583 2234
- Dr Miomir Radovanovich: 05583 30890

Taxis

- Taxizentrale Lech: 05583 2501, info@taxi-lech.at, www.taxi-lech.at
- Taxi Zürs: 05583 3110

Getting there

By car

The route finder on the tourist office website will help you find your way. There are tolls on Austrian motorways (for cars: 10 days (Fri–Sun) €7.63, 2 months €21.80, 1 year €72.67). You can pay at border crossings, petrol stations, post offices, tobacconist's, through your road recovery service or at Lech Zürs tourist office.

By plane

Innsbruck (120km)
Friedrichshafen (130km) For bus transfers E-mail transfer@airport-bus.at, or check out www.airport-bus.at. Expect to pay €30 per transfer.
Zürich (200km) Reserve your transfer at Lech travel agency (05583 3155, reservation@lech-zuers.at) or Arlberg Express (05583 2000, www.arlbergexpress.com). One way is €45, return €75.

By train

Take the Friday 16.39 Eurostar from London Waterloo to Brussels; then the Bergland Express overnight skitrain, changing in Innsbruck, to Langen, and then a local bus (25 minutes), arriving in resort at 10.33. Return fares start at £204 in a 6-berth couchette. Contact European Rail (020 7387 0444, www.europeanrail.com). Bus tickets (€3 single) are purchased on the bus.

Mayrhofen

Legendary park, lively nightlife
and good-looking town...
practically perfect

On the slopes	
Snow reliability	❄ ❄ ❄
Parks	❄ ❄ ❄ ❄ ❄
Off-piste	❄ ❄ ❄
Off the slopes	
Après ski	❄ ❄ ❄ ❄ ❄
Nightlife	❄ ❄ ❄ ❄
Eating out	❄ ❄ ❄
Resort charm	❄ ❄ ❄ ❄

The resort

Mayrhofen feels like a ski resort should feel; with a charming main street, traditional architecture, bars brimming with people from 4pm onwards, great nightlife and a snow park to rival the best in Europe. Mayrhofen has so much going for it that we can forgive it for having no runs back to town, and for the resulting queues for lifts. And if you need another reason to visit, prices are far more reasonable than at most of the top resorts.

The mountains

Height: 630–2500m

Ability	Rating
Expert	❄ ❄
Intermediate	❄ ❄ ❄ ❄
Beginner	❄ ❄ ❄

Getting about

The main riding area can be reached from the Penken gondola in the middle of town. If you can be bothered, you can skip the queues by catching a bus to Finkenberg or Hippach. Most of the riding here is geared towards the intermediate rider, the more daring should try the Harakiri piste, with a 78 per cent gradient. If you're undecided, you can pick up a leaflet that gives you a choice of five routes. The Ahorn area is a bus ride away and the place to go for peace and quiet; best suited to families and kids. The snowsure Hintertux glacier is a short drive away for more off-piste options (see Hintertux chapter, page 64).

The park

The Burton Park (www.burton-park-mayrhofen.com) has to be one of the best in Europe in terms of kickers and rails. It has three lines of kickers; choose according to your standard. The first kicker line has three jumps, ranging from 2 to 4 metres in length. The medium kicker line has two jumps, each 8 metres long. The pro line has to be one of the best around. It starts off with a 14-metre jump and then moves on to a 16-metre, with a massive 20-metre booter to finish it off. There is a rail line with up to five rails in a row and a pipe that can sometimes suffer, simply due to the low elevation of the park (1600m). There is also a mini snow skate park. The park is very well maintained – it is constantly shaped and the landings are groomed each morning so that they're not too solid.

> "The park is very well maintained – it is constantly shaped and groomed"

Off-piste and backcountry

Mayrhofen is not known for its steep and deep, more for its lively nightlife and freestyle scene. There are, however, a few areas that are worth checking out.

After a big snow fall, head to the Zell am Ziller area which is a superb place to get freshies, and look

Lift passes	
1 day	€33.50
6 days	€168
13 days	€309.50

You can also choose more flexible passes so that you can ride for 4 days in 6 (€133.50), 5 or 6 days in 7 (€157–175) or 10 days in 14 (€270). A season pass costs €484.

underneath the Larchwald trees in flat light. For getting some easy powder turns in, make your way up in the Horbergjoch area; the highest point of the mountain. Word has it, you can always find some virgin snow!

Instruction

Die Roten Profis Skischule and Snowboardschule Mayrhofen

One day in a group lesson costs €34–39 and 5 days €101–116. One day's private lesson costs €118–150.

T: 0043 (0)5285 63800
E: m.gager@tirol.com
W: www.skischule-mayrhofen.at

Ski Schule 3000

A great ski and board school offering lessons and guiding. Private lessons from €44 per hour. Group lessons from €34 for 2 hours.

T: 0043 (0)5285 64015
E: skischule@mayrhofen3000.at
W: www.skischule.mayrhofen3000.at

Skischule Mayerhofen Total

SMT is a superb ski school. One day (4 hours) costs €50 and 5 days (4 hours per day) costs €120. Private lessons cost from €93 for 2 hours.

T: 0043 (0)5285 63939
E: info@mayrhofen-total.com
W: www.mayrhofen-total.com

Snowboardschule Mayrhofen Total

A great snowboard school offering a range of disciplines. Video analysis is also available. A 2-hour lesson costs €34 and a 5-day course (2 hours a day) is €116.

T: 0043 (0)5285 63939
E: info@snowboard-mayrhofen.at
W: www.snowboard-mayrhofen.at

Other activities

Adventure pool: The adventure pool (05285 62559) has a water chute, saunas, crazy river, cascade, bubble pool, mountain lake and restaurant. Entry costs €3 for one hour and €5 for a day ticket. After 6pm an evening ticket is €8.

Adventure sports: Action Club Zillertal (0664 182 1898), www.action-club-zillertal.com, info@action-club-zillertal.com) offers loads of activities such as tobogganing evenings, skidoo driving, paragliding at €80–160, freeriding tours and snow shoes.

Aqua centre: The Aqua Centre – Fun and Spa at Hotel Strass (05285 6705) has sauna, solarium, massage, table tennis and squash. There are three indoor and nine outdoor tennis courts and three more squash courts at other venues. Contact the tourist office for more information.

Curling: There is an artificial ice rink with lanes for curling. Adult entry costs €3.

Nine-pin bowling: This can be found in La Fontana (05285 62578); open 4pm–1am on weekdays and 11am–1am at the weekend.

Paragliding: There are a couple of companies offering tandem paragliding flights. Stocky Air (0664 313 9800/0664 872 5913, www.fly-zillertal.com, toni@fly-zillertal.com) has a good range of options, costing €65–130. They fly daily at 9am and can provide you with photos and film on request. **Zillertaler Flugschule** (0664 180 2483, www.zillertaler-flugschule.com) offers flights at €65–100.

Tobogganning: A natural toboggan run starts from Gasthof Wiesenhof, with a total length of 2.5km.

Events

In January a **snow and avalanche camp** is held to introduce you to freeriding (www.saac.at). In February there is a great **street festival** on the main street with live music, street performers and shows from 6pm. At the end of March, the **Ästhetiker Tour 'Wängl Tängl' Snowboard Jam** takes place. Those not invited can attend qualifiers in an attempt to compete against the top pro boarders from America, Australasia and all over Europe. **Snowbombing** takes place right at the end of the season and lasts for a week. This mad event brings some world-class DJs to the resort such as the Audio Bullys, Soulwax, Darren Emerson, Annie Mac, Dave Clarke and Felix B from Basement Jaxx. If you are already in resort you can buy a wristband for the events or you can book the full package through Snowbombing – accommodation, transfers, event wristband, etc. There is no official ski/snowboard competition to accompany this event, although there is sometimes a jam session and a few

DJs on the mountain. Check out www.snow bombing.com for the most recent info.

Accommodation

Location is particularly important in Mayrhofen as the lifts and nightlife are all focused at one end of the main street. The 4-star **Hotel Strass** (0043 (0)5285 6705, www.hotelstrass.com, info@hotel strass.com) has the best location in town, right next to the Penkenbahn lift, and it has great spa facilities with pool, sauna and solarium. It is also home to the Ice Bar, the Speak Easy Bar, the Sports Bar and Grill and the Arena nightclub (see Bars and clubs). Rooms here cost €72–120 per person per night, half board. Ask for a room on one of the top floors to avoid the thumping music. Alternatively ask for a room in the **Aparthotel Strass**, a few doors down the road. These rooms are cheaper (€58–87), you can use all the facilities in the main hotel, the accommodation is just as nice and you are still central yet away from the noise. Contrary to the name, these rooms do not have any self-catering facilities. Another favourite is the **Sporthotel Manni** (0043 (0)5285 633010, www.mannis.at, sporthotel@mannis.at), well known

for its rooftop pool. It also has a fantastic position on the main street, just a minute or so's walk from the Penkenbahn lift. Rooms cost €70–190 per person per day depending on board basis, time of season and room type. The central **Hotel Waldheim** (0043 (0)5285 62211, www.hotel waldheim.at, hotel-waldheim@tirol.at) is a cosy and welcoming 4-star hotel, costing €55–70 per person per night. The charmingly traditional **Kramerwirt** hotel (0043 (0)5285 6700, www.kramerwirt.at, hotel@ kramerwirt.at) has lovely restaurants, and staff clad in lederhosen. The only 5 star is the beautiful **Hotel Elisabeth** (0043 (0)5285 6767, www.elisabeth

"Snowboarding brings some world-class DJs to the resort"

hotel.com, thalerfamilie@elisabethhotel.com), a little bit further out of town. The rooms have mini bars and balconies, and you can pay extra for a whirlpool, Jacuzzi and steambath. There are some very reasonable and pleasant pensions (B&Bs) in Mayrhofen and apartments for those who prefer to self cater. You can book these through the tourist office at www.mayrhofen.at.

Eating out

On the mountain

Most of the restaurants on the mountain are self-serivce. Our favourites are the restaurant on the way down from the Tappenalm lift, just by the snow park, and renowned for its schnapps, and the **Schneekar hütte** (05285 64940), at the top of the Schneekar chairlift on Horberg, cosy and traditional with good food and a great terrace.

In town

Restaurants in Mayrhofen cater to most tastes. For ribs, burgers, salads, pasta, wings, and a pint or two, in Hard Rock Café-style surroundings, **Mo's bar** is definitely the way forward. Similar snack food can be found at the curvy **Randum Café**, by the tourist office, and the **Café Tirol** in the centre of town – which unfortunately has unpredictable service, but the internet is cheap (and the food is good). All of these places are pretty reasonable. The food in the **Sports Bar and Grill** in the Hotel Strass is also very tasty. For pizza, the best are **Mamma Mia's** at the Elizabeth hotel and the pizzeria at the Hotel Mannis. For a change, head to **Singapore Chinese**, near the tourist office. For the best traditional cuisine in superb surroundings head to the **Wirtshaus zum Griena**; a

"A 400-year-old farmhouse that has been converted into an enchanting restaurant"

400-year-old farmhouse that has been converted into an enchanting restaurant. Not the place to go if you have a dairy allergy – most dishes come in a pan, covered in cheese.

Bars and clubs

The best bars for après ski are pretty obvious as you step off the lift; right opposite you is the **Happy End Bar**, and to your left is the **Ice Bar**, which is very lively, busy and bare; so you can be as rowdy as you like. The Ice Bar is part of the Strass Hotel (see Accommodation), as is the **Speak Easy Bar**, which is also popular. In the centre of town, **Mo's** is great for a pint and a bite to eat (see Eating out), and **Apropos** for a game of pool (open 8.30pm – 4am). Towards the older part of town and the tourist office, you will find the ever popular **Scotland Yard Pub** (you'll recognise it by the painted British flags and Old School English phone box). This pub has a great atmosphere and is always busy. Club-wise, you can choose between the house/techno/metal music at the **Arena**, or the more commercially biased **Schlussel Alm**, just a minute's walk from the main lift station (away from town).

Getting there

By car

Take the A12 to Wiesing, then B169 on for another 30km.

By plane

Innsbruck (75km)
Salzburg (175km)
Munich (190km)

By train

Take the Friday 16.39 Eurostar from London Waterloo to Brussels; then the Bergland Express overnight skitrain, changing at Jenbach, to arrive in Mayrhofen station, in resort, at 09.18. Return fares start at £180 in a 6-berth couchette. Contact European Rail (020 7387 0444, www.europeanrail.com).

Useful facts and phone numbers

Tourist office

T: 0043 (0)5285 6760-0
F: 0043 (0)5285 6760-33
E: Info@mayrhofen.at
W: www.mayrhofen.at

Emergency services

- Police: 133
- Ambulance: 144
- Mountain rescue service: 140

Doctors

- Dr Alois Dengg: 05285 62992-0
- Dr Simon and Katharina Gredler: 05285 62550
- Dr Jörg Ritzl: 05282 3758
- Dr Wilfried Schneidinger: 05285 63124
- Dr Armin Zumtobel: 05285 62054
- Schwaz Hospital: 05242 600
- Innsbruck Hospital: 0512 504

Taxis

- Christophorus Reisen: 05285 606
- Franky's Taxi: 0664 2500250
- Reini's Taxi: 0650 463 75 75
- Taxi Kröll: 05285 62260
- Taxi Sxhiestl: 05285 63840

Saalbach-Hinterglemm

Accessible and extensive terrain, a charming town and crazy après ski

On the slopes	
Snow reliability	❄ ❄
Parks	❄ ❄ ❄
Off-piste	❄ ❄ ❄ ❄
Off the slopes	
Après ski	❄ ❄ ❄ ❄ ❄
Nightlife	❄ ❄ ❄ ❄
Eating out	❄ ❄ ❄ ❄
Resort charm	❄ ❄ ❄ ❄

The resort

Saalbach-Hinterglemm attracts a huge variety of clients: swanky bankers roll in from Munich for the weekend to visit one of Saalbach's swish hotels, families enjoy the charming village and quaint mountain huts, ardent skiers choose the ski-in ski-out benefits of Hinterglemm and the big drinkers flock to dance on the tables all night.

Saalbach is a charming, typically Austrian town, and pulls in the mid- to high end of the market. Prices aren't cheap, but you certainly get what you pay for – the quality of accommodation is superb. Hinterglemm is slightly less glam, with fewer top end hotels, but it still has charm, and has fantastic access to the Ski Circus (see below).

The mountains are great – loads of terrain, perfect for the intermediate, but also with plenty of off-piste to keep freeriders happy. Freestylers shouldn't get too excited about the two parks – there are OK for beginners, but not for the serious jibbers.

The mountains

Height: 1003–2100m

Ability	Rating
Expert	❄ ❄ ❄
Intermediate	❄ ❄ ❄ ❄
Beginner	❄ ❄ ❄

Getting about

There are 200km kilometres of pistes covering the Saalbach-Hinterglemm-Leogang mountains, and they are immaculately groomed and pleasingly accessible. The mountains are great for all levels of skier, but intermediates will be particularly happy with the Ski Circus. This is the name for Saalbach's circuit of pistes, which covers both sides of the Glemm valley. Start wherever you like and make your way back to the beginning. Don't drag your hungover bones out of bed at midday and expect to coast round – you have to get your skates on to make it in a day.

Snow reliability is far from perfect due to altitude and the large number of south-facing slopes, but the snowmaking facilities are good.

The park

There are two snowparks: one at the base of Hinterglemm and the other in Leogang. The Hinterglemm park has a couple of jumps and a couple of rails but it's all pretty flat and aimed at the beginner freestyler. The Nitro park at Leogang is far better – it's 300m long with three rails, a box, two small jumps and two Big Airs. The tourist office isn't exactly pushing the freestyle scene.

"The off-piste is superb and check out the powder bowls around the Zwölferkogl"

Off-piste and backcountry

The off-piste is superb. It is 'off-piste' rather than backcountry – you can hop on and off pistes to your heart's content and spot your lines on the lift up. The off-piste itineraries through the trees towards Leogang are great in bad weather and check out the powder bowls around the Zwölferkogl, Seekar and Schattberg areas after a snowfall.

Lift passes	
1 day	€36
6 days	€173
13 days	€283.30

Instruction

Hinterglemm
Hinterglemmer Ski & Snowboardschule
Group lessons (ski and snowboard) cost €57 for 1 day and €134 for 3 days. A private lesson costs €54 per hour for up to 2 participants (each additional person €10) and €210 per day for up to 2 participants (each additional person €18).
T: 0043 (0)6541 63460 or 0043 (0)6542 7511-0
E: snow-fun@saalbach.net
W: www.skischule.com

Ski & Snowboardschule Activ
Group lessons (ski and snowboard) cost €60 for 1 day and €120 for 3 days. A private lesson costs €180 per day and €530 for 3 days for up to 2 participants (each additional person €20).
T: 0043 (0)676 5171325
E: info@skischule-activ.at
W: www.skischule-activ.at

Saalbach
Snowboardschule Saalbach
This snowboard school has a huge range of courses on offer. Aside from the usual the school offers Freestyle lessons (3 hours) for different levels of rider from €103 and Freeride days (3 hours), also from €103. Backcountry courses are on offer, with a theory unit and 2 days on the mountain (3 hours per day) for €125.
T: 0043 (0)6541 20047
E: school@board.at
W: www.board.at

Skischule Aamadall
One-day courses cost €57 for 1 half day (3 hours) and €146 for 5 half days. Private lessons cost from €41 for 1 hour.
T: 0043 (0)6541 668256
E:aamadall@aamadall.com
W: www.snowacademy.com

Skischule Fürstauer
Group lessons cost €122 for 3 days. Private lessons cost from €90 for 2 hours and €185 for a whole day (4½ hours). Ski guiding costs €185 for a full day (10am–3.30pm).
T: 0043 (0)6541 8444

E:fuerstauer@skischule-saalbach.at
W: www.skischule-saalbach.at

Other activities

Bowling alley: Bobby's Bowling Alley, (06541 63 89, www.bobbys-pub.at). There are four bowling alleys (€1.80 for 15 minutes), as well as darts, quiz machines, pool and table football.

Floodlit toboggan runs: The Simalalm run is 4.5km long and the price is €13, including transport up to the run, toboggan rental and welcome drink. The Spielberghaus run is 3km long and costs €7, also for transportation and rental. The Maisalm run is 1.5km long and toboggan rental costs €3. The Reiterkogel is fairly new – you can take the Reiterkogel cable car in the centre of Hinterglemm (open Mon–Sat 6.30–9pm). Rent a toboggan from the bottom for €5 (deposit €20).

Ice skating: Located after the Zwölferkogelbahn lift towards the end of the valley on the left. Entrance costs €3, skate rental €2.50 and an ice hockey stick €1.50. Call 06541 7403 for more information.

Paragliding: Air taxi (06583 8287, airtaxi@sbq.at, www.sbq.at/airtaxi) offers flights from €95. Air star (06582, airstar@sbq.at, www.airstar.at) offers a variety of flights costing €50–160.

Sleigh rides: Costs from €10.50 per person for a

1 hour trip (€6 for half an hour).

Swimming pool: This large (25 x 12.5m) indoor pool is in Hinterglemm and has a sauna. Call 06541 7131 for information.

Tennis: After the Zwölferkogelbahn lift towards the end of the valley on the left. The courts are open 9.30am–10pm. Call 06541 7403 for more information (1 hour costs €19, 5 hours €85).

Accommodation

Hinterglemm

Hotel **Theresia Gartenhotel** (0043 (0)6541 741, info@hotel-theresia.co.at, www.hotel-theresia.co.at) is superb. The water features are one of the hotel's best facilites, including a 30°C indoor pool, a 30°C Jacuzzi in the snow, and a 70m² adventure pool (outdoor). There's also an aroma grotto, salt water steam bath, and five different types of sauna. The staff are welcoming and the rooms are excellent, they even provide free soft drinks in your room. Rooms cost €104–217 per person, half board. The Aparthotel Theresia costs less (€82–142) and you still have use of all the water facilities.

Hotel **Glemmtalerhof** (0043 (0)65417135, info-glemmtalerhof@alpinparadies.at, www.glemmtaler

hof.at) has great facilities including an indoor swimming pool and sauna. The pensions are fantastic value, although check the location carefully. **Pension Blasius** (0043 (0)6541 6423, blasius@eberharter.at, www.eberharter.at) is run by a very friendly family, is centrally located and they have recently put in a small sauna and solarium.

Saalbach

The luxurious **Alpenhotel** (0043 (0)6541 6666, info@aplenhotel.at, www.alpenhotel.at) has two bars, three restautants and one nightlub, the exclusive Arena. It also has fantastic wellness facilities which include an indoor swimming pool, whirlpool, sauna and exercise room. The **Kendler** (0043 (0)6541 62250, hotel-kendler@netway.at, www.kendler.at) is another expensive luxury hotel that has an excellent location next to the Bernkogel chair. The **Haider** (0043 (0)6541 6228, info@hotel-haider.at, www.hotel-haider.at) is quaint and traditional and is also well located near the main lifts. It has a sauna and hot whirlpool. Week-long packages start at €565 and include half board and lift passes.

Eating out

On the mountain

The **Pfefferalm** (www.pfefferalm.at) is a fantastic mountain hut. It's as rustic as they come – the only light comes from candles and warm open fires, and bear skins cover the walls. The **Wieser Alm** is the place to go in the sun for views over the whole valley and the **Westernstadl Altoch** is the newest restaurant on the mountain and has a great western theme. Not just the place for carnage, the **Hinterhagalm** is also a beautiful place to dine, it serves traditional Austrian dishes and was also a backdrop for *The Sound of Music*!

In town

Most of the hotels are half board and have good restaurants.For a night out the **Heurigenstube** (06541 6345-58) in Hinterglemm is a casual restaurant, infamous for its ribs. **Wallner Pizzeria** (06541 6234) on the main street in Saalbach is good value. For meat, head to **Peter's Restaurant** (06541 6232). The Alpenhotel's (06541 6666) three restaurants serve a variety of cuisines – **La Trattoria**, is an Italian and

Spanish restaurant, **Pipamex** serves Mexican and **Vitrine** Asian wok specialities. The restaurant in the Hotel Kendler, the **Herzl Stube** (06541 6225), is highly rated for its cuisine and rustic atmosphere.

"The only light comes from candles and warm open fires, and bear skins cover the walls"

Bars and clubs

Some people come to Saalbach-Hinterglemm purely for the après ski scene. If you are staying in Hinterglemm you should commence the carnage at the **Goaßtall**. It has an outside area with patio heaters. Inside it just gets strange, with robotic goats dressed in lederhosen and real goats behind glass. There is a good restaurant too if you get peckish. In town, the **Hotel Dorfschmiede** has a great après ski bar – don't panic if the whole bar goes up in flames, they do it on purpose. The Harley Davidson and Bikers Pub has a good atmosphere and loads of motorcycle memorabilia – the bar stools are motorcycle seats, that kind of thing. The **Hexanhäusl** bar, with its weird witchcraft theme, is absolutely bizarre, check out www.hex.at. The **Tauzimal** restaurant and bar is also huge for après and later on, under it is the **London Bar** – an underground warren with pub, disco, lap dancing rooms (the lap dancing is thankfully behind closed doors so you can ignore it if you want to).

In Saalbach, you will start your evening at the **Hinterhagalm**, above the Turm T-bar on the beginners' slope, a crazy place for après, with live music and dancing on tables. Down at the bottom of the Taum T-bar, the next stop should be **Bauer's Schi-Alm** – another mad après spot. **Bobby's Pub** serves good value pints and you can have a game of pool, darts or table football, play on quiz machines or even try out the bowling alleys (see Other activities). Later on you can head to the Arena, an upscale nightclub. Live bands are often playing. Things kick off here around 11pm. The disco in **Berger's Sporthotel** is less exclusive and populated by the younger crowd.

Useful facts and phone numbers

Tourist office

T: 0043 (0)6541 6800-68
F: 0043 (0)6541 6800-69
E: contact@saalbach.com
W: www.saalbach.com

Emergency services

- Ambulance: 144
- Police: 133
- Fire brigade: 122

Doctors

- Dr Scheuch: 06541 6287
- Dr Spatzenegger: 06541 7878
- Dr Schernthaner: 06583 8447
- Dr Hartmann: 06583 8237

Taxis

Saalbach
- Taxi 6620: 06541 6620, saalbach@taxi6620.at, www.taxi6620.at
- Taxi Hörl: 06541 6573, info@hoerl.at, www.hoerl.at

Hinterglemm
- Taxi Schmidhofer: 06541 7163
- Taxi 6969: 06541 6969, info@saalbach-taxi.at, www.saalbach-taxi.at

Getting there

By car

The tourist office website has links to a route planner.
If you are travelling from the north by road, you will escape the toll charges if you use the Munich– Salzburg motorway (take the Siegsdorf exit before Salzburg–Inzell–Schneizlreuth–Lofer – towards Zell am See).

By plane

Salzburg (90km) Driving takes 1.5 hours.
Innsbruck (173km) Driving takes 2 hours.
Munich (190km) Driving takes 2.5 hours.

By train

Take the Friday 16.39 Eurostar from London Waterloo to Brussels; then the Bergland Express overnight skitrain to Zell am See station, and then a local bus (32 minutes), arriving in resort at 09.52. Return fares start at £171 in a 6-berth couchette. Contact European Rail (020 7387 0444, www.europeanrail.com). Bus tickets (€3.60 single) are purchased on the bus.

St Anton

Our top resort for 2007 - you'll get hooked on the 24-hour addictive atmosphere

Ski ARLBERG
www.skiarlberg.at

VALLUGA 2811
Knoppenjoch Spitze 2680
Weißschrofen Spitze 2752

On the slopes	
Snow reliability	❄ ❄ ❄ ❄
Parks	❄ ❄
Off-piste	❄ ❄ ❄ ❄ ❄

Off the slopes	
Après ski	❄ ❄ ❄ ❄ ❄
Nightlife	❄ ❄ ❄ ❄
Eating out	❄ ❄ ❄ ❄
Resort charm	❄ ❄ ❄ ❄

The resort

St Anton is without a doubt one of the best resorts in Europe. For competent riders with an appetite for challenging mountains and non-stop nightlife there is no better place to be. Despite its infamous party scene, the resort retains its charm, with the long, pedestrianised main street full of attractive, traditional buildings. This street is the focus of the action; the best bars and clubs and most of the restaurants are located here, and the main lifts are only a minute's walk away.

The mountains

Height: 1304–2811m

Ability	Rating
Expert	❄ ❄ ❄ ❄ ❄
Intermediate	❄ ❄ ❄ ❄
Beginner	❄

Getting about

St Anton provides 276km of pistes and 174km of backcountry runs to get your teeth into. What's more, the snowfall (and superb snowmaking facilities) is sufficient to maintain the slopes up to mid/end April. The slopes don't really suit the beginner, but all others will be ecstatic with the terrain, especially the backcountry enthusiasts, who have a wide range of options from the top of the Valluga alone. The ski routes are handy to guide those who wish to venture off-piste

without the aid of a guide, but don't expect fresh tracks, these routes are known to all. Make sure you have good insurance too, as the resort takes no responsibility for accidents on these routes.

The most demanding on-piste runs are on Schindlerkar, the Kandahar run on the Galzig and the Gampberg run on the Rendl.

The lift company have recently invested heavily in the lift system and the 06/07 season sees the opening of the spangly new Galzigbahn. This incredible piece of architecture will whip you up to the top of the mountain in no time – hopefully banishing those nasty queues.

> "You see a lot of the world's best pros filming here and making the most of natural hits"

The park

Given that St Anton is one of the best all-round resorts in the world, the park on the Rendl isn't that great, although it has improved over the last couple of winters. It has a half decent half pipe, a quarter pipe and a few kickers and rails. There is nothing that's over challenging, but it's OK for the intermediate freestyler. If you're here to push your limits, head into the backcountry and build something. You see a lot of the world's best pros filming here and making the most of natural hits; Jon Olsson, Tanner Hall and Simon Dumont have been spotted filming movie segments in St Anton's backcountry.

Off-piste and backcountry

St Anton is up there as one of the best freeriding locations in the world. We were totally blown away with what there was on offer. Like so many other resorts, especially in Austria, there are marked off-piste routes. The best, and most extreme, is the Pfannenköpfe, by

"Indiana Jones types should explore over the other side of the Valluga"

the Valfagehr chair. It is fairly challenging, and there are some good cliff drops and gullies, a perfect place to get the heart racing. Don't think that just because it's marked on the map you don't need all the proper avalanche safety gear; it's not protected from avalanches.

To step it up a level, head to the summit of the legendary Valluga and the massive powder bowl below. This eventually leads out on to another marked ski route where you have two choices: you can either traverse left and head down the Mattun route, or keep on down the steeper face, the Schindlerkar. On a powder day this is a great place to play in the steep, deep terrain, but if it hasn't snowed for a while you will probably find black run mogul fields, which are great only if you like moguls.

Indiana Jones types should explore over the other side of the Valluga (strictly with a guide; they won't let you up the last part of the lift with skis or board without one). It's hairy in places, but a very exciting area to check out. This leads you all the way into Zürs. A mountain guide is invaluable in St Anton to take you to hidden couloirs, bowls and cliffs.

Lift passes

1 day	€39.50
6 days	€189
13 days	€330

Instruction

Ski and Snowboard School St Anton
Ski courses: 1 day €54, 3 days €126, 6 days €204.
Snowboard courses: 1 day €61, 3 days €142, 6 days €220.

Private lessons cost €172 for 3 hours and €295 for 6 hours. Each additional person is €18.
One day's guiding costs €209 (€18 for each additional person).
T: 0043 (0)5446 3563
E: office@skistanton.com
W: www.skistanton.com

Ski School Arlberg
Ski courses: 1 day €54, 3 days €126, 6 days €204.
Snowboard courses: 1 day €61, 3 days €142, 6 days €220.
Private lessons cost €172 for 3 hours and €295 for 6 hours. Each additional person is €18.
One day's guiding costs €209 (€18 for each additional person).
T: 0043 (0)5446 3411
E: skischule.arlberg@st-anton.at
W: www.ski-school-arlberg.com

Other activities

Conference and sports facilities: The fairly recently built arlberg-well.com (05446 4001, www.arlberg-well.com) has an impressive combination of conference, sporting event and wellness facilities. It contains three swimming pools: an indoor pool, a children's pool and an outdoor pool, and tons of sauna facilities (Finnish sauna, kelo sauna, samarium, steam bath, two solariums and massage showers). Additionallly you will find a fitness studio and ice skating rink. Except the rink, which closes at 6pm, the facilities are open until 10pm.

Horse-drawn sleigh rides: These can take you into the Verwall valley. For reservations call Martin Tschol on 05446 2380. Sleighs leave from Hotel Mooserkreuz.

Paragliding: Tandem flights and courses can be booked through Flight Connection Arlberg (0664 141 5166, www.fca.at).

Squash and tennis: These can be played at the Raiffeisen Tennis Centre (05446 2625 or 05446 4001).

Tobogganing: The 4km floodlit toboggan run from Gampenplateau down to the valley takes 10–15 minutes and covers a 500m drop in altitude. Call the Arlberger Bergbahnen on 05446 23520 for more information.

Events

Right at the beginning of December (usually the first weekend) is the official opening of the resort when there are people partying all over the place all weekend. The **Powder 8** event (mid-January) involves teams of two competing in deep-powder skiing. The assessment criteria are technique, style, speed, synchronisation and symmetry of turn. The spring festival in April includes a freeride competiton in St Christoph. In April the **Weisse Rausch** is a Chinese downhill event in which all competitors (on boards, skis, telemark, anything) throw themselves from the top of the Vallugagrat (2650m) as fast as possible (1300m drop in altitude). The winning time last year was 7 minutes. The winning side qualifies for the World Cup in Canada.

Accommodation

St Anton really does have all types of accommodation available, from low-cost B&Bs to luxurious hotels. The tourist office claims that the cheapest room (with breakfast) costs only €30 per person (low season) and the most expensive room (half board) costs €350 per person in peak season. Unless it's high season, you are usually safe just turning up in St Anton as they have a great electronic system outside the tourist office that finds all available rooms for your required dates, and lets you know the price, location, etc. The tourist office packages are also worth checking out; the Powder Snow Weeks in January allow you to take advantage of the low season prices and more than likely fantastic snow conditions.

If you are looking for a comfy room in a great

"Take advantage of the low-season prices and more-than-likely fantastic snow conditions"

location, for the best value in town, we have the place for you. It is **Haus Flatscher** (0043 (0)5446 3603, haus.flatscher@st-anton.at), run by Emma Flatscher, who will do anything to make your holiday enjoyable. The rooms are excellent quality (with TV and phone), and an absolute bargain at €34–52 per person, including breakfast. A good 3 star is the simple but cosy **Ehrenreich** (0043 (0)5446 2353, hotel.ehrenreich@aon.at, www.arlberg.com/hotel. ehrenreich), only a minute's walk from town and lifts. A room will cost you €75–120 per person per night.

Those in search of luxury should look to either the **Hotel Alte Post** or the **Schwarzer Adler** (both are

4 star – there are two 5-star hotels but they are not particularly convenient for town or lifts). The Hotel Alte Post (0043 (0)5446 2553-0, st.anton@hotel-alte-post.at, www.hotel-alte-post.at) is absolutely stunning both outside and in, and has blended modern and traditional looks perfectly. The pool, spa and beauty facilities are incredible. Take your pick of rooms from a double (28m²), a junior suite (39–56m²), the Alte Post suite (98m²) or the Alte Post Deluxe (190m²) that sleeps 5–10 people! You will pay anything between €135 and €267 per person per night, half board. If you want B&B, there is a €14.50 reduction per person per night. The Schwarzer Adler (0043 (0)5446 2244-0, hotel@schwarzeradler.com, www.schwarzeradler.com) is an old, traditional hotel, with very similar facilities to the Alte Post. Prices range from €113 to €315 per person per night, depending on time of season and type of room.

Eating out

On the mountain

The **Rodelalm** (05446 3745) at Gampen is one of the best restaurants on the mountain for cosiness. This original Tyrolean hut has an open fireplace, a good terrace and superb local specialities. It is also open at night when the toboggan run is open. The restaurant on Rendl (05446 2353–550) serves international cuisine, including tasty wok dishes, and the ice bar outside has live music on Tuesdays and Thursdays. The Galzig run home provides lots of opportunities to stop for a meal or, more usually, a shot or two. The **Sennhütte** (05446 2048) is popular for its huge sun terrace, and sometimes has live music. The **Krazy Kanguruh** (05446 3803) serves a great burger, and a stop here on the home run is destined to mark the beginnings of a messy après ski session. At the **Mooserwirt** (05446 3588) the fun persists, and if you get the munchies, the food's good here too. In December the TV cameras hit the Mooserwirt to film the RTL Après Ski Hits programme.

In town

Some of the best restaurants are also the best bars. The offbeat **Hazienda** (05446 2968) has top notch steaks, fish, salads and pasta, which should always

be preceded by cocktails in front of the open fire. Food is served until 11pm and then the place turns into a night-time hotspot. **Bobo's** (05446 271454) similarly turns from a busy Mexican restaurant into an even more hectic bar later on. Staff and punters are all on a mission, which creates a great atmosphere, as long as you don't mind the occasional jarring of the shoulder. Sushi, sashimi and wok dishes are rife at the **Restaurant Fiu** (05446 42692), an intimate, cosy and trendy restaurant, and also a great place to stop for a perfectly prepared cocktail at the bar. **Pomodoro** (05446 3333) and **Scotty's** are both great pizzerias. For traditional food, **Fuhrmannstube** (05446 2921) is simple but cosy, and great value for money. Traditional dishes are also superb at the rustic chalet **Alt St Anton** (05446 2432) in Nasserein.

For something a little different, the contemporary **ben.venuto** (05446 30203), at the arlberg-well.com building is worth a visit to sample its fabulous food and stylish, minimalist décor. Though 'gourmet' food (an eclectic mix from Italy and the Orient), it is not super expensive; starters cost €5–15 and a main €10–26.

Bars and clubs

The **Krazy Kanguruh** (www.krazykanguruh.com) and the **Mooserwirt** are the best places to celebrate a marvellous day on the mountain and kick start the evening activities, both on the slopes just above the town. The staff at Krazy's three bars (Krazy bar, Down Under bar and Ice bar) are ready to quench that thirst but the really crazy parties are going on across the piste at the Mooserwirt (05446 3588).

Back in town you could stop for a drink at the **Anton** bar (05446 2408) right at the bottom of the slopes – a modern bar with good snacks and meals until 9.30pm. From there it's a short walk to the ever popular **Funky Chicken** (0664 4043 360), a crowded après spot, that maintains the hordes through the evening by serving dinner (tasty roast chicken or curry for €5–7), followed by the dangerous Margarita Happy Hour (11pm–midnight). The nearby **Platzl** bar is rustic, cosy, and well lit with a large open fire and live music 10pm–2am. At the centre of the main street is the **Piccadilly**, more of a British-style pub, once again with live music from 4pm. **Hazienda** is a great night spot, with perfect cocktails (see Eating out) and the tireless **Bobo's** is constantly buzzing with activity (see Eating out). **Post Keller** and **Kandahar** are the clubs to head to, and they often don't chuck you out until gone 6am.

Getting there

By car

Check out www.stantonamarlberg.com and they will plan your route for you if you type in where you're coming from.

By plane

Innsbruck (100km)
Friedrichshafen (140km) Book your transfer (bus or taxi) on www.airport-bus.at.
Zürich (200km) Book your transfer at www.arlbergexpress.com.
Munich (250km)
At weekends there are regular bus services from the airports to St Anton.

By train

Take the Friday 16.39 Eurostar from London Waterloo to Brussels; then the Bergland Express overnight skitrain, changing at Innsbruck, to arrive at St Anton am Arlberg station, in resort, at 09.51. Return fares start at £205 in a 6-berth couchette. Contact European Rail (020 7387 0444, www.europeanrail.com).

Useful facts and phone numbers

Tourist office

T: 0043 (0)5446 22690
F: 0043 (0)5446 2532
E: info@stantonamarlberg.com
W: www.stantonamarlberg.com

Emergency services

- Police: 05446 2237 / 236 213
- Mountain rescue: 140 or 05446 2970
- Ambulance: 144
- Fire: 122
- Report ski accidents by calling 2352 (or 2889 in Rendl)
- Hospital (Zams): 05442 600
- Avalanche warning: 0512 1588

Doctors

- Day Clinic Arlberg: 05446 42666
- Dr Sprenger: 05446 3200
- Dr Knierzinger: 05446 2828

Taxis

- Taxi Arlberg-Car/ Taxi Greisser: 05446 3730
- Taxi Harry: 05446 2315 or 2368, email taxi@harry.co.at
- Taxi Isepponi: 05446 2275 or 2179
- Taxi Lami: 05446 2806, taxi.lami@netway.at

Sölden

Austria's most reliable snow, and
a raucous, Ibiza-style nightlife

On the slopes	
Snow reliability	❄ ❄ ❄ ❄ ❄
Park	❄ ❄ ❄
Off-piste	❄ ❄ ❄
Off the slopes	
Après ski	❄ ❄ ❄ ❄
Nightlife	❄ ❄ ❄ ❄
Eating out	❄
Resort charm	❄ ❄

The resort

Sölden is a sprawling town, encompassing around a mile of shops and bars. The buildings are kept traditional and are mostly pretty attractive, although the busy road is a drawback. The après ski is absolutely mad and is the reason why some people flock to the place in droves, and others flee as fast as they can. Though far prettier, the general atmosphere of Sölden's 'party mile' isn't far off that of Blackpool's 'golden mile', so make sure it's your cup of tea before you book your ticket. The riding is superb for both intermediates and experts, with good on- and off-piste terrain, and an excellent park.

The mountains

Height: 1350–3250m

Ability	Rating
Expert	❄ ❄ ❄
Intermediate	❄ ❄ ❄ ❄
Beginner	❄ ❄

Getting about

Sölden's mountains have far more redeeming qualities than the town itself. Sölden can happily claim to have the largest glacier terrain in Austria, and connects three 3000m peaks by lift: Gaisloachkogl (3058m), Tiefenbachkogl (3309m) and Schwarze Schneid (3370m). It's worth taking a few hours to tour the 'Big 3 Rally', covering all the peaks. Thanks to all this,

there is good snow right until the end of the season, which is usually early May.

The 150km of pistes are mostly intermediate and can be reached by two cable cars at either end of town. The experts will also be happy with the off-piste potential and great park. For those who enjoy a spot of mogul munching, Sölden has kept areas ungroomed and you can often find some great bumps here. Beginners will be less happy, with their learning area not being particularly convenient.

"Sölden can happily claim to have the largest glacier terrain in Austria"

The park

The Base Boarders Park can be accessed by taking the Giggijochbahn cable car and then the Heinbachkar chair. The park has a good half pipe, three lines of kickers for all standards of rider, and a choice of rails that the shapers change throughout the season. These vary between a gondola rail, snake rail, wallride, two kinked rails, double-kinked rail, straight rail, two boxes, Y down rail, flat down rail and rainbow rail. There's also a boardercross here, although it's not always in the best of conditions. The park is especially good in the summer, when the BASE freestyle camps are held (www.base.soelden.com).

Off-piste and backcountry

Sölden has some great freeriding areas and there are loads of huge big open faces, but unfortunately a lot of areas are avalanche prone as they get the sun for most of the day, so watch out. When the conditions are right, start at the top of the Gaislachkogl (3058m) and make your way down the Wasserkar valley, a great spot with a few good cliffs to hook off. It's best to do this one before lunch as it does get tracked out really quickly.

Underneath the Giggijoch bubble lift is another hot spot for some powder turns. This leads out into some decent tree runs, but be careful you don't get lost as you could end up with a long walk back to town. It's also worth checking out the unpisted ski routes marked on the map; there's a good track from the top of Rettenbach (2684m) which takes you through the Rettenbachtal Valley and eventually leads back on to the piste.

Lift passes	
1 day	€39.50
6 days	€193.50
13 days	€320.50

You also have the option of buying a ticket to use 5 days out of 7 (€185.50), or 11 days out of 14 (€295.50). A deposit of €2 is required for the lift pass.

Instruction

Freeride Academy
Certified mountain guides and experienced freeriders can show you round the mountain.
T: 0043 (0)650 266 5292 or (0)650 955 8399
E: office@freeride-center.at
W: www.freeride-center.at

Ski and Snowboard School Aktiv
Prices are available on the website or by request.
T: 0043 (0)5254 6313
E: info@skiaktiv.at
W: www.skiaktiv.at

Ski and Snowboard School Sölden-Hochsölden
Group lessons (4 hours per day): 1 day €49 (ski), €51 (board), 6 days €157 (ski), €163 (board).
Private lessons for 1–2 people: 1 day: €180 (4 hours). There is a 5 per cent discount for on-line booking.
T: 0043 (0)5254 2364
E: info@skischule-soelden.com
W: www.skischule-soelden.com

Ski and Snowboard School Vacancia
Group lessons: 1 day €53 (ski or board),6 days €160 (ski or board). There is a 5 per cent discount for online booking.
T: 0043 (0)5254 3100

E: info@vacancia.at
W: www.vacancia.at

Ski and Snowboard School Yellow Power
Yellow powder organise off-piste guiding.
T: 0043 (0)5254 2203 500
E: info@yellowpower.at
W: www.yellowpower.at

If you want to improve your freestyle, the BASE summer camps in June and July are an ideal place to go. Check out www.base.soelden.com or email snowpark@soelden.at for more information or book a place on www.shop.soelden.com. Six nights B&B costs €299.

Other activities

Aqua dome: On a bad day it might be worth taking a trip down to the massive aqua dome in Längenfeld (about a 15-minute drive). An all day ticket costs €20.
Helicopter rides: Flights around the 'Big 3' 3000m mountain peaks cost €290 for 1–2 people, and €400 for 3–4, which seems a lot, as the flight lasts only 10 minutes. If you would like to book a flight call 0676 533 4050 (helicopter@wucher.at, www.wucher.at).
Ice skating: The skating rink, behind the sports centre, is open daily 2–9pm. Entrance for adults is €6/7 (with/without guest card) and skate rental €4.
Night skiing: This is usually Wednesdays – check with the tourist office – 5.30–8.30pm (last ride up). Passes cost €9.50 and can be bought at the ticket counters of the Gaislachkogl valley station.
Sledding: A 5km floodlit sledding run is open from the Gaislachalm to the Gaislachkoglbahn station.
Sports centre: The Freizeit Arena sports centre (2514, www.freizeit-soelden.com) offers a water slide, pool, samarium, sauna, steam and herb baths, fitness room, tennis, bowling, badminton and shooting.

Events

The **Back On Snow** parties kick off the season in October.

In the first week of April, Sölden hosts the 8th gay and lesbian ski week: **Gay Snowhappening**. Sölden claims this to be the hottest gay event of the Alps, and we're sure they're right. One of the week's highlights is the election of 'Mr Gay Ski Sölden'. In mid–late April,

the re-enactment of **Hannibal crossing the Alps** is pretty impressive, involving 500 actors, planes, paragliders, helicopters, bikers and fireworks. The **Winter Finale** (end April/beginning May) is a massive party weekend, with the highlight being the big air water jump, 'Queen of the Beach' contest.

Accommodation

The big and beautiful 5-star **Central Hotel** (0043 (0)5254 22600, info@central-soelden.at, www.central-soelden.at) has amazing spa facilities and beauty treatments. Prices are €158–296 per person per night. **Hotel Regina** (0043 (0)5254 23 01, info@hotel-regina .com, www.hotel-regina.com) is once again attractive and traditional and has a great pool, and beauty treatments such as wraps and special baths. The 4-star ambience may be slightly spoilt as you sip champagne on your balcony, by your full frontal view of the naked plastic mermaid on top of the Rodelhütte table-dancing club.

There are tons of good value B&Bs and pensions in and around Sölden. Your best bet is to contact the tourist office, or search online (www.soelden.com) for your specific requirements and dates of travel. If you want to be near the action, double check that the location isn't too far from the main street as some of the B&Bs are a fair way from town.

> "A massive party weekend, with the highlight being the big air water jump"

Eating out

On the mountain

At the mid station of Gaislachkogl, the **Almstubn** (05254 2214) has two big self-service restaurants, a massive sunny terrace and an ice bar. It's also open on Wednesdays during night skiing. At the top station of the Gaislachkogl, on the second floor, is **Tre Milla**

(05254 508 888), the Alps' highest pizzeria at 2058m. The views of peaks are superb from here. The quaint **Huhnersteign** (05254 2872), on the Rettenbach glacier ski route, is one of the best huts on the mountain for a good lunch in the sun.

Gampe Alm (05254 2144) and **Gampe Thaya** (0664 240 0246) on ski trail 11, between Hochsölden and Gaislachkogl, are both good rustic mountain huts with cosy atmospheres and table service. **Eugens Obstlerhütte** (05254 2186), on the run from Hochsölden to Sölden, is a great place to stop for a beer at the end of the day.

In town

The restaurants in town aren't the best selection we've ever seen, but as you'll probably be too drunk to remember them it shouldn't cause you too much heartache.

The best pizzeria in town is the **Nudeltopf** (05254 2010), and **Armin's Törggle** (05254 3535) has good-value local fare. Mexican food can be found at the **Hacienda** restaurant (05254 3526), above the tourist office. The restaurant in **Hotel Dominic** (05254 3526) is one of the smarter places to dine. There's nothing we'd get too excited about.

Bars and clubs

As you ride down the mountain at the end of the day you cannot miss the après ski hangouts, with folks clomping around on tables, happily swinging their beers. If you come down the slopes into Ausserwald, stop at **Philipp's** (05254 23510) for a few beverages.

Back in town, the atmosphere continues in many bars along Sölden's sprawling streets. **Fire and Ice**, **Bierhimml** and the glass-housed **Bla Bla** at the Dominic hotel are three of the best bars to start at. **Hinterher**, **Ötzi Keller** and **Lawine**, under hotel Tyrolerhof, are all good bar/clubs to move on to and are open late. To see some naked ladies strutting their stuff, head to the classy-looking Rodelhütte – look out for the naked plastic mermaids on the roof.

Getting there

By car

Sölden's website (www.soelden.com) has a very user-friendly route planner to help you find your way there by car.

By plane

Innsbruck (85km) Transfer time is just 1 hour. *Munich, Zürich, Salzberg and Bozen (all 210–280km)* Transfer time is 2.5–3.5 hours.

By train

Take the Friday 16.39 Eurostar from London Waterloo to Brussels; then the Bergland Express overnight skitrain, changing in Innsbruck, to Otzal, and then a local bus (60 minutes), arriving in resort at 10.15. Return fares start at £194 in a 6-berth couchette. Contact European Rail (020 7387 0444, www.europeanrail.com). Bus tickets (€6.70 single) are purchased on the bus.

Useful facts and phone numbers

Tourist office

T: 0043 (0)5254 508/0043 (0)5254 5100
F: 0043 (0)5254 510 520
E: bergbahnen@soelden.com
W: www.soelden.com

Emergency services

- Police: 05254 30399
- Ambulance (Rotes Kreuz): 05254 2360
- In the case of an accident on the mountain: 05254 508 825

Doctors

- Dr Gerhard Leys: 05254 2040
- Dr Gerhard Wutscher: 05254 2207
- Dr Wolfgang Drapela: 05254 30399

Taxis

- Taxi Quaxi: 05254 3737
- Taxi Lenz: 05254 2133

Zell am See

A small, attractive resort, geared towards the intermediate rider

On the slopes	
Snow reliability	❄ ❄ ❄
Park	❄ ❄
Off-piste	❄ ❄

Off the slopes	
Après ski	❄ ❄ ❄ ❄
Nightlife	❄ ❄ ❄
Eating out	❄ ❄ ❄
Resort charm	❄ ❄ ❄

The resort

Zell am See is a small resort by the side of a lake, full of character and Austrian charm. Despite its size, there are a decent number of good shops, bars and clubs. The mountains are just as beautiful as the town, and perfect for cruising and taking in the views. The terrain is not extensive though, and the experienced rider will cover the mountain quickly.

The mountains

Height: 755–3030m

Ability	Rating
Expert	❄
Intermediate	❄ ❄ ❄ ❄
Beginner	❄ ❄ ❄

Getting about

There are 130km of piste in Zell am See and the longest is 4km. To ski the Schmittenhöhe, avoid the main cable car from town as the queues can be pretty hideous. It's best to catch the newly extended Areit gondola from neighboring Schüttdorf direct to the Breiteck peak. If the snow suffers in Zell am See you can always head to the year-long glacier at Kaprun, beneath the peak of the Kitzsteinhorn, which is less than 10km away.

Zell am See should appeal to beginners and intermediates, but is less suited to experts. There are a couple of runs that are used for the World Cup and other downhill races, which are open to the public when events aren't on but that's about it. It is also not the place to find the steep and deep. There are a few areas just off the pistes and in the trees, but nothing major. The slopes also receive a lot of sun, so the snow can suffer.

The park

There is a small park in Zell am See, with a few kickers, a hip and a selection of challenging rails. It's not often that the park gets re-shaped so its conditions is changeable.

Lift passes	
1 day	€34
6 days	€164

Instruction

Sport Alpin Zell am See

A 2 half day course costs €63 and a 1 hour private lesson costs from €43 (€10 per extra person). These prices apply to both skiing and snowboarding.
T: 0043 (0)664 4531417
E: info@sport-alpin.at
W: www.sport-alpin.at

Ski and Snowboardschule Zell am See

Skiing: A full day (4 hours) costs €52 and 3 days €125 (4 hours per day)
Snowboard: 1 day (2 hours) costs €42 and 3 days €93 (2 hours per day)
T: 0043 (0)6542 56020
E: skischule@zellamsee.at
W: www.ski-zellamsee.at

"The mountains are just as beautiful as the town and perfect for cruising and taking in the views"

Other activities

Bowling alley: This is located at Schlosstrasse (8222)
Paragliding: Contact the tourist office for details.
Sports Centre: The Kaprun Optimum has a fitness
room and indoor and outdoor swimming pool.
Tobogganing: There is a floodlit toboggan run from
Gasthof Köhlergraben in Zell am See.

Accommodation

Hotel Berner (0043 (0)6542 799, info@berner
hotel.com, www.bernerhotel.com) is beautiful and a
great place to relax after a hard day on the slopes. It's
run by two brothers who take great pleasure in making
sure that you get well looked after. The restaurant and
food are fantastic and you can take advantage of the
outdoor pools and games room. The best thing about
the hotel is that you can ski or board right from the door.
From €84 per person per night, half board.

To bling it up, stay in the only 5 star in town, the **Hotel
Salzburgerhof** (0043 (0)6542 765, 5sterne@salz
burgerhof.at, www.salzburgerhof.at). The hotel includes
a wellness centre, sauna, swimming pool, solarium,
massage facilities and amazing food in its award-
winning restaurant. Prices from €140 per person per
night.

For cheaper accommodation, check out the excellent
Gasthof Steinerwist (0043 (0)6542 72502, office@
steinerwirt.com, www.gastlichkeit.com), a 2-star hotel
that's not far from the slopes or the main shops and
bars. Prices are €27–45 per person, B&B.

> "The Pinzgauer Diele
> is a great venue for
> après ski and it is
> also one of the bet
> spots for dancing
> until the early hours"

Eating out

On the mountain
There are some lovely mountain huts in Zell am See.
The **Ebenbergalm** (066438 14 141), on Schmittenhöhe, is a cosy hut with a small terrace, just above the
main town. The **Pinzgauer Hütte** (065497861) serves
a good variety of food, including local specialities, and
has great views. The **Schmitten Pfiff** has amazing
panoramic views. The **Berghotel** (www.berghotel-
schmitten.at) has parties on the terrace and is a good
choice of hotel if you want to be the first person on the
slopes.

In town
For a tasty steak head to the **Traubenstube** or the
Steinerwirt. **Pizzeria Giuseppe** or **Zum Caser** serve
great pizzas and the **Crazy** restaurant at Crazy Daisy's
has a Mexican restaurant attached to the bar and it's
good value food too. For award-winning gourmet food,
head to the **Schloss Prielau** (72609) or the 'Einkehr'
bistro (72363).

Bars and clubs

The most popular place in Zell am See is **Crazy Daisy's**
– there is a band playing every night and it's always
jam packed. If you want to hang around with the locals
head to the **Bierstadl**. If you're feeling a bit more
chilled, head to the **Hirschenkeller** where you can
listen to blues, rock and reggae music. The **Pinzgauer
Diele** is a great venue for après ski and it is also one
of the best spots for dancing until the early hours. The
Viva Club gets quite crazy late at night and has live
music and DJs.

Useful facts and phone numbers

Tourist office

T: 0043 (0)6542 770
E: wolf@zellamsee.at
W: www.zellamsee.at

Emergency services

- In all emergencies call 112/122
- Hospital: 06542 777

Doctors

- Dr Helmuth Barth: 06542 56766
- Dr Wolfgang Göttlicher: 06542 72136
- Dr Johann Hanl: 06542 47360

Taxis

- Taxi Rainer: 06541 6261, zellamsee@taxi-saalbach.at

Getting there

By car

From the north of Austria head towards Munich and continue on the motorway towards Salzburg. At Siegsdorf follow the street south to Lofer, Saalfelden and Zell am See. Drivers coming from the east should take the motorway Vienna – Salzburg – Bischofshofen. There get off and follow the signs through St Johann, Schwarzach, Bruck to Zell am See. Coming from the west gives you the choice between the motorway Stuttgart – Munich – Salzburg or Bregenz – Innsbruck – Wörgl.

By plane

Salzburg (100km) There is a regular bus from Salzburg to Zell am See. Check out http://engl.salzburg-airport.com/bus.html. *Munich (250km)*

By train

Take the Friday 16.39 Eurostar from London Waterloo to Brussels; then the Bergland Express overnight skitrain to arrive at Zell am See station, in resort, at 09.15. Return fares start at £171 in a 6-berth couchette. Contact European Rail (020 7387 0444, www.europeanrail.com).

France

The home of many of the big commercial resorts, with a few hidden gems

Alpe d'Huez

A great resort for
all levels of rider

On the slopes	
Snow reliability	❄ ❄ ❄ ❄
Parks	❄ ❄ ❄
Off-piste	❄ ❄ ❄ ❄

Off the slopes	
Après ski	❄ ❄ ❄
Nightlife	❄ ❄ ❄
Eating out	❄ ❄ ❄
Resort charm	❄ ❄

The resort

Alpe d'Huez is a fantastic all-round resort. The mountain is extensive, and suits all standards of rider. The resort has great snow conditions and off-piste, and it also gets a lot of sun, which can take its toll on the piste, but is great when there is a big snowfall and bluebird skies the next day.

We like the town, and find the locals really friendly, but this opinion is not universal; many people think that the resort is fairly ugly and has retained little of its traditional French charm. Alpe d'Huez is less well known than the big resorts, but it's starting to give them a run for their money, and the following of Brits who return year after year is steadily rising. It also helps that Alpe d'Huez is only an hour from Grenoble airport.

The mountains

Height: 1100–3330m

Ability	Rating
Expert	❄ ❄ ❄ ❄
Intermediate	❄ ❄ ❄ ❄
Beginner	❄ ❄ ❄ ❄

Getting about

Pic Blanc is the highest peak in the Grandes Rousses Massif at 3330m and offers breathtaking views of the national Ecrins Park and its peaks. The altitude almost guarantees good snow, although the sun can do some damage later in the season. There are 245km of pistes, offering a wealth of slopes for all levels of rider. Make sure that you explore the far corners of the ski area, such as the runs to Oz and Vaujany, as you will find some lovely peaceful slopes. The adrenaline-fuelled can either hit the backcountry, or head to the 16km Sarenne black run – the longest in Europe.

> "The adrenaline-fuelled can either hit the backcountry, or head to the 16km Sarenne black run – the longest in Europe"

The park

Alpe d'Huez has done a great job with the park in recent years. In the park at the bottom of the ski runs are the usual rails, hip jumps, different size kickers and half pipe, which is well looked after. There is another park, next to the Poutran pass, for the more advanced rider, where you will find rails, a spine jump, a big air kicker, and a skier/boarder-cross. This is higher than the original park, so it doesn't get as slushy in the afternoons.

Off-piste and backcountry

Alpe d'Huez has some of the best areas for backcountry riding in the Alps. Most of the terrain is above the tree line, which can cause a problem if there is a big storm or serious cloud cover. The Grand Sablat, which runs through the east face of the Massif des Grandes Rousses, has a descent of 2000 vertical metres. Here you will also find a few big couloirs. You will need a guide and will also need to organise transport to get back to the resort. Check with the bureau des guides for booking and more information.

Lift passes	VISALP pass
1 day	€36.20
6 days	€187
13 days	€317

Instruction

British Masterclass

The Masterclass are top ski and snowboard instructors, with a great reputation. Group lessons cost €160 for 3 half days (6 people maximum) and private lessons start at €70 for 1 hour for 1 or 2 people.

T: 0033 (0)4 76 80 93 83

E: stuart@masterclass-ski.co.uk

W: www.masterclass-ski.co.uk

Bureau des Guides

A guide costs €300 for 1 day, for 1–4 people. For more than 4 people there is a supplement of €15 per person. They also offer a number of other activities, including off-piste skiing in groups, heliskiing, ski touring and ice climbing.

T: 0033 (0)4 76 80 42 55

E: info@guidesalpedhuez.com

W: www.guidesalpedhuez.com

ESF

The ESF have a big range of ski and snowboard instructors, most of whom are English speaking. Lessons cost from €26 for a half day and €41 for a full day. Group lessons are €96 for 6 half days and €177 for 6 full days.

T: 0033 (0)4 76 80 31 69

E: info@esf-alpedhuez.com

W: www.esf-alpedhuez.com

ESI

A full day of lessons costs €47, and from €23 for half a day. Group lessons are from €115 for 6 half days and €236 for 6 full days (up to 10 people per lesson).

T: 0033 (0)4 76 80 42 77

E: mgm.international@wanadoo.fr

W: www.ecoledeskiinternationale.com

Other activities

Ice driving: The Eclose ice track is a highly specialised training ground for professional racing drivers. Here, you can have a lesson on how to drive on ice and snow, or learn more advanced skills. Individual lessons cost €35 for half an hour with a driving school car. A course in a Porsche costs €460 per person for 6 hours.

Ice skating: The rink on the Avenue des Jeux (06 88 16 60 75) offers lessons in skating and ice dancing.

Indoor heated swimming pool: €6 for adult admission into the swimming pool, open daily 11am–8.30pm.

Night skiing: The signal slalom stadium is a 950km piste, floodlit for 2 nights a week. Night skiing is free for those who have a VISALP pass for 2 days or more, but without a pass it will cost €8.50.

Paragliding: Alpe d'Huez Parapente (06 89 09 49 39), Element'air (06 73 37 03 39, www.element-air.com) and Ecole du Parapente Français (04 76 11 34 76) offer tandem flights.

Sports and convention centre: There is a wide range of activities from martial arts and orienteering to squash and tennis (04 76 11 21 41). Activities cost around €6, but many are free with the VISALP pass.

Tobogganing: The night-time toboggan run is free for those with the VISALP pass, or €1.50 per ride/ €5 per 5 rides.

Yoga: Classes cost €9 per session (04 76 79 12 33).

Accommodation

The 4-star Hotel Au Chamois d'Or (0033 (0)4 76 80 31 32, resa@chamoisdor-alpedhuez.com, www.chamoisdor-alpedhuez.com) is in a fantastic location for access to the pistes and lifts, and it is equally well suited for the shops, restaurants and bars. It has good facilities, with swimming pool, Jacuzzi and fitness room. Prices start at €195 per day for half board.

The other 4-star hotel in town is the Royal Ours Blanc (0033 (0)4 76 80 35 50, resa@eurogroup-vacances. com, www.eurogroup-vacances.com), a huge hotel, not in the prettiest building, but with good restaurants, fitness centre and swimming pool. Half-board accommodation starts from €569 per person per week. Hotel Les Grandes Rousses (0033 (0)4 76

80 33 11, hmclesgrandesrousses@hmc-hotels.com, www.hmc-hotels.com) is a beautiful and charming, 3-star, chalet-style hotel, in the centre of Alpe d'Huez, 50 metres from the lifts. Half board costs from €89 per night per person – great value!

Eating out

On the mountain

For some tasty gourmet food, head to the bottom of the Marmottes gondola, where you will find **La Cabane du Poutat** (04 76 80 42 88). The **Auberge de l'Alpette** (04 76 80 70 00) has the best omelettes and salads and the **Chalet du Lac Besson** (04 76 80 65 37) is a superb restaurant for rustic French charm, with a big open fire and a sun terrace. Make sure you book in advance. **Le Signal** (04 76 80 39 54) has some of the best views around.

In town

Alpe d'Huez has a good selection of restaurants – from high quality, gourmet cuisine, to snack bars with great value burgers and slices of pizza. **Le Génépi** (04 76 80 36 22) has superb traditional Savoyard food to be enjoyed in the cosy, rustic atmosphere. **Smithy's** restaurant (04 76 11 32 29) is one of our favourite places to stop for a bite. The Tex Mex can be a welcome break from the traditional raclettes and fondues and there is always a good, busy atmosphere. **L'Origan** (04 76 80 32 57) is the place for a good-value pizza.

"Superb traditional Savoyard food to be enjoyed in the cosy, rustic atmosphere"

Bars and clubs

Smithy's is one of our favourite bars in town, run by two brothers, who also have a Smithy's branch in Les Deux Alpes. Loads of action is guaranteed in here. Our other favourite bars are the **Pacific** bar and the **Underground**.

Live music is often on at the **Sporting** bar, or head to Crystal-owned **Vallée Blanche** or the **Roadhouse** bar to enjoy a quieter drink. To finish the night off in true fashion, you can dance the night away in the **Igloo**.

Useful facts and phone numbers

Tourist office

T: 0033 (0)4 76 11 44 44
F: 0033 (0)4 76 80 69 54
E: info@alpedhuez.com
W: www.alpedhuez.com

Emergency services

- Ambulance: 04 76 80 28 00
- Fire: 18
- Police station (Alpe d'Huez): 04 76 80 32 44
- Police station (Bourg d'Oisans): 04 76 80 00 17

Doctors

- Dr Darmon: 04 76 80 37 30
- Dr Robert: 04 76 80 69 29
- Drs Tkatchouk and Burghgraeve: 04 76 80 35 84

Taxis

- Agence de taxi S Chalvin: 04 76 80 38 38
- F Castillan: 04 76 80 61 76
- F Duclot: 04 76 80 20 81

Getting there

By car

There are 682 covered parking spaces. Call the Town Hall (0033 (0)4 76 11 21 21) for more information.

By plane

Grenoble (99km)
Lyon (150km)
Chambéry (140km)
Geneva (220km)

By train

Take the 09.09 Eurostar from London Waterloo to Paris; then by TGV, arriving Grenoble 17.32; then a bus (90 minutes) arriving in resort at 19.30. Return rail fares from £97. Contact Rail Europe (08705 848 848, www.raileurope.co.uk) or European Rail (020 7387 0444, www.europeanrail.com). Bus tickets, €5.10 single, must be purchased in advance from VFD coaches (0033 (0)4 76 60 47 08, www.vfd.fr).

Les Arcs

An extensive, versatile mountain, and some great places to stay if you do your research

On the slopes	
Snow reliability	❄ ❄ ❄ ❄
Parks	❄ ❄ ❄
Off-piste	❄ ❄ ❄ ❄

Off the slopes	
Après ski	❄ ❄ ❄
Nightlife	❄ ❄ ❄
Eating out	❄ ❄ ❄
Resort charm	❄ ❄ ❄ ❄ for 1950
	❄ ❄ for 1800

The resort

Les Arcs has four resorts at different levels: Arc 1600, Arc 1800 (which itself is split into Charvet, Villards and Charmettoger), the beautiful new Arc 1950 and Arc 2000. We don't particularly like Arc 1600 or Arc 2000. Arc 2000 has good access to the slopes but that's about it. However, we like the rest of Les Arcs and we don't want the dull parts to cloud our vision so we're going to ignore them and refer to only Arc 1800 and Arc 1950.

Arc 1800 (Charvet, Villards and Charmettoger) isn't beautiful, but it's not ugly either and there's lots going on. Charvet and Villards are centred round slightly claustrophobic open-air shopping centres and Charmettoger is prettier in the trees but it's a 10–15 minute walk to the bars in Villards.

The brand new Arc 1950 is stunning. It's still in the process of being built (due to be completely finished in 2008) by the Canadian company Intrawest, and it has a certain Canadian feel to it. The apartments are spacious and modern and the buildings are colourful. A few more restaurants and shops popped up last year, and you can expect Arc 1950 to continue to grow over the next year or two.

The mountains

Height: 1200–3326m

Ability	Rating
Expert	❄ ❄ ❄ ❄
Intermediate	❄ ❄ ❄ ❄
Beginner	❄ ❄ ❄ ❄

Getting about

In Les Arcs there are 200km of pistes (105 pistes in total) and within the whole Paradiski area (combining Les Arcs and La Plagne) there is a massive 425km. The terrain is fabulously varied, with slopes for all levels, good backcountry areas, and woodland runs for bad-weather days. Les Arcs is one of the few resorts in the world which has its own speed skiing area: the Flying Kilometre. See how fast you can go; the world record at the moment is 256kph.

The park

The Les Arcs park, named Apocalypse (www. apocalypse-parc.com), has always been popular amongst the ski and board bums who live in the resort or travel up from Bourg St Maurice, although we feel that there's some room for improvement. Three shapers are keeping it in tiptop condition, and Apocalypse park now consists of one hip, four rails, ten table tops and one pipe. We always find that this park has a great, friendly atmosphere and it's good for all standards. There's also a flood-lit half pipe in Arc 2000.

> "Les Arcs is one of the few resorts in the world which has its own speed skiing area: the Flying Kilometre"

Off-piste and backcountry

Les Arcs is a tremendous place for freeriding as so much terrain is available now that it is linked with La Plagne. If the conditions are good and the lifts are open, it's worth heading up the Aiguille Rouge cable car. Underneath there are loads of steeps and couloirs

and it's here that they hold the famous North Face Freeride competition, which attracts the best big mountain freeriders in the world. The cable car is often closed due to high winds, but on a perfect powder day, you will love it. It's an area for the experts as it is quite challenging. If the weather's not so great, it doesn't matter as there are loads of tree lines above 1600m. Also the Trans Arc cable car gives you easy access to some wicked riding that always seems to be in good condition. For more off-piste exploits in the Paradiski area, check out the La Plagne chapter (see page 206). To make the most of this amazing mountain, it's worth hiring a guide to show you all the secret backcountry hide-out spots.

Instruction

Arc Aventure (1800)

Arguably the best school in Les Arcs. Thirty instructors offer group lessons (€26 for a 2.5-hour lesson, €124 for 6 half days) or private skiing and snowboarding lessons (€37 per hour, €305 for a full day), off-piste excursions (€60 for one day, €305 for private guide and rescue equipment) as well as other, non-skiing activities.
T: 0033 (0)4 79 07 41 28
E: esilesarcs@wanadoo.fr
W: www.arcs-aventures.com

Lift passes	Les Arcs only	Les Arcs + one day in Paradiski	Paradiski
1 day	€39	N/A	€46
6 days	€186	€205	€229

You can also get an extension for 1 day's Paradiski pass with a valid Les Arcs pass (€25). There is also a discount in early or late season.

ESF Arc 1800

There are 90 qualified instructors in Arc 1800. Six half-day ski or snowboarding lessons will cost €134. Off-piste skiing/boarding costs €66 per person per day.
T: 0033 (0)4 79 07 40 31
E: esf-arcs-1800@wanadoo.fr
W: www.esflesarcs.com

Privilege (1800)

Private lessons in skiing or snowboarding cost €80 for 2 hours, €180 for half a day or €315 for a whole day. They also offer an all-day Paradiski discovery (€65) and off-piste guiding (€65). For snowboarders, Privilege offer freestyle coaching (€80 for 2 hours) and an introduction to jumping in the park (€120 for 3 hours).
T: 0033 (0)4 79 07 23 38
E: contact@ecoledeskiprivilege.com
W: www.ecoledeskiprivilege.com

Spirit 1950

Spirit 1950 offers heliskiing and freeriding as well as group and private lessons for skiing and snowboarding. Group lessons cost €30 (half day), €60 (full day), €270 (6 full days), €150 (6 half days). A day's freeride or Paradiski discovery will cost €80 for a full day and private lessons cost €90–145 for 2 hours.
T: 0033 (0)4 79 04 25 72
E: contact@spirit1950.com
W: www.spirit1950.com

Other activities

Bowling: (Arc 1800) Call the Aiguille des Glaciers on 04 79 06 97 76.
Helicopter trips: Call Heli Mountains (06 11 74 38 83, mikeb@helimountains.com, www.helimountains.com) for details of trips over Mont Blanc or the Paradiski area.
Hot air balloon rides, overnight igloo stays, dog sled trips: You can do any of these with Nordic Adventures (06 09 49 32 07, nordicaventures@free.fr).
Ice drive: Drive on ice with Ecole de Pilotage (06 08 06 67 22 or 06 07 06 34 42).
Massage: Be soothed and re-energised by 1950 (04 79 04 1950). A 45-minute massage costs €70, or pay €200 for five days (30 minutes per day).
Paragliding: Arc Adventures (04 79 07 60 02)

offer paragliding.
Skidoo: With Arc Adventures (details above) you can take out a skidoo after the lifts have shut, either as a passenger or driver (€75 per hour), led by a guide. You have to ride round a selected track and follow speed limits and safety guidelines so you won't be able to go crazy.

Events

The **North Face Freeride** takes place in Les Arcs in late February/early March, a hugely acclaimed event that attracts the world's professionals.

Accommodation

Most accommodation is in the form of apartments although there are one or two hotels. You can book apartments directly with the tourist office (0033 (0)4 79 07 68 00) and you can also expect to pay a booking handling fee, tourist tax, damage deposit and for bed linen.

1800

The best of the hotels is the smart **Grand Hotel Paradiso** (0033 (0)4 79 07 65 00, reservation@grandhotelparadiso.com, www.grand-hotel-lesarcs.com), that used to be a Mercure hotel. The hotel is about a ten-minute walk from the nearby Villards, which has more bars and restaurants than Charmettoger. Accommodation costs €240–320 per day based on a double room.

The **Golf Hotel** (0033 (0)4 79 41 43 43, arg@latitudeshotels.com) in Charvet has a good location but is in desperate need of a facelift as it looks a bit 70s. Inside are two restaurants: the Petit Zinc restaurant is massive and impersonal but the Restaurant du Golf is good. The hotel also contains the Bar Le Swing jazz bar, which again needs a revamp, and the Mont Blanc Bar, which is pretty cool. Half board is €100–170 (minus €11 for B&B).

1950

In 1950, approximately two-thirds of the accommodation (apartments) is owned by HMC hotels (0033 (0)4 79 04 19 50, arc1950@hmc-hotels.com, www.hmc-hotels.com). Apartments can sleep 2–10 people and you have the choice of paying extra for more space. For example,

standard 4-person apartments are 33–41m² (€630 in low season, €1666 in high season) and the spacious apartment is 42–56m² (€693–1848). The apartments are comfortable and well fitted, some with open fires and all with balconies. The other one-third of the apartments are owned by the 4-star Radisson SAS Resort Arc 1950 (0033 (0)4 79 23 10 00, info.arc1950@intrawest.com, www.arc1950.radisson sas.com). They have apartments with 1–4 rooms. A 2-room apartment costs €928–2495. All of the apartments for HMC and Radisson SAS have access to a health spa with a swimming pool, sauna and Turkish bath, fitness training and solarium as well as an open-air heated swimming pool and Jacuzzi and the apart-hotel has underground parking and WiFi internet connection. The tour operators Erna Low and Neilson do packages to 1950.

> "The apartments are comfortable and well fitted, some with open fires and all with balconies"

Eating out

On the mountain

The mountain restaurants in Les Arcs aren't amazing on the whole. One that is outstanding is **Chalets de l'Arc** (04 79 04 15 40), above Arc 2000. It is really cosy with a wood and stone décor and fantastic service and it's also open in the evenings. For good views, try **The Solliet** (06 13 13 13 59), above Le Pré,

or the restaurant at the **Col de la Chal**. The **Chalet de Luigi** (06 08 57 23 36), in 1950 town, has a large, south-facing terrace alongside Marmottes piste. This smart restaurant offers a welcome break from Savoyard food and burgers, with homemade pastas and proscuitto its speciality. Inside, the high ceilings and wooden beams complete the luxurious European/American chalet feel.

In town

Charvet (1800)

In Charvet (1800), the **Mountain Café** is a popular Tex-Mex restaurant with long wooden tables. A main meal (fajitas, burgers, etc) costs €12–15, and you can get a massive €16 dish of nachos. **L'Hedoniste** (04 79 01 40 02) wine bar and eatery (lhedoniste@tiscali.fr) is a tiny restaurant (14 covers) and really cute. They serve soups, oysters and a number of different boards of food such as the gourmet board (including duck and homemade foie gras), a Savoyard board or a butcher's board. A number of wines and sparkling wines are

served by the glass. **Chez Les Filles** (04 79 04 14 55) has fantastic views and is really friendly. They serve pancakes, local specialities and salads at lunchtime and traditional Savoyard fare in the evenings. The Italian-run **Casa Mia** (04 79 07 05 75) is a fantastic and charming restaurant. At lunchtimes it serves the usual pizzas, etc and at night the gastronomic Italian and Savoyard specialities are brought out. **Chez Boubou** (04 79 07 40 86) serves English breakfast for €9 and good-value burgers and chips.

Villards (1800)

In Villards (1800), **Le Triangle** (04 79 07 43 45) is really cute and the service is good. They serve omelettes at lunch and local specialities at night (€13–25 for a main). **La Marmite** (04 79 07 44 28) is small and friendly. There are loads of places serving Brit-friendly foods (pure grease!) including the **Jungle Café** and **Red Hot Saloon**. On a similar note is one of our favourites, **Benji Bar**. Here they serve a massive range of food until 4pm, including Indian dishes, fajitas,

ribs, salads and burgers (around €13 a piece) followed by a 3-hour happy hour (4–7pm).

1950

In 1950 the lovely, spacious and smart **Chalet de Luigi** (04 79 00 15 36) serves fresh, homemade pasta and other delights at lunchtimes and in the evenings. **Café Hemmingway** (04 79 04 25 51) is a nice café serving fish, meat dishes and local specialities for around €14–19.

Bars and clubs

Charvet (1800)

In Charvet (1800), the **Gabotte** is popular with the locals for a cheeky après beer. **L'Equipe** is a funky big bar, with a semi-pirate theme (barrels and the odd net). It serves good-value sandwiches, chicken wings, burgers, salads and meats, as well as offering a takeaway option. You can also check your E-mails.

Villards (1800)

The largest selection of bars is to be found in Villards (1800). **Ambiente** is a cool après bar with darts, sports on TV and extortionate €11 cocktails. **Benji Bar** gets full points for the longest happy hour (4–7pm, see Eating out). **The Jungle Café** (04 79 07 19 62) serves steaks, pastas, omelettes and not-cheap burgers. Their cocktails are great, but pricey. However, it does have a very funky jungle interior with cool murals on the walls and lots of leafy decoration. The tables can be folded up to allow dancing to the eclectic tunes. The Jungle Café opens at 9.30am and shuts at 2am. In the massive **Red Hot Saloon** (04 79 07 74 52) there's a lot to keep punters entertained: live music, theme nights, pool, and sports on big TVs. They serve salads and sarnies 12–4pm and a full menu 4–10pm, which includes steaks, burgers and smaller snacks such as wedges and garlic bread. Happy hour is 5–6pm. When you stumble out of the Saloon, head to the Apokalypse nightclub (04 79 07 43 77, www.theapokalypse.com).

1950

In 1950 **Les Belles Pintes** (04 79 07 35 42) is an 'Irish pub' (as perceived by Canadians, not the Irish) open 11am–1am. Happy hour is 5.30–6.30pm and they also have pool and darts. They serve hot dogs and sandwiches (€5), burgers and chips (€10), croque monsieurs and bruschetta (€5–10) 12–2.30pm. **Le Chalet de Luigi** (04 79 00 05 17), as well as having a top restaurant, has a bar and a nightclub, **Le Club 1950** (04 79 01 16 94). The bar is open every day from early morning until 4am. It has satellite TV, happy hours and theme nights.

Useful facts and phone numbers

Tourist office

T: 0033 (0)4 79 00 64 63 (1950) / 0033 (0)4
    79 07 61 11 (1800)
E: lesarcs@lesarcs.com
W: www.lesarcs.com/www.arc1950.com

Direct reservations 1800

T: 0033 (0)4 79 07 68 00
F: 0033 (0)4 79 07 68 99
E: reservation@lesarcs.com
W: www.lesarcs.com

Direct reservations 1950

T: 0033 (0)4 79 04 1950
W: arc1950@hmc-hotels.com, www.hmc-hotels
    .com

Emergency services

- Slopes rescue: 04 79 07 85 66
- Fire: 18

Doctors

- Centre Médical du Charvet: 04 79 07 46 41
- Centre Médical des Villards: 04 79 07 49 99
- Cabinet Médical Arc 2000: 04 79 07 30 01
- Cabinet Médical Arc 1600: 04 79 07 78 57
- Hospital in Bourg St Maurice: 04 79 41 79 79

Taxis and airport transfers

- Taxi Boirat: 06 13 61 63 10 / 06 03 22 72 68
- Borne taxis à Bourg St Maurice: 04 79 07 03 94
- Airport transfers: 04 79 07 04 49

Getting there

By car

You will need to park in the underground car park in 1950 if you drive there. Seven days will cost €73. Call 0033 (0)4 79 04 12 37 or E-mail eric.chevalier@sceta-parc.fr.

By plane

Lyon (200km) Transfers can be booked through Satobus (0033 (0)4 37 255 255, www.satobus-alps.com.
Geneva (145km) Transfers can be booked through www.alpski-bus.com or www.altibus.com (0041 (0)22 798 20 00).
Heliport transfers can also be booked on 0033 (0)6 11 74 38 83.
Chambéry (120km) Transfers can be booked through Trans'neige (0033 (0)4 79 68 32 90.

By train

Take the 17.09 Eurostar from London Waterloo to Paris; then an overnight train to Bourg St Maurice, and then a funicular train (7 minutes), arriving in resort at 08.37. Return fares from £111 in a 6-berth couchette. Contact Rail Europe (08705 848 848, www.raileurope.co.uk) or European Rail (020 7387 0444, www.europeanrail.com). Funicular tickets (€7 single, with return journey free of charge) are purchased at the station.

Avoriaz

Avoriaz has its own special charm
and the Portes de Soleil is at
your fingertips

SECTEUR SUPER MORZINE - AVORIAZ

Dents du Midi

Les Dents Blanches

Liaison Champéry-Les Crosets
(Suisse)

Liaison Champéry-Les Crosets
(Suisse)

Les Hauts Forts
2466 m

AVORIAZ
1800 m

Liaison Châtel
La Linga

Les Lindarets

Ardent

Les Prodains

On the slopes	
Snow reliability	✻ ✻ ✻
Parks	✻ ✻ ✻ ✻
Off-piste	✻ ✻ ✻
Off the slopes	
Après ski	✻ ✻ ✻
Nightlife	✻ ✻ ✻
Eating out	✻ ✻
Resort charm	✻ ✻ ✻

The resort

Avoriaz is completely unique. The design and architecture of the town is very 60s, but it was nevertheless well thought out and there is something spectacular and charming about its crazily angled structure, enhanced by its impressive setting on the edge of a cliff. One of the really exceptional features is that practically all the accommodation is ski-in ski-out. As the village is car-free and very wide, everyone whacks on their equipment outside their apartment and cruises down to the lift – a much preferable way to start the day than cumbersome bus journeys and long walks. The mountains are unquestionably superb, with Avoriaz being bang in the centre of the massive Portes de Soleil circuit that unites the slopes of France and Switzerland.

If you are looking for luxurious accommodation think again – there is only one hotel that could be described as such, Les Dromonts (see Accommodation); most of the apartments are pretty cramped.

The mountains

Height: 975–2275m

Ability	Rating
Expert	✻ ✻ ✻
Intermediate	✻ ✻ ✻ ✻
Beginner	✻ ✻ ✻

Getting about

This resort is great for mixed ability groups; beginners have some good areas on which to learn, intermediates can cruise around the 650km of pistes in the Portes de Soleil cicuit quite happily (might be an idea to ditch the unhelpful piste map and follow thc little pictures of animals – pick one depending on your ability) and experts have challenging pistes, great off-piste and superb parks to choose from.

Transportation within Avoriaz

Within Avoriaz you can get about in sledges or shuttles. You have three options when it comes to transporting you, your mates/family and your luggage to your accommodation:

You can use baggage sledges yourself for only €1. This should be fine if you are staying in the Falaise area (chalets de la Falaise, Chapka, Douchka, Elinka, Kouria, Malinka, Néve, Saskia, Tilia) as it's really close to the car park/dropping-off point.

Between 8am and 7pm you can hire a sledge to transport you for €5–13, depending on the length of journey. Between 7pm and 8am you will need a shuttle at a cost of €8.

If you are travelling on a Saturday as most people are you don't need to worry about organising or calling up for transportation, as there are assistants all over the place and they'll call a sledge for you. At any other time you will need to call 04 50 74 01 55.

The park

Avoriaz definitely knows how to build and look after its three parks. They have some big sponsors like Burton and Forum putting money behind them so they can now afford to have six full-time shapers working hard to keep it sweet! In Arare there are four decent sized kickers, two spines, seven rails, a step up and a pipe. In La Chapelle, there are six kickers of all different dimensions, five rails, a skier and boardercross and a super pipe where they hold the O'Neill freestyle pro event. The Avoriaz parks are among some of the most respected in Europe, so if parks are your thing, you should give Avoriaz a try. Check out the website www. snowparkavoriaz.com.

You also have access to one of the best parks in Europe at Les Crosets, on the Swiss side (see Champéry chapter, page 330).

"There is something spectacular and charming about its crazily angled structure enhanced by its impressive setting on the edge of a cliff"

Off-piste and backcountry

Avoriaz has a fair bit to offer in terms of off-piste, and if you get bored with this you have the whole of the Portes de Soleil to explore (see Morzine and Champéry chapters, pages 200 and 330). The top of the Combe du Machon chairlift is a great place to start. From here, you can explore either the terrain off the back of the Coupe de Monde run (with a guide/local) or the more accessible powder on the Crozets side. From the Fornet lift you can traverse to a cornice and bowl that winds up at the Valée de la Manche (Mindor lake). You can then commence the 45-minute hike down the road to Morzine, or you could arrange for someone to pick you up. The foolhardy riders can take the Cubore lift and attempt the sketchy hike to a big, fun, and untracked bowl.

Instruction

Alpine Ski and Snowboard School

Group lessons cost from €105 for 6 hours or €142 for 10 hours (beginners and improvement). Private lessons cost €120 per person for 2 hours, plus €15 per extra person.
T: 0033 (0)4 50 74 12 64
E: admin@avoriazalpineskischool.com
W: www.avoriazalpineskischool.com

ESF

The ESF teach skiing, boarding and free ride. Six half days will cost €87–113 depending on discipline and time of year.
T: 0033 (0)4 50 74 05 65
E: info@esf-avoriaz.com
W: www.esf-avoriaz.com

International Ski and Snowboard School

Six half days will cost €120, and a 3-day discovery course with 3–6 people in a group will cost €112. Private lessons cost €64–75 for 2 hours depending on the number of people. The international ski school also offers tandem paragliding from €69.
T: 0033 (0)4 50 74 02 18
E: info@ecoledeglisse.com
W: www.ecoledeglisse.com

The Avoriaz Freestyle Camps

Snowboard only. These camps are a great way to get the most out of your week.
T: 0870 800 40 20
E: andrew@step-on.co.uk
W: www.step-on.co.uk/freestyleweek.htm

Other activities

Biotrap Winter Forest Park: This adventure park was set up last year in the Lindarets Forest, designed with equipment made entirely out of wood, e.g. tree trunk slides, staircases, etc.

Lift passes	Avoriaz only	Portes de Soleil
1 day	€30.50	€37
6 days	–	€179
13 days	–	€304

Bowling, pool, table footie, video games: These activities can all be found in a bar in the Place des Dromonts (see Bars and clubs).

Diving under ice: Try the amazing experience of diving under the ice. For €60 you get your first dive, equipment and training. E-mail cameleon@cameleon-organisation .com or call 04 50 74 94 0 for more details.

Hammam and squash: Both of these can be found in the Fontaines Blanches building, open 3.30–9pm, Sunday to Friday. Squash or hammam session costs €5.30 per person for 30 minutes.

Hang-gliding, paragliding and parasailing: These are arranged by the International Ski School (04 50 74 02 18). Tandem paragliding from €69.

Hot air balloons: A 1-hour hot air balloon flight costs €245 per person (04 50 74 00 59, cameleon@ cameleon-organisation.com, www.cameleon-organi sation.com).

Ice skating: You can skate for just €5 (04 50 74 08 52).

Jacuzzis, sauna, therapies and sports hall: Check out the Altiform fitness centre (04 50 74 18 48).

Mountain biking on the snow: This involves riding down the hill to Prodains. Bike, helmet and ski pass are provided for €35.

Night sledging: This takes place every day from 6pm (except Sunday) on the Crôt slope. The cost is €17 (06 07 75 92 48).

Sledge rides: Riding in a sled pulled by dogs costs €15 for the sledge for 3 people, €80 per person for half a day and €125 for the whole day. Call 04 50 73 15 17 to book.

Events

Avoriaz hosts some of the biggest freestyle comps in Europe and attracts the biggest names on the circuit. Events include **O'Neill freestyle Pro**, **PlayStation Air Games** and the **Billabong Pro**. The comp focus is more on boarders than skiers.

Accommodation

Most of the accommodation is in the form of self-catering apartments. **Pierre and Vacances** is one of the largest rental companies (0033 (0)4 50 74 35 35), but don't expect a spacious apartment, they are usually on the cosy side. The service you will receive is also minimal – expect to make your own beds, etc. If you wind up in an apartment in Crozats with views of people passing on the chairlift up from the centre of Avoriaz bear in mind that it is a popular game with the locals to collect snow on their skis/board to hurl at unfortunate people like yourselves from the lift. Your best bet is to get yourself out on the chair and try this childish, but great, game on your neighbours.

There are just three hotels in Avoriaz. One is down in Les Prodains so not ideal if you want to sample the Avoriaz nightlife. In Avoriaz centre you have **Hotel de la Falaise** (0033 (0)4 50 74 26 00, avh@pierre-vacances.com), owned by the Pierre and Vacances group. With absolutely no atmosphere or character you are far better to get an apartment rather than stay here. The final hotel, **Hotel les Dromonts** (04 50 74 08 11 / 04 94 97 91 91, www.christophe-leroy.com/dromont.htm, info@christophe-leroy.com) is an incredible contrast to the others. From the outside it is a deceptively dull building, camouflaging itself perfectly in the less-than-stunning surroundings. However, once inside those dreary doors the innovative architecture is captivating. All rooms have something to gawp at, with crazy lines and unexpected angles fashioning fantastic spaces.

You can leave your luggage at the luggage room at the ice rink office (which also has showers) on your arrival or departure day if you have to move out of your room or apartment and don't want to lug it round everywhere. It costs €1.60 per item of luggage and €2.50 for a shower. It's open 8.30am–6pm.

Eating out

On the mountain

The **Yeti** on the slopes near Avoriaz is the place to stop for a crêpe, with deckchairs, a terrace and great après ski. There are a bunch of restaurants under the half pipe, at the top of the cable car from Les Prodains. Our favourite is **Changabang** (04 50 74 06 39), with fantastically cheap and tasty burgers. **La Tanière** (04 50 74 13 10) and **Les Trappeurs** brasserie (04 50 74 17 33) are also worth a visit. There are more restaurants at Lindarets – our favourites are **Pomme de Pin** and **Cremaillare** (04 50 74 11 68). On the Super Morzine side of town, **Les Cretes de Zorre** (04 50 79 24 73) is by far the best.

In town

If you are in desperate need of a hangover cure before you take to the slopes, the **Tavaillon** bar serves English breakfasts. The **Cabane** (04 50 74 20 60) is a popular and informal bar/restaurant that is great for food and beers. **La Falaise** (04 50 74 10 48) is the best pizzeria, with really friendly and helpful staff who are more than willing to cater for large groups. **Intrets** (04 50 74 15 45) is also good for pizza and pasta – the service wasn't as impressive as the food when we stopped, but we hope that was a one off. **Fontaines Blanches** (04 50 74 12 73) has a lovely alpine feel and serves all the usual French fare. The staff are a bit odd though. **Duchess Anne** (04 50 74 12 50) has a really nice terrace for lunch and serves pizzas, local specialities and steak haché. **Le Chalet D'Avoriaz** (04 50 74 01 30) is a really cute alpine restaurant up by the slopes, near the car park with great pierrades. For gourmet fodder, the uniquely designed **Dromonts** hotel (see Accommodation) has a fantastic restaurant. You can even attend one of Mr Leroy's three-hour cookery courses.

"The innovative architecture is captivating"

Bars and clubs

For après ski on the slopes the **Yeti** is good (see Eating out). In town, **Shooters** is the place to go, populated with Brits, Deutsch and Danish, bopping away to the live music 4.30–6pm and the disco beats until 2am. There are theme nights every week and on Saturdays

the bar is usually dominated by seasonaires. **The Place** also has live music for après. The **Wild Horse Saloon** is open 4pm–2am and has a great atmosphere. You can also grab some greasy foods – burgers, ribs, nachos, that kind of thing. For dancing until 5am, you have the choice of **Festival** or the **Choucas**, which has great live music and is our favourite place to hit the dance floor. All the best bars and clubs are around the same area so it's pretty easy to check them all out without getting too chilly.

If you fancy a change from the usual bars and clubs there is a cool and atmospheric **bowling bar** (04 50 74 06 77) with two lanes, pool, darts, air hockey and arcade games.

Useful facts and phone numbers

Tourist office

T: 0033 (0)4 50 74 02 11
F: 0033 (0)4 50 74 18 25
E: info@avoriaz.com
W: www.avoriaz.com

Emergency services

- In an emergency call 18 or 112 from a mobile phone.
- Police: 17
- Medical centre: 04 50 74 05 42 (for emergencies, general medical care, physiotherapy etc)

Taxis (for transfers)

- Hubert Buttet: 04 50 79 64 54
- Momo Cheraiet: 04 50 79 03 40/ 06 07 94 58 35
- Richard Gourvil: 04 50 75 97 12
- Laurys France Taxi: 04 50 74 69 77
- Sarl Evason: 04 50 26 29 29

Getting there

By car

When you arrive in Haute-Savoie, follow the signposts to Chamonix by the A40. Take the Cluses Exit n° 18, head towards Taninges by the D90, then follow les Gets, Morzine and finally Avoriaz. Avoriaz is only an hour or so away from Geneva. If you drive, you will be required to leave your car at the car park at the entrance of Avoriaz. The indoor car park (800 places) will cost €12.50 a day or €76 for a week. The outdoor car park (1600 places) will cost €6.50 for a day or €40 for a week. If you want to save that extra few euros and park outdoors be prepared to dig your car out of the snow when you leave. Reserve your spot on www.avoriazparkings.com.

By plane

Geneva (80km) Taxi transfer will cost around €140 (see numbers above). To find out about buses from Geneva to Avoriaz call 0041 (0)22 732 02 30. For a more 'bling' entrance into resort, a helicopter will pick you up from Geneva and drop you in Avoriaz for €993 (0033 (0)4 50 74 22 44).

By train

Take the 17.09 Eurostar from London Waterloo to Paris; then an overnight train to Cluses, and then a bus (85 minutes), arriving in resort at 10.00. Return fares from £111 in a 6-berth couchette. Contact Rail Europe (08705 848 848, www.raileurope.co.uk) or European Rail (020 7387 0444, www.europeanrail.com). Bus tickets (€15 single) must be purchased at least 7 days in advance from Altibus (0033 (0)4 79 68 32 96, www.altibus.com).

Chamonix

A base for the serious extreme community, this town has everything. Bring a car if you can

On the slopes	
Snow reliability	❄❄❄❄
Off-piste	❄❄❄❄❄
Off the slopes	
Après ski	❄❄❄½
Nightlife	❄❄❄❄
Eating out	❄❄❄❄
Resort charm	❄❄❄❄

The resort

The first thing that hits you about Chamonix is the scenery; you can't possibly drive into Cham without being impressed. Being at the foot of Mont Blanc, Chamonix was destined to be a popular resort from the start, nearly a century ago. Amazingly, Chamonix seems to have developed and matured into the perfect town, rather than being destroyed by ugly buildings and tourists like so many resorts. It has plenty of olde worlde charm, streets that you could wander round for days, a diversity of nationalities and more facilities than anyone could need. On top of the beautiful town, the mountains are the best without a shadow of a doubt and the nightlife is incredible. The commute between the town and the mountains isn't ideal but it's this fact that lets Chamonix maintain the feel of a real town, as opposed to a purpose-built resort, so we'll forgive this slight inconvenience.

The mountains

Height: 1035–3840m

Ability	Rating
Expert	❄❄❄❄❄
Intermediate	❄❄
Beginner	❄❄❄

Getting about

On one side of the valley are Flégère and Brévent, both perfect for panoramic views in the sun. Brévent can be accessed close to Cham centre and Flégère a little further down in Les Praz, although the two are linked. The Aiguille du Midi and Les Grands Montets, home of the steep and deep, are on the opposite side of the valley and Le Tour, at the far end, has some great tree runs. In total there are 155km of runs with the longest downhill run coming in at 7km.

Learning to ski/board in Chamonix

When you think Chamonix, you might not think it would be a great place to learn how to ski and snowboard and in some respects you might be right as it is geared towards the more extreme market. However, once you have been wiped out a few times by speedy riders hurtling through the beginners' slope to get to the bottom of the mountain you might appreciate the fact that Chamonix has four beginners' slopes (one attached to each of the mountains except Flégère) with no other runs going through them. Progression is difficult though, and for intermediates it's not all that great; Chamonix really comes into its own for the experts and pros.

Off-piste and backcountry

The infamous ski movie *The Blizzard of Arzhh* – starring Glen Plake and Scott Schmitt – changed the lives of every professional big-mountain skier out there and it was mainly filmed in Chamonix on the Grands Montets. There is so much off-piste and backcountry terrain in Chamonix that we can hardly do it justice. The **Grands Montets** is a good place to start. The drop is around 2000m and you don't even need to hike. Just drop over the back at the top of the gondola and you're off. One of the routes from here is actually marked on the piste map but it's completely ungroomed and gets bumped up at the bottom (you have the option of trees rather than bumps at the other side if you prefer). From the **Brévent** lift you can hike for about ten minutes to the face (marked as a black on the map). You start on a couloir that's pretty steep and has the tendency to avalanche but they do bomb it. A great run. From the **Aiguille de Midi**, the infamous Valley Blanche is a 22km descent. The run isn't too difficult, but you could probably do with a guide, especially if you want to go down some steeps. Off the back of the **Tête de Balme** are some steep and dangerous couloirs if you fancy a challenge.

Further information

The Vamos edition of *Chamonix* is a good off-piste guide book written by two mountain guides based in Cham. It's written in good English and sold in Snow and Rock.

Avalanche risk

The avalanche risks in Chamonix are less than you might think. There is a huge potential for avalanche but a fairly small chance of being caught in one. Because all and sundry want to hit the off-piste when they head to Chamonix, the local officials are very paranoid and keep everything shut unless it's safe.

Lift passes	
1 day	€44
6 days	€186
13 days	€382

The Cham ski pass allows you 2 free ascents of the Grands Montets cable car (with a 6-day pass; €5 per extra lift), 1 day in Courmayeur (with a 4-day pass or more) and the resort bus.

Instruction

The tourist office will provide you with a list of guides and schools to choose from but these are the two that we were recommended by local experts.

Chamonix Experience

A good reputation but pretty expensive: a guide for 1 day costs about €350 (EV2 costs around €280–310). To be guided in a 5–8 person group down the Valley Blanche costs €65.
T: 0033 (0)4 50 54 09 36
E: info@chamex.com
W: www.chamex.com

Evolution 2

EV2 is well thought of by the locals and can provide you with any kind of instruction or guide. A private guide costs €280–310.
T: 0033 (0)4 50 53 22 57
E: chamonix@evolution2.com
W: www.evolution2.com

Other activities

Bowling: Open 5pm–2am (earlier in bad weather), the bowling alley is situated on the Avenue de Courmayeur in Chamonix Sud (04 50 53 74 37).

Casino: Situated on the Place de Saussure, the casino (04 50 53 07 65) has slots open from noon and French and English roulette, black-jack, and poker from 9pm. The restaurant is open from 7.30pm until midnight.

Cinema: Bang in the centre of town, the cinema (04 50 55 89 98) has three screens and has several shows per day. Films are shown in French and English (with French subtitles).

Paint ball: This costs €16 per person including all the necessary equipment. Extra bullets cost €1 for 20 bullets. There are discounts for groups over five people. Call 06 07 36 01 51.

"Some really steep and dangerous couloirs if you fancy a challenge"

Panoramic flights: These are pretty popular around Chamonix. Chamonix Mont Blanc Hélicoptères (04 50 54 13 82, www.helico.fr) organise trips from €60 per person (on the Aiguille Verte) to €190 per person (for a flight over the Massive). SAF Chamonix Hélicoptères (04 79 38 48 29) organise 30-minute flights for five people.

Paragliding: This can be done on Aiguille du Midi, Brévent, and Les Grands Montets. Contact Alpine Flying Centre (04 50 54 59 63, info@flyers-lodge.com, www.flyers-lodge.com; Centre Ecole Parapente Mt Blanc (04 50 34 77 37, spirituailes@gmail.com, www.parapente-ecole.com) or Summits (04 50 53 50 14, summits@summits.fr, www.summits.fr).

Richard Bozen Sports Centre: Situated at 214 Av. De la Plage (chamonix.sports@chamonix.com, http://sports.chamonix.com), this centre contains a swimming pool, sauna and hammam (04 50 53 23 70 – €4.20 pool entry, €10.40 for sauna, pool and hammam), tennis

and squash (04 50 53 28 40 – €13.20 for 1 hour of tennis, €8 for 45 minutes of squash), skating rink (04 50 53 12 36 – €4.20 entrance; night sessions on Wednesday), weights and fitness room (04 50 53 23 70 – €8.40 inc. pool) and climbing hall (04 50 53 23 70 – entry €3.80).

Shopping: With 400 shops to choose from, shopping in Chamonix is an absolute pleasure. If you want to try on every pair of designer sunglasses available, Chamonix's your place.

WiFi for free: The tourist office has wireless connections and if you have the right equipment you can use it for free during your stay.

Events

The **Bosses de Boss** is a mogul competition without many rules; anything goes. It began 16 years ago when all the Chamonix ski bums challenged the Val d'Isère ski bums to a mogul challenge. Since then a number of the major ski resorts have become involved and enter their own teams. A resort's team must consist of five male skiers, two female skiers, two snowboarders and one telemarker. It's a great day (around mid-March) and a legendary competition.

Accommodation

High Mountain Holidays (www.highmountain.co.uk) have a number of catered and self-catered accommodations in locations across Chamonix, from dead in the centre, to quieter areas near the ski lifts. The service is superb; Glen and Caroline will bend over backwards to make sure your stay is enjoyable. The main catered chalet is **Kosciusko Lodge** in Les Praz, with eight en-suite rooms, located at the bottom of the Flégère cable car. This chalet has tons of regular guests and you can certainly see why they return. The cosy rooms, TV lounge (that has a great selection of games and movies), snug bar and dining room make this chalet really welcoming. Additionally, they always employ a qualified chef and the food is served to an incredibly high standard. Kosciusko Lodge has the benefits of a chauffeured minibus to take you to all the lifts and into

town at night, and a ski host to show you the highlights of Chamonix's mountains. A week at Kosciusko Lodge costs £418–745 per person. If you prefer self-catered accommodation or have a specific location in mind just call up Glen and he will tailor your holiday specifically – they even book alternative accommodation for you if it's more suitable for your requirements.

The **Hotel Swisse** (0033 (0)4 50 53 07 58, info@chamonix-park-hotel.com, www.chamonix-park-hotel.com) is a good 3-star hotel opposite the tourist office. A modern, new 3-star is **Oustalet** (0033 (0)4 50 55 54 99, info@hotel-oustalet.com, www.hotel-oustalet.com), near the Aiguille du Midi. **Hotel La Savoyarde** (0033 (0)4 50 53 00 77, lasavoyarde@wanadoo.fr, www.lasavoyade.com), technically a 3 star, is great value although slightly 'olde worlde'. The staff are great. You can't get a more central location than the new 4-star **Hotel des Alpes** (0033 (0)4 50 55 37 80, www.grandhoteldesalpes .com, info@grandhoteldesalpes.com) that is right smack in the centre, next to the Chanel shop. It's an excellent hotel, with swimming pool, sauna and Jacuzzi although the parking's a tad difficult.

Eating out

On the mountain

There are 14 restaurants on the mountain, and pretty much the lot have incredible views over the Mont Blanc mountain range. In the Brévent/Flégère region, **La Flégère** (04 50 53 06 13) and **Le Panoramic** (04 50 53 44 11) have amazing terraces and views over the Mont Blanc range, and not-so-bad food. **La Bergerie** (04 50 53 05 42) has a beautiful atmosphere with both table and self-service options and **Altitude 2000** (04 50 53 15 58), at the top of the gondola in Planpraz, has great food, service and terrace. On the Grands Montets, the **Plan Joran** (04 50 54 05 77) offers quick snacks, a pizzeria, a picnic area, a terrace and a smart restaurant. The **Lognan** (04 50 54 10 21) is pretty smart and has a good 'pasta corner' and the **Refuge de Lognan** (06 88 56 03 54) is rustic and off the beaten track. The food is fantastic. At the summit of the Aiguille du Midi is **Le 3842**, a café with salads, sandwiches, pies and remarkable views. Over on Le Tour, the **Charamillon** (04 50 54 09 05) is a good self-service eatery.

In town

Le Munchie on the Rue des Moulins has some of the best food in Cham. It's mid range, fresh and tasty. **La Maison Carier** (04 50 53 00 03, www.hameaval bert.fr), just out of town, is pretty smart (wear a shirt) but relaxed at the same time. The chef has a Michelin-starred reputation and for the food and service you get it's not too expensive. **Chez Valereo** (04 50 55 93 40) is a great Italian with tasty pizzas and a renowned wine list. A three-course meal can cost only €20 but the wines that are sold range from €20 to €1100! It's a popular place with the locals. The **Bistro des Sports** (04 50 53 00 46, www.bistrodessports.com) is a very French restaurant/bar right in the centre of town on the main street. Savoyard food is the speciality and the bar is legendary, and frequented by hardcore locals as well as passing tourists. The **Caleche** (04 50 55 94 68, www.restaurant-caleche.com), in the town centre (just past the cinema) is atmospheric and also serves a large selection of good traditional Savoyard food. It's a little touristy and mid price range, probably €15–50 per head before wine. For Tex Mex, the **Cantina** (04 50 53 64 20) is great. It can be found down a little back alley just off the main street and does good food at a good price. For top quality pub food, go to **Goophy's** by the station or **CyBar** in town. For a tasty takeaway sandwich and chips you can't go wrong with the **Midnight Express** in the centre of town that is open most hours of the day and night.

Bars and clubs

Since Chamonix has loads of permanent residents (about 10,000) and 180 licences, there are loads of good bars, pubs and clubs to pick from.

L'M is a hotel and restaurant in the centre of town that has a great Austrian-style après ski bar outside with big outdoor heaters and a large outdoor screen for footie and other sports.

Just opposite the station are a few cool bars. **Chambre Neuf** (04 50 55 89 81) is a classic après ski bar, popular with the locals and the Scandinavians. **Goophy's** is a real snowboarder hangout with a funky vibe and it's pretty cheap too. It's popular with the après ski crowd and has great pub grub. **Elevation** is next to Goophy's and does really good food during the day, including healthy snacks.

MBC (04 50 53 61 59, www.mbchx.com) is about 5 minutes' walk from the centre of town, has a good reputation for homemade beer and a year-round clientele, both English and French. **South Bar** (04 50 53 98 56, www.southbar.se), right at the end of town is a hip and full-on après ski bar.

The **Rue des Moulins** is a street in the centre of town, just off the main street, packed with funky bars. **Cybar** (04 50 53 69 70, www.dicksteabar.com) is massive and has a great atmosphere, open 8.30am–2.30am. The bar is on three levels. The middle floor is huge, with long wooden tables, a pool table and big comfy leather chairs that you could curl up in all day. On the top floor are a host of computers with internet access (€1 for 10 mins). Food is available 2–10pm: traditional pub fare as well as paninis, salads and nachos. The bar shows all major sporting events on a massive projector screen and for the footie matches and Six Nations they tend to do some really good offers such as burger and a pint for €8. Bargain! There is live music three nights a week and they often run comedy nights that start around 10pm. Connected to the Cybar is **Bar du Moulin** (04 50 53 08 21). It's a pretty cool little bar, with a cosy, dark kind of vibe. It opens 7pm–2am and sometimes has live music or DJs playing. **Dicks Tea Bar**, next to the Cybar, is a popular and busy club open 10pm–4am. They do all sorts of theme nights, often have live music and always have a decent DJ playing. On special nights, Cybar, Bar du Moulin and Dicks are all connected up for one massive party. A fire caused damage to these bars in 2006, but they should all be open for 06/07. **Bar'd Up** (04 50 55 80 92) attracts a more British crowd.

Useful facts and phone numbers

Tourist office

T: 0033 (0)4 50 53 00 24
F: 0033 (0)4 50 53 58 90
E: info@chamonix.com
W: www.chamonix.com

Direct reservations

T: 0033 (0)4 50 53 23 33
E: reservation@chamonix.com

Emergency services

- In a medical emergency dial 15, for the fire brigade call 18, or 112 for either from a mobile
- Mountain rescue: 04 50 53 16 89
- Ambulance: 04 50 53 46 20
- Hospital: 04 50 53 84 00
- Weather information: 08 92 68 02 74

Doctors

In Chamonix
- Drs Dartigue-Peyrou, Dehlinger and Plumerault, 350 avenue de la Plage: 04 50 53 15 27
- Dr Roncin, 10 avenue du Mont-Blanc: 04 50 55 85 74
- Drs Cadot and Richard, 275 rue des Allobroges: 04 50 55 80 55
- Doctor on call (nights, Sundays and bank holidays): 15

Taxis

- ABAC Taxi Gopée: 06 07 02 22 13, abactaxigopee@aol.com
- Cham Taxi: 06 07 26 36 62
- Taxi Monard: 04 50 55 86 28
- Taxi Rousseau: 06 07 67 88 85, www.chamonixtaxi.fr

Getting there

By car

Chamonix is really easy to access by road. From Paris take the A6 towards Lyon then the A40 towards Lyon/Geneva then N205.

By plane

Geneva (88km) is only an hour's transfer away. There is a daily coach transfer three times daily. Contact the tourist office/www.chamonix.com for timetables or call 0033 (0)4 50 53 01 15.
Lyon (220km) Bus connections are via Satobus (0033 (0)4 37 255 255).
Annecy (90km)
For taxi transfers contact the airport transfer services:
ATS: 0033 (0)4 50 53 63 97 (in France), 0709 209 7392 (in the UK), www.a-t-s.net
Chamonix Transfer Service: 0033 (0)6 62 05 57 38, www.chamonix-transfer.com.

By train

Take the 17.42 Eurostar from London Waterloo to Paris; then an overnight train, changing at St-Gervais-Les-Bains. Arrive in Chamonix, which is in the resort, at 09.25. Return fares start at £124 in a 6-berth couchette. Contact Rail Europe (08705 848 848, www.raileurope.co.uk) or European Rail (020 7387 0444, www.europeanrail.com).

Courchevel 1650

Unpretentious and unrivalled, one of the best in the Three Valleys

AIGUILLE DU FRUIT
3051 m

SAULIRE

CREUX NOIRS
2705 m

SAULIRE
2738 m

LA CROIX DES VERDONS
2739 m

ROC MERLET
2734 m

CHANROSSA

VIZELLE

ROCHER DE LA LOZE
2526 m

COL DE
LA LOZE

VALLEE DE MERIE

SIGNAL

ROC MUGNIER

CREUX

LAC BLEU

CHEMIN

MER

PRAZ-JUGET

BEL AIR

lac bleu

PRAZ-JUGET

CHANTEBISE

loze est

PRAMERUEL

VERDONS

PRALONG

LA

PLAN DU VAH

COURCHEVEL 1850

JARDIN

LA GRANDE COMBE

LUGE

COURCHEVEL 1650

ST BON 1100

COURCHEVEL 1550

FORET DU LAIDON

LA CORBIERE

COURCHEVEL 1300 - LE PRAZ

LA JAIRAZ

On the slopes	
Snow reliability	❄ ❄ ❄ ❄
Parks	–
Off-piste	❄ ❄ ❄ ❄ ❄
Off the slopes	
Après ski	❄ ❄ ❄
Nightlife	❄ ❄ ❄
Eating out	❄ ❄
Resort charm	❄ ❄ ❄

The resort

Courchevel 1650 is a great resort, and well-deserving of its own chapter. 1650 is less cosmopolitan than its Russian-favoured companion, 1850; people who come to 16 are usually more concerned with the friendly community, and easy access to (arguably) the best slopes in the Three Valleys. Convenience is high; being a small resort, you are never too far away from the slopes. Buses run frequently up to 1850 and also down to 1550 and 1300 (Le Praz).

The mountains

Height: 1850–2740m

Ability	Rating
Expert	❄ ❄ ❄ ❄
Intermediate	❄ ❄ ❄ ❄
Beginner	❄ ❄ ❄ ❄

Getting about

Courchevel has something for everyone. Beginners and intermediates will enjoy the skiing on-piste in 1650 as it is filled with beautiful, long, open blue runs, and experts will find plenty to keep them entertained with loads of off-piste and the whole of the Trois Vallées to play with.

The park

There is no park in Courchevel 1650 and even though the park in 1850 isn't far away it's not very good. However, by the Pyramids drag lifts there is plenty of natural terrain to build backcountry kickers. There are perfect spots for building gap jumps and you can often see top boarders and skiers filming movie segments here. If this sounds like too much hard work, head over to the parks in Meribel and Mottaret (see Meribel chapter, page 192).

Off-piste and backcountry

Courchevel 1650 has some of the best off-piste in the Trois Vallées area. It doesn't get as busy as 1850, so there are less people to share the powder with. In the heart of the mountain, there is the hidden valley – a favourite of the locals. The hidden valley is a huge funnel of a bowl leading down to the bottom of the Roc Mugnier chairlift and there are loads of different lines that can be fairly challenging in parts. It's better to do this run in the morning before it gets too much sun, otherwise the snow can get heavy and has been known to slide.

Another popular face can be found at the top of 1650, the Equinox, nicknamed after it was shown avalanching and taking three skiers out on the documentary programme Equinox. This is only recommended in the right conditions. There's a pisteurs' hut at the top of the Chanrossa chair where you would start your 10–15 minute hike to the top of the face and we recommend you ask if it's safe before you try it.

For an exhilarating adventure, try a firm favourite of ours, Les Avals Valley. This valley can be accessed by hiking up from the top of the Chanrossa chairlift. Once you have entered the valley you will be astounded by the breathtaking scenery and wide sections of untracked snow. If you wish you can turn this into an overnight escapade. Equipped with a warm sleeping bag and food for the evening, you can catch the last lifts up the Chanrossa, stop halfway down at a mountain refuge and spend the evening there. Early in the morning head back down towards 1650. The only drawback to this awesome trip is a fair amount of flat terrain that you have to push and walk out of. Snowboarders will find this a little harder than skiers. However, it is well worth all the effort and yields sufficient respect when you recount your adventures in the bars later. It is also essential to research snow conditions and weather fully before you attempt the Les Avals Valley.

The Chapelets area has some great off-piste riding and is described by locals as Disneyland – check out the areas in-between the trees and gulleys. The snow always keeps well.

Instruction

New Generation

Located in the centre of 1650, New Gen teaches all levels of skier and boarder. They also do gap year courses for trainee instructors.

T: 0033 (0)4 79 01 03 18

W: www.skinewgen.com

RTM

The name is made up of the initials of the three directors: Rob, Tom and Mark, or Ride The Mountain. Up to you.

The way forward when it comes to snowboard instructors, RTM employs passionate and professional snowboarders who provide the best service. By the end of the day or week your instructor will be more of a friend than an instructor.

T: 0033 (0)6 15 48 59 04

E: info@rtmsnowboarding.com

W: www.rtmsnowboarding.com

Rob Sewell

Rob is a private ski instructor who has lived in Courchevel for many years and is now one of the most respected instructors in the Trois Vallées. He is known for teaching the unteachable and also tuning up advanced skiers. If you want top results with your skiing, Rob's your man.

T: 0033 (0)4 79 08 04 17

Mobile: 0033 (0)6 10 144 762

Ski Supreme

The reputation of Ski Supreme is superb. They are the longest-serving British ski instructors in Courchevel and have led the way for those that followed (the directors are the parents of Alan Baxter, Britain's most successful alpine racer). The ski supreme team are extremely friendly and provide first-rate instruction.

T: 0033 (0)4 79 08 27 87

E: info@supremeski.com

W: www.supremeski.com

"By the end of the day or week your instructor will be more of a friend than an instructor"

Other activities

Hot air ballooning: Take a 1-hour trip above Courchevel and you get champagne and a diploma on landing. Rates: €220 per person. Call Aéro Action Aventure on 06 07 48 16 79.

Massage: Pamper Off-piste provides a large range of massage and beauty treatments. (06 17 60 89 02, enquiry@pamperoffpiste.com, www.pamperoffpiste .com). They visit you in the comfort of your chalet to relieve tired, aching bones.

Parapenting: Ski off one of the top peaks with an instructor, gliding for around 15 minutes and landing in Le Praz where you catch the lift back up. There are a number of schools offering parapenting. Craig's

Lift passes	Trois Vallées	Courchevel
1 day	€42	€35.50
6 days	€210	€170
13 days	€420	€330

Trois Vallées extension passes are available for €20.50 a day, which is good if you only want to do the full tour for one day. Children up to 13 years and adults over 60 receive a discount. Family passes are also available. It's worth getting the insurance as the emergency services on the mountain can cost an absolute fortune and if they see an insurance card the whole thing runs a lot more smoothly.

Paragliding (04 79 08 43 65, www.paraglide-alps.com) is run by the only British pilot in Les Trois Vallées. Cost: €90.

Skidoos: These can be hired for an afternoon of fun from Chardon Loisirs (04 79 08 39 60, ww.chardonloisirs.com) or Ski Vol (06 83 97 53 26, www.skivol.com). A guide will take you along the marked tracks from €75. Great fun but they won't let you go wild.

More options close by

There are lots more options very close by (see Courchevel 1850 on page 164).

Bowling: There are eight bowling lanes at the Forum in 1850 (04 79 08 23 83), which are open every day 11am–2am.

Cinema: The cinema in 1850 often shows films in English.

Ice go-karting: Literally go-karting on ice, you can do this in 1550 (06 08 73 70 58, www.kartinglace.com, asp@kartinglace.com). Really good fun but fairly expensive at €30 for only 10 minutes.

Ice skating: The rink at the Forum in 1850 is open every day 3–7pm and until 11pm on Wednesdays and Fridays. Adults pay €4.80.

Luging: Grab a sledge, available at most ski shops, and head down the specially made luge track in front of the Kalico in 1850 to the bottom of 1550. Accidents are not uncommon. Take your lift pass for the ride back up.

Raft on the Olympic ski jump: In Le Praz (04 79 08 39 60), this costs from €30 per person.

Sky diving: Available through the whole of March, all reports of this have been fantastic. If you're in Courchevel in March, do it.

Events

In 1650 is the legendary **Derby** that takes place at the end of March; contestants start at the top of the pyramids run and have to race to the bottom to claim their prize. It can turn into carnage! The Derby was an institutional event a few years back, was then cancelled and has now been reinstated. In 1850 events such as the Courchevel Freeride and Playstation Big Air are great to watch and worth a visit (see 1850, page 164).

Accommodation

Most of the accommodation in 1650 is in chalets, run by tour operators. **Cordon Rouge** (www.frenchskiholidays.com) has chalets for all sizes of group, in excellent locations. **Ski Olympic** and **Le Ski** also have good chalets and chalet hotels.

There is a beautiful new 3-star hotel bang in the centre of 1650, **Le Seizena** (0033 (0)4 79 08 26 36, www.hotelseizena.com, welcome@leseizena.com), that is stunning. It has 20 rooms, a hot tub, fitness and internet terminals. B&B accommodation costs from €270 per day per room.

The **Golf Hotel** (0033 (0)4 79 00 92 92, www.hoteldugolf-courchevel.com, info-reservation@hoteldugolf-courchevel.fr) is another good-looking 3-star building and has the best position in 1650; you can ski to the door and you're right in the centre of town. It has 47 rooms and half board costs €234–620 per day for 2 people depending on the type of room and time of season. A 2-room apartment costs €930–1900 per week. The 2-star **Edelweiss Hotel** (0033 (0)4 79 08 26 58, www.courchevel-edelweiss.com) is good for those on a budget (from €89 for 2 people B&B) and also well positioned.

Eating out

On the mountain

In 1650, try the very popular **Bel Air** (04 79 08 00 93) restaurant, which serves omelettes, salads, pasta and snails – the food is fantastic. It is advisable to book. There's a terrace on three levels with deckchairs on the bottom level and it's a great place to chill and watch the world ski and board by. **La Casserole** (04 79 08 06 35), at the bottom of the Signal chair has a fantastic terrace

but it has got a bit too expensive now for what it is and there are better places to go. The **Bubble Bar,** just off the slopes, serves superb paninis at lunchtime. **L'Ours Blanc** (04 79 00 93 93), at the base of 1650's slopes, serves the best burgers in town.

In 1850 there are some great restaurants and some ridiculously expensive ones too. Check out the Courchevel 1850 chapter for more details (page 164).

In town

Petit Savoyard (04 79 08 27 44) is the best restaurant in 1650 with a cosy atmosphere, traditional food and the best menu, food and service. It is always busy and you should really book, especially on the chalet staff's night off. **L'Eterlou** (04 79 08 25 45) is another great, traditional restaurant with superb pizzas and the friendliest staff. **La Montagne** (04 79 08 09 85), between the two mentioned above, has two parts: one smart restaurant with fish and meat dishes and a simpler, brasserie-style restaurant. **L'Alberon** (04 79 08 24 87) has a great selection of salads, meats and Savoyard specialities and the setting is lovely.

For a really smart meal or just for a change, get the bus up to 1850 where there is a superb Asian restaurant, **Le Grand Café** (04 79 08 42 97) and a very smart pizzeria, **Via Ferrata** (04 79 08 02 07), amongst others (see 1850 chapter, page 164).

"The Bubble Bar is the main meeting point in 1650 for seasonaires and holidaymakers alike"

Bars and clubs

The **Signal** bar is still the locals' choice. It has changed hands recently but the legendary Deni is still on hand to pour you a Mutzig and get you trollied. In the heart of 1650 is **Rocky's** bar which is popular with holiday-

makers. Rumour has it that Rocky's is having a revamp at the end of 2006 so could be a kicking bar for 2007. The **Bubble Bar** is the main meeting point in 1650 for seasonaires and holidaymakers alike. It's open from 8am for a morning coffee, serves a mean panini at lunchtime and live music is often playing for après or in the evenings. The Bubble kicks on until 1am. It also has internet terminals which is handy. For late-night dancing and drinking, the **New Space** bar is the way to go. The Space also has great live bands playing until the early hours and drinks are much cheaper than in 1850. There is a cheesy French nightclub in the centre of the village but drink prices are crazy and you may also be charged at the door.

Useful facts and phone numbers

Tourist office

T: 0033 (0)4 79 08 04 10
F: 0033 (0)4 79 08 15 63
E: info@courchevel.com
W: www.courchevel.com

Direct reservations (1850)

T: 0033 (0)4 79 08 14 44
E: info@courchevel-reservation.com
W: www.courchevel-reservation.com

Emergency services

• In a medical emergency dial 15, for the fire
   brigade call 18, or 112 for either from a
   mobile.
• Police: 04 79 08 34 69/ 04 79 08 26 07

Doctors

In 1650, there is one doctor (04 79 08 04 45).
   We recommend those in 1850.
• Blanc Alexandre: 04 79 08 26 40
• Cabinet Médical du Forum: 04 79 08 32 13
• Chedal Marc: 04 79 08 20 14
• Physiotherapy Clinic: 06 68 57 00 99 (Siân and
   Chris are definitely the best in town)

Taxis

• Courchevel Taxi Association: 04 79 08 23 46
• Abatrans Taxi: 04 79 00 3000
   (www.courchevel-taxi.com)
• Taxi Jack: 06 12 45 11 17

Getting there

By car

From Calais, the drive will take you about 10 hours. Car parking for the week will cost you €60–70.

By plane

Geneva (145km) From here there are a number of different options to get to Courchevel. The bus costs €109 for a return trip and takes about 3.5 hours. Contact Touriscar on 0033 (0)4 50 43 60 or visit www.touriscar.net. Best to book in advance. A taxi (1–4 people) will cost €285 and a helicopter (up to 5 people) €1450.
Lyon (180km) is also 3.5 hours away by bus. Contact Satobus on 0033 (0)4 37 25 52 55, www.satobus-alps.com. A taxi costs €330 and a helicopter €1700.
Chambéry (115km) is closer, transfer by bus costs €75 and takes 1.5 hours, a taxi is €220 and a helicopter €1000.

By train

Take the 17.09 Eurostar from London Waterloo to Paris; then an overnight train to Moutiers, and then a bus (45 minutes), arriving in resort at 08.15. Return fares from £111 in a 6-berth couchette. Contact Rail Europe (08705 848 848, www.raileurope.co.uk) or European Rail (020 7387 0444, www.europeanrail.com). Bus tickets (€11.10 single) can be purchased in advance from Altibus (0033 (0)4 79 68 32 96, www.altibus.com) or bought at the station.

Courchevel 1850

*Bling it up in the king
of the Three Valleys*

On the slopes	
Snow reliability	✳ ✳ ✳ ✳
Parks	✳ ✳
Off-piste	✳ ✳ ✳ ✳

Off the slopes	
Après ski	✳ ✳ ✳
Nightlife	✳ ✳ ✳ ✳
Eating out	✳ ✳ ✳ ✳
Resort charm	✳ ✳ ✳

The resort

Four different resorts come under the name of Courchevel: Courchevel 1850 is the highest and most cosmopolitan, 1650 is described in detail in its own chapter (see page 156), 1550 is less expensive than these and is often used as a base for those who work in other resorts and the last is Courchevel 1300, also known as Le Praz, a traditional Savoyard village where the Olympic ski jump dominates the town. There is a bubble lift in Le Praz that takes you right into 1850.

1850 has a reputation for attracting the rich and famous and many a celeb has been spotted on the slopes. This brings with it inflated prices, Michelin-starred restaurants, exclusive and well-hidden cocktail bars and plush chalets. If you have a fat wallet you'll love it here, but if not, don't stop reading yet as there is another side to the resort that isn't as elitist and the mountains have so much to offer it's worth spending an extra bob or two.

The mountains

Height: 1850–2740m

Ability	Rating
Expert	✳ ✳ ✳ ✳
Intermediate	✳ ✳ ✳ ✳ ✳
Beginner	✳ ✳ ✳ ✳

Getting about

The skiing in Courchevel is superb, with access to the massive area of Les Trois Vallées. Due to this vast expanse of pisted runs, there's plenty to keep everyone happy. No matter how experienced the skier or boarder, you would struggle to cover all the runs in a week. For most, there is more than enough terrain in Courchevel alone, so many people would be advised to buy a lift pass for Courchevel and buy extensions where necessary.

The park

The park is located at the bottom of Courchevel 1850, by the Plantry chairlift. You have a couple of quick drag lifts that allow easy access to the park. Unfortunately the park is nothing special at all, the worst in the Three Valleys due to its low altitude and lazy shapers. There is a small range of jumps and rails, and a half pipe, which is not often open. To get some wicked park action, head to Meribel and Mottaret. Come on, Courchevel, sort it out.

Off-piste and backcountry

There are some great couloirs at the top of the Saulire cable car and you can choose one depending on your ability. Directly under the cable car is the easily accessible Telepherique couloir; perhaps slightly less challenging than the rest although there are a number of shoots and drop-offs to the side of the run. Further along the path from the Telepherique is the Grand Couloir, which is marked as a black run on the piste map but is far more difficult than the average black. It is wider than most couloirs but has the tendency to transform into a mogul field in the absence of fresh powder. A short (5 minute) hike up from the Grand Couloir is the Petit Couloir, where incredible conditions can be unearthed as the short hike, though fairly easy, puts a lot of people off. Don't be discouraged by this couloir's name as the narrower width limits the sun's access to the slope, thereby preserving the snow's condition. If you fancy a slightly longer hike (around 30 minutes) head to the next couloir over, Croidex la Verdons. This has the advantages of a wide, open face, very few tracks and a long run down. Be aware of the drop-off on the right-hand side (from the riders' point of view) as it's a long fall to the rocks below. All the couloirs arrive at the Saulire piste, which leads you straight back to the cable car so you can head back up and try another. It is this ease of accessibility that makes the couloirs a great playground for the adventurous.

For some more easily accessible powder, take the Creux chairlift and traverse left to reach a vast open powder bowl (the **Creux bowl**). Cross right to the end of the bowl to a huge, pointed rock, known as the Needle. The first face you come to (left of the needle from the riders' viewpoint) is usually tracked out by mid-day as it is so easy to get to. Climb around the Needle to experience fresh powder that usually takes a good week to be tracked out after a snowfall and provides a long run down to the bottom of the Chanrossa chairlift.

"The Grand Couloir is far more difficult than the average black"

Arguably some of the finest powder in Courchevel can be found on the **Roche de Loze**. From the bottom of 1850 take the Chenus gondola and the two-man chair to the top of Col de la Loze. Turn towards your left and look straight ahead of you, where you will see the Roche de Loze. This is the site of the classic Courchevel Freeride competition that attracts the best skiers from around the world. It is not for the leisurely skier/boarder as it takes a good 45 minutes to hike to, but the ride down is well worth it and your mum will appreciate the pictures from the top. There are a number of couloirs that you can drop in from, depending on your ability, and plenty of shoots and cliffs to hook off. It's a 'safe' run to do as it rarely slides and has become popular with the locals. Manu Gaidet, the 2004 world champion freeskier, declares it to be his favourite place to train in Courchevel.

Over the back of the Freeride is a huge face known to residents of Courchevel as the butcher's run. This was named after a local butcher who climbed to the top of the face before the lifts opened each day, leaving perfect tracks. It is imperative that, should you wish to re-enact this legendary story, you follow the butcher's lead and hike up first thing in the morning as it faces the sun all day, resulting in a potential avalanche risk later in the afternoon.

Lift passes	Trois Vallées	Courchevel
1 day	€42	€35.50
6 days	€210	€170
13 days	€420	€330

Three Valley extension passes are also for sale for €20.50 a day, which is good if you only want to do the full tour for one day. Children up to 13 years and adults over 60 receive a discount. Family passes are also available. It's worth getting the insurance as the emergency services on the mountain can cost an absolute fortune and if they see an insurance card the whole thing runs a lot more smoothly.

Instruction

ESF
The ESF has around 190 instructors in Courchevel alone. It is a well respected association.
T: 0033 (0)4 79 08 07 72
E: ski@esfcourchevel.com
W: www.esfcourchevel.com

Magic in Motion
Magic has both French and British instructors but all are English speaking. They have dodgy jackets and a big mouse mascot who skis around to entertain the kids but these guys always look as if they're enjoying themselves. It is a superb school and employs lots of fun and charismatic instructors. Group lessons cost €140–170 for a 1-week course, and private lessons (ski and board) are €370 for 1 day.
T: 0033 (0)4 79 01 01 81
E: courchevel@magicinmotion.co.uk
W: www.magicinmotion.co.uk

RTM

The name stands for the initials of the three directors, Rob, Tom and Mark. The way forward when it comes to snowboard instructors, RTM employs passionate and professional snowboarders who provide the best service. By the end of the day or week your instructor will be more of a friend than an instructor. Group sessions can be booked for 5 days (€210) or 4 days (€180), and private lessons are 2 hours (€140) or 3 hours (€190).

T: 0033 (0)6 15 48 59 04
E: info@rtmsnowboarding.com
W: www.rtmsnowboarding.com

Ski Academy

Ski Academy offers skiing and boarding lessons for all abilities. One of its best ideas is to offer semi-private tuition, where you will be placed in a group of 3–5 people so you get lots of attention and can still make friends. It is also good for kids and supplies helmets for free.

T: 0033 (0)4 79 08 11 99
E: courchevel@ski-academy.com
W: www.ski-academy.com

Ski Supreme

The Ski Supreme instructors are the longest-serving British ski instructors in Courchevel and have led the way for those that followed (the directors are the parents of Alan Baxter, Britain's most successful Alpine racer). The Ski Supreme team is extremely friendly and provides first-rate instruction. Ski courses cost from €160 for 10 hours and a private lessons costs €80 per hour.

T: 0033 (0)4 79 08 27 87
E: info@supremeski.com
W: www.supremeski.com

Other activities

Artificial climbing wall: At the Forum (04 79 08 19 50), this is a 13m high wall with seven ways up.

Bowling: There are eight bowling lanes in the Forum (04 79 08 23 83) which are open every day 11am–2am.

Ice climbing: This takes place on the ice tower in between 1850 and 1650. It can be quite challenging and is dependent on conditions and temperatures.

Ice go-karting: Literally go-karting on ice in 1550 (06 08 73 70 58, www.kartinglace.com, asp@kartinglace .com). Really good fun but fairly expensive for the short time you spend on the ice at €30 for 10 minutes.

Ice skating: The ice skating rink at the Forum is open every day 3–7pm and until 11pm on Wednesdays and Fridays. Adults pay €4.80.

Luging: Grab a sledge, available at most ski shops, and head down the specially made luge track in front of the Kalico to the bottom of 1550. Accidents are not uncommon. Take your lift pass for the ride back up.

Massage: After you have indulged in all these activities, get Pamper Off Piste (06 17 60 89 02, enquiry@

pamperoffpiste.com, www.pamperoffpiste.com) to visit you in the comfort of your chalet to relieve those tired, aching bones. They provide a large range of massage and beauty treatments and come highly recommended.

Parapenting: Ski off one of the top peaks with an instructor, gliding for around 15 minutes and landing in Le Praz where you catch the lift back up. There are a number of schools offering parapenting. The best are the legendary Pascal Plazzalunga (06 09 76 50 40) and Craig's Paragliding (04 79 08 43 65, www.paraglide-alps.com), the only British pilot in Les Trois Vallées. Cost: €90.

Plane trips: These are on hand for extravagant spenders to splash some cash to see the mountains from above. The Trois Vallées circuit costs €70 per person (04 79 08 31 23, www.areoclub-courchevel .com).

Raft on the Olympic ski jump: In Le Praz (04 79 08 39 60), this costs from €30 per person.

Shopping: The shopping is great (Prends tu luge is our favourite shop).

Skidoos: These can be hired for an afternoon of fun from Chardon Loisirs (04 79 08 39 60) or Ski Vol (06 83 97 53 26). A guide will take you along the marked tracks from €75. Great fun but they won't let you go wild.

Sky diving: Available through the whole of March, all reports of this have been fantastic. If you're in Courchevel in March, do it.

Events

The **Courchevel Freeride** (March) is one of the best big-mountain freeride events in Europe. People come from all over the world to compete for big cash prizes, and it attracts some of the best-known names in the business. The freeride competition takes place on the Col de la Loze and is great for spectators as you can see it really clearly from the piste and it's pretty impressive.

The **PlayStation Big Air** usually takes place in February. It's an open competition so anyone who fancies a pop can sign themselves up. There are loads of wicked prizes so it's worth a shot. Again, it's a good one to watch as it takes place at the bottom of 1850 on a specially built jump and always attracts a big crowd.

Ice hockey matches take place on the ice rink at the Forum throughout the season and are good to watch. Courchevel vs Meribel is a popular event with the locals and workers.

New Year's Eve Party on the Piste is a great event in the centre of 1850. Hundreds and thousands turn up to boogie on the snow to the live music and wonder at the fireworks. All the bars serve drinks in plastic cups so you can wander round with them and most places stay open until the last people fall over.

Accommodation

Luxury accommodation is provided by Flexiski, Kaluma and Ski Scott Dunn, so why not bankrupt yourself for a week of sheer indulgence. In similar fashion, there are some amazing, top-of-the-range hotels that have to be seen to be believed, as do the prices. **Le Kilimandjaro** (00 33 (0)4 79 01 46 46, www.hotelkilimandjaro.com, welcome@hotelkilimandjaro.com) is a stunning, grandiose building with a piano bar, beauty salon, spa and pool. It's right at the top of 1850 and not too handy for the town although there is a good shuttle service. If you can afford to stay here, you can afford taxis. Half-board accommodation costs €690–2785 per day for 2 people depending on the season and how super-posh you want your room to be. The **Lana** (0033 (0)4 79 08 01 10, www.lelana.com, info@lelana.com) is a similar level of luxury, but cosier and it's closer to the town centre. The Lana will set you back €375–1230 per day for half board for 2 people.

If you've not quite made the rich list just yet, there are a few other places to try. **Hotel de la Croisette** (003 (0)4 79 08 09 00, www.hoteldelacroisette.com, hotel.croisette@wanadoo.fr) is well placed for the main lifts and town centre and contains the popular Bar le Jump. It's a good, 3-star hotel and rooms on the first floor tend to be slightly cheaper because of the noise from the bar so why not take advantage of the good rate and go out and join in the fun. Bed and breakfast costs €155–235 for 2 people per night. **Courcheneige** (0033 (0)4 79 08 02 59, info@ courcheneige.com, www.courcheneige.com) is a 2 star on the Bellecotte piste, very handy for the slopes but not so much for going out at night. There is a huge terrace that is busy at lunch, and reports of the staff and food are superb. Rooms cost from €200 per day for half board for 2 people. **Hotel Olympic** (0033 (0)4 79 65 08 08, www.eurogroup-vacances.com, resa@eurogroup-vacances.com) has competitive rates and contains a small bar, popular at happy hour. It's handy for town and generally good value but not much to look at. Rooms cost €70–178 per day for 2 people for B&B.

Eating out

On the mountain

The **Cap Horn** (04 79 08 33 10), next to the Altiport, is a favourite of the rich and famous and the ultimate exclusive lunch. You'd never believe you were in the mountains. It has a cosy but luxurious feel and fabulous food. Don't stumble in, thinking you'll just grab a quick sandwich – reservations are essential. The beautiful **Panoramic** (04 79 08 00 88) restaurant is at the top of the Saulire cable car and is highly recommended, again, if your wallet can handle it. The **Bouc Blanc** (04 79 08 80 26) just below the Col de Loz chair has fantastic views, a huge open deck and a great Beaufort cheese tart. It's fantastic value compared to most of the restaurants on the mountain and the food and service is excellent. The **Jump** (04 79 08 09 00) at the bottom of the slopes in 1850 serves lunch 12am–3pm and the chilli and chips is highly recommended.

In town

First come the posh places – if you've forgotten your gold card, skip to the next paragraph. The **Chapelle** (04 79 08 19 48) has a fabulous, cosy, candlelit atmosphere, focused around an open wood fire on which all the meat is cooked. If you are not a big fan of red meat this may not be the place for you as there are few vegetarian options. The **Via Ferrata** (04 79 08 02 07) is impressive and whilst you can pay top dollar for some dishes and for drinks, the pizzas are surprisingly reasonable. They may have loud music but this somehow manages to remain unobtrusive and adds to the stylish, cosmopolitan environment. The **Grand Café** (04 79 08 42 97) is one of our favourite restaurants and serves Oriental cuisine to the highest standards in beautiful surroundings. The **Mangeoire** (04 79 08 02 09) is a restaurant/bar with an ambiance second to none. Those with a poor sense of humour need not apply as it is not unknown for the barmen to open up the fancy dress box and pop a hat on your head. They will also set the bar on fire, and provide jovial entertainment, despite any language

barriers. Also be prepared for two guys/girls on stilts who surfaced whilst we were there; they are scarily amusing and fling themselves in your face with no sense of personal boundaries. The **Bergerie** (04 79 08 24 70) serves some of the best food we have tasted in the mountains and often offers live music and theme nights. It is just by the side of the piste so you can stop in for lunch or book dinner, in which case a car will come and pick you up.

Getting cheaper . . .

If you fancy some Savoyard food, head to the **Saulire** (04 79 08 07 52), which has good local specialities and the **Fromagerie** (04 79 08 27 47) which serves one of the best fondues in town. You will find many restaurants offering Savoyard food such as fondues and pierres chaudes (hot stones on which you cook your own food) but, whilst scrumptious, the novelty will wear off. When it does, we recommend the **Refuge**, which offers a range of dishes from steak and ale pie and chips to a delectable Thai curry. **Kalico** (04 79 08 20 28), the nightclub, serves good food at lunch and at night. It is less expensive than its counterparts and serves massive portions (of burgers, salads, fajitas, etc). For a tasty, good-value take-out pizza try the **End Café**. **Vache Qui Ski** is open from 10pm until the early hours of the morning and offers great burgers and baguettes for late-night clubbers. We recommend the American baguette, which contains steak and chips and tastes amazing (under the influence of a pint or two).

Bars and clubs

Make sure your wallet's looking healthy if you're after a big night in 1850 – the drinks can be pricey and dress codes may apply. The **Jump** (04 79 08 09 00) has a great atmosphere and is busy all day; for mid-morning stops, lively après ski and 10.30pm–1am, when people are getting going for the evening. It's an English-run bar that attracts both holiday makers and season workers, all mainly English. If you want to save your pennies slightly and mingle with the season workers, try **TJ's** (town centre) or **Gringo's** (at the far end of town). They have cosy, fun atmospheres and relatively cheap drinks. Flavoured vodkas are popular and can be bought by the tray and if you're lucky you might turn up on a theme night. The bar **L'Equipe** is a favourite. There is great food, thanks to head chef Darren, and there is a superb atmosphere, thanks to the new manager this year who has really made a difference to this bar. The bar is open 9am–1am.

For the high society, here are a couple to try. For a luxurious, calm atmosphere, try **Piggy's** bar (04 79 08 00 71) in the heart of 1850. While you may enjoy the thought of sipping cocktails in this 'Old English library' style atmosphere, be prepared for the bill – half a lager costs around £6. The **Mangoire** is a fantastic bar, slightly off the beaten track. Prices are high but not unjustified – a £25 cocktail may sound extortionate but, when you catch a glimpse of the size of the glass and the artwork involved, you can only be amazed. It serves as a fine dining restaurant in the early evening (if you don't intend buying champagne you won't fit in) but when dinner is over you are, surprisingly, actively encouraged to jump on to chairs, tables and any other available surfaces.

After the bars have shut, **Kalico** (04 79 08 20 28) is the only place to be for most. DJs play every night, as well as top quality bands twice a week and every night is guaranteed to be jam packed with hedonistic young people. For exclusivity, there are two places to go: **La Grange** (04 79 08 14 61), right behind the Jump bar, and **Les Caves** at the edge of 1850. These clubs attract a similar clientele – those who won't bat an eyelid at splashing out hundreds of pounds for

bottles of vodka or champagne (few people drink by the glass) which are lit by sparklers and brought to your table. For neon strip lighting and a funky, dance atmosphere hit Les Caves; for a slightly more laid back, classic club, try La Grange.

Useful facts and phone numbers

Tourist office

T: 0033 (0)4 79 08 00 29
F: 0033 (0)4 79 08 15 63
E: info@courchevel.com
W: www.courchevel.com

Direct reservations

T: 0033 (0)4 79 08 14 44
F: 0033 (0)4 79 08 33 54
E: info@courchevel-reservation.com
W: www.courchevel-reservation.com

Emergency services

- In a medical emergency dial 15, for the fire brigade call 18, or 112 for either from a mobile.
- Police: 04 79 08 34 69/ 04 79 08 26 07

Doctors

- Blanc Alexandre: 04 79 08 26 40
- Cabinet Médical du Forum: 04 79 08 32 13
- Chedal Marc: 04 79 08 20 14
- Physiotherapy Clinic: 06 68 57 00 99 (Siân and Chris are definitely the best in town)

Taxis

- Courchevel Taxi Association: 04 79 08 23 46
- Abatrans Taxi: 04 79 00 3000 (www.courchevel-taxi.com)
- Taxi Jack: 06 12 45 11 17
- Luxury Taxi Service: Poirel Thibaut, 06 09 40 19 10 (www.snowtaxis.com, thibaut@snowtaxis.com)
- Helicopter-Taxi: 04 79 08 00 91 (www.saf-helico.com, saf@saf-helico.com)

Getting there

By car

From Calais, the drive will take you about 10 hours. Car parking for the week will cost you €60–70.

By plane

Geneva (145km) From here there are a number of different options to get to Courchevel. The bus costs €109 for a return trip and takes about 3.5 hours. Contact Touriscar on 04 12 27 98 20 00 or visit www.touriscar.net. Best to book in advance. A taxi (1–4 people) will cost €285 and a helicopter (up to 5 people) €1400. Call Jeremy Hopkins (0033 (0)6 21 70 04 40, mrhoppo1@yahoo.co.uk) for a good-value transfer.

Lyon (180km) is also 3.5 hours away by bus. Contact Satobus on 0033 (0)4 37 25 52 55, www.satobus-alps.com. A taxi costs €330 and a helicopter €1700.

Chambéry (115km) is closer. The transfer by bus costs €75 and takes 1.5 hours, a taxi is €220 and a helicopter €1000.

By train

Take the 17.09 Eurostar from London Waterloo to Paris; then an overnight train to Moutiers, and then a bus (55 minutes), arriving in resort at 08.25. Return fares from £111 in a 6-berth couchette. Contact Rail Europe (08705 848 848, www.raileurope.co.uk) or European Rail (020 7387 0444, www.europeanrail.com). Bus tickets (€11.60 single) can be purchased in advance from Altibus (0033 (0)4 79 68 32 96, www.altibus.com) or bought at the station.

La Tania

We are cheating here, because La Tania didn't quite make our top 50 – but we couldn't bear to leave it out completely.

On the slopes	
Snow reliability	✳ ✳ ✳
Off-piste	✳ ✳ ✳ ✳

Off the slopes	
Après ski	✳ ✳ ✳
Nightlife	✳ ✳ ✳ ◁
Eating out	✳ ✳ ✳ ◁
Resort charm	✳ ✳ ✳

The resort

La Tania is a small, friendly resort, with a great community feel, set in the middle of a pine forest and with access to the massive Trois Vallées. The traffic-free centre does not contain huge numbers of bars and restaurants, but it still has a lively après ski scene.

The mountains

Height: 1260–2740m

Ability	Rating
Expert	✳ ✳ ✳ ✳
Intermediate	✳ ✳ ✳ ✳ ✳
Beginner	✳ ✳ ✳

Getting about

This is a great base from which to explore Les Trois Vallées and, although it doesn't have its own park, off-piste in the trees down to the bottom of La Tania comes into its own on a powdery day when the light is flat. In better conditions, try underneath the Dou des Lanches chair: good, steepish terrains with sweet cliff drops.

Instruction

ESF
T: 0033 (0)4 79 80 80 39
E: info@esf-latania.com
W: www.esf-latania.com

Magic in Motion
T: 0033 (0)4 79 01 07 85
W: www.magicinmotion.co.uk

Events

La Tania goes to town on massive snow parties at Christmas and New Year. The **Trois Vallees Challenge** in April is popular, and at the end of the season is the **La Tania Charity Day** in aid of Cancer Research, one of the most fun all-day events of the season.

Accommodation

Skideep (0033 (0)4 79 08 19 05, ferg@skideep.net, www.skideep.net) is a small chalet company with three top-quality catered chalets. **Hotel Telemark/Chalet du Sud** (0044 (0)1202 65 34 56, info@hoteltelemark. com) is a chalet/hotel with 12 spacious rooms, all ensuite. **Icicles** (0033 (0(4 79 08 81 54, info@icicles.org, www.icicles.org) have a lovely catered chalet, Chalet Helene. All rooms are a very high standard and five of the six double bedrooms have good ensuite facilities.

Eating out

On the mountain
The **Bouc Blanc** (04 79 08 80 26) is one of the best local mountain restaurants, just below the Col de Loz chair. The open deck has fantastic views.

In town
The food at the **Ski Lodge** (04 79 08 81 49) is absolutely superb – the ribs are a firm favourite and the chilli burgers are legendary. **La Taiga** (04 79 08 80 33, www.easytaiga.com) has a great menu. The bistro at **Hotel Telemark** (0044 (0)12 02 65 34 56) has some good-value fixed-price menus.

Bars and clubs

Pub le Ski Lodge (04 79 08 81 49), open 10am–1.30am, is a friendly bar and social centre. Tuesdays are the biggest nights with some great live bands; look out for theme nights. **Le Farcon** (Pub l'Arbatt) is the place to go for pool and pinball. Hotel Montana has a piano bar, and Hotel Telemark also has a bar.

Les Deux Alpes

The heart of the European freestyle community

On the slopes	
Snow reliability	❄ ❄ ❄ ❄
Parks	❄ ❄ ❄ ❄ ❄
Off-piste	❄ ❄ ❄

Off the slopes	
Après ski	❄ ❄ ❄ ❄
Nightlife	❄ ❄ ❄ ❄
Eating out	❄ ❄ ❄
Resort charm	❄ ❄

The resort

Les Deux Alpes is situated where the Northern and Southern Alps meet, in the heart of the Oisans. The nearest town is Grenoble, 79km away. The town centre is focused along the main street, which is more than a kilometre long. It's not exceptionally beautiful but the mountains, slopes and the flawless snowpark more than make up for it. It also has a strong community atmosphere, as the resort is open year-round and has a large number of permanent residents.

Les Deux Alpes was built on a marshy plateau between two villages: Mont de Lans (Les Deux Alpes 1300) and Venosc, a more traditional craft village at the far end of the resort. We will be referring to the Mont de Lans and Venosc sides of town throughout this chapter. There is also the 'Village' area (Les Deux Alpes 1800), known to the locals as the 'ghetto'. This area has been known to attract some dubious characters and isn't particularly close to the lifts or local amenities but if you're looking for a bargain it could be worth checking out.

The mountains

Height: 1650–3600m

Ability	Rating
Expert	❄ ❄ ❄ ❄
Intermediate	❄ ❄ ❄ ❄
Beginner	❄ ❄ ❄ ❄

Getting about

There are 200km of marked runs in Les Deux Alpes, 59 ski lifts, a superb snowpark, and an abundance of alternatives for the budding freestyler or freerider. There are a little more than 700 hectares of off-piste. Sixty per cent of on-piste runs are designated for beginners and intermediate skiers and boarders and 40 per cent for the more competent and experienced riders. Les Deux Alpes also has the advantage of guaranteed snow year round due to high altitude and the use of 105 snow cannons.

The Jandri Express cable car takes you up to 3200m and then the funicular up to 3425m. At the top you are greeted with a 360-degree panoramic view of the French and Italian Alps: la Meije, le Mont Blanc and many others. The Diable gondola heads up to the Tête Moute at 2800m and gives access to steep on-piste runs, including a challenging 1200m vertical mogul field.

The park

Les Deux Alpes was one of the first resorts to passionately adopt New School riding. It costs around half a million pounds per winter to maintain the New School riding zones, including 28 hours of piste grooming per day. In winter the resort's snowpark is situated at 2600m, on the Toura area which can be reached by the Jandri cable car. In the summer, the park is shifted up to the glacier.

The snowpark consists of: a beginner's zone, created for freestyle debutantes, and containing six small kickers; a half pipe zone 120m long and 4m high; a slopestyle zone with a series of hips, gaps and quarters leading to rail zones of almost 400m; BBQ; music; DJ's turntable and deckchairs.

There is a boardercross area at 2600m where official boardercross competitions are held. The length of the boardercross is 1000–1230m and there is also a new, smaller boardercross for beginners, which is situated parallel to the old one.

The **JTS (Jumping Training System)** or the 'snow air bag' was set up by Les Deux Alpes ESF snowboarding school. The air bag is 14m by 28m and allows both beginners and experienced freestylers to up the level of their tricks in complete confidence as there is less chance of injuries if you land badly. It's only €6 for half an hour and definitely worth a try. Each week there is a JTS competition where competitors battle for the biggest air.

"In the centre of the mountain is the Clot de Chalance, a big playground of open powder fields, small couloirs and cliffs"

Off-piste and backcountry

Les Deux Alpes benefits from significant heights, guaranteeing good snow. Therefore, although the resort is not known for its off-piste terrain, there are many excellent spots for off-piste freeriding, such as Chalance, La Fee, Les Vallons du Diable, Les Posettes, Bellecombes and La Selle. There are also the legendary descents to La Grave.

In the centre of the mountain is the Clot de Chalance, a big playground of open powder fields, small couloirs and cliffs. You need to be there first thing in the morning after a fresh snow fall to get first tracks – by the afternoon it's tracked out. It is often blasted by the pisteurs and is relatively safe from avalanching, but there are stories of a couple of fatal slides. If you're feeling slightly more daring, it is possible to carry on all the way down to the Lac du Chambon, located below the base of the resort. It concludes with a lengthy tree run, but this should only be done with a guide and in the right conditions.

The Diable (at 2400m) has some top quality runs after a big powder storm. Starting from the top of the Télécabine du Diable (the ones that look like red eggs), you can ride all the way back to town. The terrain isn't too challenging but great for getting freshies.

For couloirs, make your way to the Lac du Plan, which can be seen as you're heading up the mountain in the Telepheriques Debrayables and can be reached by taking the Télésiège de la Fee chair lift. Just below the lake is a variety of options, including a long, narrow, challenging couloir that is held in high regard amongst the top riders in the resort.

Make your way to the top of the glacier by catching the Funiculaire Dome Express. The Dome, nicknamed the Ice Wall, is ideal for getting fresh powder and a perfect place for building backcountry kickers. From here you can see all the terrain leading to La Grave, which has some of the best off-piste riding in the world (see the chapter on La Grave, page 184). A guide is highly recommended if you fancy attempting this terrain.

Lift passes	
1 day (21 lifts)	€16.50
1 day (54 lifts)	€34
6 days	€161.50
If you are under 5 or over 72, lifts are free.	
There is a discount on passes in early December.	

Instruction

ESF

Ecole du Ski Français and Ecole du Snowboard. Group lessons for 6 half days costs €115.50–127.50.
T: 0033 (0)4 76 79 21 21
E: les2alpes@wanadoo.fr
W: www.esf2alpes.com

European Ski School

This ski school comes highly recommended by the locals due to the quality of instruction. They limit the size of groups to 8 or 9 and all the instructors speak good English. They also offer a 'Natural Born Skiers' course with a maximum of 4 per group, lift-queue priority and video analysis (you must be a good skier). This costs €170 for 5 days (2 hours a day).
T: 0033 (0)4 76 79 74 55

E: europeanskischool@worldonline.fr
W: www.europeanskischool.co.uk

St Christophe International Ski and Snowboard School

Lessons cost €126.50 for six half days (ski), €137 (snowboard). To improve your New School riding techniques, private lessons in the park are offered from €35 per hour.

T: 0033 (0)4 76 79 04 21
E: contact@esi2alpes.com
W: www.esi2alpes.com

Ski Privilège

This school offers group and private ski or snowboard lessons by the hour or half day. Anne Millet is an ex-member of the French Ski Team and offers competitive prices with group lessons from €65 per person per week (five 2-hour sessions) or €199 with lift pass.

T: 0033 (0)4 76 79 23 44
W: http://anne.millet.free.fr

Stages Damien Albert

This school teaches only freeride, off-piste and 'bump' courses. They require that students can ski black runs. A 6-day course costs €250.

T: 0033 (0)4 76 79 50 38
E: damienalbert@wanadoo.fr
W: www.abc-skifreeride.com

Mountain Guides Bureau

The bureau offers training in avalanche rescue and snow awareness. There is also the weekly Free Respect event, which aims to heighten awareness of the risks and dangers of the mountain for off-piste enthusiasts.

E: guides2alpes@yahoo.fr

Other activities

On the mountain

Unless otherwise stated, contact the tourist office (see Useful facts and phone numbers) for more information.

Full moon parties: Combining night riding and drinking sounds pretty dangerous but it is great fun. Take the last lifts up the mountain at around 4.30pm, ski/ board as the sun sets on the glacier and enjoy a lively meal in a mountain restaurant. Then, after nightfall, ski back down towards the resort, over a drop in altitude of 1300 m with only the moon to see by (€40 includes your lift pass, meal, ice cave and mulled wine on return).

Ice Cave: Found at 3400m, this is the longest and highest in the world. The grotto was dug entirely by pickaxe, there was no use of machines, and it now contains many ice sculptures. Open winter and summer.

Night in an igloo: In the Pied Moutet area, at 1700m, in a wild mountain setting, the Kanata igloo village offers the chance to spend a night in an igloo (€60 for an adult). Access is on snowshoes in the evening or on skis during the day.

Night skiing and boarding: This takes place three times a week on the Piste de Lutins in the middle of the resort – and it's free! For more information call Deux Alpes Loisirs (04 76 79 75 01, 2alpesloisirs@2alpes.com, www.2alpes.com).

Paragliding, hang-gliding or helicopter rides: Call Ecole de Parapente Air 2 Alpes (04 76 80 19 30, j.bat.berlioux@wanadoo.fr, www.air2alpes.com) for paragliding courses (from €380) or tandem flights (€60–130). Or Ecole de Parapente des 2 Alpes (04 76 79 21 21, parapente.2alpes@free.fr) for courses from €400 or tandem flights from €55.

Snowmobiles and quad bikes: Try an evening excursion on the piste. Don't expect to go crazy – there will be a guide to keep you under control.

Tobogganing: The Alpette lift is open for tobogganing until 10pm 2–3 times a week. There are two runs, one fast and one slow.

In the town

Bowling: There are two bowling alleys and lots of games arcades. Bowling Le Strike (04 76 79 28 34) has six lanes and costs €5 before 8pm and €6.50 8pm–2am. Bowling Les 2 Alpes 1800 (04 76 80 53 99, www.clubforme1800.com) has six lanes and costs €6 before 8pm and €7 after 8pm.

Cinema: The local cinema has two screens and shows films at 6pm and 9pm.

Fitness activities: Health and fitness activities available include squash, jacuzzi, hammam, sauna, tanking, fitness circuits, slimming courses, massages, relaxation, gym, body building, cardio-training, aqua gym, solarium, UVA, spa and shiatsu.

Ice skating: There's an open-air Olympic ice rink (04 76 79 22 73). You can either ice skate (€1.80 for entrance and skate hire) or try out the dodgem cars on ice (€3.20 per ride).

Pool, spa and treatments: Aquaflorès wellbeing centre (04 76 80 56 90, www.chaletmounier.com) has an indoor pool plus spa days from €97: physiotherapy, massages, diet advice, seaweed treatments, aromatherapy, etc.

Swimming: Try the heated outdoor pool (04 76 79 25 64, www.clubforme1800.com).

Tobogganing: The Alpette lift is open for tobogganing until 10pm two or three times a week. There are two runs: one fast and one slow.

Events

The Mondial Du Snow (October/November). The Mondial du Snowboard is held at the end of October (the 17th edition). The Mondial du Ski takes place a week later (the 9th edition). There are many events during these two weekends. On the glacier, you have the chance to test an incredible number of skis and snowboards: over six days, roughly 85 brand names will be ready to give advice and loan the latest equipment, accessories and clothing from the new collections. A giant rail, more than 50m in length, will also be set up on the glacier. In the town, marquees premier the latest snow-riding films, and a massive skate ramp (12m long, 3.5m high) is set up for demos from the world's best skateboarders.

Other events include the Snowzone event (mid-March) which combines snow-riding and music. The day starts with sounds on the slopes which gradually make their way down to the resort, and then carry on into the bars and clubs. Popular DJs will be playing house, techno and electronic sounds in an extraordinary atmosphere at the bottom of the Deux Alpes slopes. The Taravana event (April) is another freestyle snowboard event, closing the winter season in the snowpark.

Accommodation

Farandole (0033 (0)4 76 80 50 45, hotel lafarandole@free.fr, www.hotel-la-farandole.com), one of the only 4-star hotels in town, is a traditional chalet, with 60 bedrooms and apartments. There is a smart restaurant, fitness club, indoor pool, sauna and Jacuzzi.

There are eight 3-star hotels, one of the best being Chalet Mounier (04 76 80 56 90, doc@chalet-mounier.com, www.chalet-mounier.com), which has a great atmosphere in an authentic chalet. There is a billiard room, spa and indoor pool with a wave machine. It is handy for the Diable gondola and the main bar scene. Prices range from €89 to €200.

There is also an enormous choice of apartments but it is very important to check their location as Les Deux Alpes sprawls over a large area.

One company that is definitely worth checking out is Scuba-Ski (0033 (0)4 76 11 03 14 (Oct–April), 0034 (0)661 323 300 (May–Sept), info@scuba-ski.com, www.scuba-ski.com), owned by Pete and Lynn Foreman, which offers both catered and self-catered apartments, for between two and ten guests.

All their accommodation benefits from a great location, right in the middle of the action (just a few minutes' walk from the ski lifts) and is priced at a very competitive rate (expect to pay around £300 per person per week depending on the time of season). They have one 10-bed chalet (comfortably fits 7), which really is home away from home with hundreds of classic videos to watch, and board games to play. It's more homely than luxurious but highly recommended. They will even arrange for your lift passes, ski/board hire and/or ski/board school to be booked and ready for you on arrival if you wish, with a 10 per cent discount! If you're looking for apartments of good standard, the **Le Prince des Ecrins** residence is situated 500m from the nearest shops and within immediate proximity of the slopes. It contains 28 apartments for 4–10 people that have a magnificent view over the Veneon valley and the Venosc and Muzelle peaks. All apartments have south-facing balconies.

Eating out

On the mountain
There are nine mountain restaurants in Les Deux Alpes. Le **Panoramic** (04 76 79 06 75) is a popular meeting point, at the heart of the action at 2600m. Choose between the restaurant or self-service. **Chalet La Fee** (04 76 80 24 13) has a friendly atmosphere, simple food and good views from the terrace.

In town
There are more than 60 restaurants in Les Deux Alpes with a wide variety of cuisines. Fast food joints and crêperies can be found all through town and offer decent burgers, kebabs, paninis and steak sand-wiches. Don't expect a bargain though, it will still cost you around €8 a piece.

Most of the restaurants in the area serve traditional French cuisine – fondues, raclettes, tartiflette, pierres chaudes, etc. **Cellier** (04 76 79 08 79, jean-luc.bisi@wanadoo.fr) has a charming wooden interior with a roaring fire. It is located at the end of town; follow the main road to the Place de Venosc and it's

just opposite. **Crepes a GoGo** (04 76 79 29 61, lescrepesagogo@lescrepesagogo.com, www.lescrepesagogo.com) is a stunning restaurant, with not bad prices for such a gorgeous place. The huge fire and cushioned benches create a very cosy and alpine atmosphere. **Le P'tit Polyte** at the Chalet Mounier (04 76 80 56 90) has a strong reputation for serving traditional Savoyard dishes.

For a change to the local fare, try these recommendations. **La Spaghetteria** (04 76 79 05 77) has good-value pasta dishes at €7–8 each. **Smokey Joes** (04 76 79 28 97, www.smokeyjoe.fr) and **The Red Frog** (see Bars and clubs) serve good, classic bar food all day until 11pm.

"The food has a fantastic, and well-deserved, reputation"

Bars and clubs

There are 30 bars, open until 2am and three clubs that are open until about 5am.

Smokey Joes (04 76 79 28 97) is right in the heart of Les Deux Alpes, a second's walk from the lifts and town centre. It is British run and is open 8am–2am every day. The food has a fantastic, and well-deserved,

reputation and it is served all day until 11pm. Choose from full English breakfasts until midday, bacon sandwiches, paninis, fajitas, wraps and many more tasty morsels. Smokeys also has internet access, DJs and regular theme nights, and is a place much-loved by locals and tourists alike. **The Red Frog** (04 76 79 23 28) is run by an Englishman, Irishman and Scotsman and always has a good busy atmosphere. Located at the Venosc end of town, it is open 7am–2am, serving food until 11pm. The Frog offers

a legendary, all day, full English breakfast as well as burgers, pasta, steaks and salads. They show all the footie on new plasma TVs and have also opened a sitting room at the back of the bar with comfy sofas to chill and watch the matches. The Frog also has a pool room and wireless laptops at broadband speed that they rent out for a bargain of 10 cents per minute.

Smithy's (04 76 11 36 79, www.smithystavern.com) is open 5pm–2am and is located next to the Avalanche club at the Venosc end of town. It's a huge, open-plan pub on two floors, the ground floor being the pub and the top floor the restaurant. The bar has a good reputation, predominantly due to the weekly DJs and live bands. It allegedly contains the longest vodka bar (with over 20 flavours of vodka shots) in the Alps, although we think the Couloir in Tignes has stolen this title. The music is an eclectic mix (anywhere from cheesy pop to hip hop, rap and house), and is usually adapted to suit the crowds. Pool and table football

tables pass the time. The restaurant (open 5–11.30pm) serves steaks, fresh fish and vegi dishes and, in the summer, BBQs are held on the outside terrace, which is used as an après ski terrace during the winter.

The Boardroom (04 76 79 08 89) benefits from a very central location on the main street and a terrace that receives the sun 1–6pm. It opens 11am–2am and serves food all day. At happy hour, usually 7–9pm, free tapas is available. Its plasma TVs show videos during the day as well as all the major sporting events. Amongst the variety of drinks and cocktails available, they also have an interesting range of absinth cocktails for the more courageous drinkers. Mezzanine (06 15 10 55 65, www.mezzaninebar.com) is a small bar, towards the Mont de Lans end of town, that does great cocktails and is the only place in town to serve the lethal 'Mutzig' beer.

There are a few clubs that are open until 5am, the best being the **Bresilien** (04 76 79 04 98) and the **Avalanche** (04 76 80 52 44). The Avalanche, towards the Venosc end of town, isn't huge but has plenty of atmosphere and regularly has DJs playing to keep the crowds entertained. It's a funky club and is right next door to Smithy's, so there's no need to get cold – just stumble on over.

Useful facts and phone numbers

Tourist office

T: 00 33 (0)4 76 79 22 00
F: 00 33 (0)4 76 79 01 38
E: les2alps@les2alpes.com
W: www.les2alpes.com
      www.2alpesexperience.com will also give you more information on the resort

Direct reservations

T: 0033 (0)4 76 79 24 38
F: 0033 (0)4 76 79 51 13
E: reservation@les2alpes.com

Emergency services

- In a medical emergency dial 15, for the fire brigade call 18, or 112 for either from a mobile.
- Police: 04 76 79 24 24/ 04 76 79 26 11
- Ambulance: 04 76 80 52 39
- Weather information: 0033 (0)8 92 68 02 38

Doctors

- Centre Clinique des 2 Alpes:
  04 76 79 20 03
- Centre Médical du Lauvitel:
  04 76 80 52 48, docteur.joly@wanadoo.fr
- Doctor Labalette, Rue des Perrons:
  04 76 80 51 40

Taxis

- Trans'Oisans Taxis: 04 76 80 06 97/ 06 09 38 38 38, transoisans@wanadoo.fr, 5–9 seater taxis
- Autocars Rouard: 04 76 80 04 21, voyages@rouard.com, can transfer 3–60 people

Getting there

By car

Take the motorway direct from Paris (643km) or Lyon (170km/2-hour drive approximately) to Grenoble (turn off N8 Briançon, Vizelle, stations de l'Oisans), then RN 91 in the direction of Briançon via Bourg d'Oisans. Turn right at Barrage du Chambon (Chambon dam) and take the D213. If you are driving from the UK, it's about 950–1130km from the channel ports.

By coach

Eurolines run a bus from London to Grenoble, where you can pick up the VFD/Satobus connection to Les Deux Alpes.

By plane

Geneva (220km) Connect to Les Deux Alpes by VDF coaches via Grenoble – 3-hour drive. *Lyon (170km)* Connect to Les Deux Alpes by Satobus – 2-hour drive. *Grenoble (110km)* is closer but is no longer serviced by a schedule airline, although charter flights still operate – 1.5-hour drive.

By train

Take the 09.09 Eurostar from London Waterloo to Paris; then by TGV, arriving Grenoble 17.32; then a bus (100 minutes) arriving in resort at 19.40. Return rail fares from £97. Contact Rail Europe (08705 848 848, www.raileurope.co.uk) or European Rail (020 7387 0444, www.european rail.com). Bus tickets, €5.10 single, must be purchased in advance from VFD coaches (0033 (0)4 76 60 47 08, www.vfd.fr).

La Grave

Freeriding heaven

La Meije 3982
Le Rateau 3809
Pointe Trifide
Pic de la Grave
Dome de la Lauze

denivelé 2150 m / 7100 feet vertical

3550

3550

Glacier
de la Girose

3200 Les Ruillans

col du lac

Glacier
du Rateau

brèche Pacave

vallons de Chancel

Glacier
de la Meije

Les
Enfetchores

Cotefine

lac de
Puyvachier

refuge Cha

2400
Peyrou
d'Amont

Chalvachère

1800

Cascades de glace de la Grave

La Lauzette

1450

1400

La Grave

vers les Fréaux

1400

On the slopes	
Snow reliability	❄ ❄ ❄ ❄
Parks	–
Off-piste	❄ ❄ ❄ ❄ ❄
Off the slopes	
Après ski	❄ ❄
Nightlife	❄ ❄
Eating out	❄ ❄
Resort charm	❄ ❄ ❄ ❄

The resort

You shouldn't come here if...

- you like cruising round between mountain restaurants.
- the idea of a steep red run sets you panicking.
- you place great importance on a resort's provision of late-night drinking holes.
- you won't stay in hotels that have less than 4 stars.
- you are a snowpark junkie.
- you can't fathom the thought of skiing (if applicable) on skis that are shorter than 195cm – they'd call you a pussy.

"From the moment you step on the lift you know that you're about to start an amazing adventure"

And, to be honest, we hope that this includes most people because if you all came, you'd spoil it. However, if you are still interested, you'll have the most amazing time of your life on this mountain. It takes the mountains back to how they used to be, and how they should be, completely opposite to the crowded, motorway-style runs that now shroud most resorts. You will not see lifts (apart from the one Old School bubble that takes you to 3200m); you will not see coloured poles marking nicely groomed runs (as there aren't any), you will not see ski patrols (there is only the great Jean-Charles who starts the morning at the bottom of the lift to provide you with invaluable info about the avalanche risk, etc – then he's off skiing); you won't see anything to warn you about rocks, cliff drops or crevasses (of which there are many); you probably even won't see other skiers or boarders; you will simply see the majestic, imposing and commanding mountains – and they're all yours. With a vertical drop of 2150m from top to bottom, the devoted freerider will be in heaven.

If you do come to La Grave you will need, without question, all the avalanche-safety gear (probe, shovel and transceiver) and enough money to invest in a guide, or know someone who knows the mountain well. It's not that it's not safe to be without one – it's no different to anywhere else, you just won't have a clue where you're going and you will, for definite, get completely lost, which would be a shame as no one's there to come and find you. You also need to be in pretty good physical condition.

The mountains

Height: 1400–3550m

Ability	Rating
Expert	❄ ❄ ❄ ❄ ❄
Intermediate	❄ ❄
Beginner	❄

Getting about

The whole mountain is available to ride, depending on your ability. There are some set itineraries but they are pretty much impossible to follow without a guide, never mind if you want to explore the couloirs and hidden areas. If, for some unknown reason, you do want to leave this beautiful mountain, La Grave is also connected with Les Deux Alpes, although there is a walk involved. If you are a beginner and you somehow end up in La Grave, La Chazelet is nearby and a good place to learn. (If you need lessons contact the ESF: 0033 (0)4 76 79 92 86.)

The one and only cable car takes you right to the top of the mountain and takes around 30 minutes in total. There are a few stops, and the usual course of action is to take the lift right to 3200m first thing and then ride down to P1 (the first stop) and take the lift back up. You'll probably manage this three to four times in one day. At first you may think the cable car is too slow but after a couple of runs you'll welcome the break and, if it went any quicker, it would allow more people to be on the mountain at once which is against the philosophy of La Grave.

Be sure that you prepare yourself with sufficient safety equipment and knowledge. For example, for some couloirs you need ropes and climbing equipment to lower yourself in – do your homework before you set off. If you have any questions, make sure you seek out the patrouilleur, Jean-Charles, as he is the best person to help you. He usually resides in the wooden chalet by the lift pass office.

"The likelihood is that you won't bump into a single person on your way down"

Backcountry

From the moment you step on the lift you know that you're about to start an amazing adventure. As you step off the lift at the top of the mountain (3200m), you can tell in an instant that you are somewhere special and unique. There are no marked pistes, no ski/board schools and no ski patrol. Therefore, it is 100 per cent certain that you need a guide, especially if you have not been here before. We bumped into a couple of people who had ventured up without a guide and they looked very confused, lost, and, if we're not mistaken, a little scared. Without a guide, you will also miss out on some of the best areas.

One of the first places to check out for your warm-up run is the classic itinerary: les Vallons (turn left as you exit the lift). If you get to do this after a snow storm, you'll be in heaven. There is challenging and fun terrain and you can really let yourself go. It's a long-lasting run and the likelihood is that you won't bump into a single person on your way down. Your guide can also show you some great couloirs if you're up for it. Our favourites are the Triffides couloirs; we checked out Triffide 1 which is at the top of Les Ruilliains. Your guide will rope you in and then it opens up into one nice shoot. You need to make sure the snow's in good condition as you wouldn't want to attempt this when it's icy or windy.

If you turn right on exiting the lift, you can set out along the Chancel, another classic itinerary, with some exciting deviations. One such digression was over to English Man Valley (nicknamed by the locals) where we skied a couloir called the Banane, approximately 150m long. It's quite steep at the top but it's easily accessible and a good ride down to a beautiful lake called Lac de Puyvachier. If the conditions are bad, and there's too much wind for them to open the top lift, panic ye not, as there are some great tree runs at the bottom of the mountain, some with good mogul lines.

There are some amazing riders in La Grave and all have a great deal of knowledge about the mountains. La Grave, we salute you!

Lift passes	
1 day	€30

Guiding
There are 28 guides in La Grave, ranging from former ski champions to locals who've lived here forever.

Bureau des Guides
On a one-day tour you will discover the classic off-piste descents of Vallons de al Meije and Chancel in a group of 1–8 people. They can also take you to couloirs and the steeper, secret spots, depending on the level of the group. Other courses include off-piste awareness courses, ice climbing, winter mountaineering, heliskiing, ski touring and paragliding (€132 per person). A private guide costs from €276 per day and a day's skiing within a group at a similar level costs €72.

T: 0033 (0)4 76 79 90 21
E: meijenet@wanadoo.fr
W: www.guidelagrave.com

Snow Legend Camps
T: 0033 (0)6 81 97 03 25
E: snowlegend@waw.com
W: www.snowlegend.com

Events

Derby de la Meije (www.derbydelameije.com) takes place around the end of March/beginning of April. It comprises the longest vertical drop of any race in the world: 2150m. There are over a thousand participants, on snowboard, skis or telemarks, dressed up or not, alone or in a team and each one chooses their own line down the mountain. For a few days La Grave really kicks off with loads of music, partying, drinking and riding, after which it returns to its idyllic state.

Accommodation

There aren't many places to stay in La Grave but there are some great ones, and nothing's too expensive. **L'Edelweiss** (0033 (0)4 76 79 90 93, info@hotel-edelweiss.com, www.hotel-edelweiss .com) is a lovely, 2-star hotel offering a great standard of accommodation in a beautiful location. There are 23 rooms that are all en suite and can house 2–4 people. The atmosphere is cosy, friendly and homely with loads of facilities: a TV room, Jacuzzi, sauna, library, games and videos. Robin and Marlan, the Scottish/Dutch couple that run the hotel, will make sure you are very well looked after. Robin can provide you with good advice about the mountain, he's had many years of experience and was the British freestyle champion (in the days of hotdogging). They offer flexible accommodation so you can book for long weekends, a week, whatever you like. The food's great (even the bread's homemade), there's a good bar, they have free internet and often have live music events – all the staff play instruments as do loads of the locals! **Chalet Dorothea** (0033 (0)4 76 79 62 47 or 0033 (0)6 24 03 10 23, ian.bowyer@alpine-xtreme.com,

www.alpine-xtreme.com) is owned and run by the very friendly hosts Donna and JJ. This is the second year the chalet has been up and running and we have heard nothing but great reports from all who stayed there last winter. Prices are £300–350 per person, per week or £45 per night.

The **Castillan** (0033 (0)4 76 79 90 04, castillan.hotel@wanadoo.fr, http://perso.wanadoo.fr/castillan) is another 2 star in the centre of town. If you're looking for self-catering accommodation, the 3-star **Les Enfetchores** (0033 (0)4 38 37 13 60, www.les-enfetchores.com, mail@les-enfetchores.com) offers good apartments with dishwasher, washing machine and TV. You can book accommodation through the central reservation office, **Meije Tours** (0033 (0)4 76 79 97 72, meije.tours@wanadoo.fr, www.meijetours.com), who will advise you on accommodation for your budget and requirements, and put you in contact with private apartment owners if necessary. They will also offer you good prices for mountain guides.

Eating out

On the mountain

There are three good restaurants up the mountain. At 3200m is a self-service restaurant, Le Haut-Dessus (06 07 56 67 25), that serves excellent pizzas, steaks, pork and all sorts. The staff are all really friendly. At full moon, there has been known to be the occasional party after everyone else has gone down the mountain. The locals congregate at 3200m, have a fair few shots and ride down the mountain in the bright moonlight – not recommended unless you know the mountain like the back of your hand. The Evarist Chancel (04 76 79 92 32, annie@refuge-chancel.com, www.refuge-chancel.com) at 2508m, just off the Chancel route, is a great restaurant and, for an experience not to be

missed, try staying there overnight. The other restaurant, at the middle station, also serves good quality food. There's nothing you'll be disappointed with in La Grave.

In town

There are two restaurants in town that are fantastic. The **Edelweiss** hotel (see Accommodation), serves a delicious, homemade four-course set menu at a very good price and, if you don't fancy what's on the menu, they also have an à la carte selection with a great three-cheese fondue. The other restaurant is the **Le Vieux Guide** (04 76 79 90 75), down a small alleyway, which is fabulously cosy and serves fantastic, traditional Savoyard food. We loved the raclette and left feeling very content. The **Bois de Fées** (04 76 11 05 48, publeboisdesfees@aol.com) bar also serves superb food if you fancy a simple but tasty pizza or gratin. It is themed in a kind of Midsummer Night's Dream fashion. If you fancy a snack after skiing you can warm yourself up with a sweet or savoury crêpe from the huge selection at the **Alp bar** (04 76 79 96 67) in the centre of town. They do all sorts of food and have good hot chocolate.

Bars and clubs

There isn't much in the way of bars in La Grave. The **Bois de Fées** (04 76 11 05 48) is one of the most popular bars with a pool table and good food (see Eating out). Apart from that there is the **Glacier Bar** which is more of a bar/café that's good for a coffee in the morning or a cheeky après ski beer. The **Edelweiss** bar is a popular choice with the locals and a really friendly place. It stays open as long as Robin and Marlon feel they want to keep it open and they often arrange music nights; the locals all seem to be top musicians as well as exceptional riders.

Whatever you do, don't brag about the 30m cliff you dropped off or the couloir you straight-lined – the 80-year-old local sat next to you probably went ten times faster yesterday and wouldn't even bother to mention it.

Useful facts and phone numbers

Tourist office

T: 00 33 (0)4 76 79 90 05
F: 00 33 (0)4 76 79 91 65
E: ot@lagrave-lameije.com
W: www.lagrave-lameije.com

Direct reservations

T: 00 33 (0)4 76 79 97 72

Emergency services

- In a medical emergency dial 15, for the fire brigade call 18, or 112 for either from a mobile.
- Police: 04 76 79 91 02
- Mountain rescue: 04 92 22 22 22
- Snow and avalanche bulletin: 08 92 68 10 20

Doctors

- 04 76 79 98 03

Taxi

- Taxi de la Meije: 04 76 79 92 87

Getting there

By car

It will take nearly 10 hours to drive from Calais. Head towards Grenoble and then take the RN91 towards Briançon. La Grave is around 80km from the motorway exit and is easily accessible.

By plane

Lyon (150km) Transfer takes around 2 hours.
Geneva (220km) Transfer takes around 3 hours.
Grenoble (100km) Transfer takes just under 2 hours.

By train

Take the 09.09 Eurostar from London Waterloo to Paris; then by TGV, arriving Grenoble 17.32; then a bus (90 minutes) arriving in resort at 19.33. Return rail fares from £97. Contact Rail Europe (08705 848 848, www.raileurope.co.uk) or European Rail (020 7387 0444, www.europeanrail.com). Bus tickets, €15.10 single, must be purchased in advance from VFD coaches (0033 (0)4 76 60 47 08, www.vfd.fr).

Meribel

Trendy, with a great atmosphere
(and great parks), if you don't
mind feeling like you are
in a pub on the King's Road

On the slopes	
Snow reliability	✻ ✻ ✻
Parks	✻ ✻ ✻ ✻
Off-piste	✻ ✻ ✻ ✤
Off the slopes	
Après ski	✻ ✻ ✻ ✻
Nightlife	✻ ✻ ✻ ✤
Eating out	✻ ✻ ✻
Resort charm	✻ ✻ ✻

The resort

Meribel is a friendly place, dominated by the Brits. It's a purpose-built resort but much more attractive than others such as Tignes, Les Arcs and Val Thorens as everything has been built in chalet style. Meribel prides itself on being funky and trendy, with some really smart bars and a good atmosphere. It can feel like you're in a bar in London, so your perception of Meribel will relate to whether you think this is a good or bad thing. Either way, the riding is fantastic, and Meribel should be especially praised for its two superb parks. Mottaret is not as charming (it's ugly), and has only a minimum of services (it's dull). However, it does have good access to the slopes.

The mountains

Height: 1450m

Ability	Rating
Expert	✻ ✻ ✻ ✻
Intermediate	✻ ✻ ✻ ✻
Beginner	✻ ✻ ✻

Getting about

There are 150km of trails in Meribel; 74 runs in total. Of these, 9 are black, 23 red, 34 blue, and 8 green. There are also 650 snow guns which assure snow coverage for 37 per cent of the ski area. This is a great help in Meribel as the resort is pretty low so the snow at the bottom is often fairly poor. The lift system is very quick and efficient.

The park

At 1800m is the Meribel **Moonpark**, which has it all. It has ten table-top jumps, ten rails, two pipes (one competition level pipe, 145m long and a 125m pipe for novices), a massive hip and a 1000m boarder/skier cross course. It is always kept in tiptop condition and is the main meeting point in Les Trois Vallées. There's a group of enthusiastic shapers taking care of the park every day and experimenting with different ideas. Check out www.moonpark.net for pictures and videos.

Meribel's little brother Mottaret, also has a great park at 2400m; the **Plattières Park**. It has five table tops, one hip, three rails, two pipes and a skier/boardercross. Having all this in the same area has to make Meribel one of the best places for freestyle in Europe. We love it!

Off-piste and backcountry

From the top of Saulire, which is famous for having amazing couloirs leading to Courchevel, you have the couloirs to Meribel. There is the central Meribel couloir, and just along from this is death couloir which is great when the snow's right, and first thing in the morning before the sun does too much damage.

The locals don't like to say too much about the favourite areas, but look out for those that have been nicknamed Super Mario Land, Rock Garden and the Spot. They are all around the Bartavelle area which you can get to by going up the Roc de tougne drag lift. The Bartavelle also has one of the best mogul fields in Les Trois Vallées, which has hosted events like the Meribel Shaker Bump competition. A favourite adventure of one of our sources is the Gébroulaz. It's best to take a guide or you might not find it. It's a good 1-hour hike via Val Thorens and has to be done early in the morning. Once you're at the top you can look forward to a 14-km run across a stunning glacier untouched by the masses.

as doing demos. Don't be surprised if you see a big orange bunny doing a massive trick off a kicker – it'll be one of the Magic team.
T: 0033 (0)4 79 08 53 36
E: meribel@magicinmotion.co.uk
W: www.magicinmotion.co.uk

New Generation
T: 0033 (0)4 79 01 03 18
E: info@skinewgen.com
W: www.skinewgen.com

Ski Academy
Ski Academy offers skiing and boarding lessons for all abilities. One of its best ideas is to offer semi-private tuition, where you will be placed in a group of 3–5 people so you get lots of attention and can still make friends. Prices are €250–330 depending on the time of season and a 15- or 18-hour course. It is also good for kids and supplies helmets for free.
T: 0033 (0)4 79 08 11 99
E: meribel@ski-academy.com
W: www.ski-academy.com

Lift passes	Meribel Valley	Les Trois Vallées
1 day	€35	€41
6 days	€166	€204

Instruction

ESF
The ESF offers freeride, freestyle and off-piste tuition as well as the usual private and group lessons.
T: 0033 (0)4 79 08 60 31
E: esf.meribel@wanadoo.fr
W: www.esf-meribel.com

Magic in Motion
Magic in Motion is well respected and loved in the local community. The Magic team consists of both British and French instructors who are a fantastic choice for all, from beginners to those who want to hook back flips in the park. Disciplines taught include skiing, snowboarding, monoski, telemarking and ski-touring. There are a lot of characters within the team! Some of France's top freestyle skiers work for Magic in Motion and have set up their own 'Team Magic' who now do the freeride and freestyle competition circuit as well

"The Magic team consists of both British and French instructors who are a fantastic choice for all"

Other activities

Cinema: Check out what's on at the cinema (0892 687 333, www.cinealpes.fr).
Climbing: The Bureau des Guides (04 79 00 30 38, guides.meribel@laposte.net, www.guides-courchevel-meribel.com) offers climbing classes – either on a frozen waterfall or on a climbing wall.

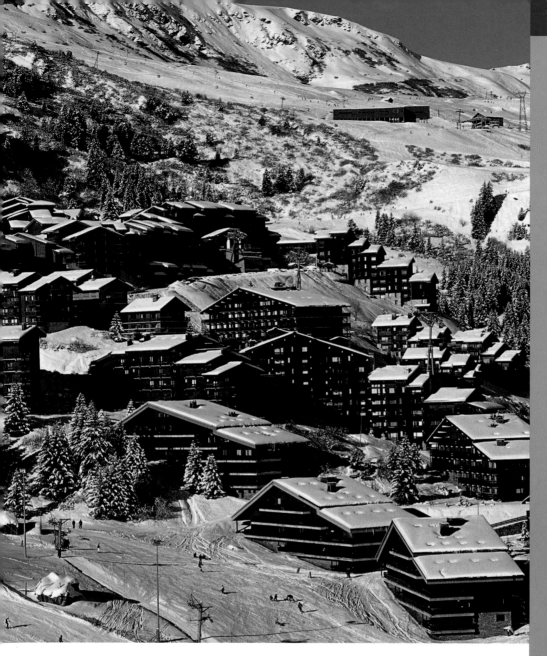

Dogsledding: This costs €50 per person for an hour (06 80 63 15 72/ 04 79 08 81 55, trianeauevasion@ wanadoo.fr).

Go-karting: On a Monday night you can have a go at driving go-karts on ice, at €20 for a 10-minute round (06 11 27 76 72, pasgirard@wanadoo.fr).

Hot air ballooning: Take a 1- or 2-hour flight for €220 (Ski Vol on 04 79 08 41 72).

Ice skating, swimming and bowling: The Parc Olympique (04 79 00 58 21, m.e.l@wanadoo.fr) is home to a number of amenities such as an ice skating rink (€4.60 plus €3.10 for skate hire), a climbing wall (free for experienced climbers), a huge swimming pool (€4.30) with spa facilities (sauna, Jacuzzi, for €13) and a six-lane bowling alley (04 79 00 36 44).

Massage: Laura and Simon Aplin are the official suppliers of massage and beauty to the Meribel

glitterati. They offer a very professional in-house massage and beauty therapy service. Contact 0033(0)6 66 88 51 43, 0033(0)4 90 04 40 5.

Mountain flying: Courses in mountain flying are available with coaching for the mountain pilot qualification from the Méribel Air Club (04 79 08 61 33, www.aeroclub-meribel.com, a.c.meribel@tiscali.fr).

Paintballing: There are special enclosures at Les Ravines for 'one on one' and 'eight against eight' games. A package of 100 paintballs and necessary equipment costs €20. Call Vincent (06 75 48 76 30, www.ampire.fr, contact@ampire.fr).

Paragliding: From the top of Saulire or La Loze pass. Contact either A-Érodynamique (06 09 92 25 80, www.parapentemeribailes.com), A Parapente (06 80 11 86 77, c.jaud@free.fr) or Tandem Top Saulire (04 79 00 45 67, astro@montagneparapente.com).

Skidoos: These can be rented in Meribel-Mottaret from Snow Biker (04 79 00 40 01, info@snow-biker.com, www.snow-biker.com).

Snowshoeing: This is offered by the ESF (see Instruction), costing €20–45. Overnight expeditions with mountain-hut accommodation are available from €62 from Raquette Passion (04 79 24 10 40, www.raquettevasion.com, info@raquettevaison.com).

Events

Magic in Motion (see Instruction) holds a competition dedicated to one of their friends who died in an avalanche in Courchevel a few years back. It's called the **Magic Dedern competition**, consists of a big air and a quarterpipe and is open to anyone. If you're around Meribel in April, check it out. Contact adam@adamj.net for more details.

It's also worth looking out for the ice hockey battles in Meribel at the **Parc Olympique** (04 79 00 58 21, m.e.l@wanadoo.fr).

Accommodation

Meribel has 36,420 beds, mostly in apartments. There is only one 4-star hotel in Meribel (another in Mottaret): **Le Grand Coeur** (0033 (0)4 79 08 60 03,

www.legrandcoeur.com, grandcoeur@relaischateaux
.com) which costs €165–317.50 per person for half-
board accommodation, depending on the time of the
season. This impressive hotel manages to be very
welcoming and grandiose at the same time.

Most tourists arrive on package holidays and there
are tons of luxury chalet companies to cater for them,
for example **Meriski** (www.meriski.co.uk) and **Kaluma**
(0870 442 8044 (UK number), enquiries@kaluma
travel.co.uk, www.kalumatravel.co.uk). They tend to be
either 'ski in, ski out' or they provide minibuses to shuttle
you about – so not too much room for concern. Look
out for chalets with outdoor hot tubs.

Le Roc (04 79 08 64 16, taverne.meribel@
wanadoo.fr, www.lataverne-meribel. com), above the
lively Taverne bar and restaurant (see Bars and clubs),
is one of the only really good-value hotels with a fantastic
location in the centre of town. The 12 rooms are comfy
and homely and the staff are friendly and helpful. B&B
costs €90–110 per night for two people.

Eating out

On the mountain
The **Rond Point** is a great place for lunch and *the* place
for après ski, with loads of live bands. If you want to chill
on a good sun terrace, head to the **Chardonnet** (04 79
00 44 81), at the mid-station of the Pas du Lac gondola.
In Mottaret there are loads of fast food joints that have
easy access from the slopes. Cruises to Courchevel for
lunch are pretty good if you've got a few quid in your
pocket. Check out the Courchevel chapter for more
info (see page 156).

In town
The smart hotels, such as **Le Grand Coeur** mentioned
above, all tend to have smart restaurants attached.
Apart from this, the **Fromagerie**, next to the 'boarder
brains shop', is highly recommended, especially for
its superb fondues, and the **Refuge** is a cosy, central
restaurant serving great pizzas. There is a **Pizza
Express** just above Dicks Tea Bar if you're missing
home. The also completely British **Cactus Café** or **The
Taverne** in town both offer simple food such as
sandwiches, cheesy chips, etc and are often really
busy as they are popular with the locals.

Bars and clubs

For après ski, the **Rond Point** is the place to be. It's
packed from 4pm with live music and lots of dancing.
Jack's Bar is also hugely popular at après ski as it's
close to the slopes and also kicks off later on, until 2am.
It has 'pitcher hours' 4–5pm and 7–8pm and then
cocktail hour 10–11pm. As well as TVs they have a 42-
inch plasma screen for showing all the big sporting
events and have DJs or live music each evening. Next
door is **Evolution**, also owned by Jack's Bar. They serve
food all day (with a variety of culinary influences),
including a great full English brekkie in the mornings.
The ingenious bit about this bar is the entertainment:
you have the usual broadband internet terminals which
double up as sports TVs for crucial matches. On top of
this is a massive plasma for movies and you can even
while away a few hours on the X-box.

Le Pub has pool tables and is a good place to watch
sports. It's a bit big and characterless though, and
they don't provide much in the way of seating in order
to try and cram in as many people as possible. **The
Barometer** is on the main street and has a number
of pool tables and a good ambience. The **Taverne**,
right in the centre of town is the hub of the local
(British) community. It's a really cool bar with a good
atmosphere and does decent food too. It also has a
few internet terminals downstairs.

If you want to escape the drunken Brits and enjoy a
more sophisticated climate, head for **Le Poste**. It is very
trendy and stylish with big leather chairs and a DJ. They
sell numerous cocktails (for about €12 a pop) and a
huge variety of bottles of champers for €60–1100.
Definitely the place to impress a potential mate.

Dicks Tea Bar (04 79 08 60 19) is the place to go later on. It's always got a good line up of DJs, and it's jam packed full of Brits up for a good laugh, although this can result in a bit of trouble now and again. The music varies from commercial pop to house music, it just depends on the night. **Le Loft** nightclub (04 79 00 36 50) is the alternative.

Useful facts and phone numbers

Tourist office

T: 0033 (0)4 79 08 60 01
F: 0033 (0)4 79 00 59 61
E: info@meribel.net
W: www.meribel.net

Direct reservations

T: 0033 (0)4 79 00 50 00
E: infos@meribel-reservations.com
W: www.meribel-reservations.com

Emergency services

- In a medical emergency dial 15, for the fire brigade call 18, or 112 for either from a mobile.
- Police station: 04 79 53 00 17
- Moutiers Hospital: 04 79 09 60 60
- Weather information: 0892 68 02 73/32 50 (www.meteo.fr)

Doctors

- Cabinet medical – Mottaret: 04 79 00 40 88
- Dr Schamash: 04 79 08 60 41
- Dr Mabboux: 04 79 08 60 41
- Dr Vabre: 04 79 08 65 40

Taxis

- Meribel: 04 79 08 65 10
- Meribel-Mottaret: 04 79 00 44 29

Getting there

By car

Take the autoroute A43 to Albertville, then the N90 to Moutiers, then follow the D90 for 18km. Meribel is 1070km from London.

By plane

Lyon (185km) Transfers take 3.5 hours by Satobus (0033 (0)4 37 255 2555, www.satobus-alps.com, mail@satobus-alps.com). One way costs €57 and a return costs €86.
Chambéry/ Aix les Bains (95km) Transfers take 1.5 hours by Cars Transavoie (0033 (0)4 79 54 49 66, www.altibus.com). One way costs €42.69 and a return costs €70.13.
Geneva (135km) Transfers are by Touriscar bus and should be booked in advance (0033 (0)4 50 43 60 02, www.alpski-bus.com).
Helicopter and plane transfers are also available with SAF (0033 (0)4 79 08 00 91 (www.saf-helico .com, saf@saf-helico.com).

By train

Take the 17.09 Eurostar from London Waterloo to Paris; then an overnight train to Moutiers, and then a bus (45 minutes), arriving in resort at 08.15. Return fares from £111 in a 6-berth couchette. Contact Rail Europe (08705 848 848, www.raileurope.co.uk) or European Rail (020 7387 0444, www.europeanrail.com). Bus tickets (€11.60 single) can be purchased in advance from Altibus (0033 (0)4 79 68 32 96, www.altibus.com) or bought at the station.

Morzine

A great resort for weekend trips,
with masses of riding potential

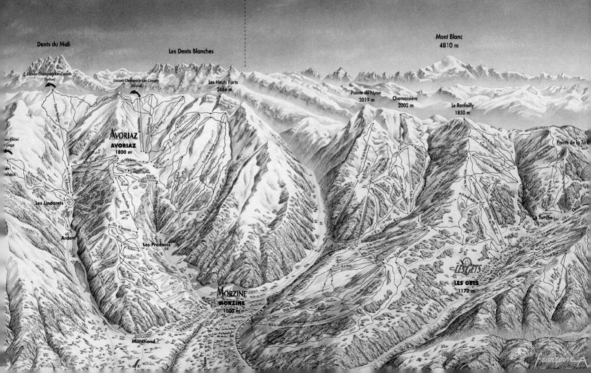

SECTEUR SUPER MORZINE - AVORIAZ

SECTEUR MORZINE - LES GET

Dents du Midi

Les Dents Blanches

Mont Blanc
4810 m

Les Hauts Forts
2466 m

Pointe de Nyon
2019 m

Chamossière
2002 m

Le Ranfoilly
1850 m

AVORIAZ
AVORIAZ
1800 m

Pointe de la Turch

Les Lindarets

La Turche

Ardent

Les Prodains

LES GETS
LES GETS
1172 m

MORZINE
MORZINE
1000 m

Montriond

On the slopes	
Snow reliability	✴ ✴ ⍕
Parks	✴ ✴
Off-piste	✴ ✴ ✴ ✴

Off the slopes	
Après ski	✴ ✴ ✴
Nightlife	✴ ✴ ✴ ✴
Eating out	✴ ✴ ✴
Resort charm	✴ ✴ ✴

The resort

Morzine is a fantastic example of how a French resort should be. You can certainly see why Morzine attracts so many of Britain's leading boarders and skiers; you have access to the impressive Portes de Soleil circuit, including some of Europe's best parks (see Champéry and Avoriaz chapters, pages 330 and 140), a great night scene, a picturesque village, and easy accessibility from Geneva.

The mountains

Height: 975–2275m

Ability	Rating
Expert	✴ ✴ ✴ ✴
Intermediate	✴ ✴ ✴ ✴
Beginner	✴ ✴ ✴ ⍕

Getting about

From Morzine town centre you can access two very different areas. The official Morzine slopes are on the Le Pléney side of town and from here you can ride over to Les Gets, etc. This area has a park and some good off-piste of its own, although many of the more proficient riders will probably head to the Super Morzine lift on the other side of town to gain easy access to the superb terrain of Avoriaz and Champéry (see below and relevant chapters, pages 140 and 330).

The park

On the Le Pléney side of Morzine is a beginners' park with a selection of rails (one box, one rail and one down-rail) and intermediate kickers. Some fantastic parks are accessible via the Portes de Soleil circuit including those in Avoriaz (see Avoriaz chapter, page 140), and arguably the best park in Europe at Les Crosets (see Champéry chapter, page 330).

"A great night scene, a picturesque village and easy accessibility from Geneva"

Off-piste and backcountry

The best off-piste on the Le Pléney side of town can be found off the back of the Pointe de Neon – you really need a guide to be able to explore this area properly. Alternatively head to the top of the Chamosa, from which you will find an accessible bowl on the left. There is some good tree skiing around the Le Pléney area too so it's a good place to head towards in bad weather.

The Portes de Soleil circuit has some fantastic terrain to unearth (see the Avoriaz and Champéry chapters, pages 140 and 330 for more ideas).

Lift passes	Morzine-Avoriaz	Portes du Soleil
1 day	€26.80	€37
6 days	€134.40	€179

Instruction

ESF

Individual classes cost €33.50 per hour (1–3 people of the same level), and €48.50 for a 1-hour group class. To hire an instructor (max. 6 people) costs €252 a day.

T: 0033 (0)4 50 79 13 13
E. info@esf-morzine.com (reservations)/
administration@esf-morzine.com (admin)
W: www.esf-morzine.com

E2SA

This ski, snowboard and adventure school offers freeride, freestyle and backcountry lessons, as well as the usual.

T: 0033 (0)4 50 79 05 16
E: info@morzineski.fr
W: www.morzineski.fr

The Guidance Office

Off-piste, helicopter trips and skiing the Vallée Blanche can be arranged through the Guidance Office.

T: 0033 (0)4 50 74 72 23
E: marcobaya@wanadoo.fr

"Proficient riders will probably head to the Super Morzine lift on the other side of town"

Other activities

Unless otherwise stated, contact the tourist office (see Useful facts and phone numbers) for more information.

Horse-drawn sleigh: You can take a short tour of Morzine or a longer tour of Montriond (€15–70).

Hot air balloon: Flights cost €245 (04 50 75 94 00, www.cameleon-organisation.com).

Ice diving: This takes place under the ice of Lake Montriond for €60. Contact Indiana ventures (04 50 74 01 88).

Night skiing: This popular activity takes place on Le Pléney.

Parapente: Try a tandem flight, with an instructor (€60–115), a discovery lesson (€120) or a course to take you from a beginner to a proficient flier, with pilot licence (€400–500). Morzine has a well-established parapenting scene. Contact Ecole de Parapente des Portes de Soleil (06 12 55 51 31, www.morzine parapente.com) or Aireole (06 07 63 16 25, www.aireole.com).

Snowmobiles: Guided tours are available for either half an hour (10km) or 1 hour (20km).

Sports centre: Facilities include a skating rink ice hockey, climbing wall and fitness centre (04 50 79 08 43).

Tobogganing: This can be organised from 6pm onwards. Contact Indiana ventures (06 75 03 05 52, www.indianaventures.com).

Accommodation

When choosing your accommodation in Morzine it is advisable to take into account the slopes on which you will spend most of your time, as cable cars set off from opposite sides of Morzine and the slopes are not connected by lifts. On one side of the valley the Le Pléney cable car takes you up to the Morzine and Les Gets slopes and on the other side of the valley the Super Morzine cable car takes you to Avoriaz and the Portes de Soleil. The street of bars is pretty much midway between the two cable cars.

At the Le Pléney side, you couldn't get closer to the lifts than the logis **L'Equipe** (0033 (0)4 50 79 11 43, www.hotelequipe.fr, morzine@hotelequipe.fr), that costs from €66 per person per night for half board, or the 3-star **Tremplin** (0033 (0)4 50 79 12 31, www.hotel-tremplin.com, info@hotel-tremplin.com). The Tremplin's dining room is basic but the lounge is comfortable with books, chess and a piano. It also has a large outdoor terrace at the bottom of the slopes that's great in good weather. Prices start at €78 per person per night, with additional costs for breakfast or half board. The **Hotel Sporting** (0033 (0)4 50 79 15 03, info@hotelsporting-morzine.com, www.hotel sporting-morzine.com), a minute or so's walk from the lift to Le Pléney, is a gorgeous and great value hotel

(with homely rooms from €67.50 per night half board). In the centre of town, one of the friendliest and cosiest hotels is **La Bergerie** (0033 (0)4 50 79 13 69, www.hotel-bergerie.com, info@hotel-bergerie.com). Rooms cost from €500 per week, rooms with kitchens €700–1350 and suites with kitchens €1100–1750.

Eating out

On the mountain

On the Le Pléney slopes **Chez Nannon** is definitely one of the best restaurants. It has a beautiful chalet atmosphere, excellent food and a good terrace. At Super Morzine, les **Cretes des Zorre** (04 50 79 24 73) is one of the best mountain restaurants on the way back to Morzine from Avoriaz. Both food and service are fantastic.

In town

Restaurant **la Chamade** (04 50 79 13 91, restaurant@lachamade.com, www.lachamade.com), in the centre of Morzine, is a gourmet restaurant, but also does basic pizzas from €9. It's really cute and cosy inside, with loads of cow-bells and other paraphernalia. The **Farmhouse** (04 50 79 08 26, info@thefarm house.co.uk, www.thefarmhouse.co.uk) is a famous chalet above the Dixie bar, down the hill. It is possible to call up and book in for dinner – the chalet can accommodate 15/16 guests, but they usually cook for around 40 people. The best pizzeria in town is **L'Etale** (04 50 79 09 29), on the strip of bars. It has great staff and serves fantastic food; massive salads and good meat dishes, as well as the wood-fired pizzas. At the other end of town is the very pleasant **Tyrolien pizzeria** (04 50 79 13 15) with a terrace and a wood-fired oven.

For a good panini or hot dog before you hit the slopes, check out the little hut **L'Anka**, just in front of the Super Morzine telecabine. If you get the munchies in town you'll want to head to the **Burger Place** (04 50 74 71 30) at the end of the row of bars (the strip), near the Le Pléney cable car. They do great burgers, hot dogs and bacon sandwiches. It's a little wooden hut with a good terrace.

Bars and clubs

For après ski you will want to be hitting one of two bars down the hill. **Bar Robertson**, a favourite with all Morzine residents, is one of the most popular après

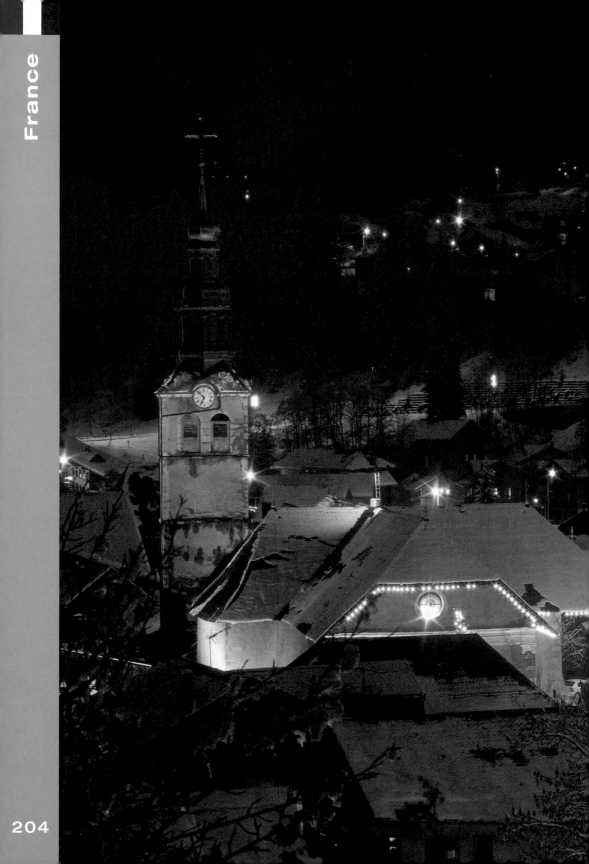

venues – largely due to the supply of Mutzig (very strong beer). The other hangout spot for après, and later on, is **Dixie bar** (04 50 79 27 83); an atmospheric and big pub (though still cosy) with a sizeable games room. If you are staying on the other side of the river to Morzine town centre you should check out the **Ridge bar** (500m from the bridge; part of the Ridge Hotel), with big TVs for sports, friendly staff, hip hop nights and a games room with free table footie. As the night moves on, you will no doubt find yourself on 'the strip': a great row of bars and clubs that always end up packed. The best are the **Cavern** (04 50 74 22 79), an atmospheric bar full of seasonaires and great for a drunken dance, and **Buddha Bar**, with some superb interior design going on (the owner makes his own furniture and it is for sale at his shop in town). As far as clubs go, you have a choice between **L'Opera** (cheesy, with cages) and **Paradis** with a dancefloor that lights up, black and pink zebra print chairs and neon lighting. If you're drunk, it could be hilarious. If not, we wouldn't recommend it.

Getting there

By car

On the Autoroute Blanche motorway, take the Bonneville or Cluses exit.

By plane

Geneva (75km) Transfer takes only an hour. Helicopter transfers can be arranged for €993 (0033 (0)4 50 92 78 21).

By train

Take the 17.09 Eurostar from London Waterloo to Paris; then an overnight train to Cluses, and then a bus (55 minutes), arriving in resort at 09.30. Return fares from £111 in a 6-berth couchette. Contact Rail Europe (08705 848 848, www.raileurope.co.uk) or European Rail (020 7387 0444, www.europeanrail.com). Bus tickets (€10 single) must be purchased at least 7 days in advance from Altibus (0033 (0)4 79 68 32 96, www.altibus.com).

Useful facts and phone numbers

Tourist office

T: 0033 (0)450 747 272
F: 0033 (0)450 790 348
E: info@morzine-avoriaz.com
W: www.morzine-avoriaz.com/ www.morzine.com

Direct reservations

T: 0033 (0)4 50 791 157
F: 0033 (0)4 50 747 318
E: reservation@morzine-avoriaz.com
W: www.resa-morzine.com

Emergency services

- Police: 04 50 79 13 12
- Ambulance: 04 50 26 26 02 / 04 50 75 93 09
- Thonon Hospital: 04 50 83 20 00
- Fire: 18

Taxis

A full list of taxis is available from the tourist office/website. An example of price for 1–4 people transfer from Geneva is €115–120. Luggage and waiting time is extra.
- Cheraiet Momo: 0033 (0)4 50 79 03 40
- Heritier Eric: 0033 (0)6 11 95 02 26
- Laury's France Taxi: 0033 (0)4 50 74 69 77

La Plagne

You won't have a problem finding virgin snow on this huge mountain

On the slopes	
Snow reliability	❄ ❄ ❄ ❄
Parks	❄ ❄ ❄ ❄
Off-piste	❄ ❄ ❄
Off the slopes	
Après ski	❄ ❄
Nightlife	❄ ❄ ❄
Eating out	❄ ❄ ❄
Resort charm	❄ ❄

The resort

La Plagne consists of about ten villages, all of varying degrees of attractiveness, from the sleepy, quiet beauty of the small village resorts of Montchavin and Les Coches to the ugly, but functional and well-placed Bellecôte and Aime-la-Plagne. The resorts also have varying numbers of services (bars, restaurants, facilities, etc). Plagne-Centre is a functional resort that has great access to the slopes (you'll be at the top of Grand Rochette in minutes) and attractive on-piste restaurants, however, the run-down indoor centre that contains the bars (all two of them), restaurants and shops needs a good face lift. Bellecôte is excellently placed for the half pipe but it is not aesthetically pleasing to say the least. If we were staying in La Plagne, we would choose to stay in Belle-Plagne as it is very central in the Paradiski area (that consists of La Plagne and Les Arcs), it's attractive and has a few good bars and the best club. Therefore, whilst we might refer to other areas, Belle-Plagne is being referred to if we don't specifically say otherwise.

The mountains

Height: 1250–3250m

Ability	Rating
Expert	❄ ❄ ❄
Intermediate	❄ ❄ ❄ ❄
Beginner	❄ ❄ ❄ ❄

Getting about

The Paradiski area (combining La Plagne with Les Arcs) is one of the largest in Europe with a total of 293 pistes over 425km (225km in La Plagne). Most of the runs are pretty cruisy (well over half the pistes are blue runs) but, with two accessible peaks over 3000m, there is a lot to keep the fervent backcountry rider happy.

The park

There are three parks in the La Plagne area. One is in the Champagny valley, and consists of two hips, four rails, ten table tops and a skier/boardercross. This is by the Télésiège de la rossa at 2300m so the snow is always pretty good and there is no excuse for them not to keep it well maintained. Montchavin also has a respectable park, which has its own skier/boardercross, six rails, two hips and six kickers. The main park is Snowpark Pro, in which you may spot the likes of Julien Regnier, Marie Martinod and Matthieu Crepel hanging out. This is the place to really push yourself. It contains three skier/boardercross courses, five rails, three hips, eight table tops, one pipe and a step up and quarter pipe! You can find this in the Bellecôte 1800 area. Definitely worth checking out.

Off-piste and backcountry

There are loads of good faces and couloirs in La Plagne if you know where to look. Although you may think you can see plenty of powder bowls from Plagne Centre, some are a bit flat for the advanced freerider – they can be good to practise a few powder turns for the freeriding newcomers though. From the top of the Bellecôte, the highest point of Paradiski at 3417m, there are exploits in all directions. For a good long powder run, take the glacier chair from the top of the Bellecôte bubble and hike for 20 minutes straight up to the backside of the glacier. From here you can ride right down the back to Champagny, which should take between an hour and an hour and a half. There is a lot of flat terrain at the end, so not a great one for boarders – skiers will be poling for about half an hour. You should take a guide, as there is a 20m drop into a river at one point, which you may not see if you don't know where it is. From the Bellecôte bubble you can also take the

Trevasse chair from which you can either hike up to tackle the challenging terrain from the Glacier de Bellecôte and end up in Nancroix (from where you will have to take a bus to Peisey and catch the Vanoise express), or you can come down to the Pointe de Friolin and ride down to the Bauches chair. Alternatively, the North face of the Bellecôte has some good lines but it is prone to sliding. From the Roche de Mio cable car, come back on yourself and you will find a few great couloirs off to the right, just below the Roche de Mio restaurant. This will bring you back down to the Bauches chair. Couloir fanatics can also head up the Funiplagne cable car from Plagne Centre, go straight ahead (under the barriers) and there are loads to choose from. You even have an easy out – you will come to a blue run that brings you down to the Versant Sud chair. Take care though as this is prone to avalanches. A 45-minute hike from the Fornalet lift above Montalbert leads you to a number of faces although this area can get a bit sun trapped.

From Aime La Plagne you can set off on a momentous quest – head up the Becoin chair and the Crêtes poma, where a traverse followed by an hour and a half hike will allow you to ride all the way down to the sleepy little village of Notre Dame du Pre. You might have to place your car there strategically before you do it though – not much passes through N.D. du Pre and the locals don't look kindly on wandering skiers and boarders.

Lift passes	La Plagne only	Paradiski
1 day	€39	€46
6 days	€186	€229

There are discounts for seniors and children. You can also pay €205 for 6 days which would include skiing in either La Plagne or Les Arcs and a one-day Paradiski extension during the period of validity. A 1 day extension costs €25.

Instruction

El Pro Belle Plagne

Multi-Snowsports Groups (one session: €45, 6 half days: €180, 6 days: €250). Snowboard (one session: €50, 6 half days: €189). Private lessons are €55 per hour and a half, €135 for half a day and €280 for a full day. They also organise guiding, bobsleigh, snowmobiling, quads on ice and parapenting (see Other activities).
T: 0033 (0)4 79 09 11 62
E: contact@elpro.fr
W: www.elpro.fr

"There are loads of good faces and couloirs in La Plagne if you know where to look"

ESF

Skiing (6 half days from €154, 6 days: €200). Snowboarding (6 half days: €142). They also have mountain guides that offer a mix between ski touring and off-piste skiing – an all day activity (€65). Prices are higher at peak times.
T: 0033 (0)4 79 09 06 68 (Belle Plagne)
E: info@esf-belleplagne.com
W: www.esf-belleplagne.com

Evolution 2 (Monchavin-Les Coches)

Skiing (5 half days: €92). Snowboarding (5 sessions: from €75, depending on ability). Private lessons are from €35 for 1 hour, from €140 for half a day and from €260 for a full day.
T: 0033 (0)4 79 07 81 85
W: www.evolution2.com

Oxygéne (Plagne Centre)

Skiing (6 half days: €152, 6 full days: €164). Snowboarding (6 half days: €158). Private lessons cost from €41 for 1 hour, €125 for half a day and €300 for a full day.
T: 0033 (0)4 79 09 03 99
E: info@oxygene-ski.com
W: www.oxygene-ski.com

Other activities

Unless otherwise stated, contact the tourist office (see Useful facts and phone numbers) for more information.

Bobsleigh: Between the beginning of December and mid-March you can ride the bobsleigh course built for the Albertville Winter Olympics. Choose from a Bob Raft (a self-steering bobsleigh with automatic braking, at about 80km/hour: €34 per person), a Taxi Bob (a four-man sleigh, driven at 100km/hour by a professional driver: €100 per person) or a Mono Bob (on your own in a self-steering bobsleigh at almost 90km/hour: €95 per person). Book at the ESF schools in resort or in advance (www.bobsleigh.net, contact@ bobsleigh.net, 04 79 09 12 73).

Bowling alley: This is located in Belle Plagne.

Cinema: Aime La Plagne, Plagne Centre, Plagne Bellecôte, Champagny en Vanoise and Montchavin-Les Coches all have local cinemas that often show films in English.

Dog sledding: In the nearby resort of Montalbert you can sign yourself up to dog sledding – call Mathias Bernal on 06 12 78 50 05.

Ice climbing wall: You can climb on the 22m high artificial wall (with or without supervision) in Champagny. There are three levels of difficulty and you will be given equipment as part of the package. It is also the venue of the Gorzderette tournament (see Events). Call the Bureau des guides (06 63 18 40 27) in Champagny-le-Haut for more details.

Ice rink: Bellecôte has a natural outdoor ice rink.

Library: The library in Plagne Centre stocks books in English.

Paintball: This can be played in Bellecôte.

Paragliding: From the top of the Grande Rochette, the Roche de Mio and Les Verdons, tandem paragliding flights can be booked. There are a number of schools to contact. For take off from Grande Rochette or Les Verdons call Plagn'Air on 06 12 73 66 56, or the ESF on 04 79 09 06 68. For take off from the Roche de Mio call Ecole El Pro on 04 79 09 11 62.

Relaxation centres: These can be found in Belle Plagne (04 79 09 26 88), Plagne Centre (04 79 09 03 45) or Plagne Bellecôte (04 79 09 22 48) and have a variety of facilities such as relaxation, spa treatments, beauty care, massage, multi-treatment courses, physiotherapy, saunas and Jacuzzis.

Snow bike circuit: Biking can be booked at Belle Plagne from the Ecole El Pro (04 79 09 11 62).

Snow quad biking, adventure trail, snowmobiling: To zip round the circuit in Belle Plagne call Ecole El Pro (see above). El Pro can also book you on to the adventure trail in Belle Plagne and organise snowmobiling.

Snowshoeing and cross-country skiing: These can be booked through the ESF schools (see above).

Sports hall, weight training, snow skating: These are all available in Plagne Centre.

Swimming pool: Bellecôte has a heated, open air swimming pool.

If you want to try an activity in another resort, the shuttle bus or gondola lift will take you between most of the resorts.

Events

A **World Cup Mogul** event takes place in late December in Plagne Centre, where they also hold **World Cup Slalom and Telemark** events throughout the season. Champagny le Haut village is host to the **Gorzderette Trophy** that brings together big air freestyle, cross country skiing, the Mont de la Guerre derby and an ice climbing contest. The **PlayStation Air Games** take place in La Plagne high level resorts in mid–late February. The **Urban Style** competition is a relatively new event on the scene and attracts many of the top, French New School riders including Julien Lopez and Julien Régnier. It's in mid February and costs €15 to enter.

Accommodation

There is loads of ski-in ski-out accommodation in La Plagne, although you should check your location carefully to be sure. Apartments take up most of the visitor beds in La Plagne, although there are some good hotels to check out if you prefer. If you wish to take an apartment it's best to go to the direct reservations office (see Useful facts and phone numbers) and let them know your specific requirements.

In Belle Plagne there are two main hotels. **Les Balcons de Belle Plagne** (33 (0)4 79 55 76 55, contact@les-balcons.com) is by far the best, in a good location with authentic wooden-chalet-style charm, great views, a cosy restaurant and bar with comfy seats and games to play. There is also a pool, sauna and gym as well as underground car parking (for €60 per week). Half-board accommodation (in double/triple rooms) costs €485–926 per person per week depending on the time of season. Bed and breakfast can be requested. There are also apartments in the same building if you prefer. **Mercure Belle Plagne** (0033 (0)4 79 09 12 09, H5627@accor.com, www.accorvacances.com) is also pretty good but bigger and less personal. It's in a great position to ski to the door.

In Plagne Centre, the **Hotel Terra Nova** (04 79 55 79 00, info@hotel-terranova.com, ww.hotel-terra nova.com) is the only one in town, pretty new and not a bad looking place. It has a fairly smart but simple restaurant serving a basic menu and plat du jour (steak and chips, that kind of thing). There is also a bar, fitness and sauna rooms, sunny terrace and a good location for riding to the door and for the town 'centre'. Prices are €714–1085 per week, half board.

In Plagne Montalbert, a small friendly resort, at the far end of the Paradiski area, there are some great chalets to stay in. One chalet (04 Le Genepy, Montalbert, 0033 (0)4 79 09 80 50 – or 01937 581287 (UK) – www.cgski.co.uk, cgski@cgski.co.uk), run by a British couple, Giles and Claire, is a fab place for either families or a group of friends (there are only a few bars and one club in Montalbert but it's a giggle if you've got a good group). The chalet sleeps 12 and costs £360–540 per person for half-board accommodation with afternoon tea. There is a cosy lounge area with a bar (the monkey bar) in which you could happily chill out all night.

In the tiny village of Montvilliers, less than 10 minutes' drive from Montalbert (which gives access to the Paradiski area), is Maison Astier (0033 (0)4 79 09 26 03, sharplespaul@hotmail.co.uk); a huge family-run guest house and the home of the lovely Paul and Monica Sharples as well as their little dog Tao. The Sharples family spent three years renovating this derelict farm house, which now accommodates 12 guests, and the open plan living/dining area has a large fireplace and a cosy, homely atmosphere. This is the perfect place for families and those who just want a few days out in the mountains at short notice.

Also if you want to experience genuine French village charm and have access to one of the best and largest ski/board areas in Europe you should come here. You will need to bring/rent a car as you will need to drive to the lifts in Montalbert. The price is approximately €55 per night (half board). There are discounts for week-long packages. Next door you can find the **Gite de Montvilliers**, another cosy place with great food. Check out www.gite-de-montvilliers.com for prices and information.

Eating out

On the mountain

On the mountain itself there are some great options. If you head towards Champagny you will find a beautiful restaurant at the bottom of the Versant Sud chairlift, called **Versant Sud** (06 21 54 39 24), which can be accessed from the hara-kiri or kamikaze runs.

This restaurant, built for the 2004/5 season, had a lot of money ploughed into it – it has a great terrace, deckchairs in which to soak up the sun and, most importantly, the best toilets on the mountain! **Le Forperet** (04 79 55 51 27, forperet@free.fr, http://forperet.free.fr), at the bottom of the Fornelet lift, above Montalbert, is an excellent, traditional log-cabin-style restaurant with a log fire, nice terrace and lovely views. **Le Vieux Bon Temp** (04 79 09 20 57), next to the Golf lift, just below Aime La Plagne, is a cute little chalet-style restaurant with lots of character. They have two open log fires and do a superb 'chocolat verte': hot chocolate with green chartreuse in it. Finally, in the middle of the Paradiski area, just above Les Coches by the Pierres Blanches lift is **Le Sauget**, a traditional Savoyard restaurant with an open fire and lots of atmosphere.

There are also some great restaurants on the piste in the town centres. In Plagne Centre, there are three big

restaurants, **Croq-neige** (04 79 09 22 03), **Chaudron** (04 79 09 23 33) and **Le Vega** (04 79 09 00 61), with massive terraces and loads of deckchairs, all serving the usual pizzas, pasta and steaks. If you fancy just grabbing a sandwich, pop inside the indoor shopping centre to **Bar La Cheminee** for a panini, sandwich or hot dog that will cost you only a few euros. In Belle Plagne, **Le Matafan** (04 79 09 09 19) is on the piste and serves delicious food and great portions. You can also eat at **Papagonne** (04 79 55 18 87) or **Face Nord** (04 79 09 01 73) which are really popular and equally good. These restaurants turn into bars at night.

In town

In Belle Plagne, the restaurants mentioned above: **Le Matafan** (04 79 09 09 19), **Papagonne** (04 79 55 18 87) and **Face Nord** (04 79 09 01 73) are open at night and all have a great atmosphere. The **Cheyenne** (04 79 09 20 72) serves great Tex Mex (see Bars and clubs).

In Plagne Centre, the **Métairie** (04 79 09 11 08) is cosy and traditional with chequered table mats, Savoyard bits and pieces on the walls and tables, and serves pizzas, salads, meat and the traditional fondues, raclettes and pierres chauds. It's just a shame that after a lovely meal you have to walk back though the battered indoor centre. **L'Etable** (04 79 09 04 82), opposite, is another cosy, traditional Savoyard restaurant serving similar fare with tables tucked into alcoves. For a quick pizza or take out, **Blu Noir**, at the end of the corridor, is open at night and pizzas cost €8–11. **Le Vega** (04 79 09 00 61) and **Chaudron** (04 79 09 23 33), mentioned above, are also popular in the evenings, serve good food and have a great atmosphere. Le Vega has fantastic fish. Also in Plagne Centre is **La Galerne** (04 79 07 73 37), a wooden restaurant with a range of tasty crêpes as well as the usual, and it has a nice, small terrace to sit on at lunchtime.

In Bellecôte, the best restaurant is **Colosses** (04 79 09 28 70), offering unusual cuisine for a resort – the chicken curry is fantastic.

Bars and clubs

In Belle Plagne, the **Tête Inn** (04 79 55 10 85), also referred to as Mat's bar, has loads of character and is atmospheric and wooden. There are big barrels to sit on, a good happy hour 4–6pm every day and live music from 5.30pm. They serve a few sandwiches at lunchtime. The **Cheyenne** (04 79 09 20 72) is a cool, unassuming bar with memorabilia hung up all over the place and fantastic Tex-Mex food. The **Saloon** (04 79 09 06 98, www.lesaloon.com) is a funky club that everyone goes to later on and is definitely worth checking out. It's open 4pm–4am and often has live music and a great atmosphere. From 4–9pm, it's BOGOF on drinks. Out of the centre of town, next to the Balcons de Belle Plagne hotel is another bar/restaurant, **Maitre Kanter** (04 79 55 76 70) that has a big and slightly impersonal bar but has a few cocktails for €6 and the restaurant is great for big groups. If you're staying nearby it'd be worth popping in at happy hour (4–6pm).

In Plagne Centre, **No Bl'm Café** (04 79 09 10 78) is the only real bar. Open from 4pm onwards, it is massive, has internet access and you sit round big beer barrels. It's wooden, atmospheric and pretty cool. After this, the only place to go is the **Luna Bar** (04 79 09 01 50, www.lelunabar.com), open from 7pm, which is funky, but might get a little monotonous after a few days.

In La Plagne 1800, there is one (and only one) bar, the **Mine** (04 79 09 24 89), but it is very cool, and has bar tables set out like a train.

Useful facts and phone numbers

Tourist office

T: 0033 (0)4 79 09 02 01
F: 0033 (0)4 79 09 27 00
E: info@la-plagne.com/
     bienvenue@la-plagne.com
W: www.la-plagne.com

Direct reservations

T: 0033 (0)4 79 09 79 79
F: 0033 (0)4 79 09 70 10
E: reservation@la-plagne.com

Emergency services

In a medical emergency dial 15, for the fire brigade call 18, or 112 for either from a mobile.
• Police: 04 79 09 22 10
• Medical surgery, Belle-Plagne: 04 79 06 93

Doctors

• Belle Plagne: 04 79 09 06 93
• Plagne Centre: 04 79 09 04 66

Taxis

Christian Bouzon (Plagne Centre) has a number of minibuses (0033 (0)4 79 09 03 41, www.taxi-bouzon.com, transport.bouzon@wanadoo.fr) and will transfer between stations in La Plagne, as well as to stations and airports. They even speak English.

Getting there

By car

La Plagne is 645km from Paris and will take around 10 hours from Calais. Head towards Lyon/Albertville on the A43 and A430 then follow signs to Moutiers, Aime, Macot and La Plagne. If you are driving from Geneva take the N201 (Cruseilles) then A41 to Chambéry, then A43 and A130 to Albertville then N90 to Moutiers and head towards Aime, Macot and La Plagne.

By plane

Geneva (149km) Take the bus with Transports Berard (0033 (0)4 79 09 72 27) or go by taxi. *Lyon (200km)* Take the Satobus (0033 (0)4 72 22 71 27, www.satobus-alps.com) or taxi or the A43 autoroute if you're in a hired car.

By train

Take the 17.09 Eurostar from London Waterloo to Paris; then an overnight train to Aime la Plagne, and then a bus (40 minutes), arriving in resort at 08.15. Return fares from £111 in a 6-berth couchette. Contact Rail Europe (08705 848 848, www.raileurope.co.uk) or European Rail (020 7387 0444, www.europeanrail.com). Bus tickets (€9.40 single from Transports Berard) are purchased at the station.

St Foy

Clever use of four lifts
opens up masses of terrain

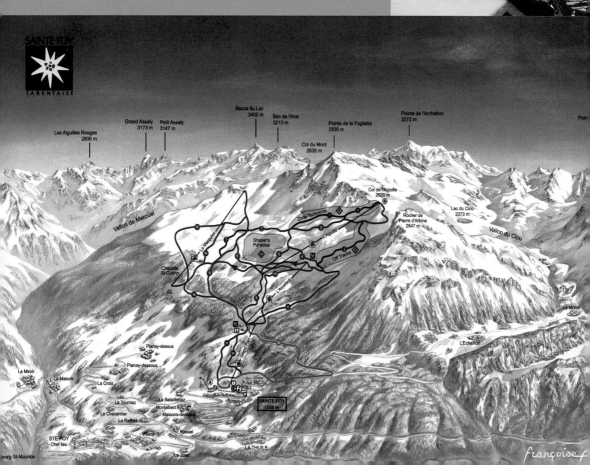

SAINTE-FOY
TARENTAISE

Poin

Pointe de l'Archeboc
3272 m

Becca du Lac
3405 m

Bec de l'Ane
3213 m

Pointe de la Foglietta
2930 m

Col du Mont
2636 m

Grand Assaly
3173 m

Petit Assaly
3147 m

Les Aiguilles Rouges
2806 m

Col de l'Aiguille
2620 m

Lac du Clou
2373 m

Rocher de
Pierre d'Arbine
2647 m

Vallon du Clou

Vallon de Mercuel

Zone Technique

Shaper's
Paradise

L'Aiguille

Off Tracks

L'Aiguille

Le Monal

L'Echaillon

Chapelle
St-Guérin

Grand Plan

Planay-dessus

Planay-dessous

Le Miroir

La Masure

La Croix

La Tournaz

La Bataillettaz

Le Chavanier

Montalbert

Le Raffort

Maisons-dessous

Villard

Rassel

STE-FOY
Chef lieu

LA THUILE

Bourg-St-Maurice

SAINTE-FOY
1550 m

Le Joiat

françoise f

On the slopes	
Snow reliability	❄ ❄ ❄
Parks	–
Off-piste	❄ ❄ ❄ ❄ ❄
Off the slopes	
Après ski	❄
Nightlife	❄
Eating out	❄ ❄
Resort charm	❄ ❄ ❄ ❄

The resort

St Foy is a beautiful, traditional and authentic alpine resort. There are none of the big, ugly buildings that plague many of the big European resorts; all of the buildings are nestled amongst the trees, and built in the traditional chalet-style, using local wood and stone. Don't come here if you are looking for crazy nights out though, as it won't happen. If you take your riding seriously and want to explore, St Foy is the place to be, as it has some of the best freeriding terrain around.

The mountains

Height: 1550–2620m

Ability	Rating
Expert	❄ ❄ ❄ ❄
Intermediate	❄ ❄ ❄
Beginner	❄ ❄ ❄

Getting about

Unless you're staying right by the lifts, you'll need to get the free shuttle bus from the main village to the slopes. St Foy is a small area, which only had three chairlifts last year. The new chairlift, 'La Marquise' (built December 2006) opens up another two runs to give a total of 14 slopes, and what it lacks in marked runs, it more than makes up for with long off picto doccontc. At tho top of tho Col do l'Aiguillo at 2612m the backcountry adventures begin. St Foy is also on the road to Val d'Isère and Tignes, so day trips are possible if you want to explore some different terrain.

The park

A few years ago St Foy decided to make a half-decent park, but they have now stopped maintaining it. There is far too much amazing terrain for this to worry you though and there are loads of great areas for building backcountry kickers if your heart is set on freestyle.

Off-piste and backcountry

St Foy is one of our favourite places for venturing out into the backcountry or off-piste. The resort is still fairly unheard of, which the regulars love as there are never any lift queues. It does, however, attract the powder hounds from Val, Tignes and La Rosière on a bluebird powder day.

As you are slowly making your way up the chairlifts, it's fairly easy to see the area's potential and spot some good lines. A guide can take you from the top of the Col de l'Aiguille through lots of little derelict villages, coming out on the main road between Val d'Isère/Tignes and St Foy (you can come back to the bottom of the resort if you know where you're going).One of the most spectacular routes takes you through the deserted farming hamlet of Le Monal, with amazing views of Mont Pourri. It is also worth employing the services of a guide in order to explore

> "One of the most spectacular routes takes you through the deserted farming hamlet of Le Monal"

the infamous 1700m vertical descent of the north face of Fogliettaz, which retains a good quality of snow long after other routes have been skied out. Lower down there are some superb tree runs.

Generally, the terrain is challenging so you should make sure that you know what you're doing. It's also advisable to hire a guide to make the most of this area. We are very lucky to have been shown the area over the years by top British photographers such as St Foy locals Mark and Holly Junak and Adrian Myers.

There have been many reports of avalanching in St Foy so be careful, be aware of the conditions and check with the pisteurs before attempting anything you're not sure about.

Lift passes	
1 day	€19
6 days	€105
Season pass	€330

For €54, you can upgrade to a 6-day 'Espace Killy Découverte' pass, which entitles you to 3 days' riding in the Espace Killy, Espace San Bernado and Grand Domaine.

Instruction

ESF

Group lessons: 6 half days €120.
Private lessons: €33 per hour for 1 person, €38 for 2 people and €45 for 3/4 people.
Off-piste to Le Monal (€120, 6 people max.) or to Fogliettaz (€200, 4 people max.).
A 3 hour off-piste lesson costs €120.
T: 0033 (0)4 79 06 96 76
E: esfsaintefoy@tiscali.fr
W: www.esf-saintefoy.com

Mountain Guides

The local mountain guides in St Foy organise off-piste trips and heliskiing.
T: 0033 (0)6 14 62 90 24
E: bureauguides.stefoy@wanadoo.fr

Other activities

Dog sledding: Drive your own sled pulled by a team of dogs, under the leadership of a professional guide. Trips are available for half a day, a whole day, or over 2 days, with a night in a refuge. For more information contact Stéphane and Véronique Lépine (06 16 48 60 47, stephanemush@aol.com).

Heliskiing: As St Foy is so close to Italy, it is one of the few places in France where heliskiing is possible, with the potential for virgin descents from 3400m right back to St Foy. Contact the tourist office for more details.
Parapente: This can be booked with Laurent Ottobon, a paragliding instructor (06 09 89 65 46, ottolaurent@yahoo.fr).
Ski biking: An initiation lesson (2 hours) costs €35 per person (ski bikes provided). Subsequent hire is €30 per day. Contact Alistair Platt: 04 79 40 11 61 or 06 75 42 40 91, info@skibike.net, www.skibike.net.
Spa: Les Balcons de Sainte Foy (04 79 06 27 20) costs €25 per day for access to the pool, sauna, Jacuzzi and fitness room. Les Fermes de St Foy (04 79 06 14 61) has the above, plus beauty treatments (prices on request). Both of these have opened recently.

"Heliskiing is possible, with the potential for virgin descents from 3400m right back to St Foy"

Accommodation

Accommodation is available at the ski resort itself, in the main village, and in many of the surrounding small farming hamlets. The chalets are often the most attractive and cosy places to stay and there are loads to choose from. Check out the list of chalets on the tourist office website (www.saintefoy.net).

We particularly like Gite de Sainte Foy Station (0033 (0)4 79 06 97 18, www.ste-foy.fr, gites.foy@wanadoo.fr) with Jacuzzi, sauna, heated ski room and DVD home cinema and Chalet Chevalier (0033 (0)4 79 06 51 69, chaletchevalier@free.fr, www.chaletchevalier.com) for a peaceful location and spectacular views. In the small

village of Villaroger, is a beautiful and cosy chalet, **Tarentaise** (08702 406 198, info@optimumski.com, www.optimumski.com), owned by the lovely Martin and Deirdre Rowe. There are nine bedrooms, all done out beautifully and all with en-suite facilities, and a sauna and in-house masseur. From Villaroger you have direct access to the slopes of Paradiski (Les Arcs and La Plagne), as well as easy access to St Foy, Val d'Isère and Tignes.

The **Auberge** (0033 (0)4 79 06 95 83, mail@ auberge-montagne.co.uk) is a lovely wood-beamed chalet/hotel in the small hamlet of La Thuile, run by a really friendly British couple. The chalet has a cosy lounge with big fire, and an outdoor hot tub and sauna. Half-board accommodation for one week costs €288–497, depending on the time of season. If you completely book out the hotel (eight rooms), they will run it as a private chalet for you. **Hotel Le Monal** (0033 (0)4 79 06 90 07, www.le-monal.com, le.monal@ wanadoo.fr) has 24 rooms, that cost from €48 per person per night. **Auberge Le Cret Folliet** (0033 (0)4

79 06 97 47, lecretfolliet@wanadoo.fr) is a traditional inn with only three rooms.

Eating out

On the mountain

The mountain restaurants in St Foy are superb and we happily stop anywhere, in the knowledge that we will not be disappointed. All of the huts are in true, rustic, alpine style. Two of our favourites are at Plan Bois at the top of the first chair lift: **Chez Leon** (06 09 57 23 88, chez.leon@free.fr) and **Les Brevettes** (06 76 35 21 70). Both have excellent Savoyard food and sunny, south-facing terraces. At the top of the Arpettaz chair is **Chalet La Foglietta** (06 17 36 10 88), a little hut where you can pick up a hot drink and a tasty panini to much on the lifts.

In town

There are few restaurants in St Foy, so here we would recommend staying in a catered chalet, and choosing a restaurant to sample on your host's day off. **Le Bec**

de L'ane (04 79 06 92 45) is a pizzeria open day and night, with a good sun terrace for lunches. Takeaway pizzas are also available. La Grange (04 79 06 90 07) is a good typical Savoyard restaurant/wine bar, popular for its wood-fired grills and La Maison à Colonnes (04 79 06 94 80), at the base of the first lift, is another excellent traditional farmhouse restaurant (see Bars and clubs).

La Bergerie (04 79 06 25 51, www.LaBergerie.tv) is a stunning, wood-beamed and candlelit restaurant with a warm and cosy fireplace. You can book the private room for a group of family or friends (16 people max.). Chez Merie (04 79 06 90 16), in the nearby village of Miroir, is one of the best restaurants in the area. Reservation is absolutely essential.

Bars and clubs

As après ski goes, there's not too much going on in St Foy. There are a couple of local bars that are cosy and relaxed, but that's about it. La Maison à Colonnes, at the base of the first lift, is a cool little bar for a beer at the end of the day. La Pitchouli is the liveliest bar around, with live music several times a week. There's table football, and the drinks are a good price. New this year is a piano bar, L'Iceberg, which also has live music.

Getting there

By car

Take the motorway A43 (dir. Lyon/Albertville) and then the main road N90 to Bourg St Maurice. From here there are signs to Tignes and Val d'Isère and on this road you will soon come to St Foy.

By plane

Lyon (215km)
Geneva (160km) Both Geneva and Lyon are approximately 2.5 hours away from St Foy.

By train

Take the 17.09 Eurostar from London Waterloo to Paris; then an overnight train to Bourg St Maurice, and then a bus (15 minutes), followed by a free shuttle bus (10 minutes), arriving in resort at 08.55. Return fares from £111 in a 6-berth couchette. Contact Rail Europe (08705 848 848, www.raileurope.co.uk) or European Rail (020 7387 0444, www.europeanrail.com). Bus tickets (€4.80 single from Autocars Martin) are purchased at the station.

Serre Chevalier

A good mountain
for cruising and for freeride

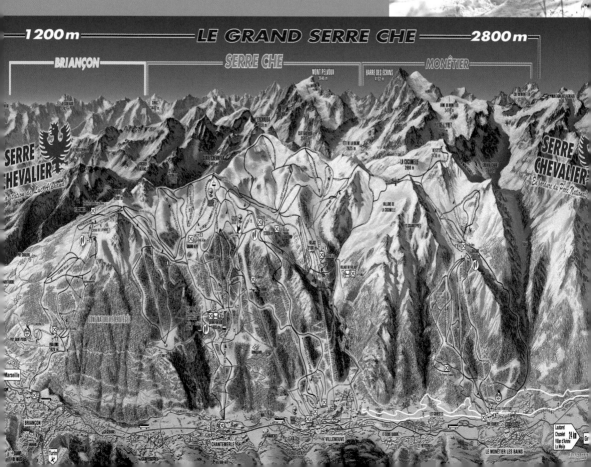

1200m ——— LE GRAND SERRE CHE ——— 2800m

BRIANÇON ——— SERRE CHE ——— MONÊTIER

MONT PELVOUX
3946 m

BARRE DES ECRINS
4102 m

SERRE CHEVALIER

SERRE CHEVALIER

On the slopes	
Snow reliability	✳ ✳ ✳
Parks	✳ ✳
Off-piste	✳ ✳ ✳ ✴
Off the slopes	
Après ski	✳ ✳ ✳
Nightlife	✳ ✳ ✴
Eating out	✳ ✳ ✴
Resort charm	✳ ✳ ✳

The resort

Serre Chevalier, more affectionately known as 'Serre Che', comprises four main areas/towns, on the main road from Gap to Grenoble, all of which have access to the massive ski area of Grand Serre Che. These towns combine traditional rustic French ambience, with new, purpose-built (and sometimes ugly) buildings. There are nine other smaller villages too but, whilst charming and pretty to look at, there's not much going on in most of them.

From Grenoble, the first town you will get to is Le Monêtier, which is more beautiful, charming and quiet than the others, but far less convenient. Next are the two main towns, Villeneuve and Chantemerle, collectively referred to as 'Le Serre Che'. Villeneuve is the hub, with some purpose-built architecture by the slopes, and a much more charming village centre. Chantemerle is a popular town and a good place

"Briançon is a very large town and the highest in France"

to look for a cheap apartment. Briançon is a very large town and the highest in France. The old town isn't convenient for the slopes, but it's traditional and pleasant to walk around. The resorts are really spread out; the closest are the 'Serre Che' resorts but these are still a half hour walk from each other.

There is a free bus service within the resorts for those with a valid lift pass, but they stop running at night. A car is not essential but we think it's worth it; there are some fantastic resorts nearby and the strange climate in this area means that if there is bad weather in Serre Che, it is more than possible that you will find decent snow wIthIn an hour of the resort. Les Deux Alpes Is a good start or La Grave, one of our favourite spots in Europe for freeriding (check out these chapters for more information, pages 174 and 184). Sestriere (Italy) and Risoul (France) are also under an hour away.

The mountains

Height: 1200–2850m

Ability	Rating
Expert	✳ ✳ ✳
Intermediate	✳ ✳ ✳ ✳
Beginner	✳ ✳ ✳ ✳

Getting about

The massive 250km of pistes covers 4445 hectares and comprises 104 runs:19 green, 28 blue, 43 red and 14 black. These slopes provide well for all levels of skier and boarder; there are good slopes for learning, travelling through the various sectors will please the cruisy intermediates and the experts can pick from some good challenging black runs, especially the steep run back to Chantemerle, which is great fun when it's quiet. Freeriders will also be more than satisfied.

The park

Until this year the park in Serre Chevalier has consisted of little more than moguls, but there is a new park on the 'Plateau de la Rouge' where you can expect to find three tables, one step-up and three boxes. There is also a 'half pipe', next to the beginners' slop in Villeneuve (The Mickey), but this is very rarely groomed and the walls are only 1.5m high.

Off-piste and backcountry

Riding through the trees is Serre Che's speciality, although it's not that steep if that's what you're after. One of the best off-piste tree runs is under the Prorel chair above Chantemerle, where there are some good lines. The trees next to the piste in Briançon are worth checking out too. You have to be careful when you are riding through the trees in Serre Che as it's pretty easy to get stuck or end up at the main road with a long walk home. Stick by the piste, or make sure you're with someone who knows where they're going.

Villeneuve and Monêtier are home to the best big mountain runs. There is a great open powder field in between the two, under the Cucumelle peak. Head up the Cucumelle chair and go for a ride. The best powder is on Monêtier, on La Montagnole. If you are very nice to the locals and buy them a beer or two, they might show you where to go within this area; it's a big secret. Avalanching is a problem here too, so you really do need a guide.

Instruction

ESF
Six half-day lessons cost €89–93 for an adult skier and €112–150 for a snowboarder. Private lessons cost €34–47 per hour.
T: 0033 (0)4 92 24 17 41 (1350), 0033 (0)4 92 24 71 99 (1400), 0033 (0)4 92 24 42 66 (1500)
E: esf-serre-che-1350@wanadoo.fr (Chantemerle), esfserreche@wanadoo.fr (Villeneuve), esf1500@esf-serrechevalier.com (Monêtier)
W: www.esf-serrechevalier.com

Instruction in Chantemerle

Génération Snow
Six half-day lessons on ski or board cost €122. Private lessons cost €51 for 1.5 hours and €68 for 2 hours. Sessions in freestyle and freeride cost €24 for half a day.
T: 0033 (0)4 92 24 21 51
E: generation-snow@freesbee.fr
W: www.generation-snow.com

Montagne Aventure
Phone or E-mail for information.
T: 0033 (0)4 92 24 05 51
E: montagne@aol.com

Instruction in Villeneuve

Axesse
Heliskiing and freeride, from 2 hours to a full day. Prices start at €80.
T: 0033 (0)4 92 24 27 11
E: info@axesse.com
W: www.axesse.com

Ecole de Ski Buissonnière
This school consists of both British and French instructors and mountain guides. Advanced and off-piste groups are limited to 6 people. Individual lessons start at €30 per hour and group lessons from €79.
T: 0033 (0)4 92 24 78 66
E: info@ecole-ski-buissonniere.com
W: www.ecolebuisse.com

Montagne à la Carte
Off-piste and touring (in a group) costs €70 for a day. Heliskiing starts at €290.
T: 0033 (0)4 92 24 73 20
E: montagnealacarte@free.fr
W: www.montagnealacarte.com

Instruction in Monêtier

Ecole de Ski et de Snowboard Internationale
Group lessons in ski or snowboard for 6 days (2 hours per day) costs €108–118. A day's freeride costs €50, and a private lesson €38.
T: 0033 (0)6 83 67 06 42
E: info@esi-monetier.com
W: www.esi-monetier.com

Montagne et Ski
Ski touring costs €46, heliskiing €130. They also organise a snowmobiling tour with a meal in Italy.
T: 0033 (0)4 92 24 46 81
E: tallaron@online.fr
W: www.montagne-et-ski.com

Lift passes	The Grand Serre Che	Le Serre Che	Monêtier	Briançon
1 day	€35	€31	€26.50	€23
6 days	€170	€150	€130	€110

It's really worth getting the Grand Serre Che pass unless you're a beginner – exploring is the best bit. There are discounts for children. This year there are also discounts for families and students.

Other activities

Unless otherwise specified, contact the tourist office for more details.

Cinemas: There are cinemas in each resort.

Drive on ice: Learn how to drive on ice using a quad or a kart; costs €12–18 for 10 minutes. Contact 04 92 24 78 44, www.slide-world.com for more information.

Horse-drawn carriage/sleigh rides: These take place on the roads or in the snow, from €5 for a half-hour excursion.

Ice climbing: Climb on gorges, chutes and waterfalls. Contact 04 92 24 75 90, www.guides-serrechevalier .com for more information.

Natural hot pools: These can be found in Monêtier.

Paragliding: Introductory flights are available from €60.

Ski jöring: Get a horse to pull you on skis. One session costs €18. Contact 06 08 93 52 87, www. clubhippique-serreche.com for more information.

Snowmobiling: Sun Scoot (04 92 24 21 79) offer snowmobile trips in which you can either be a passenger (€20) or a pilot (€65).

Events

There aren't any major on-slope activities, but there are some funny ones. The **Miss Chantemerle** contest at the end of February isn't as sexy as it sounds; it involves men dressing up as women in the Extreme Bar in Chantemerle on one of the local's birthdays. Towards the end of the season there is a **mountain bar crawl**, with only one day to visit 15 bars. It finishes in the Grotto du Yeti and you should expect some seriously drunken behaviour on the slopes. Few, if any, make all 15 bars.

"There is a mountain bar crawl, with only one day to visit 15 bars"

Accommodation

Chantemerle

The **Plein Sud** (0033 (0)4 92 24 17 01, www.hotelpleinsud.com) is one of the best bets, well placed for the centre of town and 250m from the lifts and pistes. They have mini bars and dressing gowns in the rooms and a heated swimming pool open both summer and winter. There is also a steam room and parking if necessary. The rooms are lovely and the restaurant Is good too. B&B for one week, based on two people sharing a double room starts at €670.

Villeneuve

The **Christiana** (0033 (0)4 92 24 76 33, www.le-christiana.com) is a really cute and cosy hotel, recognised by the dependable 'Logis de France'. Prices are €68–79 per person per day half board.

"A good Swedish bar where the beautiful people hang out"

Hotel du Mont Thabor (0033 (0)4 92 24 74 41, www.mont-thabor.com) is a great and attractive hotel in the centre of town, with minibars and TVs in rooms, and a solarium, sauna and hammam. It is also home to the Baïta nightclub. There are 24 standard rooms and three luxury suites; prices are €70–140.

Monêtier

Those looking for exclusivity and expensive rooms should look to the **Auberge du Choucas** (0033 (0)4 92 24 42 73, www.aubergeduchoucas.com). You can explore the charming and quiet town of Monêiter from here, but you won't be having any crazy parties.

It's pretty easy to find apartments in any town, the Serre Che tourist office will help you out and you can book on the website.

Eating out

On the mountain

Café Soleil (04 92 24 17 39), in the middle of Serre Che, doesn't look very pretty but is good value and serves great food. **Bachas** (04 92 24 50 66) above Monêtier (at the top of the Bachas chair) has good sandwiches and hotdogs, but it's not the place for a long relaxing lunch; for this you should head to **Peyra Juana** (06 81 11 40 26). This restaurant is on the blue slope Rochamout and has table service inside or on the lovely terrace. For a smart meal, with full-on main courses, book a table at **L'Echaillon** (04 92 24 05 15, www.perso.wanadoo.fr/echaillon/) on the Fangeas piste from the summit of the Casse du Bœuf chairlift. Sit on the sunny terrace or inside by the fire.

In town

In Chantemerle, the **Triptyque** (04 92 24 14 94) is a small French restaurant where you can get a fantastic three-course meal for €22. For a smart, and extremely expensive meal, look out for **Crystal** (04 92 24 03 09).

In Villeneuve the **Refuge** (04 92 24 78 08) has the best French specialities such as fondues and pierrades (cooking meat at your table on a hot stone). **Marotte** (04 92 24 77 23) is a gorgeous and tiny place, that has the best atmosphere in town and the **Vielle Ferme** (04 92 24 76 44) is the most stylish. If you're desperate for a **McDonald's**, there's one in Briançon.

Bars and clubs

It's a bit of a nightmare going out in Serre Che because everything is so far apart. If you are in Briançon or Monêtier you are pretty much stuck there as buses don't run at night, and taxis are pretty expensive. Travelling between the Serre Che resorts Villeneuve and Chantemerle is half an hour walk or a €10 taxi ride.

The best place to go is the **Grotte du Yeti** in Villeneuve, unless you don't like being stuck with all the other Brits. There are advantages to this, however; they serve a great English breakfast, or pie, chips and gravy, until 8pm every day. There's usually a live band playing – look out for the Harper Brothers, a really good English rock band. Also in Villeneuve is a good **Swedish bar** where the beautiful people hang out. They also often have a live band playing. The French clubs are pretty easy to see on the main street, but the main partying happens in the bars. The

Baïta nightclub is open 5.30pm–5am and has themed evenings every Wednesday.

If you do happen to end up in Monêtier, the **Rif Blanc** is the place to be, especially to watch sports, and in Briançon the **Rosbif** bar is a lively après ski bar at the bottom of the lifts and the **Gotcha** bar is good for a cheep beer.

A massive thank you is due here to our great guide and friend, Ben Hawker (a.k.a. Bungle), sponsored by Faction skis and Animal.

Useful facts and phone numbers

Tourist office

T: 0033 (0)4 92 24 98 98
F: 0033 (0)4 92 24 98 84
E: contact@ot-serrechevalier.fr
W: www.serre-chevalier.com
Unofficial website: www.skiserreche.com

Emergency services

- Police: 04 92 24 00 56
- Mountain rescue: 04 92 22 22 22
- Briançon Hospital: 04 92 25 34 56

Doctors

- Dr Assor (1500): 04 92 24 42 54
- Dr Cuvilliez (1400): 04 92 24 71 02
- Dr Varziniak (1400): 04 92 24 71 37
- Dr Levy (1350): 04 92 24 18 56
- Dr Revalor (1350): 04 92 24 18 13

Taxis

Villeneuve
- Jacques Caillaud: 06 13 51 17 66
- M Turco: 06 08 61 20 63
Chantemerle
- Allo Taxi Serre Chevalier: 06 09 32 22 81
- Blanchard Phillippe Taxi: 06 87 82 21 21
- Taxi Rank: 04 92 21 18 94
Monêtier
- M Bonnardel: 04 92 24 41 40
Briançon
- Allo Taxi Marion: 06 09 32 22 81
- Caillaud: 06 07 69 35 19

Getting there

By car

From Paris, Lyon, Turin or Nice take the A43 motorway (via the Frejus tunnel from the north) and exit at Oulx, Montgenèvre, 35km from Serre Che. From Marseille, and Montpellier, take the A51 motorway via Aix en Provence, and Sisteron. Exit at La Saulce, 90km from Serre Che. From Grenoble, Lyon or Paris, take the A51, and exit at Pont de Claix, 80km from the resort via the Lautaret Pass.

By plane

Turin (108km) Transfer takes just 1 hour. BA, Easy Jet and RyanAir all fly to Turin from London airports.
Grenoble (110km) Transfer takes 1.5 hours. Buses and trains regularly run to Serre Che. Buzz fly to Grenoble from London Stansted.
Lyon (200km) Transfer by bus (www.satobus-alps .com).

By train

Take the 17.09 Eurostar from London Waterloo to Paris; then an overnight train to Briançon, and then a local bus (20 minutes), arriving in resort at 09.10. Return fares from £111 in a 6-berth couchette. Contact Rail Europe (08705 848 848, www.raileurope.co.uk) or European Rail (020 7387 0444, www.europeanrail.com). Bus tickets (€3.80 single from Autocars Rignon) are purchased at the station.

Tignes

Best skiing and boarding in Europe, with stunning mountains, that are only slightly spoilt by the ugly town

Val d'Isère
Depuis 1934

TIGNES

On the slopes

Snow reliability	✳ ✳ ✳ ✳ ✳
Parks	✳ ✳ ✳
Off-piste	✳ ✳ ✳ ✳ ✳

Off the slopes

Après ski	✳ ✳ ✳
Nightlife	✳ ✳ ✳
Eating out	✳ ✳ ✳
Resort charm	✳

The resort

There are loads of reasons to love Tignes, which is why we can forgive the unsightly architecture. The slopes are the main attraction; the Espace Killy is one of the best areas in Europe for all abilities. The nightlife is good too, and the people are friendly. The self-catering accommodation can leave a little to be desired, but it's great for a cheap deal.

There are a number of areas to Tignes which can be confusing at first. Initially you will see Tignes Le Brévières (at 1550m), a traditional and peaceful town with a beautiful Baroque church.

You will then arrive in Tignes Les Boisses (at 1850m). This area is quiet at present but it has the advantage of having a few pretty chalets (comparatively speaking) and you can ski to and from it fairly easily on some nice runs. If you fancy some peace and quiet and maybe only one or two nights out up the hill, this may be worth a look. It's also worth keeping an eye on this area as there is some major redevelopment planned in the coming years, which could really make Les Boisses a very tempting option.

The hub of Tignes is focused at 2100m, which is split into another three areas: Lavachet, Le Lac and Val Claret. Lavachet and Le Lac are next to each other and it's easy to walk between them. Val Claret is a bus/car journey away from the other two. Both areas have quite a lot going on although Val Claret has better access to the slopes and good parking next to the pistes.

The mountains

Height: 1550–3455m

Ability	Rating
Expert	✳ ✳ ✳ ✳
Intermediate	✳ ✳ ✳ ✳
Beginner	✳ ✳ ✳

Getting about

There are 150km of pistes in Tignes alone. If you add this to the accessible area of Val d'Isère, the whole of the Espace Killy has 300km of pistes. There are 90 lifts and 131 pistes: 16 blacks, 35 reds, 60 blues and 20 greens. With the height of the resort at 2100m you can almost guarantee good snow all the way down to the resort.

> "Access to this area is pretty swift considering its height"

The Grande Motte Glacier has a height of 3656m, from which you can ski a number of really good red runs, in summer (mid-June to September) as well as winter (October to May).

Access to this area is speedy; the underground funicular from Val Claret takes only 7 minutes. The Tovière area is the way to head over to Val d'Isère, and there are some good cruisy runs back to Val Claret from here. Le Palet and Pramecou are in the shade of the Grande Casse mountain and the freeriding potential here is huge. Finally, there are the quieter, east-facing slopes on L'Aiguille Percée, from which you can ride all the way down to Les Boisses or Le Brévières.

The park

The park at Val Claret has two pipes and a number of rails. One of the pipes is a 120m expert half pipe that complies with FIS standards and the other a 70m beginners' pipe. There are also the necessary deckchairs and sound system without which no park is complete. There are hardly any jumps, and the park isn't the best, but there is logic behind the madness. Val d'Isère has a good park that is easily accessible from Tignes. During the Tignes Airwaves, the park is amazing, but Joe Public won't get a look-in.

Off-piste and backcountry

In Tignes, safety is an extremely important consideration because the avalanche risk here and in Val d'Isère is one of the highest in Europe. Last year, in particular, there were a lot of fatalities. It is advisable to ski or board with a guide or very knowledgeable local if you fancy testing the off-piste. Having found your guide, however, you have access to some awesome backcountry exploits.

Le SPOT (Skiing the Powder of Tignes) was developed over the last couple of years to raise awareness of exactly what is involved in going off-piste. It can be reached by the Col des Ves chair. There are seven different zones. There is also a black run left ungroomed

> "Le SPOT was developed to raise awareness of exactly what's involved in going off-piste"

to practise some tough (and more than likely mogully) off-piste and two freeride zones for different abilities. Additionally there is a boardercross course, and a backcountry freestyle zone for building your own kickers.

Tignes has excellent and extensive backcountry for the experienced freerider. As you drive into Tignes you will see the lake to your left. Overlooking this is a

massive face named the Tignes Fingers due to the appearance of the rocks and couloirs. Some of the couloirs are a lot more challenging than others, so do your research. Tignes Fingers are popular amongst the locals and seasonaires, and you can pretty much stick to the area all day long and not get bored. Remember to check out the conditions though, as there have been rumours of slides taking riders right down into the lake.

Just above Le SPOT is the Pramecou. The 45-minute hike up to Dôme de Pramecou will give you access to some challenging off-piste and this will lead you to the Grande Balme just below – another area with some superb powder. Chardonnet can be hiked to from the Col du Palet in which you are faced with a range of couloirs. There is one that is always tracked out so shop around. If you are after tree runs, the Brévière is definitely worth a look. Alternatively, from the top of the Chaudannes, you can ride off-piste all the way back to Les Boisses through some great trees.

Lift passes	Tignes	Espace Killy
1 day	€35	€41
6 days	€169.50	€197.50
Passes are free for children under 5 and adults over 75 and children aged 5–12 get a discount.		

Instruction

ESF

The ESF offers instruction and off-piste guiding.
Tignes Le Lac T: 0033 (0)4 79 06 30 28
Tignes Le Lac W: www.esftignes.com
Tignes Val Claret T: 0033 (0)4 79 06 31 28
Tignes Val Claret W: www.esfvalclaret.com

Evolution 2

Ask anyone in Tignes: these guys are definitely the best. They offer any kind of instruction/coaching for skiers and boarders, including the bumps, race training, freestyle, avalanche awareness, off-piste training or they can simply provide a guide to help you explore on- and off-piste (as well as loads of other things – see Other activities). With no more than eight in a group, video feedback presentation on all adult group lessons and lift queue priority, this school is way above the rest. You can even opt to test

next year's skis! Prices are competitive and there are too many options to go into detail here. Contact Evolution 2 with your specific requirements or check out the website.

Tignes Le Lac T: 0033 (0)4 79 06 43 78
Tignes Val Claret T: 0033 (0)4 79 40 09 04
E: reservationstignes@evolution2.com
W: www.evolution2.com

Other activities

For all the activities mentioned below (unless otherwise stated), **Evolution 2** are the people to call (04 79 06 43 78). They also organise corporate events.

Winter

Aqua Centre: (Call the Tourist Office for information, 04 79 40 04 40). This new centre was opened in July 2006, on the lakeside in the heart of the resort at 2100m. Some of the facilities in the 5000m² spa include a 25m pool, a fun pool with four 30m water slides, a leisure pool with swimming against the current, hydro-massage and a fitness room. Access to everything costs €17 a day (€58 a week), spa and pool costs €13, pool only €4.50 or spa only €8.

Gastronomic Espace Killy Tour: This usually takes place on a Friday (9am–4.30pm) so that you can treat yourselves at the end of the week. Ski the best pistes in the Espace Killy and eat in a beautiful and traditional Savoyard farm restaurant (€75).

Helicopter flights: These cost between €30 (for a 5-minute discovery flight) and €195 (for a 35-minute flight over Mont Blanc).

Horse riding. An hour and a half riding excursion with a vin chaud break costs €40.

Husky driving and rides: These take place on 2 days a week (book as far in advance as you can). It costs €30 to be a passenger, €60 for a family package, €50 to drive the pack or €130 for a half day Ste Foy Husky Experience.

Ice climbing: The keen mountaineers can use ice axes and crampons to scale a frozen waterfall (€50). You can even do it floodlit at night if you so desire.

Ice diving: This basically involves dropping through a hole cut into the ice and swimming under the ice to check out the ice formations. It is available from mid-December until early April and you don't need any prior experience (€70).

Paragliding: Longer flights are available in the summer when you can also learn to fly solo (check out www.parapente-tignes.com). Costs €65/70.

Skidoo trips: There are a variety of options, at night or during the day, and you can be a passenger or the driver for €16–79.

Ski jörring: Here the skier is pulled along the snow by a riderless horse – looks kind of dangerous, but lots of fun (€32 for 30 mins).

Snowshoe expeditions: Half a day of sheer fun – apparently (€50/70). On the more expensive tour you return by helicopter, which sounds preferable.

Torchlit descent, Les Nocturnes du Panoramic: Have dinner on the Grande Motte glacier and ski back down the Double M piste with a flaming torch. Costs from €28 per person.

Summer

Adventure assault course: Contact Evolution 2 for more information.

Canyoning: This combines abseiling, swimming, jumping and sliding through rivers and waterfalls. It costs €55–100.

Climbing the Via Ferrata: This will cost €50.

4x4 driving: You can either be driven by a pro for 1.5 hours (€90/ 125), or drive yourself with the advice of a pro (€133). You can even have a lesson with your own vehicle (€42)!

Mountain biking: This costs €30–80.

Mountaineering: Enjoy the beauty of the mountains on foot.

Quad biking: An adult pays €46 for 1 hour and €72 for 2 hours.

Rafting or riding river rapids: These activities cost €46–67.

Trial biking: For experienced or beginner motorcyclists. Private lessons cost €50, a 2-hour advanced trip costs €60 and a technique trial course €230 (hiring the bike will cost you another €220).

Events

The **Tignes Airwaves** (www.tignesairwaves.com) is a huge event and it's a fantastic one for spectators. There is an invitational skiercross/boardercross, half pipe and slopestyle for the best skiers and boarders in the business. They also have motorcross freestyle demos and 'soul flyers', who wear 'bat suits' and glide above the crowd. In 2006 the first ever Fat Face Night ski competition was held in Val Claret and was a huge success. The comp is for anyone, and even better, it's free to enter. Battle your way down the slopestyle course to win some great cash prizes. The whole event is featured on the extreme channel. Check out www.natives.co.uk for more information.

"Have dinner on the Grande Motte glacier and ski back down the Double M piste with a flaming torch"

Le Grand Raid is a long-standing event organised by Evolution 2. The idea is that, in teams of two (any combination of boarder/skier, male/female and pro/amateur), you hike to the chosen face to compete against other teams for the fastest times. The competition takes place at the weekend, and the competitors sleep in a mountain refuge. Around 60 teams compete (it is advisable to book around a month in advance) and the price (unconfirmed) includes all food and the non-luxury refuge accommodation! Contact simijohnson@evolution2 .com for more information or to book yourself on. Recently Le Grand Raid has expanded and now involves the Grand Raid Tour, which is held on six separate days throughout the season in different resorts. One day will always be held somewhere within the Espace Killy. It costs €30 per person to enter and there are usually around 50 teams

competing. There is also the newly introduced **Grand Raid Master** in which all the winners of the Grand Raid since 1992 are invited to compete.

If you are in Tignes in the summer don't miss the **beach soccer** event in which celebrity footballers have been known to make an appearance!

Accommodation

Do some research – you have the choice of peace and quiet, easiest access to the lifts, the centre of the night-time action or budget. You can get some great self-catering deals if you don't mind a slightly pokey apartment. Contact Tignes Reservations for more information (see Useful facts and phone numbers).

For a really friendly and cosy South African/Scottish-run hotel in a peaceful location, look no further than **Les Mélèzes** in Les Boisses (0033 (0)4 79 06 31 49, euan@topnotchtours.org, www.topnotchtours.org). The rooms are fairly basic with no TV or phono, but there is a TV room and a big residents' bar (open until midnight) that has Monopoly and chess. Prices for a

week's half board (per person) are €275–500 depending on the time of season (one night costs €50–85).

Les Campanules 3-star Hotel (0033 (0)4 79 06 34 36, www.campanules.com) in Tignes Le Lac is another option with a good restaurant and the Altitude Spa, which is open only to hotel guests. It includes a sauna, a Turkish bath, a Jacuzzi and a heated outdoor swimming pool with a clear view of the Grande Motte Glacier. There are also a number of specialised treatments such as hydromassage baths and chromotherapy.

The **Alpaka Lodge** in Le Lac (04 79 06 45 30, info@alpaka.com, www.alpaka.com) has a cosy chalet feel and an open fire. Everyone in Tignes loves chilling out at the Alpaka bar for a coffee during the day or a cocktail in the evening. Free WiFi is a bonus too.

The **Hotel L'Ecrin des Neige** (04 79 40 22, 50, ecrin@mgm-immobilier.fr, www.cgh-residences.com) is a beautiful hotel in Tignes Val Claret, at the entrance to the resort. Rooms cost €455–840 per person per week.

Eating out

On the mountain

The **Alpage** (04 79 06 07 42) self-service restaurant at the top of the Chaudannes has really good views.

In town

In Val Claret, the **Petit Savoyard** (04 79 06 36 23) has a great atmosphere and range of food, from meat dishes to salads and pizzas. **Daffy's Tex Mex** (04 79 06 38 75) in the centre has good fajitas, burritos and ribs. For a fairly smart night, try **Le Caveau** (04 79 06 52 32), a highly recommended French restaurant with live music.

In **Le Lac** we suggest eating at the popular **Loop Bar** (04 79 06 30 61). **Le Clin d'Oeil** (04 79 06 59 10) is a tiny restaurant that seats about 20 people. There isn't much choice but it's all very fresh and very good. **Le Bagus Café** (04 79 06 49 75), above the Angels bar, is a funky eatery serving traditional Moroccan dishes. **Croq' Burger** (04 79 06 38 80) is the perfect place to pick up a burger or American (baguette with burger and chips in it) – great with or without a hangover.

In **Le Lavachet**, **La Ferme des 3 Capucines** (04 79 06 35 10) is a farm and traditional family-run restaurant – so traditional that you can watch the cows while you eat. Set menu from €30.

Bars and clubs

There are more than 50 bars in Tignes. Here is a selection of the best in each area.

In Lavachet go to **Harris** (re-named Censored but everyone still calls it Harris), a cosy, sometimes so crammed it's a bit too cosy, wooden bar in the centre. **TC's bar** (04 79 06 46 46, www.tcsbar.com) is a small, English-run bar, open around 3pm–1am. They serve snacks such as paninis and hot dogs, and at weekends they offer full English brekkies all day long. They host a number of parties including fetish nights and the night of 1000 shots (in which TC will give away the first 100 shots, then sell the next 500, then give away 100, etc). It gets messy.

In Le Lac, the **Red Lion** (04 79 40 05 85) is a great bar to start the evening off in. **Angels Bar** is owned by three lovely English girls, and is open midday–1am. It serves tasty English food such as jacket potatoes, nachos, paninis and hot dogs all day and night. Babyfoot, a pool table, internet (€5.50/hour) and a TV provide the entertainment. On a Friday night there is a raffle where a €1 ticket might well win you a snowboard. They also have various fancy dress theme nights. The **Loop Bar** (04 79 06 30 61, alistair@theloopbar.com) is a very popular bar for a game of pool and a bite to eat at lunch (12–2.30pm) or at night (7–9.30pm). During happy hour (4–6pm) all wine and draft beers are 2 for 1 and later on you might be able to take part in some dancing on tables. For a chilled out night, with masses of cocktails, try the **Alpaka Lodge** (04 79 06 45 30). It has a big, cosy fire and two massive Irish Wolfhounds to make you feel at home.

> ## "A big, cosy fire and two massive Irish Wolfhounds to make you feel at home"

In Val Claret, **Crowded House**, run by Paul and Jaffa, is one of the best bars in town. It's open 4.30pm–1.30am and happy hour is 4.30–6.30pm. Until 10pm the bar is fairly chilled out and then after that it really heats up, with DJs every other Saturday and a mix of hip hop, cheesy classics and chart music. They also hold regular theme nights with a school disco, and a doctors and nurses night. The **Couloir** bar is another strong favourite, not just because of the 60 flavours of vodka shots, but also due to the friendly staff, ample space and well-chosen live bands. The **Fish Tank** (04 79 06 46 60) is the place to be when the sports are on.

For a late night boogie, **Jacks** (04 79 06 54 84) in Le Lac is a small, hilarious club that you are bound to end up in if you have a night out in the area. The **Blue Girl** in Val Claret is a French club, with a dodgy mirrored ceiling, zebra skin upholstery and a dancing cage to accompany the long-standing pole. The **Melting Pot** is the seasonaire hangout with good DJs but overpriced drinks. **Yorin** is a fairly hardcore techno club, quite in your face and you'll either love it or hate it. This club is owned by a massive Dutch company, who own the equivalent of Radio One, so they have the budget for some crazy laser lights, decent DJs, massive giveaways and TVs in the urinals!

Useful facts and phone numbers

Tourist office

T: 0033 (0)4 79 40 04 40
F: 0033 (0)4 79 40 03 15
E: information@tignes.net
W: www.tignes.net

Direct reservations

T: 0033 (0)4 79 40 03 03
W: www.tignesreservation.net

Emergency services

In a medical emergency dial 15, for the fire
    brigade call 18, or 112 for either from a
    mobile.
• Police: 17 (Emergency)
    04 79 06 32 06 (Gendarmerie)
    04 79 40 04 93 (Municipal police)
• Ambulance: 04 79 06 59 18/04 79 06 43 00
• Piste safety: 04 79 06 32 00
• Doctor's surgery: 04 79 06 50 07

Taxis

• Diane Taxis, Les Brévières: 06 07 05 84 85
• AA Anémone, Val Claret: 06 09 41 01 46
• Delta Taxi: 06 11 45 67 01, deltataxi@aol.com

Getting there

By car

Bourg St Maurice is accessible by Eurostar and
the snow train. From Bourg drive up the road
towards Val d'Isère and Tignes (takes about 30
minutes). Look out for the painting of Hercules
holding back the water as you cross over the
spectacular dam. Under the water in the dam is
the old village of Tignes which can actually be
seen when the dam is drained.
From Calais it will take you around 12 hours
(995km).

By plane

Lyon (235km) Transfer takes 2.5–3 hours by car.
Geneva (179km) Transfer takes around 2.5
hours.

By train

Take the 17.09 Eurostar from London Waterloo
to Paris; then an overnight train to Bourg St
Maurice, and then a bus (75 minutes), arriving in
resort at 09.15. Return fares from £111 in a
6-berth couchette. Contact Rail Europe (08705
848 848, www.raileurope.co.uk) or European Rail
(020 7387 0444, www.europeanrail.com). Bus
tickets (€10.20 single from Autocars Martin) are
purchased at the station.

Val d'Isère

Val gets top marks for snow,
off-piste, shopping and bars;
we love it

Val d'Isère
Depuis 1934

TIGNES

On the mountain	
Snow reliability	❄ ❄ ❄ ❄
Parks	❄ ❄ ❄ ❄
Off-piste	❄ ❄ ❄ ❄ ❄

Off the slopes	
Après ski	❄ ❄ ❄
Nightlife	❄ ❄ ❄ ❄
Eating out	❄ ❄ ❄
Resort charm	❄ ❄ ❄

The resort

We love Val d'Isère; it definitely lives up to its hyped up reputation and we get excited every time we come here. For a big, busy resort it's really quite attractive and full of sparkly fairy lights. The few not-so-pretty buildings are well hidden. The only slight niggle we have with this resort is us rowdy Brits. It's an awesome place to come with your mates for a week of hedonistic riding and partying (if you've got enough cash), but if you are after a romantic getaway or with your family there may be better places to go.

The mountains

Height: 1785–3300m

Ability	Rating
Expert	❄ ❄ ❄ ❄ ❄
Intermediate	❄ ❄ ❄ ❄ ❄
Beginner	❄ ❄ ❄

Getting about

Val has 300km of marked runs: 20 green, 60 blue, 35 red and 16 black. There are 90 ski lifts that are a credit to Val d'Isère.

There are three main sectors:

Bellevarde is easily accessed by the funicular at La Daille or L'Olympique gondola in town and is the route over to Tignes. The Bellevarde area contains the legendary Face run, often completely bumped up. The World Cup downhill is held on the OK run at La Daille.

Solaise is a sunny area that's really good for intermediates although there are some challenging runs back to the village.

Col de l'Iseran can be accessed from Solaise or from Le Fornet in the main valley. The runs are pretty easy and the views beautiful. From here you can also access some of the best off-piste terrain.

The park

The Val d'Isère park (www.valdisere.com/winterpark) has always been a favourite amongst the pro boarders and skiers and all the locals are at such a high level that they have to make sure this park rocks. It is situated behind the Bellevarde summit, in the Mont Blanc coomb. Gumby, who's behind the Xbox Big Day Out, is in charge of park maintenance – a massive

"The runs are pretty easy and the views beautiful"

bonus to all who ride there. The park is regularly changed so nobody gets bored doing the same stuff, and it always consists of rails, a huge hip, a quarter pipe and a range of table tops. There are two massive hits at the bottom of the park that would put a shiver down the spine of even the top riders. Word has it that the park is going to expand further during 2007 and we can't wait.

Off-piste and backcountry

La Fornet is the backcountry mecca, with access to huge areas of off-piste. The trees are fantastic and there are loads of shoots, gullies and cliffs; a great playground, especially when there's too much wind on top. The Grand Vallons, Col Pers and Pointe Pers are awesome but take care on Pointe Pers as it's steep – approaching 50° at the top. Grand Vallons is easily accessible from the Signal drag lift; for the others a guide is recommended.

From Solaise, take the Cugnai 'antique' chairlift and, rather than taking the St Jacques red run down, head over the back of the mountain to the Cugnai off-piste run. This run has some of the best back drops,

"This run has some of the best back drops, especially if you keep left under the epic cliff face"

especially if you keep left under the epic cliff face. This can warm you up for Lorès, some of the best off-piste in Val. For this though, do take a guide as it can be dangerous. To reach it, once you have skied the first half of Cugnai, hang a left and ski tour up to the Refuge des Fours. From here it's about an hour's walk to Lorès ridge, where you should stop to check out the stunning views and then head down the best powder field you'll find in Val. The Bellevarde is another huge playground with countless couloirs and bowls. Couloir des Pisteurs is a firm favourite. When looking from the top of the funicular, you are faced with a flat-topped mountain which forks into three halfway down. You can take any route, but the left fork (from the rider's

Lift passes

half day	€29
1 day	€40
6 days	€192.50
13 days	€325

The lift pass for Val d'Isère seems fairly expensive but it does cover the whole Espace Killy area. Your lift pass will also give you bad weather insurance and free access to the swimming pool. You can buy your lift pass on-line (7 days or more) and it will be delivered to your holiday home in Val. Reserve your pass at www.stvi-valdisere.com or write to STVI, Gare Centrale, 73 150 Val d'Isère. There are also 'loyal customer' discounts, so save your lift pass and you'll get a discount off next year's pass.

point of view) has some of the best powder. Another great run is the Face du Charvet; there are many routes down but it is often best in treacherous snow conditions so be warned and take a guide. To the rider's right is the most adventurous and encompasses great mini-bowls and couloirs, just don't get stuck or go over any cliffs!

Instruction

There are tons of ski and snowboard schools to choose from, so you'll easily be able to find something to suit you.

Billabong Ski and Snowboard School
This school has a good name around town, especially for boarding. It also has qualified mountain guides.
T: 0033 (0)4 79 06 09 54
E: billabong@snowboardfrance.com
W: www.snowboardfrance.com

ESF
This is the largest and oldest school in town with over 400 instructors. Some of the best skiers in town work for the ESF, but you'd be lucky to get one. It can be great, but it's a bit of a lottery.
T: 0033 (0)4 79 06 02 34
E: esf.valdisere@wanadoo.fr
W: www.esfvaldisere.com

Evolution 2
A wealth of variety and programmes are available on and off your skis.
T: 0033 (0)4 79 41 16 72
E: valdisere@evolution2.com, reservationsval@evolution2.com
W: www.evolution2.com

Misty Fly
This snowboard school has a great reputation for all aspects of boarding, including off-piste and freestyle. The shop is also pretty cool.
T: 0033 (0)4 79 40 08 74
E: lionel.surf@infonie.fr

Mountain Masters
The French and British ski instructors and guides have a great depth of experience. They are extremely popular and perhaps the best guarantee of quality

coaching whether for on-piste cruising, heliskiing or racing, etc.

T: 0033 (0)4 79 06 05 14
E: info@mountain-masters.com
W: www.mountain-masters.com

Snow Fun

Best for kids and intermediates. The first school to insist on small group sizes: max. 8 people.

T: 0033 (0)4 79 06 16 79
E: info@valfun.fr
W: www.valfun.com

Top Ski

Pat Zimmer, an ex-French-team skier, heads up a team of around 20 excellent guides and instructors, many of whom have a strong background as competitive skiers. Eric Berthan, the ex-World-Champion mogul skier is based with Top Ski.

T: 0033 (0)4 79 06 14 80
E: top.ski.val.isere@wanadoo.fr
W: www.topskival.com

Dissent

Chris Haworth, sponsored by Salomon, is a well-respected and liked face in the British Ski Industry (especially with the ladies). He takes race training camps all year round and he's the boy to coach you if you are a trainee ski instructor, or a race competitor in slalom, GS or Super GS. Chris also runs freeride, freestyle and mogul camps with Pat Sharples throughout the winter season. The feedback from these courses has been fantastic. People particularly benefit from the quality of the video analysis, which takes place with a few beers after a day's coaching. These camps are always popular and get booked up quickly, so get hold of Chris or Pat as soon as possible if you fancy joining them.

T: Chris Haworth on 0033 (0)6 03 28 11 67 or Pat on 0044 (0)79742 05852 (English mobile) or 0033 (0)6 80 23 95 76
E: christopherhaworth@hotmail.com or patsharples@hotmail.com

Other activities

Driving on ice: Fancy this? You can have a go using karts, quads, snowmobiles or a Fiat Panda (04 79 06 21 40, www.circuitvaldisere.com).

Health and relaxation spa: Hotel Christiania (04 79 06 02 90) has a health and relaxation spa that offers massages, whirlpool baths and a very expensive slimming treatment. **Yoga** lessons are available in English and French (06 03 10 63 95, charlotte@ snowrental.net). The spa at the luxury Balme de l'Ours (04 79 41 37 10) is the biggest in the Alps, and is open to the public at certain times.

Husky driving: If you've got a spare evening you could always have a go at driving a team of huskies (06 16 48 60 47, stephanemush@aol.com).

Ice skating: The rink (04 79 06 05 90) has one late night session per week.

Scenic flights: If you fancy it, take a scenic flight over the Espace Killy (06 07 22 43 97, www.marine-air-sport.com).

Shop shop shop: The shops are far better than the usual resort rubbish, and form a great way to while away a bad weather day. If you're broke, don't risk looking.

Sports hall: Located at the foot of the Bellevarde Face, the sports hall is open 9am–midday and 3–7pm. It has basketball, ping-pong, volleyball, hand-ball, badminton, trampoline, gymnastics, football, weights room and a rock climbing wall. Call 04 79 06 03 49 for more information.

Swimming pool: The indoor swimming pool is at the foot of the Bellevarde Face (04 79 06 05 90) and is free with your lift pass (if 7 days or more). It's open every day 2–7pm and there is one late night session per week.

Events

The **Xbox Big Day Out** (www.xboxbigdayout.com) takes place for five days in February and brings together some of Europe's best pro snowboarders and (a few) skiers. It's held at the bottom of Val d'Isère so it's great for spectators and the parties get pretty crazy too. The **Mad Trix** event takes place in the park and you can win dosh on the spot for pulling crazy tricks. Val also hosts the **Word Cup Downhill**, one of the toughest on the circuit, and the **Giant Slalom** and **Super Giant Slalom**. Val d'Isère is already preparing for the 2009 **World Alpine Skiing Championships**, which will take place from 30 January to 14 February, 2009.

Accommodation

Val has 28,000 beds. The main lift stations are linked by efficient, free shuttle buses. During the day they are up and down all the time but at night you might get a bit nippy waiting at the bus stop. It's worth looking around to find the best location for you. There is a huge range of accommodation available from budget to luxury.

The 4-star, luxury **Balme de l'Ours** (0033 (0)4 79 41 37 10, www.hotel-les-balmes.com, welcome@hotel-les-barmes.com) is super expensive – rooms cost €325–700 per night and suites €560–4000. The Balme de l'Ours also contains the biggest spa in the Alps. The **Blizzard** (0033 (0)4 79 06 02 07, www.hotelblizzard.com, information@hotelblizzard.com), also 4 star, is cosy and civilised with a great bar but has prices to match. It has a swimming pool, Turkish bath and Jacuzzi. The restaurant is good quality but expensive and lacks inspiration for the price.

Hotel Kandahar (0033 (0)4 79 06 02 39, www.hotel-kandahar.com, hotel.kandahar@wanadoo.fr) has 3 stars, is mid ranged and has a great location, smack in the centre of town. It has a comfortable, modern alpine décor, a great bar and a tavern downstairs that is a favourite with the locals.

Hotel Moris (0033 (0)4 79 06 22 11) is a favourite of the Brits. The food and accommodation are pretty good and the pub below is a well-liked watering hole. A popular choice, especially for those who don't place pampering high up on their priority list.

Eating out

On the mountain

The mountain restaurants in Val are surprisingly good value. Obviously we're not talking cheap but, compared to other resorts of a similar standard, Val scores very highly for value for money on the mountain.

La Fornet

Le Signal (04 79 06 03 38), at the summit of the Signal cable car, is on the top floor of the building with a cheap and cheerful self-service below. The staff are attentive and friendly and the hearty portions have an excellent reputation. The **Edelweiss** (06 10 28 70 64) is a beautiful chalet, recently constructed halfway down the Mangard blue run, with great food, ambience and service.

Solaise

Le Bar de l'Ouillette (04 79 41 94 74) is a bustling little self-service restaurant that is a huge sun trap. It is popular with instructors and has very friendly staff.

Bellevarde

La Folie Douce (04 79 06 01 47, lafoliedouce@wanadoo.fr) and **La Fruitière** (04 79 06 07 17, lafoliedouce@wanadoo.fr) are at the top of the La Daille bubble. The self-service Folie is OK for food, but better for après beers. La Fruitière, set in a restored dairy farm, is *the* place to be seen on the hill in Val d'Isère. It's often over crowded and fully booked but worth it. The best tables and service are on the upper tier inside; reservations are a must. **Marmottes** (04 79 06 05 08) is a well-positioned meeting place by the lift of the same name, overlooking the park. It is a great self-service restaurant with good portions and good value for money. Outside is a fab hot dog stand and a couple of rows of deckchairs. **Le Trifollet** (04 79 41 96 99) serves the best pizzas on the hill. If you want a good table it's best to reserve and the upper terrace is fantastic in the spring.

In town

Reservations are essential, especially in high season. The **Lodge** (04 79 06 02 01), up by Dicks Tea Bar, is a funky and cosy little restaurant that is fantastic for groups of mates, families and also for romantic dates. Great food at good prices; a pizza will cost you about €10–12 and a steak or speciality dish will cost

€18–25. The **Perdrix Blanche** (04 79 06 12 09), right in the centre of town, is popular with the locals. It's atmospheric and serves good food. **Taverne d'Alsace** (04 79 06 48 49) has good rustic food, a great atmosphere and good service, but it's pricey. **Le Grand Ourse** (04 79 06 00 19) is expensive and kitsch. **Chez Paolo** (04 79 06 28 04) has the tastiest pizzas and Italian fare in town. It can get really busy though, so it's best to pick your times. **Bananas** (04 79 06 04 23), just by the slopes, is a Tex-Mex restaurant upstairs that is really busy when people come in from the slopes and has a great bar downstairs. Two restaurants in town have embraced a no-smoking policy – **Bar Jacques** (04 79 06 03 89) combines quality, service and price, and **L'Atelier d'Edmond** (04 79 00 00 82) is a gastronomic restaurant in the style of an ancient carpenter's shop.

Bars and clubs

The **Folie Douce** (04 79 06 01 47, lafoliedouce@ wanadoo.fr) is the place to be for après ski. From lunch onwards you will often find people dancing on the tables and/or roof. There's always loud music, and sometimes a DJ, that you can hear from the top of the mountain. When you're suitably hammered you can ski/board back

"It has a fab atmosphere, loads of seating and is great at any time of day or night"

down (which we obviously don't condone) or take the lift. **Café Face**, opposite Dicks Tea Bar, is a packed après ski bar with a fab atmosphere and an inspired happy hour (from about 4pm) during which the beers are amazingly cheap; the prices get steadily more expensive as time passes. **Pacific Bar** (04 79 06 29 19) is the place to watch sports as it has plasma screens pretty much in front of every table. The **Moris Pub** (04 79 06 22 11), at the end of town, is a massive pub that has great live music, happy hours and theme nights.

Victor's bar (04 79 06 67 00), near to Dicks Tea Bar, does a huge range of great cocktails and is one of our favourite bars in town. The **Saloon Bar** (04 79 06 01 58) has a fab atmosphere, loads of seating and is great at any time of day or night. The 2 for 1 cocktail hours are a plus point too! It also has a dance floor on which to strut your stuff. **Bananas** (04 79 06 04 23) is a small bar with a good atmosphere and good cocktails. Upstairs is a popular Tex-Mex restaurant (see Eating out). **Petit Danois** (04 79 06 27 97) is a cool late-night bar that has some good DJs and is often hectic and crowded but fun.

Dicks Tea Bar (04 79 06 14 87) is the main club and gets absolutely packed. Despite Val's reputation for being a hive of late-night entertainment, if you want a boogie this is pretty much the only place to go (or at least where all the Brits go). It's worth a visit, but it is ridiculously expensive to get in (about €12) and the queues are often massive. Once inside, it's full of little alcoves and can be fun but the drinks aren't cheap – a round of four sambucas cost us €36! **La Graal** (04 79 09 64 82) is Dicks' only real competition.

Useful facts and phone numbers

Tourist office

T: 0033 (0)4 79 06 06 60
F: 0033 (0)4 79 06 04 56
E: info@valdisere.com
W: www.valdisere.com

Direct reservations

T: 0033 (0)4 79 06 18 90/ 0033 (0)4 79 06 06
     60
E: valhotel@valdisere.com/vallocation@
     valdisere.com

Emergency services

In a medical emergency dial 15, for the fire
    brigade call 18, or 112 for either from a
    mobile.
• Police: 17 or 04 79 06 03 41
• Ambulance: 04 79 06 43 00
• Slope rescue/ Ski patrol: 04 79 06 02 10

Doctors

• Médival Medical Centre: 04 79 40 26 80
• Centre Medical Centre: 04 79 06 06 11
• Val Village Medical Centre: 04 79 06 13 70
• Hospital in Bourg St Maurice: 04 79 41 79 79

Taxis

• Bozzetto: 04 79 06 02 50
• ABC taxis: 06 18 19 20 00 (abctaxi@
    wanadoo.fr)
• Taxi Nicolas: 04 79 41 01 25 (www.taxi-nicolas
    .com/ info@taxi-nicolas.com)
• Altitude Espace Taxi: 06 07 41 11 53
• Taxi Papillon: 06 08 99 93 96
• Etoile des Neiges Taxi: 06 25 89 40 53

Getting there

By car

Drive via Bourg St Maurice and take the N90
towards Tignes and then Val d'Isère. Around 10.5
hours from Calais.

By plane

Geneva (180km) Transfer 3–3.5 hours.

By train

Take the 17.09 Eurostar from London Waterloo to
Paris; then an overnight train to Bourg St Maurice,
and then a bus (60 minutes), arriving in resort at
09.00. Return fares from £111 in a 6-berth
couchette. Contact Rail Europe (08705 848 848,
www.raileurope.co.uk) or European Rail (020
7387 0444, www.europeanrail.com). Bus tickets
(€10.20 single from Autocars Martin) are
purchased at the station.

Val Thorens

If you're looking for a good nightlife and great snow and can ignore the concrete jungle, you're sorted

On the slopes	
Snow reliability	✳ ✳ ✳ ✳
Parks	✳ ✳ ✳
Off-piste	✳ ✳ ✳

Off the slopes	
Après ski	✳ ✳ ✳
Nightlife	✳ ✳ ✳ ✳
Eating out	✳ ✳
Resort charm	✳

The resort

Val Thorens is the highest resort in Europe at 2300m, making the snow as reliable as it can be. The blocks of ugly flats seriously damage the 'resort charm' factor, but it's not all ugly: the cluster of newer developments at the top of the resort contains much prettier, traditional chalets. Val Thorens is also very compact so many hotels and residences have the ski-in ski-out facility and you are never too far from the bars, restaurants and lively nightlife.

The mountains

Height: 2300–3200m

Ability	Rating
Expert	✳ ✳ ✳ ✳
Intermediate	✳ ✳ ✳
Beginner	✳ ✳ ✳

Getting about

Val Thorens' mountains are far more appealing than the town. There are 170km of pistes (66 pistes), with access to the 600km of Les Trois Vallées (328 pistes). Of the 66 pistes in VT, 5 are black, 28 red, 25 blue and 8 green. It is therefore more suited to intermediates and experts than beginners. The more challenging pistes are towards the top of the glacier with some motorway pistes that are great for intermediates. There is also plenty to keep the backcountry explorer entertained. The snow is virtually guaranteed and the lift systems are pretty

modern and quick. The disadvantages are that there is nowhere to escape to in bad weather as the trees are non existent, and the runs can get busy due to people coming over from Courchevel and Meribel. If you fancy a pretty view, head up to the Cime de Caron (at 3200m) for a panoramic view of hundreds of French, Swiss and Italian summits.

The park

Just above the 2 Lacs piste, at the bottom of the resort and accessible from the 2 Lacs chairlift, is the snowpark, which is always kept in really good condition. The jumps are not the most fierce, but are perfect for practising your latest tricks. There are lots of rails to jib on which are changed throughout the winter so the locals don't get bored and a 115m half pipe which can be pretty good after it's been shaped. This park has been used for the X-games qualifiers in the past, so it does attract some of the top pro riders.

Off-piste and backcountry

VT has a huge quantity of off-piste, and the snow stays in good condition as the mountain is one of the highest in the Alps, so you can pretty much always find some tempting powder. The Cime de Caron is one of the most popular places and has one of the best views in Les Trois Vallées. Some of the riding on the glaciers of Peclet and Chaviere can be totally mind blowing, and this is where to go after a snow storm (with someone who knows the place). If steeps and couloirs are your bag, head to le Plein Sud; these get tracked out pretty quickly but the snow's always wicked and they don't get boring. Our favourite place is the long ride over the Gébroulaz glacier down towards Meribel. You can get to this by hiking up from the top of the Col chair lift.

Lift passes	Val Thorens	Les Trois Vallées
1 day	€34	€42
6 days	€163	€210

There is a discount for children under 13 years and adults over 60. There are discounts on the normal tariff 1 November–17 December and 16 April–8 May, You can book your ski passes online at www.valthorens.com and they will be delivered to your hotel or apartment.

Instruction

ESF

The ESF provides a variety of courses, including group, private, freeride, freestyle and heliriding. As an example of price, a 6 half-days' course costs from €101.

T: 0033 (0)4 79 00 02 86
E: info@esf-valthorens
W: www.esf-valthorens.com

International Ski School

The international instructors each speak at least 3 of 10 languages. They limit groups to 7 people and offer a number of different programmes, including some with hi-tech tuition and video analysis at €30–45 for 1 morning or afternoon and €150 for 5 mornings.

T: 0033 (0)4 79 00 01 96
E: info@esivalthorens.com
W: www.esivalthorens.com

Prosneige

Prosneige offers all-inclusive packages (lessons plus lift pass and equipment) as well as private tuition, guiding and heliskiing on Italian summits.

T: 0033 (0)4 79 01 07 00
E: info@prosneige.fr
W: www.prosneige.fr

Ski Cool

Ski Cool offers carving and freestyle courses for both boarders and skiers. It also offers skiing lessons for the blind. Three-hour ice-climbing courses are available from €45. You can choose between private and group lessons or a mini group, limited to 4 people, halfway between a group and private lesson.

T: 0033 (0)4 79 00 04 92
E: mail@ski-cool.com
W: www.ski-cool.com

Thomas Diet

This X-Games freestyle competitor (in 2003), on the Dynastar Team, takes a 5 half-days' course for €99.

T: 0033 (0)6 80 88 41 75

Other activities

Unless other contact details are given, call the tourist office for more information (04 79 00 08 08).

Beauty and well being: Institut des Neiges (04 79 01 04 81, info@beauty-valthorens.com, www.beauty-valthorens.com) has moved to a new 2-storey chalet, dedicated to well-being. There are loads of treatments on offer from 1–5 day packages. Check out the website for more information.

Flying: Take a microlight flight from the base on the Moutière plateau (2500m). Costs from €45.

Ice climbing: You can take a 3-hour introduction or improvers' lesson on a natural waterfall. Equipment is provided and it costs from €45. Contact Ski Cool (04 79 00 04 92).

Ice driving: The Val Thorens Ice Driving School (03 23 72 36 36) gives lessons on general ice driving through to competition level. Beginners use cross cars and quads and can then progress to use the Mitsubishi Evo 6.

Paragliding: Tandem paraglides are available over Les Trois Vallées from €65 (06 81 55 74 94, www.libre-envol.com).

Snowmobiling: This is a fairly popular activity in Val Thorens. Val Tho Motoneige (04 79 00 21 46) has 42 snowmobiles and you can rent one for an hour from €70.

Sports centre: This freshly revamped centre (04 79 00 00 76) combines fitness, sport and relaxation. The Aquaclub has an island theme and includes a swimming pool, in which you can swim against the current. There are also several saunas, Jacuzzis and a heated solarium. The fitness centre contains a 170m² weight/circuit training room and a 110m² fitness room. Leisure activities include tennis, volleyball, football, squash, ping pong, badminton, roller skating, hockey, and a kids' play room with trampolines and ball pools. Bizarrely, the sports centre also organises fitness and aqua gym lessons for couples. Aquaclub is open 2–10pm.

Tobogganing: The highest toboggan run in Europe is situated in the Tête Ronde sector. At the foot of the Péclet glacier, this run drops 700m during its impressive 6km descent and will take around 45 minutes. It costs from €9 (with lift pass) and is accessible during the day via the Funitel of Péclet in just 8 minutes. A €50 deposit is required to hire the equipment.

Events

There aren't many major events in Val Thorens, except for a few slalom races. A popular, beginning of season party is **Boarderweek** which takes place every year, around the second week in December. It is a ski and snowboarding freestyle party with equipment testing and lots of fun parties and concerts. Check out www.boarderweek.com.

Accommodation

There are 24,500 beds in Val Thorens, all in pretty good locations, either near town and/or the slopes. There are 11 hotels; one 4-star, six 3-star, two 2-star, and two club hotels/holiday villages. There are also 15 residence chalets and almost 100 private renters (list available at the tourist office).

"A ski and snowboarding freestyle party with equipment testing and lots of fun parties and concerts"

For exclusive, self-catering accommodation try the 4-star **Oxalys** chalet complex (0033 (0)4 79 00 20 51, www.montagnettes.com), which will set you back from €1260 for a 4-person apartment (40m²) and €2540 for an 8-person apartment (95m²). Prices depend on time of season and whether you require a VIP chalet (contains whirlpool bath, video recorders, slippers…). The other glam option is the 4-star **Fitzroy** (0033 (0)4 79 00 04 78, welcome@hotelfitzroy.com, www.hotelfitzroy.com, from €185 per person per day half board) which is very posh and beautiful. For slightly less expensive beautiful apartments in a big, cosy, wooden chalet, try **Les Chalets du Soleil** (0033 (0)4 75 40 80 25, www.chaletdusoleil.com), a 4–6-person apartment costs from €774 per apartment per week. A 12–14-person apartment costs from €1859.

If you are looking for a less expensive visit, try the **Novotel hotel** (0033 (0)4 79 00 04 04, www.novotel valthorens.com). There are 104 rooms (half smoking, half non), with prices from €70 per person per night half board. It's right on the slopes, offers a ski shop and hire centre (where you can even rent ski/board clothing), a good bar and restaurant and has just had a big revamp and extension. The new spa, now teamed with Kanebo, has lots of treatments on offer. If you wish, you can take your half-board meal at lunchtime (on the huge terrace on the slopes) instead of dinner so that you are free to roam in the evenings. The Novotel attracts a large range of clients, but mostly families, attracted by the nightly entertainment for children, and family rooms with no supplement for children up to 16 years; and corporate clients, who can take advantage of the 500m² of conference and meeting facilities that the hotel offers. The hotel also offers a WiFi internet connection so you can access the net from your room if your laptop supports it.

If you prefer an inexpensive apartment, rather than a hotel, try **Le Chamois D'Or** (0033 (0)4 79 01 34 34, contact@lechamoisdor.fr, www.residchamois dor.com) in the centre of town, offering studios or apartments for 2 to 8 people. A 4-person studio will cost €404–877 per apartment per week, depending on the time of season.

Eating out

On the mountain

There are many restaurants overlooking the mountains on the slopes by the town centre. **Le Galoubet brasserie** (04 79 00 00 48) is one of the best traditional restaurants on the mountain; it has a big terrace and you can either have a quick €5 panini or opt for a fancy main meal (€12–30). **Le Scapin** (04 79 00 05 94), just behind Le Galoubet, has very friendly service and more simple food such as pizzas, pastas and steak.

On the slopes, **Chalet des 2 Lacs** (04 79 00 28 54) has a snack bar outside for hot dogs, chips and crêpes to enjoy on deckchairs in the sun. It also has a very cute, wooden restaurant with an open fire and serves good pizzas and big chunky chips. **Chalet du Génépi** (04 79 00 03 28) is another cosy chalet with a big fire.

In town

There are lots of places to eat in town, including a number of fast-food options and kebab houses. For British pub grub (fish and chips, burgers and the like), try the **Frog and Roast Beef** (04 79 00 07 17, www.thefrogandroastbeef.com). **El Gringos** serves absolutely fab Tex-Mex food and the staff are a hoot. There are long wooden benches, perfect for large groups. For a pizza, or traditional Savoyard cuisine, **La Paillotte** (04 79 00 01 02) in the town centre is very cosy and serves excellent food. Pizzas and salads are

also available at **Le Scapin** with a good atmosphere and affordable prices. If you want something less affordable but definitely memorable, try **L'Oxalys** (see Accommodation – 04 79 00 12 00). The restaurant is run by Jean Sulpice, who has recently been awarded a Michelin star, in fact the 'highest' star in Europe at 2300m. Make sure you book well in advance.

Bars and clubs

The row of bars at the top of the resort is where your night should begin. Choose an end and work your way along, picking your way through bars such as the **Frog and Roast Beef**, **Friends**, **O'Connells** and **Le Viking** (which also has internet). All of them have various happy hours and some offer tasty meals too. O'Connells happens to be the highest Irish pub in the world and was the fastest built in France – it took just four weeks to build it, ship it to the Alps and install it. **Le Chantaco** in the centre of town is another option with table football and somewhere you can usually sit for a chat.

Later on the place to be is the **Malaysia** cellar bar. It's right by the piste and looks like it's just a little wooden hut but, once inside, you walk down into a large club which has live bands all the time, and at about 1.30am the second part of the club opens up. For a very cheesy option, which is good for a laugh if you're in the mood, try the **Underground** nightclub in Place de Péclet.

Useful facts and phone numbers

Tourist office

T: 0033 (0)4 79 00 08 08
F: 0033 (0)4 79 00 00 04
E: valtho@valthorens.com
W: www.valthorens.com

Direct reservations

T: 0033 (0)4 79 00 01 06
F: 0033 (0)4 79 00 06 49
E: reserver@valthorens.com

Emergency services

- In a medical emergency dial 15, for the fire brigade call 18, or 112 for either from a mobile.
- Police station: 04 79 00 08 50
- Medical centres: 04 79 00 00 37/04 79 00 74 39 (Rue du Soleil)
- Clinique des Trois Vallées: 04 79 24 01 76
- Hospital: 04 79 09 60 60 (Moutiers)

Taxis

- Station de taxis: 04 79 00 69 54
- Favre, Pascal: 04 79 00 64 59
- Legay, Eric: 04 79 00 28 74 or 06 80 36 34 31

Getting there

By car

From Calais (209km), drive time is around 11 hours. You can't park your car in town, so either make sure your hotel/apartment has a car park or book into one (0033 (0)4 79 00 02 49, www.valthoparc.com); it's cheaper than paying on arrival. One week's parking will cost €60–64 depending on the height of your vehicle, whether you want indoor or outdoor and whether you have booked in advance.

By plane

Lyon (193km) Transfer time is around 3 hours. For bus transfers contact Satobus on 0033 (0)4 37 25 52 55.
Geneva (160km) Transfer takes about 3 hours. For bus transfers contact Touriscar on 0033 (0)4 50 43 60 02.

By train

Take the 17.09 Eurostar from London Waterloo to Paris; then an overnight train to Moutiers, and then a bus (75 minutes), arriving in resort at 08.45. Return fares from £111 in a 6-berth couchette. Contact Rail Europe (08705 848 848, www.raileurope.co.uk) or European Rail (020 7387 0444, www.europeanrail.com). Bus tickets (€14.80 single) can be purchased in advance from Altibus (0033 (0)4 79 68 32 96, www.altibus.com) or at the station.

Italy

Italy is one of the few countries in the world that allows heliskiing, and it also has some of the most incredible scenery in Europe

Alagna

This tiny town remains largely undiscovered but provides access to some of Italy's finest freeriding

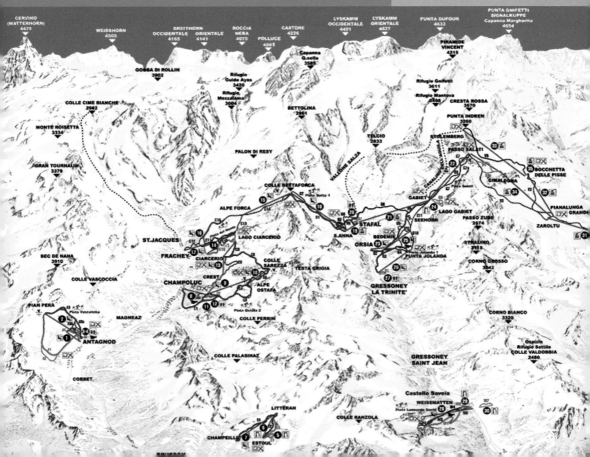

On the slopes	
Snow reliability	❄ ❄ ❄ ❄
Parks	❄ ❄
Off-piste	❄ ❄ ❄ ❄ ❄
Off the slopes	
Après ski	❄
Nightlife	❄
Eating out	❄ ❄
Resort charm	❄ ❄ ❄ ❄

The resort

'Freeriding Paradise' is written all over the lifts and town of Alagna, and for good reason. Alagna is one of the three valleys in the Monterosa area (with Champoluc and Gressoney – see Gressoney chapter, page 278), which encompasses a massive range of

"The jagged, striking mountains provide a stunning backdrop to your explorations of the surrounding peaks"

backcountry escapades. The jagged, striking mountains provide a stunning backdrop to your explorations of the surrounding peaks. If you should get bored of this magnificent area you can try heliskiing or a backcountry quest to Zermatt. Alagna's town is beautiful, centred round an eye-catching church. Beauty aside, there's not too much going on, although you can find a good glass of wine or bite to eat if you know where to look. Like its neighbouring Gressoney, Alagna is probably more suited to a weekend of intense riding, followed by a couple of relaxing evenings, than a week's holiday.

The mountains

Height: 1200–3550m

Ability	Rating
Expert	❄ ❄ ❄ ❄
Intermediate	❄ ❄ ❄
Beginner	❄

The Monterosa area is best-known for its off-piste and this extends throughout the three valleys. Now that the connecting lift between Gressoney and Alagna is completed, it makes no sense to separate them, as the Gressoney lifts lead to the Alagna off-piste and vice versa. Therefore, for information on the Alagna mountains (including lift pass prices, the park, off-piste and general info), please refer to the Gressoney chapter, page 278.

Instruction

Corpo Guide Alagna (Scuola di Alpinismo)
T: 0039 0163 913 10
E: info@guidealagna.com
W: www.guidealagna.com

Guide Monterosa
Guide Monterosa comprises 25 guides who can take you on heliskiing trips or just guide you round the mountain. They also offer a service of organising your accommodation, taxis, the works. For more information refer to the Gressoney chapter (page 278) as the company is based there.
T: 0039 0125 366 139
E: info@guidemonterosa.com
W: www.guidemonterosa.com

Lyskamm 4000
This adventure travel group offers heliskiing, freeriding, winter mountaineering, ski mountaineering and other adventure excursions as well as organising hotels and taxis if required.
T: 0039 2264 381
E: lyskamm4000@yahoo.it
W: www.lyksamm4000.com

Scuola Sci and Snowboard Alagna

A 1-hour private lesson costs €35–40 and a group lesson €25 for half a day, €45 for a full day and €110 for 5 half-days.

T: 0039 0163 91159

E: scuolascialagna@tiscali.it

Other activities

Apart from heliskiing and guiding, the only other activity is to stroll around town.

Events

In mid-February, Alagna is home to the **Telemar Karnival** (www.telemark.it) to which many budding telemarkers will flutter. The **Monterosa Skirider** (www.monterosa skirider.com) is a popular freeride competition that takes place around Easter.

Accommodation

There is a stunning 4-star hotel in Alagna called the **Hotel Cristallo** (0039 0163 922 822, info@ hotelcristalloalagna.com, www.hotelcristalloalagna .com), with top notch service and a luxurious feel. You have the choice of the lovely and colourful classic room (€160–210 per room B&B), the more roomy Prestige room (€200–260 per room B&B) or the ultimate, multi-level suite (€300–360 per room B&B). Half-board accommodation is also available. The Wellness suite, lounge and restaurant are also divine. This hotel would be a wonderful place for a romantic weekend.

The 3-star hotel **Monterosa** (0039 0163 923 209, hotelmonterosa@liberto.it, www.hotelmonterosa-alagna.it) was the first to be opened in Alagna in 1865. It is bang in the centre of the village, opposite the church and 100m from the cable car. There are 14 rooms with en-suite facilities, and an old restaurant (La Stube) with magnificent high ceilings and chandelier, although there is a feeling of eating in an archaic school dining room. Per person per day, the hotel costs €58–77 for half-board and €45–65 for B&B.

Indren Hus (0039 0163 911 52, info@indrenhus.it, www.indrenhus.it) has rooms or apartments on offer, as well as some 'panoramic attics' which boast spectacular views. All rooms have satellite TV and most have a deck or balcony. The bar and restaurant are friendly and great and there is a small fitness centre as well as a sauna and whirlpool shower. Rooms cost €35–49 for B&B and €45–63 for half-board accommodation, eating at the Dir und Don Brasserie (see Eating out) or at the Indren Stube inside the hotel. The hotel is also in association with the local wine bar (see Bars and clubs) and guests are occasionally invited to wine tastings.

Eating out

On the mountain
Rifugio Guglielmina (0163 914 44/ 0163 915 47, rifugioguglielmina@libero.it, www.rifugioguglielmina.it) has a traditional restaurant as well as accommodation, which can only be accessed off-piste. Rifugio Grande Halte (0039 0163 91104, altaquotasas@libero.it) on path no. 5, is a relaxing hut with restaurant and hotel (€45 half board) – there are 10 rooms with either 2, 4 or 6 beds. Check out the Gressoney chapter for more options (see page 278).

In town
Most of the hotels have restaurants attached, for example La Stube at the Monterosa is the place to go if you fancy a fondue or raclette. Indren also has a good restaurant. There is also a surprisingly stylish bistro in the centre of town called the Dir und Don Brasserie. This has a terrace with outside heaters and bar, and a cosy wooden interior. They serve meat, pasta, risotto and pizzas (a bargain, at €3–8). Unione is a friendly, informal restaurant and it has a good terrace. A main dish will cost €8–13.50.

Bars and clubs

As you will have guessed there's not too much going on and most people are tucked up in bed early preparing themselves for the next day. The best bar in town is the Bacher Wine Bar that's really cosy and has wine bottles covering the walls. Apart from this, the best bet is to infiltrate a local crowd and suggest that they throw a party.

Useful facts and phone numbers

Tourist office

T:	0039 0163 922 988
F:	0039 0163 912 02
E:	infoalagna@atlvalsesiavercelli.it
W:	ww.atlvalsesiavercelli.it

Emergency services

- Call 118

Getting there

By car

From Milan or Turin, take the motoway A4 or A26 and turn off at Biandrate for Gravellona Toce and Romagnano-Ghemme. Then take the main road S299 to Alagna.

By plane

Milan Linate (137km)
Milan Malpensa (98km)
Turin Caselle (170km)

All information about buses linking Alagna with Milan and Turin can be obtained by calling 0039 0163 922 988.

By train

Take the 15.11 Eurostar from London Waterloo to Paris; then an overnight train, changing at Milan and Novara, to Varallo Sesia, and then a local bus (58 minutes), arriving in resort at 09.55. Return fares from £138 in a 6-berth couchette. Contact European Rail (020 7387 0444, www.europeanrail.com). Bus tickets (€2.65 single) are purchased on the bus.

Cervinia

Not over-challenging, but great
for Sunday afternoon cruisers

KETTLER

On the slopes	
Snow reliability	✳✳✳✳
Parks	✳✳✳
Off-piste	✳
Off the slopes	
Après ski	✳✳✳
Nightlife	✳✳✳
Eating out	✳✳✳
Resort charm	✳✳

The resort

Cervina is a strange resort but regular visitors love it. The pedestrian centre is great; everything's really handy and within a few minutes' walk, there are some top bars, decent restaurants and you can ride over to Zermatt without paying Zermatt prices. On the other hand, the buildings outside of the centre are mostly pretty ugly, and the slopes aren't challenging for anyone above an intermediate level. But if you're not an expert, it will probably do you just fine.

The mountains

Height: 1525–3480m

Ability	Rating
Expert	✳
Intermediate	✳✳✳✳
Beginner	✳✳✳✳

Getting about

Cervinia has 200km of pistes of its own, and connects to the lower valley, Valtournenche, and over the Swiss border to Zermatt; in total providing 350km of accessible terrain. Most of this area is great for cruisy intermediates, but can be dull for gutsy intermediates and experts. Even though the link to Zermatt opens up some more challenging areas and good off-piste, it is really only the Schwarzsee area that is easily accessible; for the Rothorn and Stockhorn areas you have to ride down into the centre of Zermatt and then travel across town.

The park

Cervinia's park is well shaped and there is a fairly good variety of kickers. The jumps are graded, with two blues, four reds, and one black – a good 12m table with perfect transition. At the bottom of the park is a hip that you can hit from either side. Jibbers will be happy with the few rails and fun boxes. We had heard that it was only for boarders, but in fact there are just as many skiers and it has a great atmosphere. Sometimes there's a mediocre pipe, if the conditions are right. A great park for all, from learning your first jumps to pulling crowd pleasers off the big bertha.

"There's also some amazing heliskiing and boarding"

Off-piste and backcountry

Cervinia is not the place to come if all you want to do is ride off-piste. The resort gets loads of snow due to its high altitude, but it also gets strong winds, which can wreck the fresh powder. There are not many easily accessible areas, your best bet is to get a guide, and maybe head over towards Zermatt, where you will find some of the best riding in Europe. There's also some amazing heliskiing and boarding that can be done with a guide (details on page 262). Check out the Zermatt chapter (page 400) for the backcountry terrain on the Swiss side of the glacier.

Instruction

Breuil Ski School

Skiing and boarding lessons are available. Private lessons cost €30–50 per hour, depending on the number of people. Three mornings of group lessons cost €100, 5 mornings €145.

T: 0039 0166 940 960
E: info@scuoladiscibreuil.com
W: www.scuoladiscibreuil.com

Lift passes	Breuil Cervinia – Valtournenche	Inc. Zermatt
1 day	€32	€42
6 days	€174	€211
13 days	€283	€369

Discounts are made for early and late season and for children. An international daily supplement costs €27 on presentation of a multi-day pass or seasonal pass. There is a pass that can only be used in the snowpark and one for those who only use the mountains in the mornings or in the afternoons.

Cervinia Ski School

Skiing and boarding lessons are available. Private lessons cost €33–50 per hour, depending on the number of people. Group ski lessons cost €150 for 5 mornings. The school also organises heliskiing on the Monte Rosa and on the downhill from Château des Dames on the Grandes Murailles mountains.

T: 0039 0166 949 034/0166 948 744
E: info@scuolacervino.com
W: www.scuolacervino.com

Heliski Company

A drop on the Monte Rosa costs €210–260 per person and 1 day's heliskiing €330–400. Two days is €420–570 and a 3-day heliski tour of the Matterhorn and Monte Rosa costs €720–930, with a total of 8000 vertical metres of riding. The cost for a guide of the best freeriding areas is €55–65 per person.

T: 0039 0166 949 267
E: info@heliskicervinia.com
W: www.heliskicervinia.com

Other activities

Horse riding: Bepe, at the Hotel Hermitage, can take you out horse riding on the slopes (0166 948 998).
Ice skating: The natural ice skating rink is open day and night, and hockey matches are also organised here.
Night skiing: Every week guides organise a night trip in a snow-cat followed by skiing/boarding down by torchlight.
Paragliding: A half-hour paragliding flight can be organised by Fans de Sport (0347 995 018 – mobile, info@fansdesport.it). They also arrange **quad biking** on specially laid track, **kite-skiing** and **airboarding**.
Skidoos: These can be driven across the snow at night (contact Motoslitte on 0166 940 127 or 0335 565 0635).

Sports centre: Situated in Valtournenche, the Centro Polivalente has a gym, swimming pool, volleyball, tennis, 5-a-side football, a climbing wall, a sauna and a Turkish bath.

"There are some great bars, all a few minutes' walk from each other"

Accommodation

Cervinia doesn't come across as an upper-class place, but there are a load of 4-star hotels to choose from. For the ultimate in luxury, head to the **Hotel Hermitage** (0039 0166 948 998, www.hotelhermitage.com, info@hotelhermitage.com), an elegant and beautiful hotel that also manages to be welcoming and friendly. The 34 luxurious rooms and suites have fireplaces and spa baths. Facilities include a transfer service to the lifts that are 300m away, a beauty spa and swimming pool. A classic room costs €200–280, a junior suite €230–350 and a suite €320–450 (per person per night half board). Another 4-star treat is the **Hotel Europa** (0039 0166 948 660, info@htl-europa.com, www.htl-europa.com), a central hotel positioned just 600m from the minibuses to the lifts. There's a beautiful bar and a luxurious hotel lounge. A standard room costs €75–143 (per person, half board) and there is a €30 supplement for a junior suite and €50 for a suite.

www.dovesciare.it

The **Excelsior Planet** (0039 0166 949 426, info@excelsiorplanet.com, www.excelsiorplanet.com) is a lovely hotel with 35 suites and 11 rooms and is a decent price for a 4 star (€75–140 per person, half board for a standard room, supplements for a suite). They also offer short breaks. The **Sertorelli Sport Hotel** (0039 0166 949 797, info@sertorelli-cervinia.it, www.sertorelli-cervinia.it) is a 4 star that has recently been renovated. The junior suites have balconies, living rooms and whirlpools. There is also a sauna, Jacuzzi, fitness centre and beauty spa. The prices are €80–180 (per person, half-board), depending on the type of room and time of season.

For a 3-star option, check out the **Hotel Edelweiss** (0039 0166 949 078, info@matterhorn.it, www.matterhorn.it), right in the centre of town and 300m from the slopes (they have a transfer service). The layout's good, as is the bar and the prices at €64–110 per person for half board.

For 2-star hotels, **Marmore** (0039 0166 949 057, info@hotelmarmore.com, www.hotelmarmore.com) is a decent small hotel that is close to the action. They offer half-board accommodation (€495–665 per person per week), and will also rent rooms out per night if they're not fully booked. **Castelli** (0039 0166 949 183, info@aparthotel.it, www.castelli.ao.it) is an apart-hotel with 12 flats and two rooms, 300m from the slopes. A 4-person apartment costs €490–810 per week. **Petit Tibet** (0039 0166 948 974, info@petit-tibet.com, www.petit-tibet.com) has some really cheap deals for apartments (from €530 for an apartment for 4 for the week) but it is incredibly inconvenient at the top of town and you can't easily access the town centre.

Eating out

On the mountain

The refuge **Guide del Cervinio** (0039 0166 948 369), right at the top of the Plateau Rosa, is a cute and small self-service restaurant where you can pick up a sandwich for about €5–6 or a main dish for €10–23. **Les Skieurs D'Antan** is a nice restaurant right at the bottom of the mountain, just above the main cable car where you can get pasta, fish, steak or raclette (€10–23). It's also open at night. The **Igloo**, on the lower part of the Ventina run serves the best 'real meat' burgers you could hope for. Enjoy it though, it'll cost you €10 and it doesn't even come with chips!

In town

The **Copa Pan** (0166 949 140) (see Bars and clubs) has a beautiful restaurant downstairs. The pizzas are a bargain in such gorgeous surroundings, at €6–12. The **Hotel Punta Maquignaz** (0166 949 145) serves steaks and fondues in comfortable surrounds, as long as you're not put off by all the bear skins and heads in the lobby. The **Capanna Alpina** (0166 948 682) has a great, atmospheric pizzeria on its top floor, overlooking the bar. In the basement is the cosy tavern, complete with pool table and candles. The **Maison de Saussure** (0166 948 249) is tiny, snug and traditional, and reservations are a must. The **Matterhorn** (0166 948 518) is an informal but welcoming place, and serves some of the best pizzas in town. For a memorable night, try the **Baita Cretaz** (0166 949 914, baitacretaz@virgilio.it), just up the slopes from town – they will come into town on

skidoos to pick you up. One again, the food is traditional and the atmosphere relaxing.

Bars and clubs

There are some great bars in Cervinia and all are a few minutes' walk from each other to save you getting chilly in-between beers. Facing the slopes are the Yeti and the Dragon pubs. The **Yeti** (0166 949 196, www.breuil-cervinia.com/Yeti) is a dark but cosy bar with loads of big screens showing sports, internet access and good-value sandwiches, burgers and hot dogs. Between 5 and 6pm a jug of beer will cost you only €9. The **Dragon** (0166 948 085, hoteldragon@ aosanet.com) is like a big British pub. It is open 10.30am–12/1am upstairs and 2.30am downstairs. Food is served 12–3pm and 7.30–9.30pm, and the happy hours are good. It's busy at après and then again from about 9.30pm. Watch out for theme nights.

Our favourite bar for après is the **Ymeletrob** (0166 949 145), a cute and cosy wine and cocktail bar at the

end of the town centre that has chips, dips and more free snacks dotted around the bar. The prices are inflated because of the free snacks but it's worth it. The cocktail of the day tends to be a reasonable price. The **Copa Pan** (0166 940 084) has a stunning restaurant (see Eating out), a bar and a club. The bar is open 4pm–1am, and the club 10pm–3/4am. The Copa Pan attracts a mix of seasonaires and tourists and has theme nights about once a month where they really go to town; for example, on Woodstock night they laid the floor with grass and brought in tepees. The **Café des Guides** is like a big old hotel lounge with comfy, un-matching, leather chairs and a hotchpotch of patterns, pictures and memorabilia adorning the walls.

Out of town, past the cable car, towards the big apartment blocks at the top of town, there are a few shops and restaurants. There is also a fab bar and restaurant where an old cinema used to be, called the **Taverna di Gargantua** (0166 940 167). There's a massive screen that usually shows concerts and, instead of a pool table to entertain you, you can practise your golf putting.

Useful facts and phone numbers

Tourist office

T: 0039 0166 949 136
F: 0039 0166 949 731
E: breuil-cervinia@montecervino.it
W: www.cervinia.it/www.montecervino.it

Emergency services

• Police: 0166 944 311/948 103
• In a medial emergency call 118

Doctors

• Medical centre: 0166 94 01 75

Taxis and airport transfers

• Paolo Giannini: 0039 0166 62 220/0039 0335 565 3189, skitaxi@libero.it
• Pino Pession: 0039 0166 925 62/ 0039 0348 312 3036, pinopession@libero.it
• Riccardo Ferraris: 0039 0166 61 874/ 0039 0339 13 96 490, riccardoferraris@ cheapnet.it
• Sergio Meynet: 0039 0166 92 723/0039 0333 23 74 523, sergiomeynet@libero.it

Getting there

By car

From France go through the Mont Blanc tunnel and take the main road 26 from Courmayeur to Châtillon. At Châtillon, take the regional road (SR) 46 and follow signs for Valtournenche and Breuil-Cervina.

By plane

Milan (170km) Fly to either Milano Malpensa or Milano Linate.
Turin (118km)
Geneva (180km)
Transfer details can be obtained from the Consortium-Consorzio per lo Sviluppo Turistico del Comprensorio del Cervino (0039 0166 949 136, info@breuil-cervinia.it). Alternatively call a taxi transfer (see left). Car rental services, minibuses and buses can be obtained from C.A.A.R.P. (0039 0112 472 072, info@caarp.it, www.caarp.it).

By train

Take the 15.11 Eurostar from London Waterloo to Paris; then an overnight train, changing at Milan and Chivasso, to Chatillon, and then a local bus (60 minutes), arriving in resort at 10.25. Return fares from £133 in a 6-berth couchette. Contact European Rail (020 7387 0444, www.european rail.com). Bus tickets (€2 single) are purchased on the bus.

Cortina d'Ampezzo

Stunning scenery, spoilt by the pretentious town

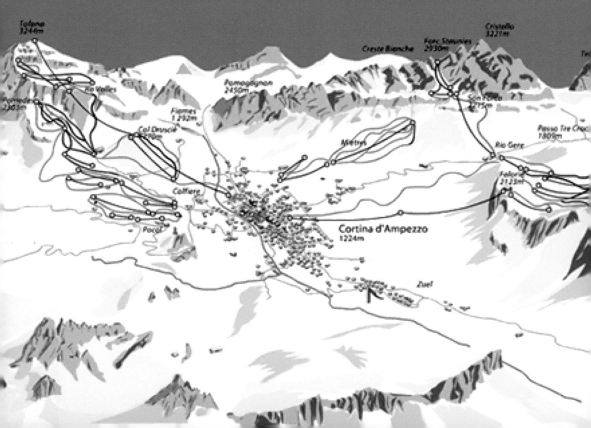

On the slopes

Snow reliability	❄ ❄ ❄
Parks	❄ ❄
Off-piste	❄ ❄

Off the slopes

Après ski	❄
Nightlife	❄
Eating out	❄ ❄
Resort charm	❄ ❄ ❄ ❄

The resort

Cortina is one of the few resorts that we really didn't get a feel for. The town is beautiful and quaint, and the Dolomite scenery some of the most dramatic and stunning in Europe, so it's not resort charm that's a problem. It's more that it doesn't feel like a ski resort, and this is largely due to the Cortina regulars. The typical lady patron of Cortina would most likely be decked out in fur at all times, and be sporting large, dark Gucci sunglasses that cover her whole face. She would not be at all fussed if she didn't go out on the mountain during the day, and would probably only make the effort to get out early in order to secure a prime deckchair spot. Come evening time she would change into even more decadent finery and walk around town three times until she was sure that everyone had seen her, at which point she could happily retire to bed to prepare for the next day. We're not trying to be cruel, everyone looked perfectly happy, and if this sounds like heaven to you, then pack your bags and trot to Cortina, but don't be surprised if you are looked down upon if you start jibbing around outside cafés in your baggy pants.

The mountains

Height: 1224–2939m

Ability	Rating
Expert	❄ ❄
Intermediate	❄ ❄ ❄
Beginner	❄ ❄ ❄ ❄

Getting about

The 115km of pistes in Cortina are a nightmare to get to – no wonder half the Cortina visitors don't bother trying. There are two main cable cars leaving Cortina town, from opposite ends of the town's fringes. It's so disjointed that you would be best off with a car, but the one-way system is so stressful and confusing that driving around is not fun. The Mandres cable car takes you up to the Faloria area, where you can find your way across to the few red runs under the

"The Dolomite scenery is some of the most dramatic and stunning in Europe"

spectacular Cristallo. Just underneath here is the separate, inconvenient Mietres that only has a few runs. From the other side of town is the cable car to Tofana, from which you can make your way over to the Socrepes area, the largest area full of cruisy blues. Cinque Torri and Passo Falzarego are two small areas that can only be accessed by car or bus, but they have the best freeride potential.

The park

Until recently this park was 'boarders only' but it is becoming a little more skier-friendly. The park is located in the Faloria area, which you can get to by catching the cable car from the bottom of the resort. There are up to four kickers (depending on the amount of snow), rails and a small half pipe. You wouldn't catch the experts and pros hanging out here, but it's good for starting off in or just having a jib.

Off-piste and backcountry

We weren't particularly inspired by this mountain as a freeride destination (apart from the incredible views,

which are hard to beat). There are places to check out, but the best bits aren't all that great, and are often inconvenient. A guide will be able to show you the areas worth visiting, which include a decent couloir at the top of Forcella Staunies (2930m), under Son Forca chair, or the narrow gorges of Bus Tofana and Canalino del Prete. Alternatively your guide could take you to the Cinque Torri or Passo Falzarego, respectable freeriding areas that can only be accessed by car or bus.

Instruction

Guide Alpine Scuola d'Alpinismo
This school can guide you round the pistes of the Sella Ronda or can teach and/or guide you in off-piste and freeride.
T: 0039 0436 868 505
E: info@guidecortina.com
W: www.guidecortina.com

Lift passes	Cortina, San Vito di Cadore, Auronzo and Misurina	Dolomiti Superski
1 day	€31	€34
6 days	€158	€171
13 days	€275	€296
Prices will be slightly less out of season and slightly more at high season. There are discounts for children and seniors.		

Scuola Sci Snowboard Cortina
Private lessons are €37–42 per hour.
T: 0039 0436 2911
E: info@scuolasciacortina.it
W: www.cortina.dolomiti.org/scuolascicortina

Other activities

Contact Cortina Adrenalin (www.adrenalincenter.it, cortina@adrenalincenter.it) for more information about the activities.

Bobsleighing: Have a go on the bobsleigh (December– February), and reach speeds of up to 75 miles an hour. If the mood takes you, you can throw yourself down the sheet ice without the aid of a bobsled, just on a crazy sledge.

> "Moonlight sledding is available too, and you get to wear a helmet with a light on it"

Ice skating and curling: The ice rink is open for skating, curling, and a crazy ice disco once a week.
Sledging: There are loads of sledging runs but most aren't that easy to get to. The handiest one can be reached by the first stage of the Mietres chairlift. This is 1km long, pisted, and reserved for sleds. You can also sledge from Rifugio Ra Stua (1668m), after an hour's walk from the car park. This 3km run has a vertical drop of 200m. The enthusiastic tobogganists should head to the Croda da Lago (2046m). The walk up is 3 hours, but you can contact the Croda da Lago refuge and see if they will get the motorsled out for you. A 4km run (550m vertical drop), starts out at the Rifugio Scoiattoli. The walk up is an hour and a half or you can take the chair from Bai de Dones, although you wind up 3.5km from where the chairlift sets off. Moonlight sledding is available too, and you get to wear a helmet with a light on it.
Snowrafting: Sit in a large rubber dinghy and fly down pretty steep snow/ice at 60 miles an hour.

Events

Cortina Winter Polo, **bobsleigh races** and the **Sleddog European Championships** are about as exciting as it gets.

Accommodation

There are two 5-star hotels: the **Cristallo** (0039 0436 881 111, info@cristallo.it, www.cristallo.it) and the **Miramonti** (0039 0436 4201, www.miramonti majestic.it, miramontimajestic@geturhotels.com). Both are beautiful big buildings but they are pretty inconvenient. The best hotel in town, in our opinion, is the 4-star **Ancora** (0039 0436 3261, www. hotelancoracortina.com, info@hotelancora cortina .com), a beautiful and traditional hotel that has won a number of awards, as well as a tribute in the *Hip Hotels Ski* book. The 2-star **Hotel Montana** (0039 0436 860 498, www.cortina-hotel.com, montana@ cortina-hotel.com) is right in the pedestrianised centre of town and is simple but cheap (€280–460 per person for 7 nights).

Eating out

On the mountain

There are lots of lovely mountain huts to stop off at for lunch, and the fur-clad contingent will head straight to them. The beautiful **Rifugio Tondi** (0436 5775) is one of the best places to lunch. You'll find it on the Tondi Normale piste (61) in the Faloria area. Under Cristallo, the **Rifugio Son Forca** (0436 866 192) has great big terraces with beautiful views and the Rio Gere (0436 3434) is a cute, family-run hut. On the other side of the valley, under Tofana, the **Pomedes** restaurant (0436 862 061) is one of the best places to stop for a bite to eat.

In town

Ra Stua restaurant (0436 868 341) do the standard pasta, risotto and meat dishes (main €9–18), and **La Botte** (0436 866 283) serves up Mexican for a change. For pizza, **Rotondo** (0436 867 777) on the main square is cosy, **Al Passetto** (0436 2254) is good, and there's a tiny little takeaway pizza place, **Al Due Forni**, opposite the cinema.

Michelin rates many restaurants around Cortina: **Tivoli** (0436 866 400) has a star and **El Toulá** (0436 3339), in a converted barn, has three Michelin forks. We liked **Restaurant Zoco** (0436 860 041), on the edge of town, as it's really cosy and serves good, smart food.

Bars and clubs

The après ski scene wasn't really our cup of tea, but there are a couple of fun places to go. The **Entoca** wine bar is the best; it's cosy and usually packed. For dancing the night away, head to the **Metro Club** or the **Limbo**.

Getting there

By car

There is a route planner on Cortina's website that will help you to plan your route.

By plane

Venice (162km)
Treviso (168km) Ryanair.
On Saturdays and Sundays there is a transfer service from Venice and Treviso airports to Cortina for the guests of Cortina Hotels. Journey time is 2 hours. You can book it on the tourist office website.
Innsbruck (156km)

By train

Take the 15.11 Eurostar from London Waterloo to Paris; then an overnight train, changing in Padova and Belluno, Calalzo di Pieve, and then a local bus (58 minutes), arriving in resort at 14.03. Return fares from £130 in a 6-berth couchette. Contact European Rail (020 7387 0444, www.europeanrail.com). Bus tickets (€2.80 single) are purchased at the station.

Courmayeur

Beautiful scenery and a gorgeous
village - one of Italy's best

On the slopes	
Snow reliability	❄ ❄ ❄
Parks	–
Off-piste	❄ ❄ ❄ ❄

Off the slopes	
Après ski	❄ ❄ ❄
Nightlife	❄ ❄ ❄
Eating out	❄ ❄ ❄ ❄
Resort charm	❄ ❄ ❄ ❄

The resort

Courmayeur is only 10 minutes away from the Mont Blanc Tunnel; a charming and picturesque village, with a maze of cobbled streets and some stylish and chic bars and restaurants. The slopes aren't extensive but

"The slopes aren't extensive but are good for cruising and posing"

are good for cruising and posing. It's a great place for people-watching too; there are some fantastic outfits walking around and most seem to have no qualms about decking themselves from head to toe in fur. If you want to parade around in the latest designer clothes, sip cocktails in classy bars and don't need a massive challenge on the slopes, this could be the resort for you.

The mountains

Height: 1210–2755m

Ability	Rating
Expert	❄ ❄ ❄
Intermediate	❄ ❄ ❄ ❄
Beginner	❄ ❄

Getting about

The slopes aren't the easiest to get to; the cable car on the edge of town takes you across the river to the mountains and most choose to take this lift down at the end of the day rather than to come down across the river and face the wait for the bus back to town. There are only 36km of slopes that are mostly cruisy runs, a few challenging pistes for the expert and no park, but there is some decent off-piste. Check out some of our favourite runs below and contact Società Guide Alpine for more information (see Instruction).

The park

We don't understand why Courmayeur doesn't have a park. There are a few areas that would be ideally suited to one. If you want to jump, get your shovel and start digging. There is a boardercross but it seems to get neglected.

Off-piste and backcountry

There's tons of good backcountry around Courmayeur. As well as loads of wicked tree riding, you will find routes to La Thuile, and to La Rosière and Chamonix in France.

The Valley Blanche Descent is one not to miss. It starts at Punta Helbronner (3462m) and ends in Chamonix (1037m); a 24km descent in the heart of the Mont Blanc Massif on the glaciers of the Colle del Gigante descending into the Valley of Chamonix. This is an amazing adventure across the Mar de Glace sea of ice that takes you through crevasses and ice tunnels. Don't do this one without a guide.

The Toula Glacier is a great place to go in the right conditions. From Helbronner point (3462m) you can get to the Toula pass (3450m) in a few minutes. Then you have to make your way up a metal staircase to get to the Toula Glacier, after which you have a 2000m descent back down to La Palud Courmayeur. You don't have to be a pro to do this, as long as you feel comfortable off-piste you should be fine, though it is recommended to take a guide.

We rate the guides from the Società Guide Alpine Courmayeur centre who can show you the routes we have described and many more as well as heliskiing and boarding. They're located in the centre of town and are reasonably priced.

Lift passes	
1 day	€34
6 days	€175
13 days	€315

Instruction

Guide Alpine del Monte Bianco
T: 0039 0165 809 469
E: carbogia@tiscali.it
W: www.giannicarbone.com

High Performance Mountain Guide Alpine
T: 0039 335 634 2771/0039 349 258 6288
E: info@guidehpmountain.com
W: www.guidehpmountain.com

Scuola Sci/ Snowboard, Courmayeur
This ski and snowboard school offers freeride, freestyle, tours and camps. Private lessons cost €30–42 per hour depending on the time of season and time of day. A 21-hour ski or snowboard camp costs €184.
T: 0039 0165 842 477
E: info@scuolascimontebianco.com
W: www.scuolascimontebianco.com

Società Guide Alpine Courmayeur
Skiers and snowboarders can discover more of the Courmayeur ski area through backcountry and freeride guides, ski-touring, heliskiing, mountaineering and ice-fall climbing. Guiding costs €64 –169 per person, depending on the location.
T: 0039 0165 842 064
E: info@guidecourmayeur.com
W: www.guidecourmayeur.com

Other activities

When not on the mountain, most people choose to wander round town in their best designer kit, elegantly sipping cocktails and looking gorgeous, but there are a few other things to entertain you.

Forum sports centre: Most of the sporting activities can be found at this huge sports centre (0165 844 096) with ice skating, ice hockey matches to watch, indoor tennis, squash, gym and climbing wall. It's across the river and contains the Planet bar (see Bars and clubs).

Ice-fall climbing This costs €157 per person in a group of 4 (see Società Guide Alpine details above).

Mountain guide museum: This is worth a look if you're interested in guiding and mountaineering in the olden days.

Paragliding, snow-biking and dog-sledding: Contact the tourist office for more details (see Useful facts and phone numbers).

Spa: Just a few kilometres from Courmayeur is the stunning spa centre of Pré-Saint-Didier (0039 0165 867 272, info@termedipre.it, www.termedipre.it). Recently transformed after 30 years of inactivity, this really is a temple of wellness and is worth a visit. The water of Pré-Saint-Didier is famous for its soothing properties (due to its low mineralisation), regenerating properties (due to the iron content) and anti-rheumatic qualities (due to moderate radioactivity).

Accommodation

There are some seriously swish and swanky hotels in Courmayeur, as you would expect, as well as a few cheaper options. The Royal and Golf Hotel (0039 0165 831 611, www.royalegolf.com, hotelroyalgolf@ventaglio.com) is smart and luxurious. There are 86 elegant rooms, all kitted out with internet connection, satellite tv and mini bar. There is also a fitness centre, gym, sauna, steam room and massage facilities. Rooms cost from €115 per person per night for half board. It's exactly what you would expect of a smart hotel, but it's pretty impersonal. We would rather stay at the Hotel Mont Blanc Perrier

"A traditional and elegant place with a welcoming and cosy atmosphere"

(0039 0165 846 555), a traditional and elegant place with a welcoming and cosy atmosphere. All rooms have video recorder and mini bar. You will find the Hotel Mont Blanc on the left of the main square as you drive into town.

Less than a minute's walk from the cable car is the retro-looking Le Grand Chalet (0039 0165 841 448, www.legrandchalet.it, info@legrandchalet.it). This apart-hotel consists of 33 apartments, including 13 studios, 17 one-bedroom flats and 3 two-bedroom flats. Prices start at €550 for a small studio. Also close to the lifts is the cosy Hotel Courmayeur (0039 0165 846 732, www.hotelcourmayeur.com, info@ hotelcourmayeur.com), which is full of character. Rooms can only be rented for a full week, Sunday to Sunday, and start at €490 per person. Try to get a room with a balcony.

Eating out

On the mountain

There are loads of choices in Courmayeur when it comes to eating on the mountain; from snacks to delicious bites in rustic huts – the most well known of which is **Maison Vieille** (0165 809 399), infamous for its homemade pasta, wood-fired oven and friendly service. For sunny terraces and snack bars, head over to the Val Veny side of the valley and try the **Grolla** (0165 869 095), **La Fodze** or **Zerotta** (0165 869 091).

In town

Cadran Solaire is a gorgeous, romantic and rustic restaurant. A main meal will cost you €14–22. **Pierre Alexis** is a smart restaurant, renowned for being an expensive place but not everything will cost you a fortune; pasta dishes start at €10. The gastronomic menus will set you back €70/€100 for a 2–4 course meal. The **Leone Rosso** is a small and charming restaurant that serves great regional specialities. Dishes include pastas, fish, meat and fondues and will cost you €10–20.

For a quick snack at après ski, head to the **Petit Bistrot**, where you can sit in a small, cosy and busy atmosphere tucking into a tasty crêpe. **Coquelicot** is one of the few places that still does beef fondues (€24), as well as cheese fondues and lots of fish. **Pizzeria du Tunnel** is a good-value and cute snack bar that serves homemade pastas, pizzas, omelettes and steaks. They also do massive pizzas for sharing (€18) and heart-shaped pizzas on request!

Mont Frety, on the road that leads from the town to the gondola, is a good pizzeria that is less pricey than most of the other options and not at the expense of quality. A pizza will cost you €6.50–10 and meaty main meals €11–18. **Poppy's Bar** (see Bars and clubs) also serves great pizzas for lunch and at night; 7–10pm you can pay €10 for any wood-fired pizza and a beer.

Bars and clubs

The **Roma** is the best bar in town, especially for après ski. It's beautiful and cosy and there is a huge amount of food out for you to munch on whilst you drink. The **Café Della Posta** looks like a regular café but if you sneak through to the room at the back you will find a huge stone fireplace with a roaring fire, a few tables and some snug sofas and chairs. **Cadran Solaire** (see Eating out) has a gorgeous, but expensive bar attached. **Ziggy's** is the place to go to check your E-mails. Down one of the winding backstreets, this dark, basement bar opens at 3pm. **Poppy's Bar** (bar/restaurant/club) is convenient, big, good value and fun. **Planet**, at the sports complex in La Villette across the river, is a huge open bar/club that has a big stage for live music and DJs; it also has pool and table football tables. It's open 11am–2am and looks very much like a student union bar with long wooden tables and a lived-in feel. It's inconvenient if you're staying in town but is a good night out and you can get a burger for under €4!

"A huge open bar/club that has a big stage for live music and DJs"

Useful facts and phone numbers

Tourist office

T: 0039 0165 842 060
F: 0039 0165 842 072
E: info@aiat-monte-bianco.com
W: www.aiat-monte-bianco.com

Emergency services

- Police: 0165 890 720/ 0165 831 334
- Medical emergency: 118

Doctors

- Dr Bahren: 0165 862 514
- Dr Di Cesare: 340 979 5327
- Dr Mannu: 0165 809 853
- Dr Rocchio: 0165 841 113

Taxis

- P.le Monte Bianco Courmayeur: 0165 842 960

Getting there

By car

Courmayeur is easy to get to from France as it is only 10 minutes' drive from the Mont Blanc Tunnel. Make sure you don't speed whilst you're in the tunnel – they'll catch you on the other side.

By plane

Geneva (100km)
Turin (150km)
Transfer from both airports takes around 2 hours.

By train

Take the 17.42 Eurostar from London Waterloo to Paris; then an overnight train, changing at St-Gervais-Les-Bains, to arrive in Chamonix station at 09.25 (this is 4 hours faster with fewer changes). Then take a taxi (30 minutes, €90 per taxi) to Courmayeur. Return fares start at £124 in a 6-berth couchette. Contact Rail Europe (08705 848 848, www.raileurope.co.uk) or European Rail (020 7387 0444, www.europeanrail.com).

Gressoney

The heliskiing capital of Europe
and a quiet, unspoilt town

On the slopes	
Snow reliability	❄ ❄ ❄
Parks	–
Off-piste	❄ ❄ ❄ ❄
Off the slopes	
Après ski	❄
Nightlife	❄
Eating out	❄ ❄
Resort charm	❄ ❄ ❄ ❄

The resort

Gressoney, in the Monterosa ski area, is a beautiful, quiet and unspoilt village; many of the local families have lived here for over 500 years. There's little to do in the evenings in this idyllic community, although this is probably for the best in order for you to keep your strength up for the next day on the mountain, as Gressoney has access to extensive backcountry terrain and some of the finest

"A long weekend of heliskiing and mountain exploration would be a first-rate trip"

heliskiing in Europe. Like its neighbour, Alagna and La Grave in France, Gressoney would not be the model resort for most. However, for the earnest skiers (Gressoney is less suitable for boarders) who value their time on the mountain more than in the pub, and would take pleasure in tranquil, yet spectacular surroundings, a long weekend of heliskiing and mountain exploration would be a first-rate trip.

Gressoney consists of two separate villages. Gressoney La Trinité is at the end of the valley where the lifts to the Monterosa ski area are located. Here you

will find a number of convenient hotels, and a couple of local facilities. Gressoney St Jean is further from the lifts (it does have a few of its own, but the reason you're here is to experience the Monterosa area so we wouldn't bother too much with these) but is larger and has more hotels, restaurants and facilities. However, this part of town does extend over a few kilometres and the restaurants and hotels require a certain amount of travel between them. Although the bus service isn't bad, we wouldn't come here without a car.

The mountains

Height: 1200–3550m

Ability	Rating
Expert	❄ ❄ ❄ ❄
Intermediate	❄ ❄ ❄
Beginner	❄

Getting about

There are 200km of pistes in Monterosa, and a landscape that consists of almost endless off-piste. Snowboarders are advised to go elsewhere – there is a fair bit of traversing on most of the off-piste itineraries. The piste map is pretty shocking, but the signs on the mountain are good so just decide where you're headed and follow the signs. From anywhere on the mountain you can also be guaranteed stunning views, not least of the striking Monte Rosa glacier.

Terrain was first opened up by the cable car connecting Gressoney and Alagna. On top of this, there are plans to enhance the available territory even further by installing a lift in Alagna from Passo Salati to Cresta Rossa and demolishing the old cable car from Bocchetta to Indren. This would extend off-piste opportunities enormously, although there is no time scale for when this might take place.

The Monterosa area tends to remain in good condition until the end of April and the later half of the season is usually the best time to visit.

The park

In between Gressoney and Alagna there is a small park which consists of two rails, one of which is kinked, one table top over a 6m gap and a pretty wicked hip jump. There are also two fun boxes at the bottom. You wouldn't come here if riding the park was all you wanted to do, but it's still good for a change.

Off-piste and backcountry

Gressoney has fantastic access to massive backcountry areas, being right in the centre of the Monterosa area, which is renowned for its backcountry expeditions. There are a number of off-piste itineraries marked on the map – we had a great long run down from the **Punta Indren** on the way back from Alagna to Gressoney. These routes are fairly easy to explore without a guide if you are a confident off-piste rider.

Understandably, many people come to Gressoney and Alagna for the heliskiing on the Monte Rosa. We highly recommend the Guide Monterosa (see Instruction), who offer guiding, touring and heli-trips, with four different drop-offs. If you are splashing out on a heli-trip try the descent down the huge Alexandra couloir or the descent right down to Zermatt. This trip usually involves a helicopter flight to the Col du Lys (4270m) and descent towards the Swiss side of the Monte Rosa (Grenz glacier) to Furi, a hamlet of Zermatt. The cable car will take you to the Matterhorn with a descent to Frachey near Champoluc and from here you will return to Gressoney using the Monte Rosa lifts.

Heliskiing is by no means the only way to get the best out of the mountain; the day, weekend or week-long excursions planned by the Guide Monterosa, are a fantastic way to explore. If couloirs are your thing, head to the Balma area, which can be reached from the Gressoney lift, or the Salza Valley, which has a huge area of powder and several couloirs. The Lost Valley and the Bettolina area in-between Gressoney and Champoluc (which involves 1.5 hours with skins on) are two vast and astonishing areas that are worth a look.

If you would like to explore the off-piste but are lacking in confidence you can ask for a special package in which you spend three days with an instructor and three days with a guide (see Instruction).

To learn how to use your avalanche equipment, visit the Ortovox training ground at the Passo dei Salati.

Lift passes	
1 day	€32
6 days	€136/170 (depending on season)

Instruction

Guide Monterosa

This guiding association has been in existence for over ten years and its guides know the mountains better than anyone. There are 25 guides who speak a number of languages and can cater for any level of experience. They offer days for experienced riders such as a day tour of the Monte Rosa where you can ski over to Zermatt and back with the use of helicopters (€215 per person, see Off-piste and backcountry above), a day exploring the off-piste (€250 for a guide for the day) or a day's heliski (€190 per person). If you wish, they can arrange an airport to airport service, including your hotel, taxis, lift pass, skis/board, guiding – the lot.

T: 0039 349 367 4950/0039 0125 366 019
E: info@guidemonterosa.com
W: www.guidemonterosa.com

Scuola Sci Gressoney Monte Rosa

Lessons are offered in skiing, boarding, carving and freeriding. A 1-hour private lesson costs €31–45 depending on the number of people. Group lessons cost €130 for 12.5 hours.

T: 0039 349 367 4950/0039 0125 366 019
E: info@gressoneymonterosa.it
W: www.scuolascigressoney.it

> ## "The cable car will take you to the Matterhorn with a descent to Frachey near Champoluc"

Scuola Sci Gressoney St Jean
Prices are as on page 280.
T: 0039 0125 355 291
E: scuolasciw@gressoneymonterosa.it
W: www.scuolascigressoney.com

Other activities

There's not a huge amount to do in Gressoney, although there is a toboggan run in Gressoney St Jean and a popular cross-country skiing track (contact the tourist office).

Events

Once every two years the **Mezzalama Trophy** (www.trofeomezzalama.org) occurs; a 45km race from Cervinia to Gressoney La Trinité over snow, rock and ice at an average altitude of 4000m.

Accommodation

There are 23 hotels in Gressoney and 1800 beds. There should be something for most tastes, be it moderately priced, romantic or convenient.

Gressoney St Jean

Situated in a small hamlet is a top quality, moderately priced hotel, the 2-star **Hotel Villa Tedaldi** (0039 0125 355 123, villatedaldi@virgilio.it), that is more like a stately home than a hotel. It's a charming building, grand and old fashioned, with eight large rooms that each have private bathroom, TV, phone and great view. The hotel offers only B&B accommodation, at €35–50 per person per night (assuming double room; there are reductions for 3rd/4th beds). The best thing about this place is that is allows short stays (which many hotels don't), which is perfect as Gressoney is the ideal place for a long weekend.

The stunning **Lyshaus** (0039 0125 356 644, info@lyshaus.com, www.lyshaus.com), has the most incredible rooms and suites – we have no idea why it has only a 3-star rating. Many of the rooms have separate lounges, hydromassage showers and a luxurious and romantic feel. And the bedrooms aren't the best feature of the hotel – this prize would have to go to the remarkable billiard room. Picture an upper

"Many of the rooms have separate lounges, hydromassage showers and a luxurious and romantic feel"

class golf club with cigar-smoking aristocracy; there are wooden floors, a massive old billiard table, panelled walls lined with expensive old wines and a small wooden bar with racks of champagne glasses and dusty bottles of champagne. It also has a beautiful, candlelit restaurant (Carducci) serving dishes such as fondues, risottos and a variety of meats. A main meal will cost you around €10–16. One night at the Lyshaus will cost €40–120 per person.

If you like to cater for yourself you could try the 4-star **Residenze des Sole** (0039 0125 357 400, reception@residenzadelsole.it, www.residenzadel sole.it) that has a number of facilities including a pool, sauna, gym, billiard room, beauty salon, cocktail bar and restaurant.

Gressoney La Trinité

If you like hopping out of bed straight on to the lifts you'll want to stay in this part of the resort. The 3-star **Hotel Jolanda Sport** (0039 0125 366 140, info@jolandasport.com, www.hoteljolandasport.com) is about as close to the slopes as you can get and is a lovely hotel. However, you can only book for the whole week and half-board accommodation is essential. The week will cost €462–710 per person. Also close to the slopes is the friendly **Hotel Dufour** (0039 0125

366 139, info@hoteldufour.it, www.hoteldufour.it), with a homely feel and a large, comfy bar area in which you can curl up with a book. The Dufour costs from €350 per week B&B and from €455 for half board.

If you're on a budget there are a number of other options. In Issime (approximately a 10 minute drive away), for example, you can stay at the friendly **Albergo Poste** (0039 0125 344 204, www.hotelpostais sime.com) for around €60 per room per night.

Eating out

On the mountain
The **Bedemie** (0125 366 429), is a cute little restaurant with a big terrace, serving simple food such as slices of pizza, sandwiches, pasta, soup and lasagne. Our favourite restaurant is the **Morgenrot**, just below the Bedemie on the way back down into Gressoney. From the outside it looks like a rowdy bar with music playing and Carlsberg banners but inside it is a beautiful restaurant with great food (homemade pastas and chunky chips) at reasonable prices (dishes cost €8–12) and lots of character. The **Gabiet** is a good, simple establishment with a terrace overlooking

the snowpark and the **Rifugio Guglielmina** (0163 914 44, info@rifugioguglielmina.it, www.rifugioguglielmina.it) has a traditional restaurant as well as accommodation, which can only be accessed off-piste. Finally the **Alpenhütte Lys** (0125 366 057), by the side of the chair from Gabiet to Passo Salati, has a stunning terrace with hand-built wooden loungers looking out on to the pistes and the mountains. A great place to watch the sun fade after a run down the Punta Indren.

In town
In **St Jean** there are a few standard restaurants; the **Flora Alpina** has a big and bright restaurant with lots of plants. The **Genzianella** is cute, wooden and good value (if you can understand the Italian menu) and **Marmotte** at the Residenza del Sole looks smart but is, once again big and bright with little atmosphere. **Carducci** at the Lyshaus hotel is one of the finest restaurants in town (see Accommodation). Another is the **Nordkapp** (http://nordkapp.too.it) in the centre of the cobbled square. This charming restaurant has a great couple in charge, and the chefs met working at Mal Maison in Glasgow! It's pretty weird hearing an Italian speak English with a Glaswegian accent. They mix local specialities with their own culinary ideas and experiences and create beautiful food. There's also a cute bar downstairs with

a little fire. In La Trinité there are only a handful of places to eat, most of them in the hotels. One great, atmospheric pizzeria is the **Walserchild**, where you can get a tasty pizza for only €5–8.

Bars and clubs

There isn't a huge choice of bars; a lot of the hotels claim to have bars but there is rarely anyone in them. In La Trinité there is pretty much only the **Schnee Blume**, opposite the Jolanda Sport hotel, that's a simple cosy bar, aimed at the local trade. The bar at the **Dufour** is big and comfy. In St Jean you have the choice of the olde worlde **Bierfall** in the centre of town – a cute, and once again local place, and the **Sport Bar**, a small place with some kind of character and a small TV.

Getting there

By car

Take the A5 motorway from Turin to Aosta, exit at Pont-Saint-Martin and take the highway for the Valle di Gressoney.

By plane

Turin (100km) has the quickest and easiest access to Gressoney.
Milan (165km)

By train

Take the 15.11 Eurostar from London Waterloo to Paris; then an overnight train, changing in Milan and Chivasso, to Pont St Martin, and then a local bus (65 minutes), arriving in resort at 10.15. Return fares from £130 in a 6-berth couchette. Contact European Rail (020 7387 0444, www.europeanrail.com). Bus tickets (€3 single) are purchased on the bus.

Useful facts and phone numbers

Tourist office

T: 0039 0125 366 143 (La Trinité)/
     0039 0125 355 185 (St Jean)
F: 0039 0125 366 323
E: info@aiatmonterosawalser.it
W: www.aiatmonterosawalser.it/
     www.monterosa-ski.com

Emergency services

- Police: 0125 355 304
- In the case of medical emergency call 118.

Doctors

- Dr Silvio Boggio (338 115 88 66) visits Gressoney every day at various times.
- Dr Aldo Mignini (339 435 13 58) also visits Gressoney.
- During the day there is usually at least one doctor available, at any other time call 118.

Taxis

- 347 578 7132
- 0125 355 957

Selva in Val Gardena

The breathtaking landscape will strike you first, then the extensive terrain and pleasant town; perfect for families

On the slopes	
Snow reliability	✳ ✳ ✳
Parks	✳
Off-piste	✳ ✳ ✳

Off the slopes	
Après ski	✳ ✳ ✳
Nightlife	✳ ✳ ✳
Eating out	✳ ✳ ✳
Resort charm	✳ ✳ ✳

The resort

Selva Gardena is just one of the villages within the Val Gardena valley. The alternative towns of Ortisei and S Cristina are just as charming, but Selva has the best access to the slopes and the best selection of restaurants and bars. The Dolomite landscape is absolutely breathtaking and the extent of the slopes is equally impressive. Intermediate cruisers will be in heaven with the far-reaching Sella Ronda circuit, that takes you on a spectacular journey round the Gruppo Sella – a magnificent limestone massif.

At first you will probably be confused by the language, no matter how good your skills are, as many locals still speak the age old dialect of Ladin. Fortunately all speak Italian and German as well and English is also pretty widespread. Road signs are also often expressed in the local dialect so expect to see signs for Wolkenstein (Selva) and Gröden (Val Gardena).

The mountains

Height: 1250–2520m

Ability	Rating
Expert	✳ ✳ ✳
Intermediate	✳ ✳ ✳ ✳ ✳
Beginner	✳ ✳ ✳ ✳

Getting about

The 510km of pistes will more than satisfy the adventurous intermediate, but the experts and beginners are also pretty well catered for. The serious experts

should give heliskiing a go or perhaps try the more demanding Porta Vescovo trail from Arabba.

The Sella Ronda circuit can take up to 6 hours depending on queues and how speedy you are, so don't crawl out of bed hungover at midday and decide to give it a shot; you might end up paying for a taxi back. You can set off clockwise or anticlockwise.

The park

There is a park in Selva that has a mediocre half pipe and a couple of hits that would be OK to learn some tricks or just have a jib, as well as a little park for kids by the euro chair.

"Exploration requires a guide here, or you will get lost"

Off-piste and backcountry

Despite most of the terrain being fairly flat, there are some easily accessible bowls that are great after a snowfall. Exploration requires a guide here, or you will get lost. Ask them to show you the Mezdi Valley, the 'Grand Canyon' of the Dolomites, and a freerider's heaven with enough terrain for a whole day's riding in untracked snow (in good conditions).

Instruction

Ski and Boarders Factory

A 1-hour private lesson costs from €30–42 for 1 person (€9–10 for each additional person). Costs rise in high season. A course of 6 half days costs €133/160 (low/high season respectively).
T: 0039 0471 795 156
E: info@ski-factory.it
W: www.ski-factory.it

Ski and Snowboard School '2000'

A private lesson will cost from €30 and a group lesson from €35 for 1 day (3 hours), €85 for 3 days (9 hours) and €113 for 5 days (15 hours). Expect to pay more in high season. They can also offer you a package with equipment included.

T: 0039 0471 773125
E: snowboardvalgardena@hotmail.com
W: www.snowboardvalgardena.com or
www.skischool-valgardena.com

Val Gardena Mountain Guide Association

This guiding school offers everything from guiding, touring, ice climbing, off-piste and freeride, to glacier hiking.

T: 0039 0471 794133
E: info@guidegardena.com
W: www.guidegardena.com

Other activities

Climbing: There are two climbing walls. The Iman Sports Centre in S Cristina (0471 793 793) has a climbing wall but you cannot hire climbing equipment.
Horse-drawn sleighs: On the top station of the cableway Alpe di Siusi there are horse-drawn sleighs. Fares are approximately €28–45 for 1 hour.
Ice climbing and glacier hiking: Val Gardena Mountain Guide Association offers ice climbing and glacier hiking as well as many other exhausting activities. For contact details see Instruction.
Ice skating: There's an ice stadium in Selva (0471 794 265).
Nativity: The biggest nativity in the world is exhibited in the Sport Centre Iman of S Cristina. Each year new figures are added.
Night skiing: Every Tuesday, Thursday and Friday at 7.30pm Taxi Gardena (0335 560 6141, www.taxigardena.com) organises night skiing on floodlit slopes followed by après ski at Richy's Igloo. Transfer back to the hotel is included (at about 11pm).
Shooting: Facilities at the shooting centre.
Sleigh rides by night: Taxi Gardena (see Night skiing) organise sleigh rides by night. They take you to the Seiseralm, where you make an ascent by snowcat to the Dialer Lodge and then have dinner at 2145m. Depart at 7pm and return to your hotel at 11pm.
Swimming: There is an outdoor and indoor pool with wellness facilities.
Tennis: The massive tennis centre incorporates six tennis courts, two squash courts, billiards, bowling and a fitness centre.
Tobogganing: If tobogganing is your thing, there is a 6km sled run from the Rasciesa chairlift in Ortisei. The middle station allows you to go down the first part as many times as you like. You can hire sleds when you get there.

Events

There aren't too many New School events apart from a **Big Air Comp** that is usually held in late March. The **FIS World Cup (Super G and Downhill)** is also held in Val Gardena in December. The **Ski Jörring** event in February is a good one to watch. In this event 16 ski instructors, pulled by horses, compete against each other for the champion's title. If you see girls dressed up as witches don't be alarmed, it may just be the **Watch out for Witches** day; just one of the strange customs of Val Gardena.

Lift passes	Val Gardena (as far as Passo Sella and Passo Gardena)		Whole of the Dolomites	
	Low season	High season	Low season	High season
1 day	€31	€35	€34	€38
6 days	€158	€180	€171	€194
13 days	€275	€312	€296	€337

There are discounts for passes bought in December and for children and seniors. You can also buy tickets that will allow you 10 days out of 14 on the mountain so you can have a few chill-out days in town. The cards now have a chip in them for handsfree access to lifts – to get these free, book online at www.DolomitiSuperski.com.

Accommodation

The 5-star **Alpenroyal Sporthotel** (0039 0471 795 555, www.alpenroyal.com, info@alpenroyal.com), on the outskirts of town, is a large and smart complex, although it does have a slight 80s tinge to it. There is a swimming pool and a games room with a pool table and table footie. It's not too handy for town but they do have a shuttle service. The lovely **Hotel Aaritz** (0039 0471 795 011, www.val-gardena .com/hotel/aaritz, aaritz@valgardena.it) has a fantastic location in the centre of town and right opposite the lift. The pool, sauna and gym are another advantage.

We loved the beautiful **Hotel Freina** (0039 0471 795 110, www.hotelfreina.com, info@hotelfreina .com), a stunning chalet hotel just a couple of minutes from town and right next to the lifts. The rooms are huge (especially superior rooms and suites: 35–44m^2) and the whirlpool and sauna are a great place to relax after a hard day on the slopes. Prices are €76–138 per person per day for half-

board accommodation. **Hotel Laurin** (0039 0471 795 296, www.malleier.com, info@malleier.com) is the place to stay if you want to be in the centre of the action. Right in the centre of town, this hotel contains the popular après bar and restaurant Laurinkeller as well as a sauna, steam bath, Turkish bath, whirlpool and gym. Prices start from €70 per night but can be up to €125 depending on the type of room you are looking for.

Eating out

On the mountain
There are tons of cute and cosy huts dotted all over the Sella Ronda circuit. Our favourite was the **Baita Vallongian** (0471 794 071) that can be found on the route from Ciampino to Plan de Gralba. It is a stunning spot to sit and relax, either in the deckchairs or on the big wooden benches outside. The food is superb and it's the sort of place you could sit all afternoon – until the Italian folk music takes its toll. Other favourites are the

Piz Setëur (335 613 9112), especially for an après ski beer and the **Panorama** (0471 795 372) for its cosy and rustic atmosphere. For value, you can't beat the restaurant at the top of the cable car from Selva, where you can pick up a slice of pizza for €3.

In town

Pizzas, pasta and local dishes are the staple food of the restaurants in Selva. **L'Medel** (0471 795 235), on the outskirts of town, has loads of character and charm, and is well worth a very short taxi ride or drive. It has a really cute little bar and the restaurant serves hundreds of fantastic pizzas. Another stunning place to enjoy a pizza is the **Sun Valley** (0471 771 508, www.hotel sunvalley.it). Its classic wooden feel creates a superb, cosy atmosphere. For more casual surroundings, head to **Rino's** (0471 795 272), **Laurinkeller** (0471 795 004) for ribs, steaks and snacks or **La Bula** (0471 795 208), a pizzeria/club at the Hotel Stella. The restaurant at **Hotel**

Freina (0471 795 110) is really lovely and serves a huge range of tasty food.

Bars and clubs

One of the great things about Val Gardena compared to many other European resorts is the prices, so get drinking. For après, the liveliest haunt is the **Luislkeller**, which you may never leave.Both the Luislkeller and **Laurinkeller** are kicking at all times of the evening – expect lots of beer swinging and dancing to the DJ's beats. Other options for après ski are the cosy **La Stua**, where you will often find live folk music, or the **Goalies Irish Pub** that also has live music to entertain the après crowd. Goalies has a proper pub feel and serves Guiness, Carling and Murphy's. Those looking for a dance later on should boogie on to **La Bula**; the pizzeria-turned-club at the Hotel Stella.

Useful facts and phone numbers

Tourist office

T:	0039 0471 795 122
F:	0039 0471 794 245
E:	selva@valgardena.it
W:	www.valgardena.it

Emergency services

- In an emergency call 118
- Police: 113
- Avalanche information: 0471 271 177
- Medical Services Selva: 0471 794 266

Taxis

- Autosella: 0471 790 033, taxi-autosella@val-gardena.com
- Bauer Martin: 335 560 6141, www.taxigardena.com
- Wienen Schmalzl M: 0471 796 543

Getting there

By car

Use the Brenner Motorway (A22) and take the Chiusa/Val Gardena exit. You should reach Selva after 20–30 minutes.

By plane

Bolzano (40km)
Innsbruck (120km)
Verona (190km)
Airport transfers can be arranged by bus or taxi (see above) or by helicopter! Check out www.elikos.it for more information.

By train

Take the Friday 16.39 Eurostar from London Waterloo to Brussels; then the Bergland Express overnight skitrain, changing in Innsbruck, to Bolzano, and then a local bus (80 minutes), arriving in resort at 13.02. Return fares start at £215 in a 6-berth couchette. Contact European Rail (020 7387 0444, www.europeanrail.com). Bus tickets (€5 single) are purchased on the bus.

Norway

Small, quiet resorts that
perk up at the weekend

Hemsedal

The best-known resort in Norway, with reliable snow but limited terrain

Totten 1497 m

Tinden 1444 m

Rogjin 1370

HEMSEDAL

Rv 52

skistar.c

On the slopes	
Snow reliability	❄ ❄ ❄ ❄
Parks	❄ ❄ ❄ ❄
Off-piste	❄ ❄ ❄
Off the slopes	
Après ski	❄ ❄ ❄
Nightlife	❄ ❄
Eating out	❄ ❄
Resort charm	❄ ❄

The resort

Hemsedal is the best place for riding in Norway, but this still doesn't make it a real player in comparison to the resorts in France, Austria and Switzerland. The snow is really reliable but there's not a lot going on in the resort, with most visitors popping in for a weekend. The ski area is a few kilometres from the village centre but the free bus service isn't bad.

The mountains

Height: 625–1920m

Ability	Rating
Expert	❄ ❄
Intermediate	❄ ❄
Beginner	❄ ❄ ❄

Getting about

Hemsedal has the highest alpine point of Scandinavia, at 1500m above sea level and a vertical drop of 810m. There are 43km of slopes with the longest slope at 6km. The terrain is limited, and not the best for cruisy intermediates but the beginners' slopes are pretty good and experts can amuse themselves on the eight black slopes, off-piste or in the fantastic park. Make sure you get wrapped up; it's cold.

The park

Hemsedal is very proud of its freestyle park, and rightly so. Each year money is pumped into expanding and developing it, ensuring that it is up there as one of the very best.

In the main park they have catered for all standards of rider. They have a red line for advanced skiers and boarders, and a black line for the experts and pros. The 600m-long park contains two half pipes, jumps, table tops, quarter pipe, big air, boxes and rail slides.

More recently, Hemsedal built the Blue Park for beginner freestylers and those looking for a gentle jib. This has a blue line with the same sorts of jumps, table tops and rails as the main park, only smaller.

The parks are groomed every day and the pipes are re-shaped two or three times a week. On top of this, the elements are painted and outlined every day to make them visible.

> "The parks are groomed every day and the pipes are re-shaped two or three times a week"

Off-piste and backcountry

Off-piste conditions are usually pretty decent as Hemsedal gets a good share of snow. The top of the Totten summit (1450m) is the best place to head for freeriding, where you are more than likely to find some fresh snow, and fun cliff drops. There is also a popular couloir that is fairly steep and long, but it's not over-fierce. There's no shortage of trees and there are some good routes amongst them. You can also find some off-piste just to the side of the pisted areas, from the top of Hamaren.

Lift passes	
1 day	NOK 320
6 days	NOK 1320

Instruction

Hemsedal Ski School

Group lessons for 5 days (90 minutes per day) costs NOK 745. A course in the park for 3 days (90 minutes per day) is NOK 625. Private lessons cost NOK 670 for one person for 100 minutes, including video analysis. A personal trainer for 1–5 people costs NOK 995 for 3 hours, and NOK 1795 for 5 hours, both with video analysis.

T: 0047 32 05 53 90
E: skiskolen@skihemsedal.no
W: www.skistar.co/English/hemsedal

Kruse Topptur

For more information, see the website.

T: 0047 41 41 96 82
E: info@topptur.no
W: www.topptur.com

Norske Opplevelser

One day a week there is a 6–8 hour guided mountain tour to one of Hemsedal's peaks. They also offer off-piste guiding, which costs NOK 1050 for 4 hours for 1 person. The 2nd person costs NOK 595, the 3rd NOK 450 and the 4th–10th NOK 495. A beginner's course (2.5 hours) costs NOK 295.

T: 0047 32 06 00 03
E: info@norskeopplevelser.no
W: www.norskeopplevelser.no

Other activities

Bowling, pool, darts and games: The activity centre, Experten Sportsbar (0047 32059 715), has four bowling lanes, pool, darts, games and a big TV for sports. Bowling costs NOK 45, and shoes are NOK 10 a pair.

Drive a pack of dogs: A great drive over 10km of frozen lakes and forest. Adults pay NOK 600, inclusive of snow shoes. Book at Hemsedal tourist office one day in advance (32 05 50 30).

Horse sleigh ride: Elvestad Fjellridning (90 88 45 45), Flaget Farm (91 51 70 82), Gjedokk Hestesenter (95 73 40 44) or Hemesedal Hestensenter (32 06 02 02) all offer sleigh rides. Most will take you through the forest and some provide food and drink round a camp fire. Usual cost is NOK 150 for an adult.

Ice climbing: Norske Opplevelser (32 06 00 03, info@norskeopplevelser.no, www.norskeopplevelser.no) offers ice climbing lessons for beginners (NOK 595 for 3 hours). Hemesedal tourist office (32 05 50 30, info@hemsedal.com) offers 2.5 day beginners' courses and instruction on more advanced ice waterfalls for those with experience. Cost is NOK 2000.

Kiteskiing: Wintersteiger Norge (33 11 77 73, post@kiteaction.no, www.kiteaction.no) will teach you how to fly a kite on your skis/board. Bring your own board/skis and helmet. Cost is NOK 2000.

Night skiing: For 4 days a week the slopes of Hemsedalsløypa (red no.10), Såhaugløypa (black no. 8) and the children's and beginners' area are open for night skiing 5.30–9pm. Adults pay NOK 95 per night. Call Hemsedal Skisenter (32 05 53 00, skisenter@skihemsedal.no) for more information.

Overnight stay in a Lavvo (wigwam): Take a horse sleigh ride into the forest and have supper around an open fire. Have a warm bath in a hot tub and sleep on a reindeer skin around an oven in the centre of the lavvo. Arrive back at midday. NOK 1600. Book through Flaget Farm (0047 32 06 24 00/0047 915 17 082).

Paragliding: Oslo Paragliderklubb (www.opk.no) organise tandem flights (90 96 58 95, 92 81 95 45) for NOK 1000 and intensive courses (22 15 08 18, kurs@opk.no) for NOK 6900.

Snowmobile: You can either drive a snowmobile behind a guide on the mountain for NOK 350 for 45 mins (32 05 53 90, skiskolen@skihemsedal.no) or you can drive on race courses (32 06 02 02, hest@hemsedalhestesenter.no, www.hemsedalhestesenter.no). The race course below the ski centre on powerful mobiles costs NOK 150 for 15 minutes or you can drive on the big race track in Lykkja forest and over fields. This costs NOK 150–200 for 15 minutes and NOK 600 for 60 minutes.

Events

Hemsedal hosts its own freeride and slopestyle competitions. Burton back one of the slopestyle competitions. Check out events on www.skistar.com/hemsedal and click on 'EVENTER'.

Accommodation

The best hotel around is the **Skarsnuten Hotel** (0047 32 06 17 00, booking@skarsnuten.dvgl.no, www.skarsnutenhotel.no). It has great modern, stylish architecture, and is made entirely out of rocks, steel and lots of glass. There are 37 rooms (35 double and 2 suites) and a superb restaurant, fitness room and sauna. The only problem is that it is at 1000m altitude, on the slopes at Skarsnuten, so it's not too convenient

> "It has great modern, stylish architecture, and is made entirely out of rocks, steel and lots of glass"

for Hemsedal centre. In Hemsedal village, the **Norlandia Skogstad Hotel** (0047 32 05 50 00, service@ skogstad.norlandia.no, www.norlandia.no/skogstad) is massive and has a good pool, sauna, jacuzzi, solarium as well as a few restaurants, bars and a nightclub. The **Hemsedal Hotel** (0047 32 05 54 00) is good too, but not actually in Hemsedal; it's 3km from the ski area and 6km from the village centre.

If you want to be right in the centre of the action, the **Hemsedal Café Skiers' Lodge** (0047 32 05 54 10) is in the same building as the very popular Hemsedal Café. There are four apartments for 4–6 people and four apartments for 7–9 people. Some apartments have a fireplace and balcony. **Hemsedal Fjellandsby** (0047 32 05 50 60) have a number of apartment blocks (Alpin, Staven, Tinden and Trotten) next to Hemsedal ski centre. Up on the slopes you can stay at **Harahorn Hyttegrend** (0047 32 05 51 10), next to Solheisen Ski Centre, or **Lykkja Feriesenter** (0047 32 06 18 20), well placed for cross-country skiing.

Tour operators organising holidays to Hemsedal include Crystal (0870 160 6040), Ski Norway (0207 917 6044), Neilson Ski (0870 333 3347) and Thomson (0870 606 1470).

Eating out

On the mountain
There is one self-service restaurant and a few huts, which are better for picking up a quick snack rather than relaxing over a nice lunch.

In town
There's not a huge choice of restaurants, many of them are in the hotels (see Accommodation); the **Bistro** at Skogstad Hotel is good. **Peppes** (32 06 06 00 or 22 22 55 55 for takeaway) serves tasty pizzas. The food at the **Hemsedal Café** (32 05 54 10) is popular; the burgers and breakfast are particularly good. The restaurant at the **Skarsnuten Hotel** on the slopes (see Accommodation) is very smart.

Bars and clubs

The best bar for après ski is the **Hemsedal Café** (32 05 54 10) that gets absolutely packed. The **Elgen Bar** at the Skogstad Hotel, the **Oxen** and the **Garasjen** are also popular bars. The **Experten Sportsbar** is good for games (bowling, darts, etc, see Other activities) and for watching sports.

Useful facts and phone numbers

Tourist office

T:	0047 32 05 50 30
F:	0047 32 05 50 31
E:	info@hemsedal.com
W:	www.hemsedal.com

Direct reservations

T:	0047 32 05 50 60
F:	0047 32 05 50 61
E:	booking@hemsedal.com

Emergency services

- Police: 32 05 55 11
- Ambulance: 113
- Emergency: 112
- Emergency at night time or weekends: 32 02 95 00
- Red Cross: 32 06 04 77

Doctors

- 31 40 89 00
- Night time or weekends: 32 06 07 88

Taxis

- 32 06 01 80

Getting there

By car

From Oslo take the E-16 to Sandvika, then the E-16 to Hønefoss, the R-7 to Gol and finally the R-52 to Hemsedal.

By plane

Oslo (220km) Oslo Airport Gardermoen is the main airport. There are direct buses to Hemsedal on Fridays and Sundays. Ryanair flies to Oslo Torp from Glasgow or London. Torp is 280km from Hemsedal.
Lavik (290km)

Oppdal

Popular with the locals at
weekends for its snowsure runs

On the slopes

Snow reliability	❄ ❄ ❄ ❄
Parks	❄ ❄
Off-piste	❄ ❄

Off the slopes

Après ski	❄ ❄
Nightlife	❄ ❄
Eating out	❄ ❄
Resort charm	❄ ❄

"You can find some steeps and cliffs off the pisted areas and some decent freeriding too"

The resort

Oppdal, located between the Dovrefjell mountain plateau and the Trollheimen mountain range, isn't well known, but it is Norway's largest downhill skiing area so deserves some credit. Norwegian resorts aren't huge and, as such, Oppdal only has a handful of bars, restaurants and hotels. The après ski and atmosphere is good at the weekends though. Heliskiing is another attraction.

The mountains

Height: 550–1350m

Ability	Rating
Expert	❄ ❄
Intermediate	❄ ❄
Beginner	❄ ❄

Getting about

Snow reliability is great in Oppdal, but extent isn't. There are only eight blues, five greens, nine reds and five blacks. There are three resort centres: Vangslia (0047 72 40 44 80), Stølen (0047 72 40 41 50) and Hovden (0047 72 40 41 92). Hovden is the best place for experts to head to, or check out the off-piste.

The park

There is a very small park in the Vangslia area, with a couple of kickers and the odd rail. There's also a half pipe, but the resort doesn't seem to push the freestyle scene and the park does get neglected. Oppdal is all about downhill alpine, which is a little bit of a shame.

Off-piste and backcountry

The great snow conditions in Oppdal mean that there is some decent freeriding to be had. Stolen Valley is a popular place for getting some fresh tracks, but it does have a high avalanche risk and the patrollers often close the area before you get a chance to check it out. You can find some steeps and cliffs off the pisted areas and there's some decent tree riding too. Everything gets tracked out really quickly after a fresh snowfall, but on the whole it's not a bad mountain.

Lift passes

1 day	NOK 280
6 days	NOK 1190

Instruction

The standard price for group lessons is £70–80 for 5 days, with 90 minutes each day and £65 for 100 minutes of private lessons.

Oppdal Skiskole Vangslia
T: 0047 72 40 44 85
E: oppdal.skiskole@oppdal-booking.no

Ski Akademit
T: 0047 72 40 41 70
E: skiakademi@opplev-oppdal.no

Other activities

Gymnasium: Access to gym and training equipment costs NOK 155. For more information contact Merete Nylende (72 40 16 09, merete.nylende@oppdal.kommune.no).

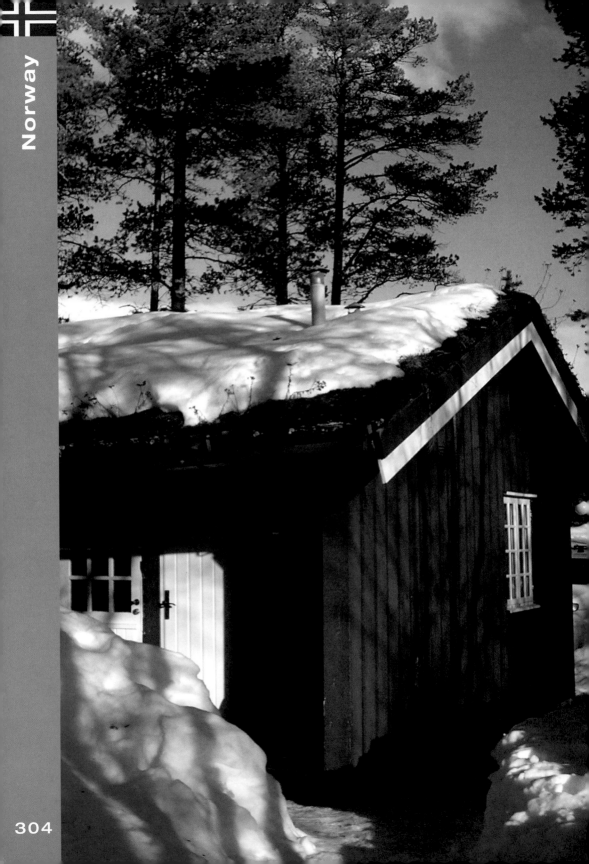

Oppdal Husky Resort: A half-day trip costs NOK 800 and a full day is NOK 1100. You can drive your own sled or simply be a passenger. For more information and booking contact Julie (95 92 96 08) or Øyvind (97 02 86 14, post@islandbreezecrew.com, www.islandbreezecrew.com).

Other sports: For information about kite skiing/ boarding, ice climbing, sled rides and tandem hang-gliding contact the tourist office.

Accommodation

Unless otherwise stated, call the Oppdal booking line to reserve hotel rooms (0047 72 40 08 00, post@oppdalbooking.no).

The **Quality Hotel Oppdal** has 75 rooms, including 20 rustic suites with four-poster beds, as well as a steakhouse, the Caledonian Bar and George's Pub and Bar. **Hotel Nor** has a nice bar and a lounge with a big fireplace. The **Vangslia Fjelltun** has top quality log apartments for 2–4 people, with private sauna,

> "Hotel Nor has a nice bar and a lounge with a big fireplace"

magnificent views, and the ever-useful dishwasher. Most have a balcony. They are 3km from the centre of town.

The cheapest accommodation in town is **Oppdal Vandrehjem** (0047 72 40 40 90, booking@sletvold-stolen.no), a partner of Norwegian Youth Hostels. There are 16 apartments, each with four beds, bathroom, mini kitchen and TV. Linen and towels can be rented. They are within walking distance of Oppdal centre.

Eating out

On the mountain

Generally, you'd only stop at a mountain hut to grab something to eat, not to spend any time there, but **Rockoss** (72 40 41 53) is good, especially for après ski.

In town

Pizzas, pasta and takeaways can be found at **Møllen's** (72 42 18 00) and steaks at **Perrongen Steakhouse** (72 40 07 00) at Quality Hotel Oppdal. The hotel restaurant at the **Quality Hotel** (72 40 07 00) has good fish dishes. **Oppdalsporten** (72 40 06 40), 10km north of the centre, serves great homemade food.

Bars and clubs

The **Rockoss** on the mountain is a good place to start, and back in town the **Loftet** (99 64 29 05) and the **Opp & Ne** après ski bar (93 86 80 00) get packed out later on at the weekend.

Useful facts and phone numbers

Tourist office

T: 0047 72 40 04 70
F: 0047 72 40 04 80
E: post@oppdal.com
W: www.oppdal.com

Direct reservations

W: www.oppdal-booking.no

Emergency services

• Police/Mountain rescue: 112
• Ambulance: 113

Doctors

• Medical centre: 72 42 11 00

Taxis

• 72 42 12 05

Getting there

By car

National road no. 70 comes from Kristiansund in the west of Norway and joins the E6, which runs through the centre of Oppdal.

By plane

Trondheim (150km) You can book a bus by calling 23 00 27 30, see www.nsb.no.
Oslo (320km) Book a bus by calling 81 54 44 44.

Sweden

A mecca for party-going Swedes, who will welcome you as if you were one of their own

Åre

By far the best Swedish resort,
with great riding, park, events
and nightlife

On the slopes	
Snow reliability	❄ ❄ ❄
Parks	❄ ❄ ❄ ❄
Off-piste	❄ ❄ ❄
Off the slopes	
Après ski	❄ ❄ ❄
Nightlife	❄ ❄ ❄ ❄ ❄
Eating out	❄ ❄
Resort charm	❄ ❄ ❄

The resort

Åre is awesome. It's popular with everyone, from families and couples to groups of young party people. There aren't too many Brits around but the Swedes are fun, speak good English and know how to party. The centre of town has a great atmosphere and it's a charming and beautiful place, made up of stylish wooden buildings. Some awesome talent has originated in this area too, such as Jon Olsson (see Events), which gives the resort an even better profile and may be one of the reasons that many of the Scandinavian jetset head here for their holidays.

The mountains

Height: 380–1270m

Ability	Rating
Expert	❄ ❄ ❄
Intermediate	❄ ❄ ❄ ❄
Beginner	❄ ❄ ❄ ❄

Getting about

Åre has around 100km of groomed runs, which are split over four areas: Åre and Åre Björnen (a fairly big area with the main slopes and off-piste) and Duved and Tegerfjäll (connected, but not massive). The variety of riding is good and should suit most. Darkness shrouds the resort for most of the days in early winter; the best time to come is March or later.

The park

We expected Åre's Land Park to rock as so many of the world's best riders grew up here, and we weren't disappointed. Everything is well set up, with the kickers organised like a slopestyle course. The jumps were in tiptop condition and there were hits for all abilities. There are also some big-ass hip jumps and quarter pipes and a wicked half pipe, all well maintained by the shapers. The ideas tank is pretty good too, with locals designing their own rails and bringing them to the park. There's a boardercross, but it's not as popular as the rest of the park.

Off-piste and backcountry

Åre is a pretty good freeriding destination. There are steeps, wind lips and cornices to play on that are pretty obvious from the pistes or you can explore more unchartered terrain. One popular local adventure is to hitch a ride with a piste basher or skidoo to the top of Åreskutan and go exploring. There is some amazing backcountry terrain that you can reach from here (and a 1000m vertical drop) but it is very easy to get lost, so watch out or check it out with a mountain guide first. If everything goes to plan you will come out at the bottom of the resort.

As in Riksgransen, the heliskiing is mind-blowing, but it's not cheap. It's a good idea to get a group of three or four of you together and do a deal with your heli guide.

Lift passes	
1 day	310 SEK
6 days	1545 SEK

Instruction

Skidåkarna

A 1-hour private lesson costs 460 SEK for 1 person and 210 SEK for each extra person.
T: 0046 (0)771 840 000
W: www.skistar.com

Other activities

Contact Åre tourist information for more information on any of these activities (0046 (0)647 177 20).

Åre Sleddog Adventures: A fantastic company with over 50 well-trained Alaskan Huskies. A 2-hour tour costs 500 SEK, half a day is 600 SEK and a whole day 850 SEK (0046 (0)647 303 81, info@ aresleddog.se, www.aresleddog.se).

Gyms: A few of the hotels have gyms that are open to the public including Hotell Årevidden (6km east of Åre). Åre also has a training centre.

Horse riding: Try horseback riding on an Icelandic horse. One-hour or half-day trips are available and a half-day ride will cost around 500 SEK per person.

Ice fishing: There are good ice fishing grounds at Åresjön, Fröåtjärn in Åre Björnen, Greningen above Duved and Hensjön in Edsåsdalen. A fishing permit is required and can be bought at tourist information or at an agent in any of the villages. Fishing permits cost 50 SEK per day.

Indoor climbing: Indoor climbing is available in the sports hall in Duvedshallen (book though the tourist office) or at the Lokalen in Åre. At Ristafallet you can climb the frozen waterfall.

Reindeer sledge: Drive a sledge driven by reindeer; you can even catch and harness them yourself if you like. A 1-hour trip costs 400 SEK and a half-day 700 SEK. Husky sleds are also an option.

Snowmobiling: This can be combined with ice fishing or dinner. Choose between a 1.5-hour trip, a 3-hour trip or a whole day trip. A short trip costs 375 SEK with 2 people on the snowmobile.

Tobogganning: A toboggan course runs from Hotel Fjällgården down to the square. You can toboggan at night on Wednesdays 6–9pm. For 60 SEK you can rent a toboggan, and spend 3 hours on the track.

Events

In 2005, Jon Olsson held his first Invitational Big Air event in Åre, where he gathered together the world's best New School skiers. This year he has done it again with even bigger jumps, more pro-riders, and a whole lot of prize money. The **Jon Olsson** Invitational is now the world's most prestigious and talked about Big Air event, with over 10 000 spectators watching the action each year. If you are planning a holiday to Åre, try to make it the same time as this event. Check out www.jonolsson invitational.com. In April, 20 of the world's best snowboarding girls compete in the **Candy Jam** weekend. There is a big end of season finale in April, when the elite New School riders, photographers and film-makers all meet up in Åre, with sessions, DJs and great après ski in the square.

"One popular local adventure is to hitch a ride with a piste basher or skidoo to the top of Åreskutan"

Accommodation

The **Holiday Club** (0046 (0)647 120 00, info@ holidayclub.se, www.holidayclub.se) is one of the best hotels in town, and a short 5-minute walk from the town centre and the lifts. It is a huge complex that has everything including a great restaurant and bar, games room, free internet, a bowling alley, spa and sauna world and an awesome water world complete with a horizon pool with views of the mountains and 67m of waterslide! All rooms have TV, mini-bar, internet and views of the peak or lake. Prices are 8310–13500 SEK for one week, Sunday to Sunday.

If you would prefer to stay in the centre of the resort the **Åregården** (0046 (0)647 502 65, www. diplomathotel.com) is the best and most popular. It's a beautiful and stylish place, with good rooms and friendly staff. The breakfasts are worth getting up for and the smart restaurant is popular in the evenings. Prices are 7195–11530 SEK for one week, Sunday to Sunday.

Eating out

On the mountain

Buustamons (0647 531 75, bokning@buustamons
fjallgard.se, www.buustamonsfjallgard.se), a hut in the
woods with an outdoor heated tub, is the best
restaurant, and you can book a meal at night too. Give
them a call and they will arrange to pick you up on a
skidoo. You can stay overnight if you like.

In town

The **Karolinen** (0647 320 90) is one of the best
restaurants in town, cosy and intimate with good
traditional food. **Broken** attracts a younger crowd for
burgers and steaks and has plasma screens playing the
latest ski and snowboard movies. The hotel restaurants
(see Accommodation) are good and the burger huts in
the centre of town serve fantastic fast food.

Bars and clubs

The après ski rocks on from 4pm and most people head
straight to the **Diplomat** where they have live bands.
This gets really crowded and it's great fun but not the

"Most people head straight to the Diplomat where they have live bands"

place for a quiet drink. You can also pick up snacks; the
burgers and chips taste superb after a few beers. Around
10–11pm the night really starts. The **Bygget Club** is
one of the best clubs ever, and it's the place to rub
shoulders with the Scandy jetset. It's absolutely massive,
and includes a restaurant serving great sushi, and loads
of rooms playing different types of music: live bands,
60s and 70s music, techno, hip hop… The atmosphere
is completely crazy. It's definitely worth putting up with
the long queues and extortionate drinks' prices to get
in. Another club that is worth checking out is the **Country
Club**, which has live bands.

Useful facts and phone numbers

Tourist office

T: 0046 (0)647 177 20
E: info@areresort.com/info@areturistbyra.com
W: www.skistar.com
See also www.visitare.se and www.compare.se

Direct reservations

T: 0046 (0)771 840 000
E: reservations@areresort.se

Emergency services

• Police station in Järpen (22km from Åre):
   0647 105 55 or 112 in an emergency

Doctor

• Hälsocentralen: 0647 166 00

Getting there

By plane

Östersund (100km) There are regular bus
services from Östersund to Åre.
From Stockholm you can reach Östersund by air
or you can take the sleeper train, which brings
you almost right into Åre.

Riksgransen

Heliski in the Midnight Sun, but don't expect much from the resort - it's all in one hotel

On the slopes	
Snow reliability	❄ ❄ ❄ ❄
Parks	❄ ❄ ❄
Off-piste	❄ ❄ ❄ ❄ ❄

Off the slopes	
Après ski	❄
Nightlife	❄
Eating out	❄
Resort charm	❄

The resort

Riksgransen is in Lapland, 300km north of the Arctic Circle and most visitors are there for the seemingly endless heliskiing. If you can, take your trip in May, when the sun never sets, and hit the mountain at midnight. The mountains are more majestic than most resorts in Scandinavia, with the jagged landscape you would expect to see in the Swiss or French Alps.

Back in resort, there is simply the Riksgransen Hotel, which contains the shops, restaurants, bars and nightclub. This is the resort; there is nothing else.

The famous ice hotel (and the world's biggest igloo) is in Jukkasjärvi, about half an hour from Kiruna, the closest airport to Riksgransen. We definitely recommend a little stop off on the way there or the way back, for a quick drink in the Absolut Ice Bar, and maybe a night stop for the full experience.

The mountains

Height: 520–910m

Ability	Rating
Expert	❄ ❄ ❄ ❄ ❄
Intermediate	❄ ❄ ❄
Beginner	❄

Getting about

The ski season doesn't actually start when the winter does; nothing happens in the first winter months as Riksgransen is in complete darkness. Only in February are there sufficient daylight hours to kick off the season. The hours of sunshine gradually increase until midsummer's day, when the sun never goes down. It's pretty difficult to sleep when the sun's pouring through the window but there is another alternative – you can get your skis or board out and head up the mountain to ride the powder at midnight. At these times, lifts are open 10pm–1am; check with the tourist office for exact dates.

On piste there are 34 descents, but if you are looking for cruisy pistes you should really be elsewhere.

"The whole mountain is geared towards freeride and there are loads of accessible steeps, cliffs and shoots"

The park

The freestyle scene in Riksgransen is pretty big. Dedicated freestylers are up on the hill each day spending hours building huge gap jumps and crazy hips. Jon Olsson (X Games gold medallist) is often in the park working hard and helping all the up-and-coming rippers. There's a selection of rails that are moved around to different spots and they do build a slopestyle for the King of the Hill event, however it's difficult to predict whether it will be shaped. There is a half pipe and a quarter pipe that are used for the Swedish Snowboard Cup and for all the freestyle camps that are held here.

Off-piste and backcountry

When the conditions are right (the weather is a tad unpredictable), this crazy mountain becomes a freerider's heaven. The whole mountain is geared towards freeride and there are loads of really accessible

steeps, cliffs and shoots, on which they hold the Scandinavian Big Mountain Champs.

A good route to explore is called Lilla Ölturen, or 'The Little Trip for a Beer' (there's a nice place for a beer at the end). You start from the summit of Riksgransen and head down to the bottom of the Norweigian Björnfjell railway station. You should definitely take a guide to show you the best spots to find untracked powder. If you embark on a half-hour trek from the top lift station you can get to the fantastic Mörkhåla snow bowl. There are also some marked trails on the map: Branten, Ravinen and Gränsängarna.

To get the most out of these amazing mountains you definitely need a guide and a helicopter. The heliskiing here is out of this world and you are dropped off in areas that look like man has never touched them. We used Krister from Alpine Madness and his avalanche-trained dog kept up with us down some steep faces in 2 metres of powder. Superb.

Lift passes	
1 day	SEK 300
6 days	SEK 1414

Instruction

Book instruction, off-piste guiding, and heliski trips at the Riksgransen Hotel (0046 (0)980 400 80, info@riksgransen.nu, www.riksgransen.nu).

Other activities

All activities can be booked at the hotel (0980 400 80).
Driving dog sleds and ice climbing: Both of these are fun options at Riksgranen.
Snowmobiles and ice fishing: You can either rent snowmobiles and go off on your own or combine the outing with ice fishing in a frozen mountain lake.
Spa: If your bones are aching, visit the spa, which has massage, treatment pools, sauna, Tai Chi, yoga, Qi gong, facials and body treatments. They also offer Lappish Zen, a unique treatment that involves cleansing, deep relaxation, hot stone massage, birch oils and stones from the Torneträsk river bank. The hotel offers good ski and spa packages.

Events

At the **Scandinavian Big Mountain Championships** (SBMC) the best freeriders fight it out to become national champion. It is one of the oldest extreme competitions in the world, and has now reached its 16th year. The **King of the Hill** is a slopestyle event for skiers and snowboarders who battle it down a course full of kickers, rails and quarter pipes. This was one of the first events to push New School skiing and attracts the world's best.

Accommodation

The one and only **Hotel Riksgransen** (0046 (0)980 400 80) isn't anything amazingly special, but it's comfortable and cosy, and you're handy for everything. The hotel has apartments and rooms; a double room (Saturday to Saturday) costs €438–713 and a 4-bed apartment €818–1340.

Eating out

In town

Restaurant **Lapplandia** is the smartest restaurant in the Riksgransen Hotel, and has won awards for food and service. There is also **Café Lappis**, a pizzeria with a wood-fired, Italian stone-oven. For a quick hot dog or burger, head to the **Katterjaure Café** or the **Nordalskiosken**.

Bars and clubs

Grönan is a fairly decent après ski bar and club; it's a casual place, but can get pretty nuts. They often have live music at après, and the place kicks off properly from about 11pm.

Getting there
By car
From Kiruna, take the Nordkalott Highway (E-10) for about 3 hours.
By plane
Kiruna (130km) Domestic flights from Stockholm fly to Kiruna. *Stockholm (1500km)* Fly to Kiruna or take the 18-hour overnight train.

Useful facts and phone numbers
Tourist office
T: 0046 (0)980 400 80 F: 0046 (0)980 431 25 E: info@riksgransen.nu W: www.riksgransen.nu
Emergency services
• Call 112
Doctors
There is a ski doctor in the hotel during the winter season.

+ Switzerland

Swiss Tourism have their finger
on the button - fault them if you can!

Arosa

A good, intermediate mountain,
and a great town for everyone –
from families to party people

Arosa schneesicher

Anlagen / Facilities

A	Hörnli-express
B	Hörnli
C	Plattenhorn
D	Carmenna
E	Inner joui-Tschuggen
F	Tschuggen-Ost
G	Brüggerhorn
H	Tschuggen-West
J	Riet
K	Tomli
L	Pränzli
M	Weisshor n 1. Sektion
N	Weisshor n 2. Sektion

Pisten / Slopes

- Leicht / Easy
- Mittel / Intermediate
- Schwer / Difficult
- Winterwanderweg / Walking path
- Schlittelweg / Toboggan run
- Langlaufloipe / Cross country

- Heimfahrtziele / Home Runway
- Wildschutzzone
  Forest and Wildlife pr tection ea
- Freeride-Checkpoint
  Befahre n auf eigene Gefahr
  Use on your own risk
- Tschuggengebiet / T schuggen ar es

- Alpen Club Micky Maus

T Ticket-V erkaufsstellen
   Tickets Point of Sale
P Arosa Ber gbahnen AG
i Information

On the slopes	
Snow reliability	✽ ✽ ✽ ✽
Parks	✽ ✽
Off-piste	✽ ✽

Off the slopes	
Après ski	✽ ✽
Nightlife	✽ ✽ ✽
Eating out	✽ ✽ ✽
Resort charm	✽ ✽ ✽

The resort

We had a superb time in Arosa; it has a certain charm that we really fell for. The town is quite pretty, but it's the atmosphere that we loved: the people, the restaurants, the bars, everything. Most of the action is around the Obersee/Untersee area so this is the region we deal with. It seems to attract all sorts of people – families, a few fur coats, some trendies and some party people (Arosa has a great night scene if you know where to look). The mountain's not bad either; it's a wide, open area, perfect for blue and red run riders but not challenging enough for the expert.

The mountains

Height: 1800–2653m

Ability	Rating
Expert	✽
Intermediate	✽ ✽ ✽
Beginner	✽ ✽ ✽

Getting about

Arosa's 100km of pistes (60km of prepared pistes, 40km of freeride trails) are great for beginner and intermediate riders. There are lots of gentle slopes to get you started and then you'll be cruising all over the mountain. However, if you are a good intermediate or expert you will probably cover the terrain in a couple of days. The park might entertain you for a while

though. There are the same number of hiking trails as there are pistes so get used to sharing the mountain with walkers.

The park

The park is located in a fairly small area near to the Sit hütte restaurant at the top of the Tschuggen-Ost chairlift. It is OK for beginner freestylers but there isn't much choice. There are two very small table tops and one very small rail. However, the massive new super half pipe is an incentive for freestylers to hit Arosa.

> "The massive new super half pipe is an incentive for freestylers to hit Arosa"

Off-piste and backcountry

In the right conditions, there are some easily accessible and good spots for freeriding. A favourite place of the locals is towards the resort Lenzerheide by the Hornli area, where you can often find fresh tracks. Avalanching is a problem though, so do take a guide.

Lift passes	
1 day	CHF55
6 days	CHF256
13 days	CHF400

You can also get a beginners' pass that just lets you on to the easier runs; perfect for a first timer. This costs CHF35 for 1 day and CHF161 for 6 days.

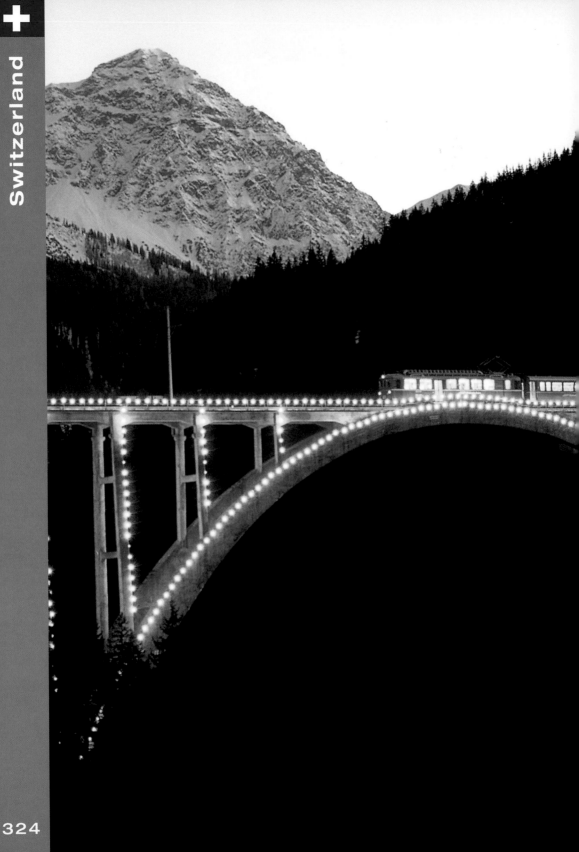

Instruction and equipment

ABC

Private lessons cost from CHF130 for 2 hours and group lessons are CHF40–50 for a half day; 5 full days costs CHF240 for snowboarders and CHF360 for skiers.

T: 0041 (0)81 356 56 60
E: abcschneesportschule@spin.ch
W: www.abcarosa.ch

Bananas

Bananas is a great snowboard school for budding freestylers. A 2-hour group lesson costs CHF40 and a 5-day package costs CHF435, including lift passes.

T: 0041 (0)81 378 75 00
E: bananas@sssa.ch
W: www.sssa.ch

Swiss Ski and Snowboard School

Private lessons cost from CHF140 for 2 hours, or CHF350 for a whole day (6 hours). There is also a Mickey Mouse club for kids.

T: 0041 (0)81 377 11 50
E: fun@sssa.ch
W: www.sssa.ch

Ski Shop Beck

This is located at the bottom of the cable car and chairlift. It's the perfect location for picking up your hire equipment and you can even leave it in the hut outside the shop when you come down from the slopes so you don't have to lug it around town. You can also pick up the essentials like socks, glasses, goggles, etc. The staff are very friendly and helpful.

T: 0041 (0)81 377 34 48
W: www.skishopbeck.ch

Other activities

Balloon trips: At weekends these trips are available over Arosa, the Grisons alps or in the low lying hills, with prices staring at CHF350. Call Walter Vollenweider on 0041 (0)52 214 37 14.

Friday night skiing: Takes place in Inner Arosa (Tschuggen chairlift) 4.30–10pm and costs CHF10.

Ice skating: You can ice skate on the open air rink (081 377 17 45) until 5pm (night skating on Mondays and Wednesdays) and on the natural ice rink at Inner Arosa (081 377 29 30). Adults pay CHF4.50 for skating, CHF6 for skate rental and CHF4 for ice hockey stick rental. You can rent the whole ice rink for CHF160 per hour if you fancy your own ice hockey match, or you can learn how to curl for CHF48 per hour.

Moonlight skiing: Takes place 7–10pm on one day each month and costs CHF15 (free with season pass).

Paragliding: This costs CHF190 per person per flight. Call Jogi Engewald (079 449 88 13). You can buy a gift certificate at the Swiss Ski and Snowboard School by the bottom of the cable car.

Sleigh rides: By the station you will find horses and sleighs all ready to take you for a ride. The Prätschli-Maran round trip for 2 people costs CHF80 and longer circuits can cost up to CHF160.

Sunrise on Weisshorn summit: The trip costs CHF32 and includes breakfast at the Weisshorngipfel.

Sunset and fondue nights: Take place on the Weisshorn twice a month in January, February and March and cost CHF49. For reservations call 0041 (0)781 378 84 84.

Tobogganing: There are a number of toboggan runs in Arosa, with a variety of lengths, and one that is floodlit (Prätschli-Scheiterböden-Obersee). You can take the bus from Postplatz.

Events

At the end of March/beginning of April is the World Junior Half Pipe Championships and this year Arosa will host the FIS Snowboard Championship on 13–20 January. Check out www.arosa2007.ch. Arosa has another claim to fame in the world of the half pipe, as it is the home of snowboarder Gian Simmen, the World Half Pipe Champion for three years running (2000–3) who became the half pipe Olympic winner in Nagano in 1998.

As well as events on the mountain, Arosa seems to hold a fair number of music events, from rock concerts, to popular DJs and hip hop events. On 28 January check out the Alpine Hot Air Balloon week.

Accommodation

If money was no object, there would be no question of where we would stay in Arosa; the **Hotel Eden** (0041 (0)81 378 71 00, info@edenarosa.ch, www.edenarosa.ch) is by far the best place in town. From the outside the hotel looks fairly standard, but take a look inside and you will find yourself at the cutting edge of interior design (check out www.designhotels .com). The bar is gorgeous and the atmosphere is perfect. In addition, one of the best clubs in town, the Kitchen Club, resides in the hotel's basement (see Bars and clubs). The individually designed rooms range from the slightly odd to the completely absurd. The Garden Eden room has a tree above the bed and rocks and gorges around the whirlpool. For an interesting Valentine's Day why not book yourself into the Lilly Tiger room, complete with velvet, fur, a cage bed and an open bathroom. Prices start at CHF85 per person per night for a classic kitchen room and extend to CHF210 for a 50m^2 design apartment. In high season, add another CHF45. Not cheap, but an experience.

Another smart and more classic hotel is the **Hotel Cristallo** (0041 (0)81 377 22 61, www.crisalloarosa.ch, cristalloarosa@swissonline.ch) on the main road. It has a lovely smart restaurant and you can hire DVD players and films for a quiet night in. Prices start at CHF120 per person per night. The large **Post Hotel** (0041 (0)81 378 50 00, mail@posthotel-arosa.ch, www.posthotel-arosa.ch) is in a good location and has a spa as well as a range of different restaurants in the same building including a pizzeria, the Mexicalito Mexican, and a classic eatery. It's pretty 70s, but in an endearing way. Prices start at CHF119 per person per day.

The 5-star **Tschuggen Grand Hotel** (0041 (0)81 378 99 99, reservations@tschuggen.ch, www.tschuggen. ch) is set to have a new spa for 2007, designed by the famous architect and designer Mario Botta. The spa, Botta Berg Oase, will be set within a mountain and will be linked to the hotel by a glass bridge. The £15 million investment will cover four floors and 4000m^2 with numerous pools, saunas and treatment rooms. More exotic features include a grotto where guests can enjoy a programme of seasons – summer rain, a winter storm or pure sunshine – and a Kneipp Path where

guests will walk over natural stones through a knee-deep stream of ice cold and hot spots, stimulating their blood circulation and nervous system.

If you're looking for a bargain, your best bet is probably to get an apartment. The tourist office has a good selection on the website. We rented an apartment in Haus Bristol and loved it; we had a great view and a great location.

Eating out

On the mountain

Our favourite bar on the mountain on a sunny day is the very accessible bar on the **Brüggerstuba** (081 378 84 25) at the top of the cable car from Obersee. This is a great place to sit and have a few beers after a hard day on the mountain. If you're peckish, they also cook up a tasty hot dog. In bad weather, a big umbrella-type cover keeps you out of the snow. The **Sit hütte** (079 407 89 38), at the top of the 'park' is the place to sit back and look cool. There are big, loungy cushions on the snow and a palm tree with sofas round it. There's

also table football and good snack food. At **Tschuggenhütte** (081 378 84 45), by the colourful tented Mickey Mouse club, there is raclette bar, snack bar, ice cream hut, massive terrace and huge double loungers to relax on. If you're a bit knackered, take a good book and chill out here. The restaurant at the top of the **Weisshorngipfel** (081 378 84 02) lacks atmosphere inside but has amazing views from the outside. Surprisingly the food isn't *too* expensive. As well as traditional dishes, they serve the simpler sausage and chips or spag bol.

In town

There are some great restaurants around town. In the centre one building contains three of the best. On the middle floor, the pizzeria **Grottino** (081 377 17 17) is a cosy and friendly place with a busy atmosphere. The restaurant below it, **Schnüggel** (081 377 17 17), is small and romantic. Order one of the house meat spits, where you can choose two sauces and three side dishes to accompany it. On the top floor is a raclette/fondue restaurant: **Alpträumli** (081 377 06 06), also under the same ownership. The cheese

fondue is absolutely superb and the raclettes good, although you don't have the satisfaction of melting the cheese yourself which is a shame; they do it in the kitchen and bring it out to you.

Head to **Mexicalito/Boomerang Bar** (081 378 50 00) for a strange mix between Australian and Mexican cuisine, with Kangeroo burgers and fajitas on offer. The decorations are slightly confused, but the food, atmosphere and service are all fantastic. For Thai, head to **Chilli's** (081 377 13 66) at the top end of town, and for a smart meal, try the Italian in the Casino building, the traditional **Le Bistro** restaurant in the **Crisallo** (081 378 68 68) or the funky restaurants at the **Hotel Eden** (081 378 71 00), where you can choose between a fondue at the **Roggenmoser** or an Italian at **Sapori**.

Bars and clubs

One of the best bars in town is **LOS Café Bar**, which is great for a game of Pacman or table footie and for a fairly quiet après ski beer. Later at night it's heaving and fun. Other good places for après ski are the **Sitting Bull** and **Bellini's** café bar (for a chilled out glass of wine). The **Boomerang** Bar (see Eating out) is great for games and tequilas. The **Casino** building may have you reaching for your poker chips but hold your horses, there's no blackjack or roulette, just a few slot machines. There is a really nice smart bar though, and the **Nuts Club** for dancing later on.

Our absolute favourite bar is the **Eden Bar** in the Hotel Eden, a smart place where it's great to chill out and chat in the midst of candlelight and sushi. On one night there was a massive bed adorned with Egyptian sheets, and a glam crowd smoking a sheesha pipe. Downstairs is the unique **Kitchen Club** which looks just like an old kitchen with a couple of bars put in. The drinks are really expensive but it has a great atmosphere and music, and the hip hop nights are superb.

Useful facts and phone numbers

Tourist office

T: 0041 (0)81 378 70 20
F: 0041 (0)81 378 70 21
E: arosa@arosa.ch
W: www.arosa.ch

Emergency services

• Police: 117 or 081 377 19 38/ 081 378 67 17
• If you have an accident on the piste call 081 378 84 05
• Snow reports: 0041 (0)81 378 84 50

Doctors

• Drs V Meyer and M Walkmeister: 081 377 27 28
• Dr M Röthlisberger: 081 377 14 64

Taxis

• Taxi Keller: 081 377 35 35
• Taxi Obersee: 081 377 11 33

Getting there

By car

The road to Arosa is pretty dreadful. It takes almost an hour from Chur on a windy and narrow road and accidents are not uncommon. Best avoided if possible.

By plane

Zürich (163km)
Friedrichshafen (around 170km) for Ryanair flights.
Transfer from Zürich and Friedrichshafen will take around 1.5 hours. Your best bet is to avoid the awful road and take the efficient and beautiful Rhaetian Railway up to Arosa from Chur.
Milano (217km)

By train

Take the 17.42 Eurostar from London Waterloo to Paris; then an overnight train, changing at Chur. Arrive Arosa station, in resort, at 09.09. Return fares start at £168 in a 6-berth couchette. Contact European Rail (020 7387 0444, www.europeanrail.com).

Champéry

Part of the Portes de Soleil circuit, Champéry has extensive terrain and one of the best parks in Europe

On the slopes	
Snow reliability	❄ ❄ ❄
Parks	❄ ❄ ❄ ❄ ❄
Off-piste	❄ ❄ ❄

Off the slopes	
Après ski	❄ ❄ ❄
Nightlife	❄ ❄ ❄⊰
Eating out	❄ ❄ ❄ ❄⊰
Resort charm	❄ ❄ ❄ ❄ ❄⊰

The resort

Champéry is an undiscovered gem. The resort itself is a charming place, full of ultra-friendly people. There are great places to stay, fantastic restaurants, good access to the Portes de Soleil circuit (the largest internationally connected ski area in the world), and one of the finest snowparks we have ever seen.

The mountains

Height: 975–2466m

Ability	Rating
Expert	❄ ❄ ❄ ❄
Intermediate	❄ ❄ ❄ ❄
Beginner	❄

Getting about

The slopes have a lot going for them. Intermediates and experts will have a whale of a time, whether exploring the 650km of pistes in the Portes de Soleil, tackling the more challenging steep and mogully Swiss wall or attacking the massive kickers in the incredible super-park. However, Champéry is not suited to beginners; there are very few gentle enough slopes for your first venture on to skis or board. The other disadvantage is the inability to ride back into the centre of town; you can come all the way back down into Grand Paradis (there are free buses all day to the village), but to get straight to the centre of Champéry you will have to take the cable car down and then possibly a bus if you're not staying near the lift.

The park

At the end of 2004 one of the best parks in Europe was formed in the Les Crosets area. The park is high and has a huge selection of kickers for all standards of riders ranging from small table tops to 30m gap jumps. There are four hip jumps, at a variety of heights, ten rails, including a massive rainbow rail and a couplc of flat-downs. A big bonus is the gap jump to a big snow block to drop off, then a quarter pipe with a rail on top to finish off. A jibber's paradise. World-famous pro boarders Travis Rice and Roman Dimarchi have been spotted filming for their latest flick. If parks are your thing, check this place out, it's arguably the best park in Europe. At least visit the website www.superpark.ch – if your French isn't up to scratch, you'll have to settle for the pictures.

Off-piste and backcountry

Though not its strongest feature, Champéry does have something to offer in the off-piste sector. Les Crosets and Chavanette are good places to start looking. The sun can kill the lovely powder, so if there is an area that you spot and want to ride, make sure you check it out first thing. Also at Chavanette is the legendary Swiss wall: a marked black run that gets the best moguls on the mountain. This is a pretty steep face and can be amazing after a big snowfall. You may want to seek out some spots in Avoriaz, Chatel and Morzine for the off-piste.

Lift passes	
1 day	CHF56
6 days	CHF270
There are discounts for children, teenagers, students and the over 60s.	

Instruction

Freeride Co.

Snowboard, ski, freestyle and telemark. Private lessons (1–2 people) cost CHF60 per hour (discounts for 3–6 hours), and semi-private lessons (3–5 people) cost CHF150 for 2 hours.
T: 0041 (0)24 479 10 00
E: info@freeridecompany.com
W: www.skichampery.com

Swiss Ski and Snowboard School

Ski, snowboard, telemark, racing, freeride and heliskiing. A 2-hour private lesson costs CHF120 for 1 person and CHF20 for every extra person. Group lessons cost CHF190 for 5 half days and CHF50 per day.

T: 0041 (0)24 479 16 15
E: ess@champery.ch
W: www.esschampery.ch

Other activities

Unless other contact details are given, call the tourist office for more information (024 479 20 20).

Night skiing: This takes place twice a week and is actually really good fun; 5km of ski runs are open until 10pm.

Paragliding: Tandem flights, training flights or initiation courses can all be arranged.

Snow-kiting: To try your hand at this call 079 409 22 75.

Sports centre: The Champéry **Palladium** (024 479 05 05) has pool, fitness room, curling rink and ice rink.

Tobogganing: This takes place on the Grand Paradis. Rent your toboggan from Berra Sports (024 479 13 90) or Borgeat Sports (024 479 16 17).

Trampolining: There are two bungee **trampolines** and one normal trampoline to play around on.

Events

In the first week of February is the **Chavanette Session;** a race which takes place on the densely moguled Chavanette piste, also known as the Swiss wall. As part of this festival is the **Derby**, a great competition in which teams of three race to finish the 5km course from Pas de Chavanette (2180m) to Grand-Paradis (1055m). There is also **The Wall**, an individual race on the Chavanette. The snowpark hosts events all winter long – check with the tourist office for the latest information. At the end of the season is the **Champéry Snow Mix**, with a big air ski/snowboard comp, a waterslide or a snowskate contest. The après ski and party scene is great, with a number of good DJs.

Accommodation

The rustic and charming chalet-hotel **Auberge de Grand-Paradis** (0041 (0)24 479 11 67, rhondsworld @aol.com, www.grandparadis.ch) is right on the slopes and the only hotel in Champéry that boasts ski-in ski-out accommodation. This does mean that it's a 20 minute walk into the centre of town, but avoiding the après-ski jostle to catch the cable car and bus more than makes up for this. Paul and Rhonda, the British proprietors, will welcome you into one of their ten spacious bedrooms (which share five bathrooms), and it's fantastic value at CHF110 per room per night. If you require half board, you will pay an extra CHF32.50 per head for a four-course meal. The food is superb, as both Paul and Rhonda are excellent chefs. One of the highlights is raclette night, when Rhonda stands in front of the fire in the cosy, rustic dining room, dishing out melted cheese.

In town, the newly refurbished **Beau-Sejour** (0041 (0)24 479 58 58, www.bo-sejour.com, info@bo-sejour.com) is a great option, with some beautiful rooms and a games room with PlayStations. A room will cost CHF160–255 for a double with B&B. The **Hotel Suisse** (0041 (0)24 479 07 07, www.champery .com/hotelsuisse.shtml, hotelsuisse@netplus.ch) is right in the centre of town and has charming rooms. It also contains the Bar des Guides and Les Mines D'Or (see Bars and clubs). A double room costs CHF187–270.

Eating out

On the mountain

Restaurant Coquoz (024 479 12 55) at Planachaux is one of the best places to stop for a bite to eat. **Les Marmottes** (079 691 07 00) is a cosy alpine chalet towards Chavanette and Ripaille. On the French side, Avoriaz has some great places for lunch (see Avoriaz chapter, page 140).

In town

The best restaurant in town is, without a doubt, **Mitchell's** (024 479 20 10, mitchells_champery@ hotmail.com, www.mitchells-champery.com). Tree trunks grow through the restaurant, and the lighting is perfect, with well-placed spot lights and candles. The menu is beautifully composed. For lunch choose between a homemade burger, grilled sandwich (big or small), wrap, beef or fish noodle wok, or delicious salad. In the evening you will have a really tough time choosing between the mouth-watering dishes. If you go to Champéry, you must eat here at least once.

Another good restaurant is **Café Centre** (0041 (0)24 479 15 50, www.cafeducentre.com), open all day. The top floor serves only their gourmet menu (CHF28–48), but downstairs serves just as delicious dishes, such as Thai green curry, Indonesian stew, fish and Cajun Chicken. The **Auberge de Grand Paradis** (just at the bottom of the slopes at Grand Paradis) serves lunch – choose from burgers, spag bol, steak and ale pie, chilli, etc. Similar fare is on offer for dinner – if you plan to visit on the popular raclette night (see Accommodation), make sure you book. The **Gueullhi** (024 479 35 55, info@legueullhi.ch, www.legueullhi.ch) café-restaurant, by the cable car station is a decent place to stop for lunch or dinner. The menu and food is fantastic but the service a bit slow at peak times. For a good pizza, try the **Farinet**, a restaurant 7pm–1am, with fondues, steaks and salads and pizzas, and a club 11pm–4am (see Bars and clubs).

Bars and clubs

Champéry isn't massively into its boozing, but the bars there are, are good. In the Hotel Suisse is the **Bar des Guides**, full of locals enjoying après ski, and the **Mines D'Or**, a wicked bar, with cavernous hideaways – a great place at all times of night for a cosy pint and live music. **Mitchell's** restaurant (see Eating out) also has a great bar, with massive comfy sofas and it is a popular meeting point for the Champéry community. After hours, you will find the locals at **Le Farinet** and the riders at **La Crevasse** (www.la-crevasse.com).

Useful facts and phone numbers

Tourist office

T: 024 479 20 20
F: 024 479 20 21
E: info@champery.ch
W: www.champery.ch

Emergency services

- Police: 024 479 09 18
- Ambulance/mountain rescue: 144
- Medical centre: 024 479 15 16
- Hospital de Monthey: 024 473 17 31
- Hospital d'Aigle: 024 468 86 88

Taxis

- Serge Rey-Bellet: 0041 (0)79 430 15 15
- Closillon Tours: 0041 (0)79 622 22 24

Getting there

By car

From Geneva take the Lake Geneva motorway past Lausanne to Monthey and follow signs to Champéry.

By plane

Lausanne (62km)
Geneva (126km) Transfer around 1.5 hours.
Zürich (250km)

By train

Take the 17.42 Eurostar from London Waterloo to Paris; then an overnight train, changing at Zürich, Lausanne and Aigle. Arrive Champéry station, in resort, at 10.20. Return fares start at £168 in a 6-berth couchette. Contact European Rail (020 7387 0444, www.europeanrail.com).

Crans Montana

Sunny cruising on the slopes and a town you'll want to come back to

CRANS MONTANA®
Ski & Golf
SWITZERLAND

Wildstrubel
3243

Rohrbachstein
2950

Weisshorn
2948

Gletscherhorn
2943

Glacier
Plaine Morte
3000

Les Faverges
2968

Plaine
Morte

Tubang
2826

Mont Bonvin
2995

Petit Bonvin
2400

Bella Lui
2543

Col du
Pochet

La Toula

La Tza

La Flèche

Les Violettes
2250
CAS

Les Taules

Vallon de
l'Ertenze

Cry d'Er
2267

Colorado

La Barmaz

Aprili

Chetseron
2100

Mont Lachaux
2140

Cabane
de Bois

Plumachit

La Cure

Merbé

Pas du Loup

Amadeus 2006

Les Marolires

Aminona

Verdets

Signal

S.M.C

Arnouvaz

S.M.C

Les Barzettes

Plans Mayens

Tom Pouce

Vermala

Barzettes

Grand Signal

Lac de Chermignon

La Combaz

Lac Grenon

Randogne

Montana

Bluche

CMA
DOMAINE SKIABLE
CRANS - MONTANA

On the slopes	
Snow reliability	✳ ✳ ✳
Parks	✳ ✳ ✳
Off-piste	✳ ✳ ✳
Off the slopes	
Après ski	✳ ✳
Nightlife	✳ ✳ ✳
Eating out	✳ ✳ ✳
Resort charm	✳ ✳ ✳

The resort

The two resort centres of Crans and Montana have a definite charm about them; the town doesn't have the 'chocolate box' feel of a number of Swiss resorts but the mountains are stunning, and the resort has a certain character and warmth. Crans is full of Paris-style boutiques, and has some top-class restaurants and hotels. Most of the good bars and clubs are in Crans too, although there are a couple in Montana, as well as the massive Casino. It's not too British either; we make up only 3.5 per cent of visitors to Crans Montana giving it a cosmopolitan feel that many resorts lack. The slopes are dominated by fur-clad skiers searching for a nice restaurant before cruising back down to town for a massage. However, the area does have more to offer.

The mountains

Height: 1500–3000m

Ability	Rating
Expert	✳ ✳
Intermediate	✳ ✳ ✳ ✳
Beginner	✳ ✳ ✳

Getting about

The Crans Montana mountains have some truly stunning views. They are, however, geared to the cruisy intermediate with a preference for pretty paths through the trees rather than steep and challenging terrain. Saying this, there are a few slopes for the expert skier/boarder and there are a number of options for the enthusiastic powder hounds, and these areas rarely get tracked out as few Crans Montana regulars are interested in exploring the surrounding backcountry.

The park

The Aminona Snowpark is a decent size, with a good range of jumps and rails for all standards of rider. There are several small kickers in different lines, according to the level of the rider and a reasonable range of rails, including a rainbow rail and C-rail. There's a fairly easy skier/boardercross course and two huge big-air jumps in the centre of the park, which are very well looked after. New in for last winter were a steel-made quarter pipe and a 6m long box slide. The shapers and designers are enthusiastic and do a great job. There is also a snack bar and BBQ hang-out spot. Check out www.evilplayers.ch/snowpark/.

Off-piste and backcountry

There aren't loads of backcountry areas to explore in Crans Montana, but there is a lot of really easily accessible off-piste to be had. Just off the side of the pisted runs are some sweet faces. There are a couple of narrow couloirs (experts only) and a steep face by the Bella-Lui area. We recommend that you only do this with a guide or knowledgeable local. Some easier spots can be found beneath La Tza and Chetseron. Beware of the sun; most of the mountain is exposed to the sun and the snow can get very heavy by lunchtime, resulting in some nasty slides.

Lift passes	
1 day	CHF56
6 days	CHF274
13 days	CHF468

Instruction

Crans Montana official guide office

These are the guys to call if you want to explore Crans Montana's off-piste potential. They can take you ski touring, off-piste skiing, on avalanche courses, and heliskiing. They also offer semi-private lessons (min. 4 people, max. 6) in ice climbing and freeride.
T: 0041 (0)27 481 14 80
E: info@essmontana.ch
W: www.essmontana.ch

Ecole Swiss de Ski de Crans

One week of group skiing lessons (15 hours) costs CHF170 and snowboarding lessons (12 hours) cost CHF200. Alternatively you can pay CHF55 for 1 half day. Private lessons cost CHF60–90 per hour depending on the number of people.

T: 0041 (0)27 485 93 70
E: esscrans@quick-soft.ch
W: www.cranskischool.ch

Ecole Swiss de Ski de Montana

One week of group lessons (18 hours) costs CHF185 or you can pay CHF55 for 1 day. Private lessons cost CHF60 for 1 person per hour; add CHF10 for each extra person.

T: 0041 (0)27 481 14 80
E: info@essmontana.ch
W: www.essmontana.ch

Ski and Sky

Ski and Sky will teach you skiing, boarding, snowbiking and telemarking. Their hourly rate is CHF60 for private lessons for 1; add CHF10 for each extra person. They also organise tandem paragliding.

T: 0041 (0)27 480 42 50
E: info@skiandsky.ch
W: www.skiandsky.ch

Stoked

Private lessons in skiing or boarding cost CHF198 for 2.5 hours (plus CHF20 for each extra person) and group lessons (max. 6 people) cost CHF95 for 2 half-days. Costs rise to CHF375 for 5 whole days.

T: 0041 (0)27 480 24 21
E: crans-montana@stoked.ch
W: www.stoked.ch

Swiss Mountain Sports

This company can organise all-in-one packages including accommodation, activities, transport and meals. Ski and snowboard lessons cost CHF360 for 1 week (20 hours) of group lessons, CHF190 for 1 week (10 hours) of half-days. Private lessons are CHF60–90 per hour. Tandem paragliding, paintball, telemarking, free ride, heliski and sledging are also available.

T: 0041 (0)27 480 44 66
E: info@swiss-mountain-sports.ch
W: www.swiss-mountain-sports.ch

Other activities

Casino: This is most definitely worth checking out (see Bars and clubs).

Curling: There are a few curling rinks, on which you can have lessons (027 485 04 04).

Hot air ballooning: Flights can be arranged by the Club Aérostatique de Crans-Montana (079 206 84 35/ 079 332 02 93) at a cost of CHF300 per person.

Ice climbing and snow-kiting: Adrenatur offer these activities, as well as riding a snow monster (a kind of scooter).

Ice skating: There are two ice skating rinks – the Ycoor in Montana (027 481 30 55) and Sporting in Crans (027 485 97 95). An adult pass is CHF5 and a 20-minute lesson is CHF28.

Indoor bowling: Another great way to while away an evening (027 481 50 50, barlebowling@netplus.ch). There are four lanes, and the cost for one adult is CHF9.

Internet cafes: There are a number of places to check your E-mails and surf the web – Avalanche (which also has a wireless hotspot), Café 'Au Garage', Club 360, Restaurant Le Farinet and Bar Number Two, Hotel Olympic, and the New Pub.

Night skiing: This takes place on Friday nights on the floodlit slope of Verdets (via the cable car Grand Signal), 7–10pm, and costs CHF15.

Paintballing: This can be arranged with Paralook (079 606 46 28, www.paintball-center.ch, paralook@netplus.ch) and costs CHF30 for 1 hour, including 100 shots, clothing and equipment.

Paragliding: Tandem paragliding flights can be booked with Ski and Sky (see Instruction), or Paralook for CHF140 (see above).

Shopping: For shopoholics with cash to splash, there are some seriously chic boutiques to mosey around. Not the place to pick up the slope fashions though – it's more Prada and Chanel than Oakley.

Squash: There are two squash courts (027 481 16 15, www.leregent.ch) which cost CHF10 for half an hour.

Swimming: A number of hotels have swimming pools available to the public – Hotel Aïda-Castel (Montana, CHF15), Alpina and Savoy (Crans, CHF15), Hôtel Etrier (Crans, CHF15) and Hôtel de la Forêt (Montana, CHF9).

Tennis: Crans Montana has the largest tennis centre in the Swiss Alps (027 481 50 14) with five indoor courts and six outdoor courts. Court hire costs

CHF28–38 and CHF85 for a private lesson.

Tobogganing: There is a 6km toboggan run from Petit Mt-Bonvin (2400m) to Aminona (1500m). Sledges can be hired for CHF10/14 (2 hours/4 hours) and one trip on the Télécabine will cost you CHF16.

Wellness centres: There are a number of centres offering treatments, swimming pools, etc. The Centre de santé et beauté Mességué-Phytotherm at Hôtel Crans Ambassador (027 485 48 48, www.crans-ambassador.ch, info@crans-ambassodor.ch) has a pool, sauna, hammam, solarium, and a number of beauty treatments and slimming treatments. Other centres offering similar treatments include Dabliu Beauty Farm (next to Hotel du Golf, 027 480 34 81, www.dabliu.com, dabliu.crans@bluewin.ch), Centre thérapeutique 'Medica' (027 480 40 41, medica@bluewin.ch) and Centre de 'Bien-être' (027 481 26 12, www.club-hotel-valaisia.ch, valaisia@datacomm.ch).

"The Crans Montana Snowgames combines a big-air jam session, a water slide contest and a sumo contest"

Events

Crans Montana has a number of good events, from the **Crans Montana Snowgames** (www.cransmontanasnow games.ch) which combines a big-air jam session, a water slide contest and a sumo contest, to **Caprices**, the music festival (www.capricesfestival.ch) in which 60 concerts are scheduled over nine days. In February 2005 Texas played on the slopes and there was a huge marquee packed with spectators.

Accommodation

Crans

If price isn't an issue, the best place to stay is the **Hostellerie du Pas de L'Ours** (0041 (0)27 485 93 33, www.pasdelours.ch, pasdelours@relaischateaux.fr) which has nine suites, including junior suites, that are all individually decorated and absolutely stunning. Each suite has a fireplace, mini bar and Jacuzzi and will set you back CHF380–900 for the room per night, depending on the time of season and the type of suite (the most expensive is a 4-person suite). There is one restaurant in the hotel and another beside the main building, Bistrot des Ours, which is equally as stunning, and equally as expensive.

The larger **Hôtel de l'Etrier** (0041 (0)27 485 44 00, hotel.etrier@bluewin.ch, www.hoteletrier.ch) next door shares the newly built spa, massage and pool complex. It's slightly less expensive; a room will cost CHF140–440 depending on the room and time of season. The **Hotel Alpha** (0041 (0)27 484 24 00, www.hotel_alpha.ch, hotelalpha@bluewin.ch) is a great hotel within a few minutes' walk of Crans centre and about 10 minutes' walk from the lifts. It's pretty 60s looking from the outside but the staff are mega friendly, the rooms comfortable and spacious with stunning views and the restaurant has a really cosy, alpine feel. There is an outdoor swimming pool in the summer. We highly recommend it.

Montana

Montana has some more reasonable hotels. **Hôtel Olympic** (0041 (0)27 481 29 85, hotel-olympic@ bluewin.ch, www.amadeus-holidays.ch) is a simple hotel in the centre of Montana, right next to loads of the bars and the casino and only 300m from the slopes for CHF65 per person per night for B&B. **Hotel Mirabeau** (0041 (0)27 480 21 51, www.hotel mirabeau.ch, contact@hotelmirabeau.ch) is well placed, pretty nice and not too expensive with a double room costing CHF190–330 per night depending on whether you want a bath or shower, and on the time of season.

Slightly more off the beaten track is the **Grand Hôtel du Parc** (0041 (0)27 481 41 01, www.parc-hotel.ch, hotel.parc@bluewin.ch). It's a big ugly building on the outside but inside it's really nice, the staff are friendly and the views are incredible. The prices are always

changing so it's best to check with the hotel. The **Bella-Lui** (0041 (0)27 481 31 14, www.bellalui.ch, info@bellalui.ch) is in a quiet area in the trees but it's not too far from everything. Again it's not beautiful, but the views are. B&B accommodation costs CHF55–100 per person per night depending on the type of room.

The 4-star **Alpina and Savoy** (0041 (0)27 485 09 00, www.alpinasavoy.ch, info@alpinasavoy.ch) is bang in-between Crans and Montana, but close to the lifts, and it's pretty retro inside. There's a spa centre, a pool and comfy rooms that will cost from CHF200 per person per night.

You can book your accommodation directly on the Crans Montana website (www.crans-montana.ch) and they give you cheaper prices for booking earlier (December). They are perfectly happy for you to book for 3 or 4 days and not the whole week.

Eating out

On the mountain

The **Plumachit** (027 481 25 32) is tucked away in the trees on the path to Aminona with a huge terrace and stunning views. The service can take a while on busy, sunny days, but once you've managed to get your order in, the food arrives fairly quickly. The run down is a very flat path so it attracts a lot of walkers too. Other favourites of ours with outdoor bars and terraces are the restaurant at **Merbé** (027 481 22 97), at the first

stop of the gondola from Crans Montana, and the **Amadeus** (027 481 24 95), above Montana.

In town

In Crans, **Le Chalet** (027 481 05 05) is a stunning restaurant in the centre of town that serves a fantastic raclette and other tasty treats. If raclette is your cup of tea you may also want to try **La Dent Blanche** (027 481 11 79), whose cheese is like no others. **Raphaele** (027 480 31 50) is the best pizzeria in town, opposite the post office. It has a beautiful interior and a large wine cellar. A pizza will cost you CHF13–19. **Hotel Alpha** (see Accommodation) has a good rustic restaurant in its basement. **La Channe** (027 480 39 19) is one of our favourite restaurants in town. It serves fantastic Mexican food in a romantic, candlelit atmosphere. Alternatively, you can also sit at or near the bar and have some tapas, which is great if you get sick of big meals. For gourmet cuisine you should head to the **Bistrot des Ours** at the Hostellerie du Pas de L'Ours (027 485 93 33) and get your favourite credit card ready.

In Montana the **Farinet** (027 481 36 15) is a lovely pine-clad restaurant serving traditional food including raclettes, fondues and the like. The **Mayen** (027 481 29 85, www.amadeus-holidays.ch), under the Hotel Olympic, is similarly traditional and has an alpine feel. Rostis are their tasty specialities. At the end of town, the **Micheal Angelo Pizzeria** (027 481 09 19) is simple and cheery, with checked tablecloths. You can get a pizza for CHF14–18. The **Gerber,** on your left as you come into Montana from Crans, has a large terrace that gets the sun at lunchtime and is also beautiful inside. A great place for lunch or dinner. There is also a café area and patisserie.

Bars and clubs

In Crans, If you're looking for somewhere to take your grandpa, head to **Bar 1900,** a nice enough place that does a good club sandwich and chips for CHF12.50. If you're looking for somewhere a bit more lively head to **Le Pub** (027 481 54 96), also known as George and

Dragon – the busiest bar, open 4pm–2am. **Tapas ex La Channe** (see Eating out) also has a cosy bar where you can snack on some tapas as you drink. From 11pm there are a number of lively options to choose from: **Punch Bar** (027 481 20 83, www.plazapunch.com), **Absolut** (027 213 61 39, www.absolutclub.ch), **Le Barocke** (079 221 16 35, www.barockeclub.com) and the very funky **Leo's Bar** (027 481 98 00, www.leosbar.com). The best thing about all the bars in Crans is that they are only a few steps away from each other.

Most of the good bars are in Crans but there are a couple in Montana that are worth checking out. The **Amadeus** bar (027 481 29 85) has concerts on Sundays and a jam session every Thursday (days may change). It's open 4.30pm–1am. The **Grange** is a bar to stay away from – it's pretty dingy, amazingly smoky and full of old locals. When the bars close, head to the **Number Two** bar/club (027 481 36 15) under the restaurant Mayen. One of the best places to while away an evening in Montana is the **Casino** (027 485 90 40, www.casinocm.ch, info@casinocm.ch) with roulette, blackjack and slot machines as well as a great restaurant and a bar open 3pm–3am. Remember to take your passport.

Useful facts and phone numbers

Tourist office

T: 0041 (0)27 485 04 04
F: 0041 (0)27 485 04 60/61
E: information@crans-montana.ch
W: www.crans-montana.ch

Direct reservations

T: 0041 (0)27 485 04 44
F: 0041 (0)27 485 04 60

Emergency services

- Police municipale: 027 481 81 81
- Police cantonale: 027 486 65 60
- Medical centre: 027 480 40 40
- Medical emergency: 144
- Weather and snow information: www.mycma.ch

Doctors

- Dr Bonvin Louis: 027 481 35 35
- Dr Kunz Ariane: 027 481 32 32
- Dr Vouilloz Patrick: 027 481 42 74

Taxis

- Emery, Jean: 027 481 19 19
- Morard, Jaques: 027 481 53 65
- Pott, César: 027 481 13 13
- Pott, Michel: 027 481 71 71
- Taxi Philippe: 079 422 29 85
- Taxi Sylvio: 079 400 75 45

Getting there

By car

From Geneva/Lausanne, take the A9 motorway to Sierre, then follow signs to Crans-Montana

By plane

Geneva (180km)
Milan (260km)
Zürich (300km)

By train

Take the 08.12 Eurostar from London Waterloo to Paris; then by train, changing at Lausanne, to Sierre; and then a funicular train, arriving in resort at 18.57. Return fares from £140. Contact European Rail (020 7387 0444, www.european rail.com). Funicular train tickets (CHF11.40 single) are purchased at Sierre station.

Davos

Great mountains, with a city where the resort should be

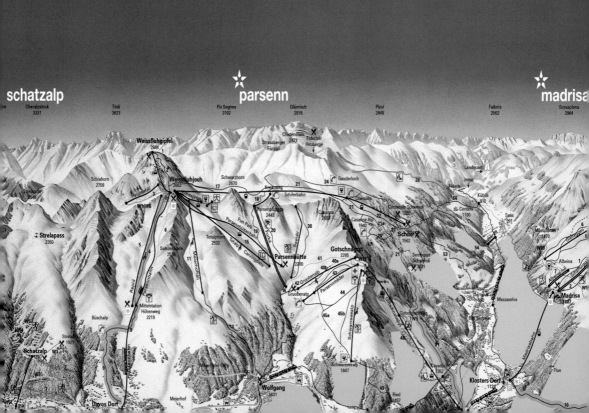

schatzalp

★ parsenn

★ madrisa

On the slopes	
Snow reliability	❄ ❄ ❄ ❄
Parks	❄ ❄ ❄ ❄
Off-piste	❄ ❄ ❄ ❄

Off the slopes	
Après ski	❄ ❄ ❄
Nightlife	❄ ❄ ❄ ❄
Eating out	❄ ❄ ❄ ❄
Resort charm	❄ ❄

The resort

There's no doubt about it, Davos is a bizarre place. On the plus side the mountains are incredible. There are five main mountains in the Davos-Klosters area which present stacks of opportunities for all sorts of riding, from unlimited on-piste opportunities to masses of freeriding and the best pipes around. Travelling from, to and between the mountains can be a bit of a laborious task though and you really have to make use of the mountains to make it worthwhile. You certainly wouldn't visit Davos to experience resort charm. It's not ugly, but its city feel doesn't create a particularly endearing atmosphere. There are loads of restaurants, bars and clubs as well as the kind of designer shops, museums and other facilities that you expect in a large town or city but it's almost eerie in that it's fairly rare to see people moseying around town.

The mountains

Height: 1124–2844m

Ability	Rating
Expert	❄ ❄ ❄ ❄ ❄
Intermediate	❄ ❄ ❄ ❄ ❄
Beginner	❄ ❄ ❄

Getting about

There are 103 pistes (310km) in the Davos-Klosters region, with 54 lifts to serve them. There are four different mountains to be accessed from Davos, each with their own clientele. **Parsenn**, accessible from Davos Dorf (also from Klosters) is the best mountain for cruising around on well-groomed slopes and checking out the stunning scenery. The restaurants are great, there's some fantastic off-piste and it's generally a great place. The only run back down, though, is to the outskirts of Dorf.

From the centre of Davos Platz, you can get to **Jakobshorn** mountain, home of the park, fun restaurants and good, wide pistes. **Rinerhorn** and **Pischa** both take a bit of travelling to get to from Dorf or Platz. Rinerhorn is good for cruising around in the sun. Pischa, for the 2006/7 season, will be purely a freeride mountain; two ski lifts and the cable car will be open, but the pistes will not be prepared.

"Jakobshorn is the main hangout spot for the freestylers"

The park

Jakobshorn is the main hangout spot for the freestylers. It has two superb pipes; one super pipe is located in the village in the Bolgen area and is floodlit for night-time riding, the other is at the top of Jatz with the park. There are a lot of world-class riders who hang out in the area, including Dani Castandaché, who organises the SB Jam, sponsored by O'Neill and these guys make sure that the pipes are always perfectly shaped. There's a good range of kickers, from small table tops to big booters and plenty of rails to jib. The Rinerhorn and Pischa mountains each have a park and there's supposed to be a pipe at Parsenn, but they need the right conditions in order to build it. Davos rocks for freestyle.

Off-piste and backcountry

On Pischa, the freeride mountain, you have a choice. You can hit the accessible, unpisted runs, but if you are prepared to hike for 2 hours maximum you can drop down the back of the mountain and have access to everything: cliffs, bowls and couloirs. From there you end up in the middle of nowhere though so a car is handy. Parsenn has some of the best off-piste; you can pretty much access powder from every lift. There's not much hiking involved and plenty to do. The Totalphorn area, between the Meierhoftäli and Totalp chairlifts, is superb, but does get sketchy if the snow isn't great and bad accidents have been known to happen in these conditions. Don't let that put you off: on a perfect powder day it's definitely worth checking out. If the visibility is bad, there are loads of tree runs to play in on the Gotschna side and on Madrisa.

The Weissfluh, a north-facing slope, is one of the most famous off-piste runs. It's around a 500m drop with a 15-minute hike out. You can also take a guided tour to Arosa and Lenzerheide from the Weissfluh – there is no walking involved, although you do have to buy different lift tickets. Definitely take a guide with you for this one. We recommend contacting Lukas Dürr at Swiss Freeride (www.swissfreeride.ch).

There is an avalanche training centre at the top of the Carjöl lift (Fuxägufer) on the **Jakobshorn**. Here you can practise using your avalanche equipment under realistic conditions. For further information and group reservations contact Fun Mountain Holidays (081 414 90 20).

"The Weissfluh, a north-facing slope, is one of the most famous off-piste runs"

Lift passes	
1 day	CHF61
6 days	CHF282
13 days	CHF488

Children and teenagers get reductions. You can order your pass in advance on the internet at www.davosklosters.ch.

Instruction

Ski School 'New Trend'

Lessons can include off-piste and there are freeride camps that offer video coaching.
T: 0041 (0)81 413 20 40
E: info@newtrenddavos.ch
W: www.newtrenddavos.ch

Snow and You

Reto Cahenzli is a local ski teacher who offers carving, guiding and powder skiing.
T: 0041 (0)79 636 70 30
E: snowdesign1@bluewin.ch

Swiss Snowsport-School Davos

This school offers the usual lessons including off-piste and telemarking and freestyle boarding.
T: 0041 (0)81 416 24 54
E: info@ssd.ch
W: www.ssd.ch

Top Secret Snowboard School

Freestyle, freeride and off-piste courses are available and include video coaching.
T: 0041 (0)81 413 40 43
E: info@topsecretdavos.ch
W: www.topsecretdavos.ch

Other activities

Remember to get a guest card from your hotel as it entitles you to a number of discounts on activities as well as unrestricted use of the Landschaft Davos public transport network.

Non-sporting activities

Casino: This is located at the Hotel Europe in Davos Platz, offering blackjack, American roulette and 70 slot machines. Remember to take your passport for ID.

Cinema: Four or five films are shown daily. Call 0900 900 123 for information about the programme or check out www.diesewoche.ch.

Museums: There is a choice of visiting a cultural museum, a doll museum, a folk museum, a winter sports museum, a mining museum or a museum of medicine. Don't exhaust yourself with all that culture.

Wellness centres:

Arabella Sheraton Hotel Seehof (081 416 12 12) has a sauna, steam bath, whirlpool, exercise room, beauty farm and solarium and offers massage.

Bad Alvaneu (081 420 44 00) has a sulphur bath, steam bath, solarium and sauna, and offers various therapies, massage, and exercise facilities.

Bad Serneus (081 422 14 44) has a 34° sulphur bath, an aqua gym, sauna and solarium, and offers mud packs and medical care.

Bristol Wellness (081 416 31 33) has a sauna, steam bath, whirlpool and solarium, and offers massage and shiatsu.

Turmhotel Victoria (081 417 53 00) has sauna, steam bath, whirlpool, solarium, health club and beauty parlour.

Waldhotel Bellevue (081 415 37 47) has steam grotto, whirlpool, sauna, steam bath and brine bath, and offers massage.

Sporting activities

Hang-gliding and paragliding: Choose from tandem flights, passenger flights or a weekly course over Jakobshorn or Parsenn from a number of schools: Luftchraft Paragliding School (079 623 19 70, info@ luftchraft.ch, www.luftchraft.ch); Flugcenter Grischa (081 422 20 70); Paragliding Davos (079 236 19 70, www.paragliding-davos.ch).

Horse riding: Lessons and treks can be booked for both beginners and advanced riders. Call either Hans Lenz (081 413 19 55) or Andreas Stiffler (081 416 46 82).

Ice skating: Europe's largest natural ice rink (over 18 000m^2), an outdoor ice rink and an ice stadium are all top venues for ice hockey, ice skating, speed skating, curling and Bavarian curling. Admission for skaters is CHF4 for adults with guest card and it's CHF20 for a 20-minute lesson (081 415 36 00).

Sports complex and gymnasium: This is open to the public for a range of activities including athletics, football, handball, volleyball, basketball, streetball, etc. If you're staying in Davos you can use the facilities free of charge but you should make a reservation (081 415 36 00, sportzentrum@davos.ch).

Swimming: The public pool is in Davos Platz (081 413 64 63) and has a sauna and solarium. The Hotel Sonnenberg in Davos Dorf (081 417 59 00) and the

"The Spengler Cup Ice Hockey Tournament is the most important ice hockey event on the international calendar"

Waldhotel Bellevue in Davos Platz (081 415 37 47) also have public indoor swimming pools.

Tennis and squash: Phone to book courts on 081 413 31 31.

Tobogganing: There are toboggan runs on Schatzalp, Rinerhorn, Madrisa and Parsenn (totalling 22km of runs).

Swissraft (081 911 52 50) offer a range of activities to try, from **balloon trips** to **canyoning** and **hydrospeeding**.

Events

The **Spengler Cup Ice Hockey Tournament** is the most important ice hockey event on the international calendar, and is held annually in Davos between Christmas and New Year (www.spenglercup.ch). The **O'Neill Snowboard Jam** is also held at New Year in Davos on the Bolgen area at Jakobshorn. It has become one of the major events on the freestyle snowboarding calendar. The qualifying heats are open to all, and the best up-and-coming boarders can challenge the pros at the Grand Show Finale which should not be missed.

For further information regarding events in Davos contact the tourist office (see Useful facts and phone numbers, or E-mail events@davos.ch).

Accommodation

There are 71 hotels in Davos, with a total of 24 000 guest beds and there is something for any budget. In Davos Platz, **Hotel Europe** (0041 (0)81 415 41 41, www.europe-davos.ch) is a great place to stay – just to be near all the action. With restaurants, bars and a casino in the one place, who'd want to go anywhere else? It's a 4-star hotel and one night's B&B costs CHF110–145. The **Alte Post** (0041 (0)81 414 90 20, www.fun-mountain.ch) is really handy for Jakobshorn and is cosy and attractive. It costs CHF150–210 for 1 night's B&B.

In Davos Dorf, **Hotel Parsenn** (0041 (0)81 416 32 32, www.hotelparsenn.ch) is an attractive, 3-star hotel, right opposite to the Parsenn railway so in a perfect position for the slopes. It costs CHF595–994 for 7 nights' half-board and CHF85–147 for 1 night's B&B. The **Snowboarders' Palace** (0041 (0)81 414

90 20) provides the cheapest, dormitory style accommodation and is handy for the Schatzalp funicular.

Eating out

On the mountain

The restaurant at the **Höhenweg** (081 417 67 44, www.gourmetdavos.ch), just up the Parsennbahn train from Davos Dorf, has a massive terrace and bar and it's a great place to chill out with some top nosh. Also on Parsenn, **Bruhin's** (081 417 66 44) is a fancy restaurant right at the top of the Gipfelbahn cable car. It has stunning views but there is no terrace which is a bit of a shame on a sunny day. The **Gruobenalp** (081 422 62 30) is a traditional chalet-style restaurant, just down from Gotschnagrat; perfect on a sunny day as the terrace has a gorgeous view. The **Alte Schwendi** (081 332 13 24, www.freeridelodge.ch, freeridelodge@E-mail.ch) is the best mountain restaurant in which to hang out due to the great music and atmosphere. It's located at Chesetta, just above the Schifer. There's a massive terrace, great traditional food, a cosy chalet inside and really friendly staff. If you just fancy grabbing a good burger, the restaurant on the **Weissfluhjoch** (081 417 66 44) has the best in town.

On Jakobshorn, the **Bolgen Plaza** is where the après ski dancing is to be found and **Jatzhütte's** (081 413 64 01, www.jatzhuette.ch), near to the terrain park, is pretty funky and madly themed with fake palm trees and other paraphernalia.

In town

There is a great variety of cuisine in Davos if you know where to look. **Tab Tim Siam** (081 416 32 52) in Davos Dorf is a really popular and friendly Thai restaurant, full of only slightly tacky, brightly coloured decorations. **Bistro Angelo** (081 416 59 79) is a simple but cool restaurant. In Davos Platz there are lots more opportunities to track down a decent meal. If you have a taste for some oriental cuisine you will not be disappointed with **Zum Goldener Drachen** in the Hotel Bahnhof-Terminus (081 414 97 97). Hotel Europe (081 415 41 41) also has a stylish Chinese eatery, **Zauberberg**, and the same building houses another restaurant, **Scala**, which serves some good-

value and tasty dishes until midnight. If you're peckish in the early hours of the morning try **After Hours** (081 413 63 76), for 24-hour takeaway munchies including pizzas, sandwiches and hot dogs. If you're too lazy to move from your room, **Hotel Albana** (081 413 58 41) deliver pizzas to your door.

Bars and clubs

Pick the right bars and clubs, and you can have a great night out in Davos. The crowd is young and there is a good mix of tourists and locals around. **Bolgenschanze** (081 413 71 01, www.bolgen schanze.ch) is the snowboard hangout. It has great deals on pitchers and shooters and plays a range of music: hip hop, rock and the like. It's a big place, gets pretty busy and has a young, hip atmosphere. **Chämi**

"The crowd is young and there is a good mix of tourists and locals around"

Bar (081 413 55 55) is one of the most popular bars in Davos Platz and tends to be fairly hectic and jam-packed. **Ex Bar** (081 413 56 45) is a good late-night bar, especially if you have the munchies as you can eat until 6am. The **Hotel Europe** is right in the centre of the action and comprises a number of restaurants and cafés (see Accommodation), the casino, a comfy and chilled out piano bar, **Toxic,** where the top people tinkle out their tunes, and the two main clubs: **Cabanna Club** (081 415 42 01, www.cabanna.ch) and **Cava** (081 413 23 57, www.cava-davos.ch).

Useful facts and phone numbers

Tourist office

T: 0041 (0)81 415 21 21
F: 0041 (0)81 415 21 00
E: info@davos.ch
W: www.davos.ch/ www.davosklosters.ch

Emergency services

- Fire brigade: 118
- Police (emergency): 117
- Local police: 081 414 33 11
- Cantonal police: 081 413 76 22
- Rescue and ambulance: 144
- Hospital: 081 414 88 88
- Snow and avalanche report – 187
- Weather information: 081 415 21 33/162

Doctors

There are nearly 30 doctors and dentists in Davos so we shall name only a few.
- Dr P Flurry (081 413 71 28)
      Promenade 33A, Davos Platz
- Dr B Knöpfli (081 415 70 70) Scalettastrasse 5, Davos Platz
- Dr R Stocker (081 416 61 62) Bahnhofstrasse 15, Davos Dorf
- Dentist – Dr A Bader (081 413 34 30)
      Promenade 41, Davos Platz

Taxis

- Angelo's Taxi: 081 416 73 73 or 079 416 59 05
- Express Taxi: 081 410 11 11

Getting there

By car

It takes about 12–13 hours to get to Davos from Calais, so it's probably easier to fly unless you're going to take a few days over the drive.

By plane

Zürich (150km) is the easiest place to fly to and it takes under 3 hours to get from the airport to Davos by train or car. You can get the train straight to Davos Dorf or Platz but you will have to change trains a couple of times. For CHF20 per bag you can send your luggage to the appropriate station from Zürich airport. For more info contact the railway on 0041 (0)81 288 32 50, www.rhb.ch, davos-platz@rhb.ch.

By train

Take the 17.42 Eurostar from London Waterloo to Paris; then an overnight train, changing at Landquart. Arrive Davos station, in resort, at 08.55. Return fares start at £168 in a 6-berth couchette. Contact European Rail (020 7387 0444, www.europeanrail.com).

Flims

A freestylers' mountain and
a pretty Swiss resort, spoilt
by a constant flow of traffic

On the slopes	
Snow reliability	❄ ❄ ❄
Parks	❄ ❄ ❄ ❄ ❄
Off-piste	❄ ❄ ❄
Off the slopes	
Après ski	❄ ❄ ❄
Nightlife	❄ ❄
Eating out	❄ ❄
Resort charm	❄ ❄

The resort

The Flims-Laax-Falera mountains are fantastic. They are particularly perfect for the budding freestyler, and there's some good off-piste into the bargain that you can find with or without guidance. It's a little flat, but you'll forgive that when you see the park. The town, however, is not for the fun-crazed freestyler; there are a couple of very cool après ski bars but little to entertain you later on. It is quite attractive in the way that all the buildings have an appealing, chalet-style look, but the resort is hugely disadvantaged by the endless traffic that runs through the centre of the town at all hours of the day. Also many of the interiors of hotels and restaurants look like they need bringing into the 21st century. If you want to ride these mountains we suggest you stay in Laax Murschetg (see Laax Murschetg chapter, page 366); it has easier access to the park, and the best bars and places to stay.

The mountains

Height: 1100–3018m

Ability	Rating
Expert	❄ ❄ ❄
Intermediate	❄ ❄ ❄ ❄
Beginner	❄ ❄ ❄

Getting about

Flims is located at the far end of the Alpenarena (which combines Flims, Laax and Falera), providing access to 220km of slopes. The mountain is pretty flat so it's great for cruisy intermediates, though there is a fair bit of fresh powder that you can see from many of the pistes. The park is located at Crap Sogn Gion and there are some freeride routes marked on the piste map. As the mountains in the Alpenarena are the same, the details on the park and the off-piste can be found in the Laax Murschetg chapter, page 366.

Lift passes	
1 day	CHF61
6 days	CHF301
13 days	CHF443

You can get a park and pipe pass for CHF38 per day. Teens and children get a discount.

Instruction

Mountain Fantasy

These are the best mountain guides in town for skiers, boarders and anyone else who wants to explore.
T: 0041(0)81 936 70 77
E: bergsport@mountain-fantasy.ch
W: www.mountain-fantasty.ch

Ski Schule

Five days in ski school will cost CHF300.
T: 0041 (0)81 927 71 71
W: www.laax.com/skischule

Snowboarding School

Five days will cost around CHF460. They also offer a taster course on a Sunday afternoon to find out whether you like snowboarding or not.
T: 0041(0)81 927 71 55
E: fahrschule@laax.com
W: www.laax.com/fahrschule

Other activities

Curling: There is a curling stadium in Flims (081 911 19 50) with four rinks and a heated spectator stand. You can pay to rent the stadium or for lessons.

Full-moon skiing: In January, February and March you can ski under the full moon; contact the tourist office for more details and exact dates.

Golf: There is an indoor driving range at the Park Waldhaus Hotel (081 928 48 48) if you can't stand a week away from your golf clubs.

Helicopters: These can be hired for pleasure trips or as a taxi (081 911 52 50).

Ice skating: There are two ice skating rinks; the natural rink can be skated on from December until February and the other until the end of March.

Paragliding or delta flying: Training and trial days paragliding or delta flying can be arranged by a few companies including Swissraft (081 911 52 50) and X-Dream Fly (081 921 28 47).

Sports centre: The sports centre (081 920 91 91) has an ice rink, fitness room, basement shooting range, solarium, table tennis, outdoor ice rink, Bavarian curling and an interestingly named 'Vibra bed'.

Tobogganing: There is a 3km tobogganing run from Foppa to Flims (081 927 70 78).

Wellness centres: There are loads of wellness centres to check out with the best two being La Mira at the Hotel Adula (081 928 28 28) with an outdoor hot tub, and Delight at the Park Hotel Waldhaus (081 928 48 48).

Events

The best events are in the park; these are detailed in the Laax Murschetg chapter, see page 366.

Accommodation

Waldhaus

The **Park Hotel Waldhaus** (0041 (0)81 928 48 48, www.parkhotel-waldhaus.ch, info@parkhotelwaldhaus.ch) was awarded Hotel of the Year in 2004 by Gault-Millau, a very prestigious Swiss award. It was awarded on the completion of the Delight spa and beauty wellness centre which is stunning and needs to be seen. The 'water world' area is made up of three different pools with a total of 355m^2 of water. The hotel (that's really more like a self-contained village) is massive, with acres of long corridors. It is pretty impersonal, despite being impressive. We would prefer to stay in the beautiful **Hotel Adula** (0041 (0)81 928 28 28, www.adula.ch, info@adula.ch), a more

friendly and cosy kind of luxury. The spa (La Mira) has a gym, pool and outdoor spa and the restaurants are the best in town (see Eating out). The spa facilities in both the Park Hotel and the Adula are open to the public.

For a slightly less expensive alternative try the pleasant and comfortable **Arvenhotel Waldeck** (0041 (0)81 928 14 14, www.waldeck.ch, info@waldeck.ch) or **Hotel Garni National** (0041 (0)81 928 14 74, www.national-flims.ch, info@national-flims.ch) – both owned by the same company.

"The spa facilities in both the Park Hotel and the Adula are open to the public"

Flims Dorf

The best hotels are in Waldhaus but there are some in Dorf that are worth a look, and they do have the advantage of being closer to the lift station. The cosy and friendly **Meiler Hotel Prau da Monis** (0041 (0)81 920 93 93, www.meiler-pdm.ch, hotel@meiler-pdm.ch) is in a fantastic position for the slopes and après ski bars (it is attached to the Stenna Bar). Most rooms have a balcony or terrace and will cost you CHF144–290 per room per night for B&B. They also offer half-board accommodation.

If you're not into late-night partying (and if you are, you really shouldn't be in Flims in the first place) and enjoy the tranquillity of isolation, one of the best places to stay is the **Fidazerhof** in the nearby town of Fidaz (0041 (0)81 911 35 03, www.fidazerhof.ch, info@fidazerhof.ch). It is a short bus ride from the town and slopes (the buses run every half hour during the day) and has a spectacular view from the terrace. It's really friendly, has great rooms and a restaurant, and a wellness suite that offers a large variety of treatments.

Eating out

On the mountain

If you're hitting the park and pipe you will be eating and drinking at the popular bars at Crap Sogn Gion: **Rock Bar** and **Café No Name** (081 927 73 44). These bars are just above the half pipe and they are great places to hang out. For a cheeky beer, hit the terrace of Café No Name right at the top of the park and for a great cheeseburger head upstairs to the café **Gastro-Zentrum** (081 927 73 73). There are tons of deckchairs and comfy outdoor seating at the Rock Bar so you'll always be able to find a place to relax with a beer. There's even a free games room in the basement with an Xbox and table football. The restaurant at **Foppa** (081 911 16 50) is a good place for lunch, just above Flims, and can be reached by foot or on skis or a board. If you like small, family-run chalet-restaurants,

turn off the route from Startgels to Flims to **Runcahöhe** (081 911 15 88).

In town

Most of the decent restaurants in Flims are in hotels and take a little searching for. In Waldhaus, the **Hotel Adula** (081 928 28 28, info@adula.ch) has two of the best restaurants in town. **La Clav** is a small and smart Italian restaurant that serves top quality pasta and risotto (no pizza). The cream of the crop is the **Barga**, a very beautiful and quaint French restaurant; perfect for a smart celebration. There are two restaurants in the Hotel Bellevue, the most atmospheric of which is the **Caverna-Keller** (081 911 31 31, info@bellevueflims.ch), a 425-year-old cavernous basement perfect for a romantic candlelit dinner. If you tire of the traditional cuisine, try the fantastic **Little China Restaurant** (081 928 48 27). If you fancy a pizza, you can head to the **Pomodoro** (081

911 10 62) in Waldhaus for a wood-fired pizza or the cheery **Pizzeria Veneziana** (081 929 90 10) in Flims Dorf.

A 5-minute drive away in Fidaz is the **Fidazerhof Hotel** (081 920 90 10) that has a pleasant restaurant with stunning views from the terrace. For something unusual, take a trip up the slopes to the **Startgels Alpenrose** (081 911 58 48); when you book they will arrange to come and pick you up in a piste basher from outside the Legna Bar on the slopes. Every Tuesday and Thursday evening, the **Foppa** restaurant (see Eating out on the mountain) is open; enjoy a raclette or fondue and then a sledge ride back to town.

Bars and clubs

The best bars are the après ski bars in Flims Dorf. The **Legna Bar** is right on the slopes in Flims Dorf and has a great après ski vibe. Stylish and simple, it's the perfect place to get drunk. Moving on down a few stairs you will come to the **Iglu**, a small dome that is very cool and cosy. If you're still standing, the **Stenna Bar** isn't too bad, but it does need a revamp to keep up with the times. There's a bar outside too but the scenery's not great as you're overlooking the main road. The **Livingroom** is nearby, has a lounge with a fireplace, and offers good food all day. Flem Massiv plays hip hop, reggae and dancehall. Check out www.flemmassiv.ch for the event programme.

If you want to hear some top class DJs in action, take a taxi to Laax Murschetg where you can find the über-cool **Riders Palace** lobby bar and club complete with neon lighting (see Laax Murschetg chapter, page 366).

Useful facts and phone numbers

Tourist office

T: 0041 (0)81 920 92 00
E: tourismus@alpenarena.ch
W: www.alpenarena.ch

Emergency services

- Police: In an emergency call 117, if not call 081 928 29 40/081 911 11 64
- In an emergency on the mountain call the SOS central office on 081 972 70 01
- Hospital in Chur: 081 256 61 11
- Fire: 118

Doctors

- Dr B Durschei: 081 911 26 66
- Dr A Lötscher: 081 911 10 55
- Dr Michel: 081 911 12 07
- Dr P Reiser: 081 911 13 13

Taxis

- Taxi Mario: 081 941 22 22

Getting there

By car

Don't try to drive from Geneva via Andermatt; we did and it became a 4-hour detour – halfway along the road it stopped; it's only completely open in summer. You best bet is to fly to Zürich or Friedrichshafen. From there you can hire a car or catch a bus.

By plane

Zürich (150km)
Friedrichshafen (140km) for Ryanair flights.

By train

Take the 17.42 Eurostar from London Waterloo to Paris; then an overnight train to Chur, and then a local bus (42 minutes), arriving in resort at 08.40. Return fares start at £168 in a 6-berth couchette. Contact Rail Europe (08705 848 848, www.raileurope.co.uk) or European Rail (020 7387 0444, www.europeanrail.com). Bus tickets (€8.30 single) are purchased at the station.

Klosters

Klosters has an impressive
returning population, and it's
not hard to see why

On the slopes	
Snow reliability	✽✽✽
Parks	–
Off-piste	✽✽✽✽

Off the slopes	
Après ski	✽✽✽
Nightlife	✽✽
Eating out	✽✽✽✽✽
Resort charm	✽✽✽✽

The resort

Klosters has a distinguished reputation as the choice of the rich, royal and famous. Whilst this is not an unfair statement, and it obviously attracts an opulent clientele, there are few signs of pretentiousness. The striking characteristic of Klosters is the returning population and although it can appear a bit cliquey, if you are willing to put in the effort you can infiltrate the scene pretty easily and a new world will open up. Klosters is also an ideal place for young families and the facilities are fantastic. In fact, the mountains have something for everyone; you are unlikely to be disappointed.

The mountains

Height: 1124–2844m

Ability	Rating
Expert	✽✽✽✽
Intermediate	✽✽✽✽
Beginner	✽✽✽✽

Getting about

There are two mountains that can be accessed from Klosters: Parsenn, a large ski area connected to Davos, and Madrisa, a smaller, family-orientated zone that has some fantastic off-piste potential.

The Parsenn mountain is beautiful, the acres of pistes are always well groomed and it is the perfect place for intermediates to cruise around. The runs back down from Parsenn to Klosters and the surrounding areas are not the easiest runs (beginners might be advised to catch the lift back down), but they are great. Alternatively you could embark on the 12km-long run down to Küblis. You'll need to catch the train back to Klosters, but the transport system is superb so it shouldn't pose too much of a problem. The only disadvantage is that the mountain can only be accessed from the Gotschnabahn lift from Klosters which can mean really big queues in busy holiday periods.

"The acres of pistes are always well groomed and it is the perfect place for intermediates to cruise around"

Madrisa is a smaller mountain, but has a lot to offer and it has the added benefit of being far quieter than Parsenn. The lift system on Madrisa is being totally modernised; the Old School red bubbles have just been replaced with smart new blue ones that are much faster and more comfortable. Madrisa could almost be classed as a separate resort as there are locally based ski and snowboard schools, a great restaurant and different play areas for the kids. Madrisa is filled with T-bar lifts which can be a little hard for beginners but if that doesn't bother you, you can take full advantage of this superb area. There's something for everyone; for starters it's perfect for learning to ride using the magic carpet and special beginners' lifts, there are also some great groomed slopes for carving and loads of untracked areas for freeriding. Madrisa is the perfect area for young families. Mum and dad can leave their child in the care centre and go off for a bit of on- or off-piste action (for children 2–6 years old it costs CHF10 for the first hour and CHF5 after that). There is also a room in which you can supervise your own child that is free of charge.

There are three mountain regions of Davos (Jakobshorn, Rinerhorn and Pischa – purely a freeride mountain for 2007) that are fairly easily accessible from Klosters (see Davos chapter, page 344).

The park
Last season a much-requested park opened in town on the Selfranga lift, which is open during the day and is also floodlit for two nights of the week. The park currently contains three kickers ranging from 6 to 14m, a flat down box, an up box and two flat boxes. However, there are plans to extend this considerably in the 2006/7 season. Check out www.duty.ch.

Off-piste and backcountry
The off-piste in Klosters is fantastic. You can almost always find good snow, even if there has been no snow for a month, due to the large numbers of north-facing slopes and countless tree runs. Disadvantages include more often than not having to catch a bus, train or taxi from wherever you end up as few of the runs actually end up in Klosters. We were shown the ropes by Chris Southwell, a professional snowboarder sponsored by Oakley, and Lukas Dürr, a local and well-respected mountain guide.

On a sunny day Madrisa is the place to hit the backcountry. From the top of the mountain is the long run down to San Antonien that is superb. A 5–10-minute walk takes you to a big open powder field. It's not too hard (although there are some steeps if you fancy it) and can be done with the whole family if you feel confident. However, it should be done with a guide so you don't get lost. Once in San Antonien there is a beautiful restaurant to sample and then you'll need to take a taxi back.

On Parsenn you can pretty much access powder from every lift. The Totalphorn area, between the Meierhoftäli and Totalp chairlifts, is superb but does get sketchy if the snow isn't great. Don't let that put you off completely; on a perfect powder day it's definitely worth checking out. If the visibility is bad, there are loads of tree runs around. The Weissfluh, a north-facing slope is one of Klosters' most famous off-piste runs. It's around a 500m drop with a 15-minute hike out. You should take a guide with you for this one. We recommend contacting Lukas Dürr at Swiss Freeride (www.swissfreeride.ch).

Lukas can also take you on a guided tour to Gargellen, a village in Austria, starting from the top of Madrisa. The tour involves about 2 hours of walking in total but the terrain isn't too challenging and the scenery is incredible. Don't forget your passport if you do give it a go.

Lift passes	
1 day	CHF61
6 days	CHF282
Discounts are available for children, teenagers, seniors, groups and early birds.	

Instruction

Boardriding
T: 0041 (0)81 420 26 62
E: office@boardriding.ch
W: www.boardriding.ch

Duty Board and Bananas Head Office
Swiss Snowboard School, Klosters
T: 0041 (0)81 422 66 60
E: boardshop@duty.ch
W: www.duty.ch

Swiss Ski and Snowboard School Klosters
A 3-day course (Mon–Wed) costs CHF215 for skiing or boarding. A 5-day ski course is CHF460.
T: 0041 (0)81 410 28 28
E: info@sssk.ch
W: www.sssk.ch

Swiss Ski and Snowboard School Saas
Costs are similar to those above but may not be identical. Contact the school for more information.
T: 0041 (0)81 420 22 33
E: sssssaas@bluewin.ch
W: www.sss-saas.ch

Other activities

Paragliding and delta-gliding: Contact the tourist office about taxi flights, lessons and test days.
Shopping: There isn't too much in the way of shopping in Klosters, even though it's a great place to wander round. They are hoping to attract more shops though with the opening of the new bridge and tunnel that will almost free Klosters of traffic by allowing the Davos traffic to bypass the town, restoring the quiet charm of the resort.

Sports centre: The sports centre has artificial ice rinks for skating and ice hockey, skating lessons, curling for beginners and ice stick shooting (Bavarian curling).

Swimming: There are five public indoor swimming pools in local hotels.

Tennis and badminton: There are several courts (you can play for 1 hour a day free with the guest card).

Tobogganing: There are a number of runs: 8.6km from Saaseralp (Madrisa) to Saas, 3.5km from Gotschnagrat to Klosters, 2.5km from Melcheti to Aeuja and 2.5km from Alpenrösli to Klosters Platz.

Events

Klosters doesn't have too many fixtures organised in town. There are often events for the disabled though and in mid-March the popular and highly entertaining **Wild Girls on Snow** charity spectacle. Celebrities, models and local stars are invited for a 3-day event involving lots of dressing up, larking around and looking gorgeous. Each year the event is run for different charities and follows different themes, for example one of the latest was 'What Not to Wear Skiing'. The event includes a ski race with past and present racers from the Swiss National Ski Team so there's loads to watch on the mountain but at night the partying tends to happen behind closed doors.

Contact the tourist office for more information about the events in Klosters.

Accommodation

Klosters isn't huge on the whole tour operator thing, you're better off booking directly with hotels and organising your own transfer. Renting apartments is also popular in Klosters; there are 6600 beds in rented and privately owned flats and houses and 1900 in hotels. Contact the tourist office for specific information about renting.

The 4-star hotel **Alpina** (T: 0041 (8)1 410 24 24, Г: 0041 (0)81 410 24 25, www.alpina-klosters.ch, hotel@ alpina-klosters.ch) has everything that anyone would

want from a hotel. It has the most amazing location in town and it is absolutely stunning. The pool and wellness area contains sauna, steam bath, solarium, beauty salon and fitness area. The rooms are beautiful and if you want to splash out there are some great suites available with dressing rooms and the works. Call the number above to request a brochure and price list for the various types of room.

Hotel Rustico (0041 (0)81 410 22 88, info@ rusticohotel.com, www.rusticohotel.com) has 11 rooms (10 rooms and 1 junior suite) and is a 3-star hotel. All of the rooms have a really cosy, alpine feel. The guys who run the hotel, Al and Renee Thöny, will bend over backwards to make sure that your stay is enjoyable. The restaurant is also superb (see Eating out).

The Hotel Vereina (0041 (0)81 410 27 27, www. vereinahotel.ch, klosters@vereinahotel.ch) is a top quality 4-star establishment. It was rebuilt fairly recently

"Everything about the hotel is superb, from the gourmet restaurant to the amazing views, to the wellness area and spa"

and is a majestic and splendid building. Everything about the hotel is superb, from the gourmet restaurant to the amazing views, to the wellness area and spa. If you want to splash some serious cash, ask for the queen's or president's suite with their balconies, fire places, office areas, etc.

Silvapina (0041 (0)81 422 14 68, www.silvapina.ch, hotel@silvapina.ch) in Klosters Dorf is a family-run hotel and it's a lovely place for families to stay. Breakfast and dinner are provided so it's more like a chalet than a hotel. It's good value (prices are CHF49–123 per person per night), but it's probably not for those who want to be out on the town every night because it's pretty far away.

Eating out

On the mountain
On Madrisa, the Saaseralp (0041 (0)81 410 2180, www.madrisa-gastro.ch) restaurant is a superb place, with really tasty traditional Swiss food (we recommend the homemade rosti). It has a separate restaurant for large parties, usually dominated with ski school groups,

and rooms where kids can play around, supervised by you or their staff.

Bruhin's (081 417 66 44) is a fairly fancy restaurant right at the top of the Weissfluhgipfel on Parsenn, (via the Gipfelbahn cable car). It's a smart restaurant with stunning views but there is no terrace which is a bit of a shame on a sunny day. Book a table by the window to get the best views.

If you're looking for a traditional, chalet-style restaurant, the Gruobenalp (081 422 62 30), just down from Gotschnagrat on the other side to Klosters, is perfect, especially on a sunny day as the terrace has a gorgeous view. The Alta Schwendi (081 332 13 24, www.freeridelodge.ch, info@freeridelodge.ch) is the best mountain restaurant for hanging out in. It's located at Chesetta, just above the Schifer. There's a massive terrace, great food, a cosy chalet feel inside and really friendly staff. Be careful though, it's pretty easy to end up staying all afternoon; in fact you can even stay overnight if you like! Below the Schifer, on the way back to Klosters Dorf is the Serneuser Schwendi (081 422 12 89, www.schwendiserneus.ch, hotel.lohner@ bluewin.ch) which has recently changed hands and is

now run by locals, so is serving some great traditional Swiss cuisine. It is also a mountain hostel. If you just fancy grabbing a good burger, the restaurant on the **Weissfluhjoch** (081 417 66 11) has the best in town.

In town

Hotel Rustico (081 410 22 88, www.rusticohotel.com, www.rusticohotel.com) has a superb restaurant. It manages to create a stylish and luxurious atmosphere whilst remaining cosy and friendly. The staff are charming and the unusual (and tasty) cuisine falls under a Euro-Asian theme with Japanese, Asian and international specialities. It's open for lunch and dinner but is very popular in the evening so it's a good idea to book a little in advance. In addition to the main restaurant is a cosy Stübli for fondues and raclettes.

The **Alpenrösli** (081 422 13 57) is a beautiful restaurant. You have to walk up to it, which can take about half an hour from Klosters Platz (or you can catch a cab) and then you toboggan back down after a few cheeky drinks. The excellent rosti dishes are their speciality.

The **Chesa Grischuna** (081 422 22 22) is a chic restaurant with a very smart bar. The funky and stylish hotel attached is featured in *Hip Hotels*, along with only a handful of others throughout Europe.

There are also loads of pizzerias around where you can get a pizza for about CHF18. If you are feeling lazy, the following restaurants offer a takeaway option: **Pizzeria Grottino Al Berto** in Klosters Dorf (081 422 30 20), **Alte Post** in Platz (081 422 17 16) and **Pizza Fellini** also in Platz (081 422 22 11).

Klosters has a glowing reputation for gourmet food and in the summer they arrange a gourmet circus (www.gourmetcircus.ch), which encorporates a Cirque de Soleil-type circus and a gourmet meal whereby each of the best chefs from the region cooks a different course.

The tourist office also provides a great gastro-guide which gives a good summary of all of the restaurants in town and shows you exactly where they all are.

Bars and clubs

The **Brasserie**, in the super smart Vereina Hotel, is probably the best bar in Klosters. Its friendly staff, headed up by Claudia, are great. There's often live music, DJs, pianos and lots more. For a classy place it's quite surprising the carnage that goes on! **Chesa** is another really smart bar that is great fun. The beers in these bars can be pretty expensive, approximately CHF8.50 for a pint – much cheaper beverages can be found in the local bars such as the **Bistro**, next to the train station, or the **Rössli** bar in the centre of town. Later on, the most famous and prestigious club to be seen at is the **Casa Antica**, where William, Harry and those boys hang out. Have a boogy, chill with the cool kids, but try to work it so that it's someone else's round when you get there – a bottle of Heineken costs a whopping CHF18 and it's even more for spirits and mixers.

Useful facts and phone numbers

Tourist office

T: 0041 (0)81 410 20 20
F: 0041 (0)81 410 20 10
E: info@klosters.ch
W: www.klosters.ch

Emergency services

- European emergency number: 112
- Fire brigade: 118
- Police: 117
- Ambulance: 144/081 422 17 13
- Medical care: 081 422 49 49
- Police station: 081 423 36 80

Getting there

By car

It takes about 12–13 hours to get to Klosters from Calais, so it's probably easier to fly unless you're going to take a few days over it.

By plane

Zürich (140km) is the easiest place to fly to and it takes under 3 hours to get from there to Klosters by train or car. For more info contact the railway on 0041 (0)81 288 32 50, www.rhb.ch, davos-platz@rhb.ch.

By train

Take the 17.42 Eurostar from London Waterloo to Paris; then an overnight train, changing at Landquart. Arrive Davos station, in resort, at 08.55. Return fares start at £168 in a 6-berth couchette. Contact European Rail (020 7387 0444, www.europeanrail.com).

Laax Murschetg

Laax is becoming known as the best freestyle hangout in Europe

On the slopes	
Snow reliability	❄ ❄ ❄
Parks	❄ ❄ ❄ ❄ ❅
Off-piste	❄ ❄ ❄
Off the slopes	
Après ski	❄ ❄ ❄
Nightlife	❄ ❄ ❄
Eating out	❄ ❄
Resort charm	❄ ❅

The resort

Laax was relatively undiscovered by the Brits until the British Championships moved here in 2005, bringing it on to the map. Laax itself is a small town with several separate areas, and Laax Murschetg contains all of the important bits – i.e. lifts, bars and clubs. Laax is a sanctuary for the avid freestyler: the park is second to none in Europe, you can stay here pretty cheaply (although drinks will set you back a fair bit) and the nightlife is cool (as long as you are). You should have second thoughts if you spend much of your time moseying around town (although Flims is a short bus ride if needs be – see Flims chapter, page 352) or if you get bored going to the same restaurants and bars every night. If these things don't bother you, you should definitely give Laax a whirl.

The mountains

Height: 1000–3000m

Ability	Rating
Expert	❄ ❄ ❄
Intermediate	❄ ❄ ❄ ❄
Beginner	❄ ❄ ❄ ❅

Getting about

Laax is at the centre of the Alpenarena, providing good access to its 220km of slopes. From Laax Murschetg it is a quick cable car ride to Crap Sogn Gion and you'll be in the park in a matter of minutes. The mountain is pretty flat so it's great for cruisy intermediates, though there is a fair bit of fresh powder to be had, which you can see from many of the pistes, and there are some freeride routes marked on the piste map.

The park

This is one of our favourite parks in Europe. The guys looking after it are keen and park-proud. There are two different areas to the park, on either side of the café/bar/hostel at Crap Sogn Gion. The riders loved the slopestyle area at the Brits; it consists of a selection of rails, including 10-metre down rails, a C-rail and a fun wall ride. You can hit three different kickers on the way down, with a choice of sizes at each hit. In total there are six jumps (5–25m tables). The other side of the park has a fantastic selection of rails. There's an S-rail, C-rail, rollercoaster, and big gap jumps to a 5-metre high rail. There are also six straight boxes, one 4-frame rail, one kinked box, and four rainbow rails. To finish it off there are two super pipes (one 80m and one 140m) in mint condition.

"The other side of the park has a fantastic selection of rails"

Off-piste and backcountry

Most of the Alpenarena's off-piste terrain is pretty accessible and not bad at all considering the shallow gradients of the mountain. Like many other resorts, they now provide 40km of unprepared but marked and avalanche-controlled slopes for freeriders to play on. These runs lead from the summits of the three main peaks: Vorab Pign (2897m), La Siala (2810m), above Laax, and Cassons (2675m). Cassons has been recommended, not just for the marked run there, but also for the off-piste terrain surrounding it (which would require a guide). If you do want to hire a guide for a day or so they can show you more of the area contact Mountain Fantasy (see Instruction). From Cassons, they can take you into the backcountry to Seghesgkecier or down to Bargis. Alternatively, you can start your trip from the Vorab Gletscher (3018m), above Falera, and skin (hike) to the Bündner Vorab (3028m), from which you can expect a great ride down a big open valley, ending up in Alp Ruschein (1774m). These expeditions should only be undertaken with a qualified guide.

Lift passes	
1 day	CHF62
6 days	CHF351

You can also buy just a park and pipe ticket for CHF39 if that's all you're interested in or a beginners' ticket for the same price that gives you access to all the beginners' areas.

Instruction

Mountain Fantasy

These are the best mountain guides in town for skiers, boarders and anyone else who wants to explore. The office is located in Flims.

T: 0041 (0)81 936 70 77
E: bergsport@mountain-fantasy.ch
W: www.mountain-fantasty.ch

Ski Schule

Five days in ski school costs CHF300.

T: 0041 (0)81 927 71 71
W: www.laax.com/skischule

Snowboarding School

Five days costs around CHF460. They also offer a taster course on a Sunday afternoon to find out whether you like snowboarding or not.

T: 0041(0)81 927 71 55
E: fahrschule@laax.com
W: www.laax.com/fahrschule

Other activities

There isn't too much to do in Laax Murschteg. If you need other activities, such as paragliding and sledging, Flims is your best bet (see Flims chapter, page 352).

Full-moon skiing: In January, February and March there is full moon skiing (weather dependant) on Crap Sogn Gion (081 927 70 00); from 8pm you can take the gondola lift up and take a guided moonlit tour down.

Ice skating and curling: You can ice skate and do Bavarian curling on Laax lake (081 921 51 53).

Wellness centre, pool and tennis: The Hotel Signina (081 927 90 00) in Laax Murschetg has a wellness suite, Laguna pool and tennis courts that are open to the public. Hotel Laaxerhof (081 920 82 00) has a public pool and sauna. If you don't mind catching the bus to Flims the wellness centres at the Park Hotel and Adula are well worth a look (see Flims chapter, page 352).

Events

The superb and well maintained park means that there are a crazy number of events that take place in Laax. Most of the after parties take place later on in the Riders Palace so if you're competing, or watching, this is the place to book into.

To start the season there is the **Ski and Snowboard Open** in October (when the snowpark is moved on to the Vorab glacier) with DJs, new equipment to be tested and the Burton Team demo. The **Snow Groove Party** in November is another freestyle party which is repeated in early December when the Monster Pipe is re-opened.

"Most of the after parties take place later on in the Riders Palace so if you're competing, or watching, this is the place to book into"

In January the **Burton European Open** takes place. In total 600 athletes compete – pros, amateurs and juniors – in the super pipe and slope style. In one bizarre but great competition, Microsoft Xbox and Laax team together to fund the **Amped Champ**. This unique contest looks for champion snowboarders, both real and virtual. The qualifiers are in early February and the best real and virtual boarders will battle it out in the Amped Champ finals in early April. For more information, check out www.amped champ.ch.

In early March the **FIS Freestyle World Cup** (skier cross and ski half pipe) takes place. In mid–late March the **British Ski/Snowboard Championships** kick off, a must for British boarders and skiers. This competition attracts both pros and up-and-coming riders, all trying to make a name for themselves. It consists of skier and boardercross, slopestyle, big air and half pipe. There are cash prizes for the top three in each category, but the title is the main trophy. Check it out on www.orangebrits.com.

Accommodation

The coolest place to stay is the **Riders Palace** (0041 (0)81 927 97 00, www.riderspalace.ch), a funky, glass, neon-lit hotel/bar/club, full of ultra-cool clientele. Rooms vary from basic dorms to stylish multimedia rooms and suites with DVD player, games consoles, Sky and projector screens. One night's stay and a 1-day ski pass will cost you CHF60–200 per person, depending on the type of room. They do deals for weekends and for 4–7 days, all including lift pass. For example, 7 nights and 7 days of lift passes will cost you CHF473–1678.

"This unique contest looks for champion snowboarders, both real and virtual"

It's the best place to stay if you are going to be partying every night as it's all in the building, but it's not the place to get a quiet night's sleep.

If you really want to be the first to hit the park you can stay in the **Mountain Hostel** on Crap Sogn Gion (0041 (0)81 927 73 73, www.mountainhostel-laax.ch), at 2228m. Five nights in a room with 4 beds, including a 6-day lift pass, dinner, breakfast and sauna, will cost from CHF435 per person. The **Laaxerhof** (0041 (0)81 920 82 00, www.laaxerhof.ch) is a pretty smart hotel with an elegant restaurant and good pool and sauna. Prices are CHF155–255 per person for half-board accommodation, depending on the type of room

(lowest price is for 6 people in a room). The **Hotel Signina Sport Golf** (0041 (0)81 927 90 00, www.signina.ch) is another great traditional hotel with a wellness suite and tennis courts that are open to the public. Prices are CHF120–180 per person per night.

Eating out

On the mountain

If you're hitting the park and pipe you will be eating and drinking at the popular bars at Crap Sogn Gion. **Rock bar** and **Café No Name** (081 927 73 44). These bars are just above the half pipe and they are great places to hang out. For a cheeky beer, hit the terrace right at the top of the park and for a great cheeseburger, head up to the café. There are tons of deckchairs and comfy outdoor seating so you'll always be able to find a place to relax with a beer.

At **Plaun**, the old chairlift station has been converted into a bar with deckchairs outside in good weather, and they barbeque sausages and serve good soup.

On the way back down to Laax there are two superb restaurants: **Togia Curnius** (081 927 99 30) and **Tegia Larnags** (081 927 99 10), both with cosy, traditional atmospheres, sizeable sun terraces and local foods.

In town

There are very few restaurants in Laax Murschetg, although you can eat in most of the hotels. Restaurant **Muhbarack** (081 927 99 40, muhbarack@laax.com), above the Crap Bar, serves great pasta and local specialities, including fondues and raclettes.

Pizzeria Cristallina (081 921 22 52, casaselva@kns.ch) is a fantastic pizzeria at the bottom of Laax Murschetg on the main road. It cooks superb pizzas on a big open wood fire and also does takeaways.

If you need something a little more gourmet, you should take a short bus ride to Flims where you will find a few really good restaurants such as **La Clav** and **Barga** at the Hotel Adula and the **Little China** if you're bored with local food (see Flims chapter, page 352).

> "There are tons of deckchairs and comfy outdoor seating so you'll always be able to find a place to relax with a beer"

Bars and clubs

There are only a handful of bars in Laax; for après ski, head to the **Crap Bar** at the bottom of the slopes, built with 24 tons of granite. For a change, you could come down into Flims Dorf and have some beers in the **Legana** and **Iglu** bar (see Flims chapter, page 352) and then catch a bus back to Laax. After this, you should head to the neon-lit **Riders Palace Lobby Bar**, kitted out with leather sofas, internet and a huge bar. Unfortunately the huge bar rarely has enough staff on a busy night but apart from that, it's wicked. Downstairs is the massive (and expensive) Ministry-of-Sound-run **Palace Club** where the cool kids hang out. Later on the music ranges from hip-hop to trance and house. If you prefer rock and pop try the **Casa Veglia** club.

Getting there

By car

See the directions for getting to Flims, page 357.

By plane

Zürich (150km)
Friedrichshafen (140km) for Ryanair flights.

By train

Take the 17.42 Eurostar from London Waterloo to Paris; then an overnight train to Chur, and then a local bus (44 minutes), arriving in resort at 08.42. Return fares start at £168 in a 6-berth couchette. Contact Rail Europe (08705 848 848, www.raileurope.co.uk) or European Rail (020 7387 0444, www.europeanrail.com). Bus tickets (€9.50 single) are purchased at the station.

Useful facts and phone numbers

Tourist office

T: 0041 (0)81 920 81 81
E: tourismus@alpenarena.ch
W: www.alpenarena.ch

Emergency services

- Police: In an emergency call 117, if not call 081 928 29 40/081 911 11 64
- In an emergency on the mountain call the SOS central office on 081 972 70 01
- Hospital in Chur: 081 256 61 11
- Fire: 118

Doctors

- Dr P Schneller: 081 921 48 48
- District nurse: 081 921 55 05

Taxis

- Taxi Mario: 081 941 22 22

Saas-Fee

The perfect Swiss 'chocolate-box' town, this resort is a favourite, especially in summer

On the slopes	
Snow reliability	✳ ✳ ✳ ✳ ✳
Parks	✳ ✳ ✳ ✳
Off-piste	✳ ✳ ✳ ✳

Off the slopes	
Après ski	✳ ✳ ✳ ✳
Nightlife	✳ ✳ ✳ ✳
Eating out	✳ ✳ ✳ ✳
Resort charm	✳ ✳ ✳ ✳ ✳

The resort

The village of Saas-Fee does not feel, as many do, like a functional resort built purely to support the winter sports; it is a magical place that you can easily fall in love with. The unique atmosphere is traditional and romantic, and the entire town is surrounded by 13 imposing, 4000-metre peaks, including the highest mountain in Switzerland, the Dom (4545 metres above sea level).The traffic-free town and the chalet-style buildings contribute to the relaxing pace of this charming glacier village. And it manages to provide a varied and rich nightlife. In the winter the village can be very cold; conditions are best for autumn or spring skiing when there is plenty of sun and snow. Saas-Fee is also the perfect resort for summer skiing on the glacier.

The mountains

Height: 1800–3600m

Ability	Rating
Expert	✳ ✳ ✳
Intermediate	✳ ✳ ✳ ✳
Beginner	✳ ✳ ✳ ✳ ✳

Getting about

Take two Alpin Express cable cars to Felskinn at 3000m. From here you can either enjoy some long, sweeping red runs back to town or take the highest underground funicular in the world, the Metro Alpin to the Mittelallalin glacier (3500m). When visibility is good

you can apparently see the lights of Milan. We couldn't, but maybe your eyesight's better than ours. It will take you around 40 minutes to reach the top.

Winter

There are 100km of marked pistes in Saas-Fee in the winter, most designed for the beginner/intermediate skier or boarder. The 32 runs comprise 13 blue trails, 14 red and 5 black. Saas-Fee has a great reputation for maintaining the runs in tiptop condition, allowing the intermediate riders a great base from which to push themselves to the next level. The unprepared mogul piste under the Längfluh chairlift puts those knees to the test.

"It is a magical place that you can easily fall in love with"

Summer

The glacier provides 20km of ski slopes for summer skiing, geared to high-standard riding. It is best to get out early, as the glacier closes some time between 12pm (in high summer) and 2pm. The runs are pretty good but if you're not doing slalom training or hitting the park, you may end up twiddling your thumbs. If you are hitting the park, you will not be disappointed. Get used to the T-bars and draglifts; chairlifts are difficult to manoeuvre and so are not practical with the moving glacier.

The park

There is a park in the winter, but it is far better maintained in the summer. Saas-Fee was one of the first resorts to put real money in to develop the park and skier/boarder cross. It is, therefore, renowned for hosting many of the major competitions such as the Rip Curl Challenge and the World Cup Half Pipe events. Professionals often train here in the summer, and ski and board manufacturers are regularly spotted testing their products.

The park is changed regularly but always consists of a super half pipe, three big kickers ranging from 6m to 12m gaps and a huge range of rails. There are plenty of table-top jumps for learning and practising new tricks, before stepping it up to the bigger ones. The atmosphere in the park is superb; a DJ often plays at the bottom and photographers and cameramen are frequently spotted filming for the latest movies.

" From the top of the Alpin Express you can find the Morenia, great if you like the steeps, and it's hardly ever touched"

Off-piste and backcountry

It is wise to be cautious when exploring the off-piste around a glacier due to the crevasses and concealed dangers. However, this does not mean that there aren't any off-piste opportunities to be had. There are three pistes that are marked as yellow or off-piste runs, but there are a few more. The absence of glacier on the Plattjen makes it a great place to find fresh tracks through the trees. The trees also shelter the snow, so it stays in good condition all day. Be warned though, this area can be quite challenging!

The Maste 4 is another good place to keep you out of the way of crevasse dangers. It is a relatively easy powder run – a perfect place for cruising. From the top of the Alpin Express you can find the Morenia, great if you like the steeps, and it's hardly ever touched. It is very important only to attempt this after a good snowfall and, even then, it must be done early in the morning. The Hannig, at the other side of town to the Alpin Express (used for hill-walking and sledging), is a great place for an early morning hike. There is a lift from the bottom of the resort but they won't let you on with your board or skis so it is a bit of a trek. If you fancy a backcountry adventure, set off early from Brittania Hutte and enjoy the legendary, 1.5-hour

freeride down to Saas-Almagell. This is pretty challenging, especially at the beginning, and is only recommended with a guide.

Lift passes	Summer	Winter
1 day	CHF61	CHF60
6 days	CHF303	CHF299
13 days	CHF517	CHF509
CHF5 for a deposit for the key-card.		

Instruction

Eskimos Snowboard School

This is a well-known school. Taster courses are run on Sundays for 2 hours for CHF35. Courses range from basic to freestyle/carving, 3 days costs CHF115 and a week (10 hours) is CHF165. Private instruction costs CHF70 for 1 hour, for one to two people.

T: 0041 (0)27 957 49 04
E: info@eskimos.ch
W: www.eskimos.ch

Saas-Fee Ski and Snowboard School

This school comes highly recommended by locals. Not that there is a huge amount of choice. All instructors speak a variety of languages.

Ski lessons

Class instruction: 1 day CHF52 for 3 hours, 1 week CHF183 for 15 hours. Private instruction is available; prices vary. For example, one person for 1 hour will cost CHF60.

Snowboard lessons

Class instruction: 1 day CHF49, 1 week CHF169. Private instruction is available, one person for 1 hour will cost CHF60.

T: 0041 (0)27 957 23 48
E: info@skischule-saas-fee.ch
W: www.skischule-saas-fee.ch

British Freeski Camps

These run for 3 or 4 weeks in the summer every year, and are organised by Warren Smith. You can sign up for the whole time or any one week. On the camp, you have the choice of hitting the park, perfecting the skier cross course or getting your carving up to scratch. The top professional skiers in Britain gather

together for these camps, some coaching and others training, so it's a great place to introduce yourself to the British ski scene.

T: 0044 (0)1525 374757
E: admin@snowsportsynergy.com
W: www.britishfreeskicamps.com

Popcorn shop

For **buying or renting** snowboards or freestyle skis we highly recommend this shop, located right in the centre of town near the clock tower. They always have the latest equipment and clothing and are also happy to offer their expert advice.

Other activities

Always ask if there is a discount with a guest card, obtainable from your hotel or apartment landlord.

Winter and summer

Bobsleigh: The Feeblitz Bobsleigh is a 900m long toboggan run. Great fun for all the family. It can be adapted to suit the adrenaline junkie – although not 'officially' recommended, it has been known not to apply the brakes and keep your eyes closed. We didn't tell you to do it though (CHF5.30 with guest card, CHF6 without).

Ice grotto: Visit the Allain Ice Pavilion – the biggest ice grotto in the world. It can be accessed from the Metro Alpin top station hall at 3500m above sea level. Entry CHF4.

Mountain climbing: The mountain climbing schools offer a number of activities for keen climbers, or those who fancy giving it a go. Rock and ice climbing, canyoning, glacier trekking and mountaineering are available for both beginners and advanced climbers. For a James Bond-type activity, the 'Alpine Gorge' is an opportunity to be seized. This is a mountain descent from Saas-Fee to Saas-Grund, where you make your way down with the aid of a guide, fixed steel ropes, ladders, three Tyroliennes and a suspension bridge. It costs CHF100 to do the full canyon and CHF70 for half. A final option is to conquer one of the three Via Ferratas (secured climbing routes). The Mittaghorn is fairly easy and good for families, the Jägihorn is pretty difficult and should be undertaken with a guide and the Via Ferrata del Lago is recommended as a 2-day tour.

For further information contact Active Dreams (027 957 14 44, www.weissmies.ch, weissmies@rhone.ch) or Bergführerbüro Mountain Life (027 957 44 64, www.mountainlife.ch, info@mountainlife.ch).

Tennis and badminton: There are two indoor tennis courts and four indoor badminton courts available.

Wellness centre: If you're looking for a good way to while away a bad weather day look no further than the Bielen Wellness Centre. There is a 25m swimming pool

as well as a sauna, solarium, whirlpool, steam bath, solar sun bathing, fitness room, table tennis and table football. It costs CHF13 to use the swimming pool with a guest card (CHF14 without). The 5-star Hotel Ferienart contains the Paradisa wellness centre and non residents can pay for a day's spa package. We'd love to tell you what it was like but we couldn't afford it.

Summer only

Adventure forest: This opened in 2004. You can swing from tree to tree using rope swings and zip wires and walk across hanging bridges. There are a couple of routes to choose from and depending on which you prefer it will cost CHF22–29.

Crazy golf: A fantastic way to pass an hour or so! Not a course to be sniffed at, it really is quite difficult and should be taken very seriously. Costs CHF4 with guest card (CHF4.50 without).

Golf: A 9-hole alpine golf course can be found just behind the Kalbermatten sports field.

Hiking: There's loads of hiking to be had in and around Saas-Fee. Contact the tourist office for all the details.

Mountain biking: Bikers will be in their element in the summer, as there are around 70km of trails. The marked trails suit a range of abilities. Contact the tourist office for a detailed mountain bike map.

Sports: The Kalbermatten sports ground offers football, basketball, volleyball, a mini skate ramp for skateboarding and in line skating and tennis courts. Pit Pat (a weird combination of snooker and crazy golf) is located nearby, at the Hotel Waldesruh.

Winter only

Heliskiing and snow touring: These are definitely worth checking out later on in the season.

Husky tours: These run several times a week from 4.30am. It costs CHF40 per adult and can be booked at the tourist office.

Ice skating: The natural ice rink is open 8am–10pm from mid-December to the end of February and costs CHF4. Snow bowling on the rink costs CHF20 an hour.

Sledge run: A 5km sledge run can be found at Hannig. On Tuesdays and Thursdays (6–9pm) you can sledge at night. A single run costs CHF18. Sledge rental is CHF8 and head torch rental CHF3. There is also an 11km run in the nearby town of Saas-Grund – the longest in Europe.

Snow shoe trekking: This is organised daily. Contact the tourist office.

Snow tubing and air boarding: This looks mighty fun. It costs CHF8 and occurs several times a week.

Events

Saas-Fee is a very popular venue for a wide variety of events because the height of the glacier pretty much guarantees snow all year round. The **FIS World Cup** (24–26 November) has been held in Saas-Fee for many years with disciplines for skiers and boarders in the half pipe and skierboardercross. The Dutch and British Championships have also been held here over the years. The **Saas-Fee Ride** takes place every summer, usually at the end of July, and many of the best freestyle skiers in Europe turn up for the event. If you fancy your chances at entering the competition or if you just want to improve your style, why not book on to the **British Freeski Camps** (www.britishfreeskicamps.com) which take place in the few weeks running up to the Saas-Fee Ride.

The **North Face Ice Climbing World Cup** (1–3 February 2007) is one of the biggest events in Saas-Fee. The world's best ice climbers strut their stuff on a 30m high wall of ice in the car park of Saas-Fee.

Accommodation

There are a variety of packages available to suit all budgets and it is a good idea to contact the tourist office with your particular requirements. Renting an apartment is often a good option; you will pay anything from £250 a week. Bear in mind that the north end of the village is a bit of a hike from the lifts so always make sure you check the location before you book.

For a funky, unique, well placed and friendly hotel call the **Dom Hotel** (0041 (0)27 957 51 01, relax@uniquedom.com, www.uniquedom.com). Its mad décor and the fact the rooms contain PlayStations and CD players, really do make this the ultimate choice. The rooms are minimalist and funky with wooden floors, and the balconies have stunning views. The hotel also contains the hugely popular Popcorn bar and the Living Room, a stylish chill-out bar. It will cost you (depending on the season) CHF216–338.

"It has a beautiful location sitting above a deep creek and contains a charming restaurant"

If being near the slopes is of utmost importance to you, check out **La Gorge** Apart-Hotel (0041 (0)27 958 16 80, www.lagorge.ch, la.gorge@saas-fee.ch). It has a beautiful location sitting above a deep creek and contains a charming restaurant. It is only 100m from the lifts and is also close to all the facilities of the town. The rooms are fairly basic but contain a little kitchen so you can save money on food. Depending on the season it will cost CHF200–270 per night for two people.

For a luxury apartment at a decent price check out the 5-star **Shangri-La Apartments** (contact Pamela Andermatten on 0041 (0)27 958 15 15, zum.lerch@rhone.ch, www.rhone.ch/zumlerch). The apartments are huge (47–83m^2) and contain Sky TV, a DVD player, internet connection, a coffee machine, a dishwasher, a washing machine, a massive balcony and there is a

sauna and whirlpool room for the use of guests. A 2-room apartment will cost CHF560–1120 for the night. Larger apartments are also available.

If price is no object and you enjoy fancy hotels, it has to be the 5-star **Hotel Ferienart** (0041 (0)27 958 19 00, info@ferienart.ch, www.ferienart.ch). It has all the charm and splendour and prices that you would expect with six restaurants, a piano bar, dance hall and beauty spa. The spa and beauty salon are very nice. Expect to pay CHF396–786 per person per night for half-board.

Eating out

On the mountain

The world's highest **revolving restaurant** is at the top lift station on the Mittelallain glacier. It spins all the way round about once an hour. The views are stunning, the food is tasty and we think it's pretty good value too. It's definitely worth doing at least once and you should book if you want a table by the window – call 027 957 17 71.

Other restaurants to check out are the popular, rustic **Gletschergrotte**, halfway down from Speilboden (book on 027 957 21 60) and the more trendy hangout, **Popcorn Plaza** at Längfluh (027 957 17 71) which has dramatic views that can be enjoyed from comfy deckchairs on the huge terrace.

In town

La Ferme (027 958 15 69) is a superb restaurant in the centre of town. It has a traditional, rustic and charming atmosphere and all the staff don the traditional dress. It's not cheap, but is good value as the food is fantastic.

The **Bodmen** restaurant (027 957 20 75) takes 10–15 minutes to walk to along a beautiful woodland path and is well worth the trip. It's a beautiful place to sit at lunchtime in the summer as the huge terrace has marvellous views and goats scuttle in-between the tables. In the evening it's not too formal and has

great food, from fondues to fillet steak. If you wish, you can request the table next to a glass panel with views into a barn so you can see lots of chickens and other farmyard animals strutting their stuff whilst you eat. It's not advisable to ask for this table if you fancy tucking into a chicken dish. To find the restaurant, walk past the Alpin Express lift station, in the opposite direction to town, and you will see a sign pointing you towards the Bodmen.

The **Fletschhorn** restaurant (027 957 21 31) is highly recommended by gourmands and is highly expensive. **Boccalino's** (027 957 17 31) is a great pizza restaurant on the main street serving pizzas, pasta and risottos. Probably the best value in town, this is a great place to eat if you're on a budget.

Bars and clubs

Saas-Fee has a very good night scene. The laws have also recently changed so that there is no specific time at which a bar should close; if it's busy they will open

until it's time to hit the slopes again. Dangerous stuff.

The **Popcorn** bar is definitely at the centre of the action with good après ski, European DJs, live bands and the odd 'Diva Night' when they play all the classic cheesy music. Dressing up is optional. It's not cheap here though, a pint will set you back CHF9, and a cocktail CHF14. The younger crowd tend to hang out at the **Happy Bar**, at the north end of town, where the drinks are cheaper, especially during happy hour.

If you are in the 25+ category you might favour **The Living Room** in the Dom Hotel, which is more of a chill-out bar with sofas and candles. If the mood takes you later on, you can always head downstairs to the Popcorn for a drunken boogie. **Poison** nightclub is popular and good fun. Again, it's more for the 25+ age group. Opposite the Popcorn is the **Alpen-Pub,** which has live music in the winter and on quieter nights is a great place to have a cosy beer and a game of darts.

The **Metropol** is a typical American diner with a number of pool tables and table football along with an 80s-style dance floor. You can also have a delicious burger to soak up the alcohol. If you intend to do your partying indoors, watch out for the 'hush police' who parade the streets after 10pm and can collar you into a fine of about CHF120 if they think you're making too much noise.

Useful facts and phone numbers

Tourist office

T: 0041 (0)27 958 18 58
F: 0041 (0)27 958 18 60
E: to@saas-fee.ch
W: www.saas-fee.ch or www.saastal.ch

Direct reservations

T: 0041 (0)27 958 18 68
F: 0041 (0)27 958 18 70
E: to@saas-fee.ch. Online booking at
   www.saas-fee.ch

Emergency services

- Police: 117
- Police station (by the car park): 027 958 11 60,
  polizei@saas-fee.ch
- Ambulance: 114
- Breakdown service: 140
- Weather information: 0900 57 30 70
  (CHF1.49/min)

Doctors

- Stefan and Stephanie Kuonen, Saas-Fee: 027
  957 58 59
- Medical Centre, Saas-Grund: 027 957 11 55
- Pharmacy, Saas-Fee: 027 957 26 18
- Dentist, St Imseng: 027 957 20 52

Electro-taxis

- Ambros: 079 439 10 29
- Taxi Anselm: 079 220 21 37
- Bolero: 027 958 11 35
- Center Reisen: 027 958 11 33
- Imseng 027 957 33 44

Getting there

By car

From Calais, it will take around 10 hours to drive to Saas-Fee. Enter Switzerland above Lausanne and from there follow signs for Sion, and then Brig, where you are signed to Saas-Fee.

The village itself is car-free, so you will have to use the car park (open air or covered).

The car park prices decrease the longer you are staying and are cheaper if you have a guest card, which can be obtained from your hotel or apartment owner on arrival. (Winter: 1 day CHF14.50, 1 week CHF77.50, 2 weeks CHF126.50 with guest card. Summer: 1 day CHF11, 1 week CHF56, 2 weeks CHF98 with guest card.)

There are free phones in the unloading areas to call your hotel for a free lift or to call a taxi (free phone numbers are by the phone).

The recommended price for all taxis from the car park to a hotel/apartment is CHF18–28 (plus luggage and waiting time).

By plane

Geneva (234km) Transfer from Geneva is approximately 3 hours by car. If transfer is by train, change in Brig (or Visp) for the postbus, which takes you right to Saas-Fee. There are hourly connections from Brig from 06.15 to 20.05 and from Visp from 06.35 to 20.25. Reservations may be necessary with the post bus (0041 (0)27 958 11 45).
Zürich (246km) There are regular transfers to Brig or Visp. The transfer is approximately 3 hours.

By train

Take the 17.42 Eurostar from London Waterloo to Paris; then an overnight train, changing at Zürich, to Brig, and then a local bus (57 minutes), arriving in resort at 11.02. Return fares start at £168 in a 6-berth couchette. Contact Rail Europe (08705 848 848, www.raileurope.co.uk) or European Rail (020 7387 0444, www.europeanrail.com). Bus tickets (CHF17.60 single) are purchased on the bus.

St Moritz

Glitzy, glam and exclusive –
and the riding's pretty good too!

On the slopes

On the slopes	
Snow reliability	❄❄❄❄
Parks	❄❄
Off-piste	❄❄❄❄

Off the slopes	
Après ski	❄❄❄
Nightlife	❄❄❄❄
Eating out	❄❄❄❄
Resort charm	❄❄❄❄

The resort

St Moritz is absolutely fabulous: stunning mountains, fantastic freeriding and a striking resort. Set over the beautiful Lake San Murezzan, St Moritz Dorf is one of the most famous and exclusive resorts in Europe. The majority of the hotels are 5 and 4 star and are frequented by fur-clad guests and small poodles. And if you need more evidence of exclusivity than the Versace and Chanel shops, St Moritz is host to the Cartier Polo World Cup on Snow. It was the upper crust Brits who established the style of the resort, and they're never too far away. Amazingly though, it's not too pretentious; you'd be mad not to love it.

The mountains

Height: 1327–4354m

Ability	Rating
Expert	❄❄❄❄
Intermediate	❄❄❄❄
Beginner	❄❄❄

Getting about

From Dorf a funicular takes you up to the sunny slopes of Corviglia. From St Moritz Bad you can get a gondola up to these slopes and there is the advantage that you can ride back down into town. However, if you place value on nightlife and shopping, we would still recommend staying in Dorf. The other slopes on Corvatsch are a bus or car ride away which is worth it if you like cruisy reds or a blast in the park. The best time to check out this mountain is for the Snow Night Parties each Friday, during which 5km of pistes are floodlit. The parties carry on until 2am and are more focused on drinking than riding. Diavolezza is also considered to be part of the St Moritz ski area but it's a half hour drive away. The avant-garde lift system and 350km of pistes are impressive, but it is a shame that the areas aren't linked.

"St Moritz is host to the Cartier Polo World Cup on Snow"

The park
The Mellowpark on the Furtschellas area, has a half pipe and a couple of jumps, rails and a hip, but it can be neglected on occasion. Rumour has it that they are pumping more money into it in the years to come to attract more freestylers, so watch this space…

Off-piste and backcountry
The off-piste possibilities in St Moritz are great, but not obvious, so it's a good place to invest in a guide if you want to make the most of the area. The powder hounds should head straight to the peaks of Piz Nair (3057m) or Piz Corvatsch. There are some tricky spots, but the snow usually stays in good nick. Get there early after snow fall if you're after fresh tracks. Some steep and deep can also be found opposite the Marguns lift.

Lift passes	
1 day	CHF57–70
6 days	CHF265–339
13 days	CHF441–560

Instruction

Suvretta Snowsports School
Private instruction costs CHF330 per day.
T: 0041 (0)81 836 36 00
W: www.suvrettasnowsports.ch

Swiss Ski School

Private instruction costs CHF320 per day; a class costs CHF70 per day.

T: 0041 (0)81 830 01 01

W: www.skischool.ch

Other activities

Bobsled: Pros can get up to speeds of 85mph on the natural bobsled run. The races and the championships are great to watch and if you fancy it, you can have a taxi ride driven by a pro or you can have a go yourself with instructions. The bobsled run has seen the Swiss European Championships, Bobsled World Championships and two Olympic Winter Games. Call 081 830 02 00, or check out www.olympia-bobrun.ch. The 100-year-old unique **Cresta Run** (www.cresta-run.com) is another chance to reach speeds of 85mph – but only if you're a bloke. The British clientele of St Moritz have managed to keep a firm grip on male chauvinism. To race down sheet ice, grabbing hold of a 'skeleton' sled, the gent will fork out £200 for 5 rides over a season. Events on the Cresta Run to look out for include the Heaton Gold Cup, Curzon Cup, Grand National and Gunter Sachs Challenge Cup.

Casino: The casino in St Moritz Bad is definitely worth a look (081 837 54 54, www.casinostmoritz.ch).

Curling: Rink rental at the Curling Centre (081 833 45 88) costs CHF25 per person for 2 hours. A 45-minute lesson is CHF50–100. Group instruction costs CHF20–25 per person. Events held here include the Jackson Cup and the St Moritz Grand Prix.

Horse-drawn sleigh ride: Take a romantic horse-drawn sleigh ride over the frozen lake and through the

Staz forest. You can find the sleighs in St Moritz Bad, next to the church. A half-hour ride for 1–4 people costs CHF55 and CHF95 for an hour.

Horse riding: Indoor horse riding (081 833 57 33) costs CHF60 and group trail riding CHF60 per hour.

Ice skating and hockey: Open air ice skating, hockey and curling takes place on the Ice Arena; CHF5.50 for adults (CHF3.50 for kids) and CHF5 for ice skate rental (081 833 50 30).

Medical centre: For some pampering, head to the Medical Therapy Centre, Heilbad St Moritz (081 833 30 62), where you can take a mineral or aromatic bath, beauty treatment, mud bath or pack, massage, physical therapy, stone therapy (new) and a solarium. Massages costs from CHF54 and carbonic acid mineral baths from CHF35.

Museums: If you like your museums you can head to

"Take a romantic horse-drawn sleigh ride over the frozen lake and through the Staz forest"

either the Engadin Museum, Segatini Museum or Mili Weber's House.

Paragliding and hang-gliding: These take place every hour 10am–4pm, from Corviglia mountain top (0041 (0)79 353 21 59, www.luftarena.ch). It costs CHF230.

Shopping: A favourite activity of visitors to St Moritz – bring your best credit card with you.

Sledging: If the boblsed runs all sound a bit too much for you, there is some normal sledging (a 2.5km run) from Muottas to Punt Muragl. Sledges can be rented from the bottom of the Muottas Muragl funicular. It is open every day 9.30am–4pm.

Snow night parties: These Friday night parties on Corvatsch are a great place to go for riding, drinking and partying. Have a bite to eat at the charming Alpetta Hut and a few beers at the Hossa Bar.

Snowkiting at Silvaplana: Beginners and pros welcome. Rates for lessons on request. Call 0041 (0)81 828 97 67 or check out www.kitesailing.ch.

Tennis and squash: Courts can be found in the Corviglia Tennis Centre in St Moritz Bad (081 833 15 00). One hour of tennis costs CHF49 and 45 minutes of squash CHF19.

Events

Get the latest on the hundreds of events that take place in St Mortiz at www.stmoritz.ch. Dates subject to change.

Events in St Moritz take a rather unique slant with a focus on traditional British high society events on the St Moritz frozen lake.

The **Concours Hippique**, an international equestrian jumping tournament on snow (www.stmoritz-concours.ch) is on 14–21 January. This annual event sees more than 100 horses competing in 15 tests, including ski jöring (with a riderless horse pulling a skier).The amazing **Polo on Snow** (www.polostmoritz.com), in which around 60 polo horses and 24 of the world's best polo players compete, takes place on 25–28 January.

Cricket on Ice (www.cricket-on-ice.com), 2–3 February, has been played on the lake since 1989 and **Winter Golf** since 1978. Red golf balls and white greens signify the Winter Golf Tournament in Silvaplana (www.silvaplana.ch). **White Turf Horse Races** take place the first three Sundays (4, 11, 18 in 2007) in Febuary (www.whiteturf.ch). There are short-distance, flat, trotting and ski jöring events and each winter the prize money totals a whopping CHF500 000. On 25 February international **greyhound races** are held, with traditions dating back to the 1930s.

The **gourmet festival**, 29 January to 3 February 2007, (www.stmoritz.ch/gourmetfestival) is yet another long-standing tradition, in which the best chefs from all over the world inspire young talented chefs from St Moritz hotel kitchens. The Grand Gourmet Finale once again takes place on the St Moritz frozen lake.

Engadin Cross-country Skiing Marathon is on the second Sunday in March, and 13,000 participants will take part in this 4.2km race. Check out www.engadin-skimarathon.ch.

Accommodation

The place to stay is St Moritz Dorf, unless you are happy to sacrifice the atmosphere and nightlife for the benefit of being able to ride back to town, in which case you should stay in St Moritz Bad.

There is a huge range of 5- and 4-star hotels to choose from. On the whole, the 5-star hotels were a tad too grand for us. For example, on walking into the distinguished and impressive **Badrutts Palace** (0041 (0)81 837 10 00, reservations@ badruttspalace.com, www.badruttspalace.com), there are two people swinging the revolving door for you which is, in our opinion, slightly excessive. The **Kulm hotel** (0041 (0)81 836 80 00, info@kulmhotel-stmoritz.ch, www.kulmhotel-stmoritz.ch), which celebrated its 150th birthday in 2006, is another imposing one; remarkable to look at, but again we didn't feel too comfortable here.

We much preferred the smart, comfortable and friendly 4 stars in the centre of town. The **Schweizerhof** (0041 (0)81 837 07 07, reservation@ schweizerhofstmoritz.ch, www.schweizerhofstmoritz.ch) is one of the best, with amazing staff, a beautiful dining room, and a relaxation room on the top floor where you can chill out in your dressing gown after a nice sauna and read a magazine, looking out at the beautiful river through the glass windows. It has one of the best locations, one of the best restaurants and three of the best bars in town. Smart, luxurious, and you are allowed to open the door yourself. The **Steffani** (0041 (0)81 836 96 96, info@steffani.ch, www.steffani.ch), across the road, is another great option and the 4-star **Crystal** (0041 (0)81 836 26 26, stay@crystalhotel.ch, www.crystal hotel.ch) is superb, and is as close to the funicular as you can get.

Most of the less expensive hotels aren't in the best locations and still aren't cheap. The 3-star **Hotel Arte** (0041 (0)81 837 58 58, info@arte-stmoritz.ch, www.arte-stmoritz.ch) is one of the most inexpensive, yet central, hotels but don't expect a bargain. You can also contact the tourist office (0041 (0)81 837 33 99), who are incredibly helpful, and will be happy to help you find a hotel or apartment to suit your budget.

Eating out

On Corviglia

If your parched mouth will sip nothing but champagne alongside a soupçon of caviar, and you managed to squash your platinum credit card into your white fur-lined ski suit without spoiling the lining, swish your way over to the **Marmite** restaurant (081 833 63 55), where your palate and wallet are in for an exquisite shock. **Paradiso** (081 842 63 03) and **Trutz Lodge** (081 833 70 30) are both charming, traditional and have beautiful views.

On Corvatsch

The **Hossa Bar** (081 828 96 44) is a heated tent with music and a packed terrace. This place is perfect on the Snow nights, when it stays open until late. The **Hahnensee** (081 833 36 34), on the run back down to St Moritz Bad, is great for lunch, après and evening meals. The **Alpetta** (081 828 86 30) is charming and rustic.

In town

Secondo (081 834 99 90) is one of our favourite restaurants, and a break from the swanky white tableclothed eateries. It is stylish and colourful, with a busy atmosphere and a wide range of food, from tapas and Mexican to pasta and local dishes. **California bar** is good for a quick burger or snack, as is **Bobby's Bar** (081 834 42 83), with hot dogs, burgers and chicken nuggets. You should also pop into the renowned **Hanselmanns** at tea time; it's part of the St Moritz history and everyone goes there at least once.

Of the smart places to eat, the **Acla** (081 837 07 07) at the Schweizerhof is superb. The **Grissini** (081 836 26 66) at the Crystal is not as extortionate as it looks – the most expensive main you can get is CHF52. **Cascade** brasserie (081 833 02 01) serves pasta, meat, salads and risotto, and a main dish will cost CHF24–41. For posh pizza head to the beautiful and cosy **Chesa Veglia** (081 837 28 00) where pizzas cost around CHF30. For a night of pure indulgence, take a 5-minute taxi to **Jöhri's Talvo** in Chamfér (081 833 44 55). In a converted hay barn, you will find a beautiful, cosy, candlelit restaurant on two levels. If you are planning a romantic night, ask for one of the two tables on the separate balcony. It is definitely recommended to book, especially in high season. If caviar, foie gras and lobster with black truffles make your mouth water, you're in the right place. A fancy steak will cost you CHF88 and the six-course menu CHF230. Add on a couple of bottles of wine and you'll need a stiff drink to face the bill. The **Post Haus** is a new restaurant/bar lounge designed by thc famous architect Lord Norman Foster. It is the first part of a new complex 'The Murezzan', due for full completion by 2007.

Useful facts and phone numbers

Tourist office

T: 0041 (0)81 837 33 33
F: 0041 (0)81 937 33 77
E: information@stmoritz.ch
W: www.stmoritz.ch

Direct reservations

T: 0041 (0)81 837 33 99
E: reservation@stmoritz.ch

Emergency services

• Police: 117
• Medical emergency: 144
• Heli-rescue:1414

Doctors

• Dr P R Berry: 081 833 79 79
• Dr P Hasler: 081 833 83 83
• Dr F Kuthan: 081 833 18 48
• Dr C Riederer: 081 833 30 30
• Dr P F Signotell: 081 833 69 43
• Dr P O Steiner: 081 833 17 77

Taxis

• Cattaneo Taxi: 081 833 69 69
• Erich's Taxi: 081 833 35 55
• Taxi Alessandro: 081 833 70 49
• Taxi Angelo: 081 833 13 93
• Taxi Bären: 081 833 72 72

Bars and clubs

Après ski is good at the outdoor **Roo Bar** (081 837 50 50) in the main square in good weather. Later, there are loads of bars to choose from, with varying degrees of exclusivity. **Bobby's Bar** (081 834 42 83) has a British-pub feel, with a comfy 'outdoor' area indoors and pool tables. The **Cava bar** in the Steffani (081 836 96 96) is a cavernous bar with a relaxed and friendly feel, and over the road in the Schweizerhof Hotel, you will often find live music in the packed and great fun **Stübli bar** and the country-style **Muli bar** (081 837 07 07), and live jazz in the **Piano bar**. If you're still going, head to the bar/club **Diamond**, opposite the Kulm hotel, or the **Vivai** (081 833 69 39) back at the Steffani. At the **Bailando Dancing Bar** (081 834 47 40) you can Latino dance the night away. If you have infinite cash, and popped your jacket and tie into your ski or board bag, you could head to the **Kings Club** at Badrutts Palace, or to the **Casino** down in St Moritz Bad.

Getting there

By car

The road to St Moritz seems to go on forever but it is well maintained. From Zürich the driving time is approximately 3 hours, from Milan about 3 hours and from Munich about 4 hours.

By plane

Zürich (200km) Transfer will take you 3 hours by car, 4 by bus.
Basel (290km) Transfer takes 4 hours by car.
Munich (360km) Transfer takes 4 hours by car.

By train

Take the 17.42 Eurostar from London Waterloo to Paris; then an overnight train, changing at Chur. Arrive at St Moritz station, in resort, at 09.58. Return fares start at £168 in a 6-berth couchette. Contact European Rail (020 7387 0444, www.europeanrail.com).

Verbier

Ride hard, play hard. Come and experience one of the best mountains in Europe

On the slopes	
Snow reliability	❄ ❄ ❄ ❄
Parks	❄ ❄ ❄
Off-piste	❄ ❄ ❄ ❄ ❄
Off the slopes	
Après ski	❄ ❄ ❄ ❄
Nightlife	❄ ❄ ❄ ❄
Eating out	❄ ❄ ❄ ❄
Resort charm	❄ ❄ ❄

The resort

Verbier is a fantastically fashionable resort and has an equally fierce mountain. If you're a keen freeriding skier or boarder you won't get bored with the mountain or the nightlife, even if you're there for the season. You might tire of the prices though. It's a beautiful, but sprawling resort, with lots of cute chalets, but few people are moseying around enjoying the view – everyone's on a mission. Get lots of sleep before you arrive.

The mountains

Height: 1500–3330m

Ability	Rating
Expert	❄ ❄ ❄ ❄ ❄
Intermediate	❄ ❄ ❄ ❄
Beginner	❄ ❄

Getting about

Verbier is at the far side of the Quatre Vallées, connecting 412km of pistes. The skiing area of the Quatre Vallés links the ski runs of Verbier, La Tzoumaz, Nendaz, Veysonnaz, and Val de Bagnes/Entremont. The Mont Fort Glacier keeps the area pretty snowsure. Beginners should head to The Moulins or Les Esserts pistes and intermediates to Savoleyres, where you will find excellent snow on the Tzoumaz side and maximum sun on the Verbier side. Les Attelas and Les Ruinettes are also good for cruisy carvers. Experts will find Mont-Fort the steepest and most challenging.

The park

The park, at La Chaux, has been around for a while now, and has a good team of shapers working on it. The terrain is a little strange and the run-ins to some of the kickers are somewhat flat which makes it hard to get the speed to clear the gaps. However, it does have a few good kickers at the top of the park and a good selection of rails including a C-rail, wall ride and up-flat-up. There is also a great big hip jump located at the bottom of the park. It's not the best place for learning freestyle, but advanced riders will enjoy it. The Verbier Ride Slopestyle event is held here and attracts Europe's best New School skiers. To see this park being ridden at its best, check this event out on www.verbierride.com.

> ## "The Verbier Ride Slopestyle event is held here and attracts Europe's best New School skiers"

Off-piste and backcountry

Verbier is the freeriding capital of Europe. It is a test for even the world's best big-mountain riders; Seth Morrison has said that this is his favourite area as there is so much challenging terrain. The Bec des Rosses face (home of the O'Neill Xtreme event, see Events) is one of the hardest faces in the world and should only be attempted by seriously good riders, with a guide. Mont Gele is the home of the Verbier Ride event, and once again has extreme terrain and some massive cliffs. There is a cable car up there but it's rarely open so you usually have a 40-minute hike.

The back of the Mont Fort is another favourite. On a powder day this is the perfect spot to find amazing steeps, gullies and cliff drops. Getting out is quite hairy though, as there is a long traverse along the side of the dam on the way. Its difficulty varies depending on whereabouts you go, though we would not recommend it to anyone who wasn't a competent rider. For those who don't mind a steep climb, check out the Stairway to Heaven. It starts near the Col de Gentianes and takes you right over into the next valley. This place is known for its incredible snow conditions and you won't see many other riders around. If you need shelter from the weather, head across the valley to Bruson, the perfect place to ride through the trees.

Verbier also provides marked ski routes that are not groomed or patrolled. They are great for riders wanting to improve their off-piste riding. Good routes are the Vallon d'Arby and Col des Mines. You can get to these areas from the Lac des Vaux.

We highly recommend that you always carry the right equipment: avalanche transceiver, shovel, probe, helmet, back protector, etc. Also, if you are venturing into the unknown, take a qualified mountain guide to ensure that you get the best out of Verbier's incredible terrain.

We would like to thank Warren Smith, Chris Southwell and Nick Southwell for showing us round and helping with our research.

Lift passes	Quatre Vallées	Verbier
1 day	CHF62	CHF54
6 days	CHF319	CHF277
13 days	CHF569	CHF493
There are discounts for children, young people, families and groups.		

Instruction

Adrenaline Ski and Snowboard School
A Swiss school; recommended.
T: 0041 (0)27 771 74 59
E: info@adrenaline-verbier.ch
W: www.adrenaline-verbier.ch

European SnowSport
This is a good British-run school.
T: 0041 (0)27 771 62 22
E: info@europeansnowsport.com
W: www.europeansnowsport.com.

La Fantastique
T: 0041 (0)27 771 41 41
E: lafantastique@verbier.ch
W: www.lafantastique.com

La Maison du Sport
The Maison du Sport is the official Swiss school and good, though Old School.
T: 0041 (0)27 775 33 63
E: info@maisondusport.ch
W: www.maisondusport.ch

Powder Extreme
T: 0041 (0)76 479 87 71
E: info@powder-extreme.com
W: www.powder-extreme.com

Warren Smith Ski Academy
Run by one of Britain's top performance coaches, this is the perfect school to bring your skiing to the next level.
T: 0044 (0)1525 374757 (UK office)
  0041 (0)79 359 65 66 (Swiss office)
E: admin@snowsportsynergy.com
W: www.warrensmith-skiacademy.com

Other activities

Adventure trail: There is an adventure trail open in both winter and summer with a climbing wall in the summer and ice climbing in winter. Call La Maison du Sport on 027 775 33 63.

Heliskiing/boarding and off-piste: For off-piste guiding or heliskiing/boarding call La Maison du Sport on 027 775 33 63 or La Fantastique on 027 771 41 41.

Paragliding: Call the paragliding centre (027 771 68 18) for an introduction to paragliding, lessons, licence courses and tandem flights. Other paragliding schools are: Fly Time (079 606 12 64, www.fly-time.ch, info@fly-time.ch), Verbier Summits (079 313 56 77), Max biplace (027 771 55 55). A tandem flight will cost CHF100–250 (10–45 mins). It will cost you around CHF240 to learn how to fly solo.

Sports centre: At the Sports Centre (027 771 66 01, www.verbier-sport.ch, info@verbier-sport.ch) you can enter the pool for CHF8 (with access to whirlpools), or CHF20 (with access to sauna and steam bath). As well as ice hockey events you can go ice skating yourself for CHF7 (equipment extra), squash is CHF15 for 30 minutes and tennis is CHF10/20 for an hour (upper/lower courts respectively). You can get a 7-day holiday package for CHF40 including pool and ice skating. There are also six artificial curling rinks at the multi-sports centre.

Tobogganning: Take a sled down the 10km toboggan run from Savoleyres-Tzoumaz (call Téléverbier on 027 775 25 11).

Events

24 Heures Freeride, in mid-December, is a 24-hour charity event to launch the winter season. Participants ski in teams of four, accumulate as many kilometres as they can and convert them into Swiss francs. It's also a chance to party for 24 hours with live concerts and DJs set up at Médran.

The **Verbier Ride** in February (www.verbierride.com) is Europe's leading New School skiing event. Top skiers compete in two disciplines: Big Mountain Freeride (from the awe-inspiring Mont Gelé) and Big Air in the snow park at La Chaux. The event was started in 2000 by British freeski pioneer Warren Smith and it's now a world-recognised event. It attracts the biggest names from around the globe and the Big Mountain is part of the World Tour. If there is one competition you are going to see this year, check out the Verbier Ride. Over the last couple of years Warren has extended the series by adding two more events. In July on the glacier of Saas-Fee is the Saas-Fee Ride (see Saas-Fee chapter, page 374 and www.saasfeeride.com) and a new addition is the London Ride (www.thelondonride.com), held at the Metro Ski Show in October; an indoor event.

The **O'Neill Xtreme** usually takes place mid–late March (www.xtreme-snowboard.com). Launched in 1996, this competition brings together the finest freeriders (two-thirds snowboarders, one-third skiers) to compete at Bec des Rosses, opposite Col des Gentianes, on gradients between 45 and 55 degrees, with couloirs and cliff drops. The **Ultime Session**, at the end of April, is a great finish to the winter season. There is a speed skiing race at Le Mont Fort, big air, waterslide concert, equipment testing and loads more going on in bars and clubs later on.

Accommodation

Verbier has a huge number of guest beds: over 15 000. The only 5-star hotel is **Le Chalet d'Adrien** (0041 (0)27 771 62 00, www.chalet-adrien.com, info@chalet-adrien.com), right next door to the Savoleyres lift, but a little walk from the centre of town. For a smart hotel it's very homely, cosy and welcoming, but it does come at a seriously hefty price. Expect to pay CHF450–1030 per room/suite per night, and add CHF40 per person for breakfast and another CHF85 per person for half board. The balconies overlooking the valley are well worth requesting and the view from the outside terrace is absolutely stunning. You should also take advantage of the gym, sauna and hot tub, as well as the new indoor swimming pool, which has views over the mountains. The other super smart hotel is the 4-star **Rosalp** in the centre of town (0041 (0)27 771 63 23, www.rosalp.ch, rosalp@relaischateaux.com). It has a gorgeous restaurant, but we found the staff a little surly.

If we could stay in any hotel in town, we would choose to stay in the 3-star **Farinet** hotel (0041 (0)27 771 6626, www.hotelfarinet.com, farinet@axiom.ch). It has one of the best locations, bang in the centre of town, only a few minutes' walk from the main cable car. In recent years it has had a complete revamp and the interior is amazing. All rooms have plasma screen TVs, iPods, free wireless internet, a DVD player, and there is a DVD library downstairs from which you can help yourself. There's even a menu of pillows for you to choose from! There are 16 rooms (all with underfloor heating and south-facing balconies) and four big apartments. A double room costs CHF230–395 per room per night and an apartment CHF460–795. Not only is it the best place to stay, it's also the best place to enjoy après ski and late-night dancing (see Bars and clubs) and to eat (see Eating out).

"It has one of the best locations, bang in the centre of town, only a few minutes' walk from the main cable car"

The **Bunker** at the Sports Centre (0041 (0)27 771 66 02, sleep@thebunker.ch, www.thebunker.ch) is really cheap, dormitory accommodation for individuals and groups, 800m from the village square. It has 128 beds starting at CHF25 including entrance to the swimming pool, whirlpool and ice rink. Remember to bring your own sleeping bag! It's a great budget option, but not great accommodation; as it's an old nuclear fall out centre, there are no windows and it's not particularly pleasant. A better option, for not too much more money, is the **Summer House** next door, which has much more pleasant dormitory accommodation, starting at CHF35.

You may also be able to grab a bargain at the 3-star Verbier Lodge (0041 (0)27 771 66 66, info@verbierlodge.ch, www.verbierlodge.ch) – new for 2007 is a reservation system whereby rooms are auctioned off to the highest bidder on www.gast-club.ch.

Eating out

On the mountain
One of the best mountain restaurants is the **Cabane du Mont Fort**, which serves local Swiss specialities (as well as the odd hot dog) on a beautiful sun terrace with great views of the valley. **Chez Dany**, slightly off the beaten track, is a cosy, friendly chalet, again with a great terrace for bathing in the rays. For a quicker, and less expensive, burger and chips, head to the less attractive **Les Attelas** or **Les Ruinettes** restaurants.

In town
Verbier has loads of restaurants offering a wide variety of food, for a wide variety of budgets. If you've too much cash on your hands, you could palm some of it off on the very expensive, very smart and Michelin-starred **Restaurant Pierroz** in the Hotel Rosalp. Slightly less expensive, but in a similar budget category, is the more cosy and Swiss **Le Caveau**. Enjoy local specialities in the less formal, and more comfortable surroundings. **Au Vieux Verbier** serves more innovative and unusual food; it's a really fun and good restaurant, but once again prepare yourself for the bill.

In the **Farinet's** relaxing, cosy and romantic lounge bar you can choose from one of the mouth-watering platters or a simple snack of bread and hummus. For an inexpensive, but superb meal, head to the **Fer à Cheval** in the centre of town. Enjoy a pizza or local dish, and the very friendly service. The Fer à Cheval has a great little terrace for eating in the sun at lunchtime, if you're not on the mountain. You can also enjoy a great meal downstairs at the **Pub Mont Fort**, whose food is much smarter than the usual pub grub, or failing that, head to the beautifully cosy **Al Capone's**, towards the Savoleyres lift. It has fantastic pizzas, made in the open, wood-fired oven, and you will be welcomed with a smile every time. **Offshore**, by the Medran lift, has a great surfy atmosphere inside, and it serves the best breakfasts in town (that you pay CHF20 for). It's great for an informal lunch or dinner, and is a local hangout spot. For a swift burger, at any time until 1am, head to **Harold's** in the centre of town (also an internet café). For something a bit different call **Chez Dany's** mountain restaurant (027 771 25 24); you get a skidoo up there and can toboggan back down.

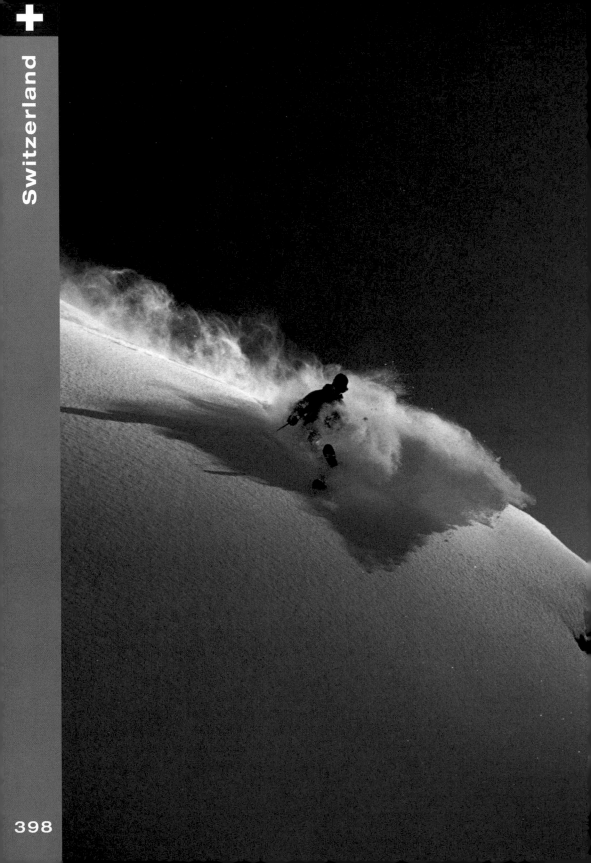

Bars and clubs

Après ski in Verbier is difficult to beat. To start the fun, stop off at the **1936** bar on the mountain, basically a big tent on the piste and a great place for a beer in the sun and a little something from the barbeque. When down the mountain, head straight to the **Farinet** for the rousing live music. Feel free to stomp on the bar in ski/board boots if the mood takes you. If the music gets a bit much and you actually want to talk to the people you're with, either head inside to the Farinet's lounge bar or sit outside in the sunshine next door at the 'London-esque' **Central T Bar**. The massive **Pub** **Mont Fort**, open until 1.30am, is popular at all times of the evening; it plays great music, has a great atmosphere and is a staple part of the Verbier scene – no night is complete without a beer here.

There are a few clubs to choose from that are open until 4am. Most popular is the **Casbah**, under the Farinet, which has a number of rooms playing different music, from rock, to pop, to hip hop. **Tara's** (Taratata) is a big club full of party people, jiving away to the usual commercial sounds. The rich and famous should head to the **King's** bar and the **Farm Club**, ridiculously exclusive and expensive, but fun nevertheless.

Getting there

By car

The tourist office website has links to a route planner and information about the current road conditions.

By plane

Geneva (170km) Transfer costs CHF58 and takes around 3 hours.
Zürich (300km) Transfer costs CHF94 and takes around 4.5 hours.
For a timetable and more information contact CFF on 0900 300 300 or www.cff.ch.

By train

Take the 08.12 Eurostar from London Waterloo to Paris; then by train, changing at Geneva and Martigny to Le Chable, and then a local bus (25 minutes) arriving in resort at 20.15. Return fares from £144. Contact European Rail (020 7387 0444, www.europeanrail.com). Bus tickets (CHF5.40 single) are purchased at Le Chable station.

Useful facts and phone numbers

Tourist office

T: 0041 (0)27 775 38 88
F: 0041 (0)27 775 38 89
E: info@verbier.ch
W: www.verbier.ch

Emergency services

- Police: 117 in an emergency or 775 63 20 (Police cantonale)/775 35 45 (Police municipale)
- In a medical emergency call 144 for an ambulance
- Pharmacy: 771 66 22/ 771 23 30

Taxis

- Bruchez: 079 221 06 66
- Carron Vincent: 776 28 29
- May Taxis Excursions (24h): 771 77 71
- Taxi Edelweiss: 079 460 67 60

Zermatt

A cosmopolitan town with amazing skiing, boarding and nightlife - love it!

On the slopes	
Snow reliability	✻ ✻ ✻ ✻ ✻
Parks	✻ ✻ ✻
Off-piste	✻ ✻ ✻ ✻

Off the slopes	
Après ski	✻ ✻ ✻ ✻
Nightlife	✻ ✻ ✻ ✻
Eating out	✻ ✻ ✻
Resort charm	✻ ✻ ✻ ✻

The resort

Zermatt is a beautiful resort. The 38 4000-metre peaks surrounding Zermatt, make for impressive views, not least due to the trademark of Zermatt – the 4478m high Matterhorn. The terrain that these mountains provide is also superb.

The town is car free, but there are loads of electric cars and buses whizzing round so it's not quite as relaxed as you might imagine.

There are plenty of hotels, restaurants and bars to suit all tastes. You will not be disappointed with this resort.

The mountains

Height: 1620–3899m

Ability	Rating
Expert	✻ ✻ ✻ ✻
Intermediate	✻ ✻ ✻ ✻
Beginner	✻ ✻

Getting about

There are 394km of marked runs and acres of backcountry terrain. There is something for everyone, except perhaps for the complete beginner. In Zermatt alone there are 18 black and yellow pistes (70.5km), 33 red pistes (106km), 19 blue pistes (17.5km); if you include the runs from Zermatt to Cervinia in Italy (mostly red pistes) you get the total of 394km of marked runs.

The slopes are well-groomed and there are many long, scenic runs, perfect for cruising. It used to be a big grumble that you could not always ride back to the resort but snow cannons have been installed all the way to the bottom so it doesn't matter if it has been a little short on snow.

The lift systems in general are not great; on sunny days and weekends there are usually pretty nasty queues to get on to crammed gondolas that will leave you hot, flustered and unable to move. This would be a big setback but, luckily for Zermatt, the memories of the horrendous lift journeys are soon forgotten.

Zermatt consists of three separate areas, two of which are well linked.

The **Sunnegga** area (including Blauherd and Rothorn) is reached by the underground funicular which is located about 5 minutes' walk from the station.

The **Gornergrat** area (including Hohtälli and Stockhorn) is linked to the Sunnegga area by a 125-person cable car linking Gant to Hohtälli. Gornergrat can be reached directly from Zermatt by trains (Gornergrat-Monte Rosa railway, GGB) that leave every 24 minutes and take 30–40 minutes. The views from this train are definitely worth a look if you're not in a hurry. The red runs from Gornergrat and Hothälli to Gant are beautiful.

The **Klein Matterhorn** area (including Trockener Steg and Schwarzsee) is the highest region and includes the glacial area used for summer skiing. There are tenuous links to the other regions but you really need to head back down to the main valley in order to get to a different mountain. The Klein Matterhorn also gives you access to Cervinia in Italy (see Cervinia chapter, page 260) – for which you need to buy an international pass or pay a daily supplement on your lift pass. The Klein Matterhorn glacier (now called the Matterhorn Glacier Paradise) is the highest summer ski area in the Alps. It consists of 36km^2 of pistes, six in total, and is at a height of 2900–3900m. There are also six drag lifts and a cable car. The glacier is open until 2pm depending on snow conditions.

Park

There are two parks in Zermatt, as well as a separate pipe at the Gornergrat which benefits from a bar in the shape of an igloo. The Gravity Park is above the Trockener Steg in the Klein Matterhorn area and the other slightly lower down, used more in the winter as it can get very cold at the top. The parks contain some great rails from easy wide 5m rails to some 8m kinks. Unfortunately there aren't many jumps, but the couple of table tops that there are, are always in good condition.

Off-piste and backcountry

The glacier does limit the extent to which you can freely explore the backcountry terrain on the mountain tops but there are plenty of areas to check out.

At the top of the **Höhtalli** lift is an amazing area for freeride. This always has great snow, and you can get fresh tracks three or four days after a snowfall. The best moguls around can be found on the slopes between Höhtalli and Gant, at **Triftji**, where the Triftji bump bash is held each year, organised by the local pros. Above the Höhtalli and Triftji areas is the **Stockhorn** region, which has been designated as a freeride area. The runs are marked, but not prepared, and not checked at the end of the day. However, the Stockhorn area often doesn't open until around February.

The **Rothorn** area has diverse terrain and there are loads of amazing and challenging faces to ride. There is a hidden valley in the Rothorn area, but you should hire a guide or local who knows it well if you are going to check it out.

A guide is definitely recommended if you want a full day of adventure on the **Schwarzsee** tour. It is a good 1.5-hour hike round the back of the glacier and 3–4 hours of non-stop riding back down.

Zermatt is also famous for its extensive **heliskiing** opportunities with trips up to the **Monte Rosa** at 4250m (a fantastic run down through stunning glacial scenery to Furi), the Alphubeljoch at 3728m and up to the Plateau Rosa at 3479m. Trips cost from CHF450.

Instruction

Independent Swiss Snowboard Instructors

Private instruction for 1 to 2 people, including video analysis, costs CHF160 for 2 hours, CHF 220 for 3 hours and CHF 360 for a full day (5 hours). A full day's guiding costs CHF360 for 1–4 people.

T: 0041 (0)27 967 70 67
E: info@issi.ch
W: www.issi.ch

Stoked AG Ski and Snowboard School

T: 0041 (0)27 967 70 20
E: info@stoked.ch
W: www.stoked.ch

Summit Ski School

Call Paul for information on 0041 (0)79 616 74 53.

The Swiss Ski and Snowboard School

T: 0041 (0)27 966 24 66
E: info@skischulezermatt.ch
W: www.skischulezermatt.ch

Other activities

Bowling: Contact the tourist office for information about the bowling alley.

Cinema: This is located at Vernissage (see Bars and clubs).

Climbing: There are both outdoor and indoor walls. Alternatively, the Gorge Adventure is a dynamic secured climbing route in the Gorner Gorge (contact the Alpin Centre for more information on 027 966 24 60).

Fitness centre: Contact the tourist office for more information.

Heliskiing: Extensive heliskiing is available in the area (see Backcountry and off-piste).

Lift passes	International pass (inc. Cervinia)	Zermatt only
1 day	CHF75	CHF67
6 days	CHF374	CHF332
13 days	CHF648	CHF576
Season pass	CHF1516	CHF1346
Children aged 9 or younger receive free lift passes and 16 or under pay only 50 per cent.		

Ice grotto: The grotto at the Klein Matterhorn Glacier is the highest glacier palace in the Alps at 3810m. It contains various sculptures and information about glaciers, geology and climbing. Special events can be held in the ice grotto. It is open in both summer and winter.

Ice skating and curling: There are both natural and artificial skating rinks and a curling rink. Contact Obere Matten sports arena on 027 967 36 73.

Moonlit skiing/boarding: This can be arranged from the Rothorn area.

Night in an igloo: The igloos on Gornergrat are decorated with artistic sculptures by a local Inuit, and can be rented for the night (see Accommodation).

Night skiing/boarding: This requires headlamps and takes place from Schwarzsee.

Paragliding: Contact the Air-Born Flight School on 027 967 67 44, moskito62@bluewin.ch, www.paragliding-zermatt.ch.

Saunas, solariums and massages: These are on offer at a number of hotels at various prices. Hotel Arca (027 967 15 44), Hotel Christiania (027 966 80 00) and Mont Cervin (027 966 88 88) are good places to start looking.

Sledding: There are 2.5km of sledding runs. Sledding can also be done at night, with a number of additional options such as a party at a mountain hut or a fondue party.

Squash: Call the Hotel Alex on 027 966 70 70.

Swimming: There are indoor swimming pools at various hotels including Hotel Christiania (Roger Moore's hotel of choice! – call 027 966 80 00) and Hotel Eden (027 967 26 55).

Tennis: Both indoor and outdoor courts are available.

Torchlit skiing: Ski at night by the light of flaming torches, then move on to a fondue party.

Winter hiking: There are 30km of prepared paths.

Summer only

Climbing: Contact the tourist office for more information.

Golf: There is a 9-hole golf course at Zermatt-Randa (027 968 10 75, www.golfclubmatterhorn.ch) and also a mini golf course.

Hiking: There are 400km of marked hiking paths.

Mountain biking: There are 80km of mountain bike trails.

Sports field: Football, volleyball, basketball, tennis and unihockey can all be played here. Contact Obere Matten sports arena on 027 967 36 73.

Events

The **Triftji Bump Bash** mogul competition is held every year on the infamous mogul runs.

Accommodation

In 1838 the local surgeon opened the first guest house that could accommodate three people, called the Hotel Mont Cervie (which was later changed to Monte Rosa). Zermatt can now accommodate 14 000 guests in 112 hotels (6800 beds) and around 2000 holiday apartments. There are three 5-star hotels, thirty-six 4-star, and forty-five 3-star. The other twenty-eight hotels are 2-star or less.

You should take care when choosing the location of your hotel/apartment as the resort does sprawl a long way. The best location is probably near the Gornergrat and Sunnegga railways, as here you are close to two of the lifts and the main street. You will need to take a bus to the Klein Matterhorn lift from here unless your hotel offers a free shuttle.

On a budget there are few decent places to stay. There is a **youth hostel** in Zermatt, located about 400m from the main lifts in the centre of town. This is fairly cheap and offers half-board accommodation.

For an average-priced hotel in a good location, we recommend the **Admiral Hotel** (0041 (0)27 966 90 00, info@hotel-admiral.ch, www.hotel-admiral.ch), a very friendly, 3-star hotel, with lots of character and charm (and a health and spa room). The rooms are cosy, and all of the 20 double rooms have fantastic views of the Matterhorn from their balconies. There are also four single rooms. A double room will cost

CHF80–360 per room per night, depending on the season. This price is for bed and breakfast only; if you would like full board you will pay an extra CHF40 per night for a four-course dinner on five nights and a gala dinner on one night. The hotel is located right next to the Sunnegga-Rothorn lifts, and 5 minutes' walk from the centre of town. The bus stop for the Klein Matterhorn is a few seconds' walk away.

For sheer luxury, book yourself into the stunning, 5-star **Mont Cervin** (0041 (0)27 966 88 88, www.seilerhotels.ch/montcervinpalace) in the centre of town. A double room could cost you CHF294–910 per room per night, for half board, depending on the time of season and standard of room.

For a bizarre experience, stay in an igloo village below the Gornergrat, at 2700m! There are romantic suites for two people, or group igloos sleeping six. There is also a whirlpool to relax in whilst enjoying the awe-inspiring views above Zermatt. You can find more information on the igloo village at www.iglu-dorf.com, info@iglu-dorf.com or telephone 081 862 22 11.

Eating out

On the mountain

There are 38 restaurants on the mountain, with nearly every one having a reputation for serving excellent food. It is also difficult not to have beautiful scenery on the mountains of Zermatt, even the couple of ugly concrete restaurants have stunning views. At Findeln, below Sunnegga, are several busy, rustic and atmospheric restaurants. Of these, **Chez Vrony** (027 967 25 52, www.chezvrony.ch) is the most widely esteemed. Between Furi and Zermatt is another hamlet of restaurants including **Simi** (027 967 26 95) and **Zum See** (027 967 20 45, www.zumsee.ch), which are both fantastic. Also at Furi, the **Farmerhaus** (027 967 39 96) is a beautiful, traditional rustic chalet with a big log fire inside. Outside you will find a large terrace with a bar and pizza hut. This place really comes into its own after 4pm for après ski when the live music starts. The food ranges from pizzas and crepes to pastas and steak. To get to this cluster of restaurants you need to take the red run from Schwarzsee to Furi. This is a very scenic route through the trees and there are cannons to make sure that there is always decent snow cover.

Further down the mountain is **Hennu Stadl**, another

great place for loud live music during après ski. The hotel restaurant at **Schwarzsee** (027 967 22 63), right at the foot of the Matterhorn, has a massive terrace with incredible views of the Matterhorn and glacier. Booking is recommended.

In town

There is no doubt that Zermatt is an expensive place to eat. If you are on a strict budget then you should hit the supermarkets (or even McDonald's – not that this is particularly cheap). However, as there are around 100 restaurants in Zermatt with a huge range of cuisines, it would be rude not to indulge a little.

Grampis is right in the centre of town; you can't miss it for the sparkling fairy lights. It has a funky bar/club downstairs and serves good pizzas and pastas upstairs at decent prices. **The Brown Cow Snack Bar** in the Hotel Post serves good burgers and sandwiches and always has a busy, fun atmosphere.

Hotel Abana Real (www.hotelabanareal.com) contains two restaurants: **Rua Thai** (027 966 61 81) and **Fuji** (027 966 61 71), a Japanese restaurant where teppanyaki dishes are prepared in front of you. These restaurants are located on the river; turn at the church on the main street, and cross the river. Walk along this side of the river and you will come to the Hotel Abana Real. For something very different, **Restaurant Riffelalp** is a 5-star hotel and restaurant that produces pizzas in the shape of the Matterhorn – 10 points for originality go to them.

The 5-star restaurants have posh nosh if you fancy it. Try **Prato Borni** in the 5-star Zermatterhof (027 966 66 00, www.zermatterhof.ch) and **Mont Cervin** (027 966 88 88, www.seilerhotels.ch/montcervinpalace). These restaurants are no doubt a gourmet treat but are the same as other 5-star restaurants that you would find anywhere around the world. For superb food in very smart but cosy surroundings, we highly recommend **Le Mazot** (027 966 06 06, le.mazot@reconline.ch, www.lemazotzermatt.ch). This restaurant has been owned by Roger for the last 13 years, and he is there evening after evening to welcome customers, oversee the running of the open kitchen,

and generally ensure that every aspect of the food and service is carried out to the highest level. The owner's pride in the restaurant and dedication to service is what makes it really stand out above the rest. The cuisine is dominated by lamb, the restaurant's speciality, and we can't speak highly enough of the mixed lamb plate for main course. To complement these dishes is a menu of 150 different European wines (CHF40–150). You should book a few days in advance and expect to pay CHF70–100 per person for two courses and wine.

Bars and clubs

Zermatt has 44 bars and a buzzing, year-round nightlife.

For a good après ski scene, try **Papperla** (027 967 40 40, info@papperla-pub.ch) where the club downstairs is popular with the workers. **The Country Bar** (027 967 16 96, www.olito zermatt.ch) offers the internet, karaoke and a game of pool. If you fancy

drinking and eating with the seasonaires, **The North Wall** bar hosts the Natives' party each year as well as numerous fancy dress nights (Facstnacht). Sunday and Tuesday are the nights to be with the locals, whilst Saturdays are more touristy. For great snack food to accompany your beers, **The Pipe** (079 758 53 24, www.gozermatt.com/thepipe) is open from 4.30pm every day and has a great surfy-type atmosphere and the friendliest staff. For getting drunk quickly, **Z'Alt Hischi** (027 967 42 62, www.rhone.ch/hischi) pours the biggest measures ever. For drunken partying later in the evening, **Hotel Post** has loads of bars and restaurants to check out, but the main partying tends to occur in the cave-type club at the bottom of the building, the **Broken Bar**. Everyone should go to **Vernissage**. (027 967 66 36, www.vernissage-zermatt .com). This mega trendy bar needs to be seen. Its bizarre décor really works, with chandeliers made out of chains, loads of candles, and comfy sofas. It serves food at night and downstairs you will come across an art gallery and cinema! You can take your drinks downstairs for the film

and later on the chairs move away, a DJ gets on stage and it turns into a club.

For the more discerning drinker, **Pink** at Hotel Post (027 967 19 31, www.hotelpost.ch) has live jazz music every night and a great atmosphere. It's also in the same building as the cheesy parties, so when you're done being civilised you can join in the carnage. **Elsie's** bar (027 967 24 31, www.elsiebar.ch), opposite the church on the main street, is tiny but atmospheric. It tends to attract the 25+ age group, who have enough cash to splash out on a decent bottle of plonk. Elsie's also serves as a restaurant with fresh oysters every day.

Useful facts and phone numbers

Tourist office

T: 0041 (0)27 966 81 00
F: 0041 (0)27 966 81 01
E: zermatt@wallis.ch
W: www.zermatt.ch

Emergency services

• Fire brigade: 118
• Police: 117
• Ambulance/rescue service: 144
• Police station: 027 966 22 22 (community police), 027 966 69 20 (cantonal police)
• Mountain Guide's Office: 027 966 24 60
• Avalanche situation: 187 (excluding foreign mobile phones)

Doctors

• Dr Ch Bannwart: 027 967 11 88
• Dr J Bieler und Dr P Brönnimann: 027 967 44 77
• Dr E Julen: 027 967 67 17
• Dr N Lutz: 027 967 19 16
• Dr D Stoessel: 027 967 79 79
• Dr Hermann Steffen (dentist): 027 967 34 67
• Hospital in Visp: 027 948 21 11
• Hospital in Brig: 027 922 33 33

Electric taxis

All four Zermatt taxi companies have amalgamated to form 'Taxi Zermatt'. Call 0848 11 12 12.

Getting there

By car

The drive time from Calais is 10 hours (1070km). From Geneva, take the N1/N9 via Sion to Sierre. Then take the E62 to Visp, where you will turn and head towards Zermatt via Stalden.

Cars have to be left in a car park in Täsch in open-air or covered car parks. A shuttle train runs from the car park to Zermatt every 20 minutes and this will set you back CHF15.60 for a return (www.mgbahn.ch). If you would prefer a taxi to pick you up from the car park there are a number of options – try Taxi Eden on 027 967 64 44 or Taxi Schaller on 027 967 12 12.

By plane

Geneva (244km) Transfer by bus (around 4–5 hours) or train (4 hours, see www.rail.ch), or car (3.5 hours).
Zürich (248km) Transfer is 5 hours by train, 3.5 hours by car.
Milan (234km) Transfer is nearly 4 hours by train, 3 by car.
You can take trolleys on to the train up to Zermatt and wheel them off the other end which can save a lot of hassle. Your hotel should arrange an electric car to pick you up from the station, just give them a call on the free phones at Zermatt station. If not, taxis are available (see left).

By train

Take the 17.42 Eurostar from London Waterloo to Paris; then an overnight train, changing at Zürich and Brig. Arrive at Zermatt station, in resort, at 11.24. Return fares start at £168 in a 6-berth couchette. Contact European Rail (020 7387 0444, www.europeanrail.com).

Ski and snowboard banter

Backcountry

Some people use the terms off-piste and backcountry interchangeably, but backcountry really refers to riders heading out into the really remote and untouched areas of the mountain.

Backcountry kicker

You will sometimes see skiers and boarders building their own jumps in the backcountry. This enables you to hand pick your location, size and landing, and many people will session these kickers for hours.

Big booter

A massive jump that really stands out from the rest.

Box

Budding freestylers will practise sliding on boxes in the park before progressing to rails.

Cornice

A big chunk of snow (caused by wind and such like) that is dangerously balanced on the side of the mountain. Look out for cornices in the backcountry; whilst it may seem enjoyable to jump off them, they are very unstable and have a tendency to break and cause an avalanche that could sweep you away in the process.

Couloir

A gully in the mountain. Couloirs range from little more than a narrow run that many people could have a bash at, to steep and tight shoots only to be attempted by experts.

Drop-off

This involves riding off a cliff on your board or skis.

FIS standards

The FIS (Fédération Internationale de Ski) organise world-class events so if something is to FIS standards it means it's pretty damn good.

Freeride

Freeriding has been attributed to many different kinds of riding – when we use the word 'freeride', we are referring to backcountry, big-mountain and off-piste riding.

Freestyle

Freestyle can mean anything from skiers in the moguls to skiers and snowboarders hitting the jumps in the park. Sometimes freestyle is related too closely to the park; many freestyle riders enjoy jibbing off natural hits all over the mountain.

Freshies

You can get freshies if you are the first person up the mountain immediately after a fresh snowfall, as they refer to the first tracks in fresh powder.

Gap jump

This is when a rider has to clear a gap from the take-off to the landing.

Half pipe

Take a big pipe, cut it in half and put snow in it – voilà. Variations are a quarter pipe (take a big pipe, cut it in half, and cut that half in half so that you just have one wall to hit) and a super pipe (take a really really big pipe, cut it in half and put snow in it). These pipes have massive walls and are used in all the world-class comps.

Hip

A hip is the same as a spine.

Hit

A jump.

Hook

To hook is to throw yourself off something, a cliff, for example. If somebody refers to you as a 'hooker' it's not necessarily a compliment, as hookers will throw themselves off anything, but without any element of control or style.

Jibbing

This is when riders play around on the pistes or in the park. In the park you might jib on rails or fun boxes whilst on the piste you might be doing nose or tail presses or playing on natural hits wherever you might spot them.

Line

As well as being a top brand of ski, the term 'line' also refers to the route you take down the mountain. In big-mountain competitions, judges rate the line a competitor chooses, as well as their technique, style, etc.

Mogul field or bumps

A slope covered in natural or manmade bumps.

New School

This is a term that has emerged fairly recently in the skiing world, referring to the new movement in freestyle skiing. Skiing has gone through a huge change in the past decade, and the gap between skiing and boarding has closed in. There is no longer the rift between skiers and boarders that there used to be, and there is no real difference in the image, or desires of freestyle skiers and boarders. As always, it will take probably another decade or so for the new style of skiing to be recognised by everyone – some resorts are still seriously Old School, only allowing snowboarders into their parks and other guidebooks have separate sections for skiers and boarders, or deal exclusively with one or the other. We are the first to acknowledge that the new generation of rider, whether skier or boarder, is after the same thing.

Off-piste

This is the natural terrain, outside the marked areas of the piste.

Pisteurs/ski patrol/ski monitors

These are the lifeguards of the mountain. They will come and help you if you've injured yourself on the slopes and they know everything there is to know about the mountain and weather conditions. These are the people to consult before you venture off-piste as they will inform you how safe it is and which areas should be avoided.

Powder

Good, light, deep snow.

Rails

These are just like hand rails that you see in the street and you'll mainly find them in parks. Skiers and snowboarders use them to slide down, or up, and they come in many different shapes and sizes, such as a rainbow rail, kinked rails (flat-down, up-flat-up, Y-down, etc), C-rail, S-rail or rollercoaster rail. If you want to start learning rails, most parks provide a fun box on which to learn and practise.

Rider

We use the term 'ride' or 'rider' to refer to both skiers and boarders. We don't differentiate between them; we all ride the same mountain.

Sessioning

This means hitting a jump or rail once, walking back up and repeating this process for as long as you fancy.

Shapers

These are the people who maintain and look after the park. Some resorts leave their parks to fade away once they have been built, whilst others employ a number of shapers, who take huge pride in their work and are a great asset to the resort.

Skiing switch

This means skiing backwards.

Slopestyle

A course of jumps, rail slides and other obstacles.

Spine

A jump shaped like a spine, where you can land on either side of the landing.

Step up

A type of jump where you land at a higher point than where you took off.

Table top

A jump with a platform that you must clear to reach the landing. Table tops are less intimidating than gap jumps and small ones are suitable for learning on.

Wall ride

A steep wall, found in the park, for boarders and skiers to ride up and jib around on.

Index

Page refs for (rated) facilities are in **bold** for 5 star rating; ordinary type for 4 star rating. Resorts: (And) = Andorra (Aus) = Austria (Fr) = France (It) = Italy (Nor) = Norway (Swe) = Sweden (Sz) = Switzerland

accommodation
   chalets 151, 161, 173, 180, 197, 210, 216
   family friendly 37, 85, 210, 251, 286, 359
   ski-in ski-out 141, 210, 247
   see also apartments; hotels; igloos; wigwams
airboarding 380
Alagna (It) 256–259
Alp d'Huez (Fr) 126–131
Alpenarena 353, 367
apartments
   Andorra 37, 43, 52
   Austria 73
   France 135–136, 145, 179, 188, 196, 210, 225, 251
   Italy 259, 263, 275
   Norway 299, 305
   Switzerland 327, 380
après ski (rated) 13
   Austria 71, 77, 91, **105**, 113, 119
   France 175, 193
   Switzerland 375, 393, 401
Arcs, Les (Fr) 132–139
Åre (Swe) 310–315
Arinsal (And) 34–39
Arosa (Sz) 322–329
avalanche safety 21, 26–27
   training 42, 49, 177, 230, 280, 337, 346
Avoriaz (Fr) 140–147

backcountry 13, 65, 410
   see also freeriding; off-piste
Bad Gastein (Aus) 58–63
balloon rides 36, 78, 135, 143, 158, 195, 202, 325, 339, 349
   Alpine Hot Air Balloon Week 325
beauty treatments 62, 72, 86, 248, 319
beginner facilities (rated)
   Andorra 35, 41, **47**
   France 127, 133, 157, 165, 175, 207, 221
   Italy 261, 267, 287
   Sweden 311
   Switzerland 359, **375**
bobsleighing 209, 269, 377, 386

cameras 24
canyoning 232, 349, 378
casinos 63, 150, 339, 346, 386
celebrity-spotting *see* rich and famous

Cervinia (It) 260–265
Chamonix (Fr) 148–155
Champéry (Sz) 330–335
charm, top 5 resorts 13
cheapest resorts, top 5; 13
children's instruction 167, 194, 241, 325
   see also under accommodation; family resorts
Christmas 173, 288
cinemas 150, 159, 179, 194, 209, 223, 347, 402
   360 cinema 60
climbing 129, 186, 223, 232, 288, 305, 319, 378, 402, 405
   frozen waterfalls 61, 194, 223, 231, 248, 274, 298, 312
   ice towers 168
   walls 168, 194, 209, 288, 312, 394
conference facilities 106, 129, 251
cookery courses 145
Cortina d'Ampezzo (It) 266–271
Courchevel 1650 (Fr) 156–163
Courchevel 1850 (Fr) 164–172
Courmayeur (It) 272–277
Crans Montana (Sz) 336–343
Cresta Run 386
cricket on ice 389
cross-country skiing 49, 210
curling
   Andorra 49–50
   Austria 60, 66, 72, 78, 87, 93
   Italy 269
   Switzerland 325, 339, 348, 353, 386, 403

Davos (Sz) 344–351
delta-gliding 354, 360
Deux Alpes, Les (Fr) 174–183
diving under ice 143, 202, 232
dodgem cars on ice 179
dog driving 298
dog sledding
   France 195, 209, 216
   Italy 275
   Sweden 312, 319
Dolomites 267, 287
driving 129, 223, 232, 241, 248
   see also go-karting; quad bikes

eating out (rated)
   Austria 71, **85**, 99, 105
   France 149, 165
   Italy 257, 273
   Switzerland 359, 375, 385, 393
equipment guide 16–25, 29
etiquette 29

expert facilities (rated)
  Austria **105**
  France 127, 133, 165, 173, 175, **185**, 193, 201, 215, 229, **239**, 247
  Italy 279
  Sweden **317**
  Switzerland 331, 345, 385, **393**

family friendly resorts 37, 91, 210, 251, 286, 359
fishing 312, 319
fitness centres 78, 179
  see also sports complexes; wellness centres
Flims (Sz) 352–357
flying 169, 196, 241, 248
freeriding 410
  Austria 71, 77, 85, 105–106, 113
  France 133–134, 176, 185, 207, 229, 230, 239
  Italy 257, 273, 280
  Norway 297, 303
  Sweden 311, 317–318
  Switzerland 346, 360, 367, 385, 393, 402

Gastein (Aus)
gay events 114
glaciers
  Austria 65, 113
  France 176, 207, 247
  Italy 273, 288
  Switzerland 375–376, 401
go-karting 49–50, 159, 168, 195
golf 353, 379, 389, 405
Grandvalira *see* Pas de la Casa; Soldeu
Grave, La (Fr) 184–191
Gressoney (It) 278–285

hang-gliding 143, 179, 305, 347, 387
Hannibal crossing the Alps 115
Healing Gallery 61
helicopter flights
  Andorra 42, 49
  Austria 87, 114
  France 135, 150, 179, 202, 231
  Switzerland 354
heliskiing 13
  France 129, 135, 186, 216
  Italy 257, 262, 274, 280, 287
  Norway 303
  Sweden 311, 318
  Switzerland 332, 337, 380, 394, 402
Hemsedal (Nor) 296–301
Hintertux (Aus) 64–69
horse riding 231, 262, 312, 347, 387
hotels (4 star and above)
  Andorra 37, 43, 51–52
  Austria 61–62, 67, 72–73, 81, 87, 94, 101–102, 109, 115, 121
  France 129, 153, 169, 179, 225, 242, 251

  Italy 258, 262, 269, 275, 282, 290
  Switzerland 326, 341, 349, 354, 361, 381, 389, 396, 405
husky driving 241
husky sled trips 42, 49, 231, 305
husky tours 380
hydrospeeding 349

ice caves 178
ice grottos 378, 403
ice hockey matches 169, 196, 349
ice rinks
  Andorra 49–50
  Austria 60, 66, 72, 79, 87, 101, 106, 114
  France 143, 159, 168, 179, 195, 209, 241
  Italy 262, 269, 288
  Switzerland 325, 332, 339, 348, 354, 380, 387, 403
igloos
  building 42, 49
igloo village 405
  overnight stays in 178, 403
instruction
  avalanche training 42, 49, 177, 230, 280, 337, 346
  for blind people 248
  camps 114, 142, 187, 241, 274, 346, 376–377
  child friendly 167, 194, 241, 325
  for trainee instructors 158, 241
  video analysis 93, 176, 230, 241, 248, 298, 346
intermediate facilities (rated)
  Andorra 41, 47
  Austria 59, 71, **77**, 91, 99, 105, 113, 119
  France 127, 133, 141, 157, **165**, **173**, 175, 193, 201, 207, 221, 229, 239
  Italy 261, 273, **287**
  Sweden 311
  Switzerland 331, 337, 345, 353, 359, 367, 375, 385, 393, 401
Ischgl (Aus) 70–75

Jump Training System (JTS) 175–176

kiting 298, 305, 332, 339, 389
Kitzbühel (Aus) 76–83
Klösters (Sz) 358–365

Laax Murschetg (Sz) 366–373
Lech (Aus) 84–89
libraries with English books 209
lift passes 13
luging 159, 168

Madrisa Mountain 359, 360
massages 135, 158, 168–169, 195, 387, 403
mates, top 5 resorts for 13
Matterhorn 280, 401
Mayrhofen (Aus) 90–97

Meribel (Fr) 192–199
moguls 113, 193, 332, 375, 405
Monêtier *see* San Chevalier
Mont Blanc 149, 273, 277
Monterosa 280, 402
    see also Alagna; Gressoney
Morzine (Fr) 200–205
mountain biking 143, 232, 379, 405
mountaineering 186, 232, 257, 274, 378
museums 274, 347, 387
mushing 36, 42, 49
music events 72, 325

New School riding 175, 177, 312, 319, 393, 395,
    411
New Year 169, 173
night skiing
    Austria 114
    France 129, 178, 179, 202, 232
    Italy 262, 288
    Norway 298
    Switzerland 325, 332, 339, 353, 403
night sledging 143
nightlife (rated) 13
    Austria 71, 91, 99, 105, 113
    France 149, 165, 175, 201, 239
    Sweden 311
    Switzerland 375, 385, 393, 401

off-piste (rated) 13, 411
    Austria 85, 99, **105**
    France 133, **149, 157**, 165, 173, **185**, 201, **215**,
        229, 239
    Italy 257, 279
    Sweden 317
    Switzerland 345, **393**, 401
Olsson, Jon 312, 317
Oppdal (Nor) 302–307
orienteering 42, 49

paintballing 42, 49, 150, 196, 209, 339
Pal *see* Arinsa
Paradiski *see* Arcs, Les; Plagne, La
paragliding
    Andorra 36
    Austria 60, 66, 79, 87, 93, 101, 106, 121
    France 129, 135, 143, 150, 158, 179, 186, 196,
        209, 223, 232, 248
    Italy 262, 275
    Norway 298
    Switzerland 325, 332, 339, 347, 354, 360, 387,
        394, 403
parapenting 42, 49, 158, 169, 202, 216
parasailing 143
parks (rated) 13
    Andorra 35, 47
    Austria 71, 91

France 141, **175**, 193, 207, 239
    Norway 297
    Sweden 311
    Switzerland **331**, 345, 353, 367
Parsenn Mountain 359, 360
Pas de la Casa (And) 40–45
Plagne, La (Fr) 206–213
pop concerts 72, 325
Portes de Soleil Circuit 142, 331
Praz, Le *see* Courcheve 1850

quad biking 179, 210, 232
Quatre Vallés 393

raft on the Olympic Ski Jump 159, 169
rafting 232
reindeer sledges 312
resort charm (rated) 13
    Austria **59**, 71, **77**, 85, 91, 99, 105
    France 133, 149
    Italy 273
    Switzerland 331, 359, **375**, 385, 401
rich and famous 13, 76, 84, 156, 358, 384
Riksgransen (Swe) 316–319
romantic resorts, top 5; 13
rules 29

Saalbach-Hinterglemm (Aus) 98–103
Saas Fee (Sz) 374–383
safety *see* avalanches; equipment
St Anton (Aus) 104–111
St Foy (Fr) 214–219
St Moritz (Sz) 384–391
scenic resorts
    Austria 58
    France 148
    Italy 256, 267, 287
    Switzerland 336, 384, 393, 401
Selva in Val Gardena (It) 286–293
Serre Chevalier (Fr) 220–227
shooting ranges 66, 288
shopping
    Andorra 35, 41, 42, 49
    Austria 78
    France 151, 169, 241
    Switzerland 339, 360, 389
skating *see* ice rinks
ski jöring 223, 232
ski touring 129, 186
skibiking 36, 216
skidoos 93, 135, 159, 169, 196, 232, 262
skis 18–20
sky diving 159, 169
sledding 114, 143, 269, 280, 389, 403
sleigh-rides
    Austria 66, 72, 78, 87, 101, 106
    France 202, 223

Italy 288
Norway 298
Switzerland 325, 386
snow biking 61, 210, 275, 338
snow reliability (rated) 13
    Austria **65**, 71, 85, 105, **113**
    France 127, 133, 149, 165, 175, 185, **229**, 239,
        247
    Italy 261
    Norway 297, 303
    Sweden 317
    Switzerland **375**, 385, **401**
snow touring 380
snow tracks (driving) 42, 50
snow tubing 280
snowmobiling 42, 49, 179, 202, 210, 223, 248,
    298, 312, 319
snowrafting 269
snowshoeing 42, 49, 93, 196, 210, 232, 380
Sölden (Aus) 112–117
Soldeu (And) 46–55
spas 60–61, 79, 216, 231, 241, 275, 319
speed skiing 133
sports complexes
    Andorra 42, 50
    Austria 66, 87, 93, 106, 114, 121
            France 129, 150, 202, 210, 241, 248
            Italy 262, 274
    Switzerland 332, 348, 354, 361, 379, 394
sports events
    Billabong Pro 143
    Bosses de Boss 151
    British Ski/Snowboard Championships 369
            Courchevel Freeride 166, 169
    Derby de la Meije 187
    FIS Nokia Snowboard World Cup 61
    FIS Snowboard Championship 325
    Freestyle Festival 51
    Grand Raid, Le 232
    Jon Olsson Invitational 312
    Kitzbühel Hahnenkamm Downhill 79
            Mezzalama Trophy 281
    Mondial Du Snow 179
    North Face Freeride 134
    O'Neill Freestyle Pro 143
    Playstation Air Games 143, 210
    Playstation Big Air 169
    Polo on Snow 389
    Powder 8; 107
    Scandinavian Big Mountain Championships 319
    Ski Jörring 288
    Sleddog European Championships 269
    Snowboard World Cup Half Pipe Event 66

Snowbombing 93
Snowgames 43
Snowzone Event 179
Spengler Cup Ice Hockey Tournament 349
Tignes Airwaves 232
Trois Vallées Challenge 173
Verbier Ride 395
Weisse Rauch 107
World Cup downhill 242
Xbox Big Day Out 242
SPOT, Le 230
summer activities 379, 405
swimming pools 36, 60, 93, 101, 106, 114, 129,
    179, 195, 210, 241, 339, 348, 361, 403

Tania, La (Fr) 173
telemarking 331, 338, 346
tennis courts 72, 101, 106, 288, 339, 349, 361,
    389
    see also sports complexes
thermal water centres 36, 50–51, 60–61, 223
Tignes (Fr) 228–237
tobogganing
    Austria 60, 61, 66, 72, 79, 87, 93, 101, 106, 121
    France 129, 179, 202, 248
    Italy 269, 288
    Sweden 312
    Switzerland 325, 332, 341, 349, 354, 361, 395
trampolining 332
tree runs
    Andorra 35, 49
    Austria 71, 93, 99, 114
    France 149, 201, 215, 221, 239
    Italy 273
    Norway 297
    Switzerland 376
trial biking 232
Trois Vallées 157, 165, 173
    see also Courchevel; Meribel; Motteret

Val d'Isère (Fr) 238–245
Val Thorens (Fr) 246–253
value for money, top 5; 13
Verbier (Sz) 392–399

wellness centres 62, 67, 79, 106, 143, 179, 209,
    288, 341, 347, 354, 368, 378
wigwams, overnight stays 298

yoga 129, 241

Zell am See (Aus) 118–123
Zermatt (Sz) 400–409